Ou Chaoquan (欧潮泉) was born into a Dong-nationality family in Guizhou province, China, in 1930. From an early age, he developed a love of learning.

In the course of time, Ou became a lecturer, and later professor, in anthropology at the Qinghai Institute for Nationalities in Xining. He spent 14 years, between 1965 and 1979, doing hard labour. In 1995, he retired to Guizhou, but continued writing and publishing until ill health intervened in 2011.

Professor Ou currently lives with his third wife.

GW00546357

Ou Chaoquan

RED
AUTOBIOGRAPHY OF OU CHAOQUAN

To

Monday prayer group

with thanks for prayers

Ruth & Norman

4 October 2021

AUSTIN MACAULEY PUBLISHERS™

LONDON · CAMBRIDGE · NEW YORK · SHARJAH

A CIP catalogue record for this title is available from the British Library.

ISBN 9781528912587 (Paperback)
ISBN 9781528960175 (ePub e-book)

www.austinmacauley.com

First Published (2019)
Austin Macauley Publishers Ltd
25 Canada Square
Canary Wharf
London
E14 5LQ

Before I left Guiyang with my family at the end of July 2007, Professor Ou Chaoquan asked if I might be interested in translating his autobiography. At first, I said no. He had never spoken to us about what had happened in his his life before 1995. I had no idea and no inclination.

A decade of working together on academic projects, however, had led to mutual friendship and respect. When I realised the professor was in earnest, I agreed. Now I know his story deserves to be told.

Thanks to my wife, Ruth, who helped with early proofreading and has been supportive throughout the translation project.

In addition, thanks to the following for their feedback on some or all of the draft: William Geary (my brother), Philip Saunders, Hannah Waine, Mandy Engelsma, Ginny Larson, Keith Slater and Alistair Kennedy. Responsibility for any mistakes or clumsiness in the translation remains mine.

I'm grateful for the kind encouragement of Leo Semple (deceased), who supported the project without ever having read the manuscript.

Thanks, finally, to Professor Ou, for his friendship over these 20 years.

–   Norman Geary (Translator)

Chapter 1
Growing Sense of Foreboding
(Xiangye, 1930-49)

Xiangye consisted of about 120 households, all Dong. This was large compared with other villages in the vicinity. It was well endowed with paddy fields and forest. In front of the village, there was a continuous line of fields from west to east and all year around, water in the fields rippled in the breeze. Fish and shrimps were raised there. Between spring and summer, frogs croaked. At night, children carried homemade torches, made by wrapping fuel-soaked cotton around the tips of sticks, to search for sleeping fish and shrimps. They'd use pitchforks and vegetable knives to make the kill.

In the summer of 1930, I was born in Xiangye, in County Jianhe of Guizhou Province, China. That's where I grew up, speaking the Dong language and immersed in Dong culture.

A stream flowed silently from west to east between the paddy field embankments, forming a spectacular waterfall in the east, falling into a deep valley. The stream divided Xiangye into two parts: Big Village in the south, with over 100 households, and Small Village in the north, with around a dozen households. People from one side heard the barking of dogs and crowing of cocks on the other, and for generations residents of both sides had regarded each other as friends and neighbours. My family lived at the centre of Big Village.

Xiangye was in a long, narrow valley surrounded by mountains, but was still higher than other neighbouring settlements. It was densely inhabited, overlooked by paddy fields. This panorama often surprised newcomers: such a large village, with so many fields around.

There were no roads linking Xiangye with the outside world and access was difficult. For generations, people had reached the village via mountain paths, crossing streams. Mountains and forests, along with language and cultural differences, made Xiangye an independent, semi-autonomous place.

Strangers often took advantage of the village's isolation. Plunder, extortion and blackmail were rife and recurrent. In the face of such injustice, women would weep. When children heard that 'Han people are coming!' or 'Miao people are coming!' they would burst into tears and run away. Even adult men would groan with fear.

The village originally had no name in Chinese. The story goes that a local Chinese squire, observing how Xiangye people were often weeping and groaning, said to his people: "Our town is called Liujin. Xiangye people always seem sad. We'll call their place Liu'ai (*liu* means 'willow tree', *ai* means 'grieve')." The name caught on and was adopted by Han people in the region.

In the 1940s, another local Chinese leader objected that *ai* was inauspicious and might influence village well-being; so he changed the name from Liu'ai to Liukai.

Xiangye in Dong means 'village of honest people'. We liked this. The Chinese called us 'Dong'. As far as they were concerned, Dong people were obedient and easy to govern. We called ourselves 'Kam' (pronounced 'gum' as in 'chewing gum'), meaning people who live in remote mountain valleys.

Some Miao people lived in adjacent mountains. Cultural or economic ties with them, however, were few and far between, with little intermarriage.

From about 1935 onwards, Xiangye people were mobilised for a couple of days every year in spring to fix paths and bridges leading to two Han towns; Nanshao (twelve kilometres northeast) and Taiyong (ten kilometres north). Villagers would cut down vegetation and growth blocking the paths, to facilitate the passage of people with carrying poles or on horseback.

With time, military personnel used these two paths more frequently and we began to observe them coming and going, often escorting townspeople who had been arrested and bound.

Ten kilometres to the south was Langdong, a town in the adjacent County Rongjiang. This had been accessible to the village for many decades. Rongjiang people came along a mountain path to buy rice, while others carried goods for sale, such as needles and threads. Yet others came to beg for food.

We often observed Han strangers entering the village and later sitting on the paddy field embankments eating barbecued fish, or sitting in homes by the fire waiting for their hosts to serve meat and rice wine. Such strangers often didn't converse.

On one side of the small wooden bridge joining Big Village to Small Village, there was a bullfighting arena. When I was about five years old, we celebrated the Eating Bull Intestines festival. Each clan bred a bull, and bullfights were convened for three days. Two clan bulls would lock horns on the arena, with two sets of young men egging them on, banging gongs and drums.

During the festival days, crowds of people stood on the mountain slopes around the irrigation channels, watching the fateful bullfights. At the close of each fight, irrespective of the result, clan members would fall in behind their bull and go home.

After my father's generation, there were no more bullfights and the arena became simply a playground for children and a meeting place for adults.

Further down from the arena, there was a wind-and-rain bridge across the stream, with a tiled roof, and benches on either side. As a child, I often observed men and women who had been working in the fields come running to the bridge for refuge from rain. Tired pedestrians would divert there from the path for a rest. Young men also liked to sit there, furtively sizing up the girls as they passed by.

At one end of Big Village, there was an ancient evergreen tree which in its season was laden with red fruit. Along with friends, I'd often climb up to pluck the fruit. Its trunk was so thick that two grown men couldn't reach right around. Its leaves served as great umbrellas, providing shelter and shade.

There was a natural round well close to the tree trunk, gushing water day and night. It never ceased to flow, even during years of drought and famine. In the event of a shower on a summer's evening, there would often be an accompanying rainbow. At such times, a dragon seemed to lean over to the mouth of the well, its tail flung over to the other side of the sky. Adults said that the dragon king was stooping over to quench his thirst…so this year there would be a drought.

The well's water was pure and clear, even a little sweet, and food would taste better for having been cooked in it. Most villagers would ladle a drink from the well several times a day. Those about to breathe their last would gasp for a drink of well water before setting off on their journey in the afterlife. Any time I returned to the village in winter or summer holidays, the first thing I'd do on reaching the veranda would be to quench my thirst with some well-water from a bucket there.

An ancient maple tree grew behind Big Village, said to have been planted by founding elders of the village. Villagers regarded it as hosting the spirit of a god. No one could say exactly how old it was. It stood nobly and imperiously stretching into the sky. On muggy afternoons, cicadas on the tree would make a racket, as if informing the villagers that the red bayberries were ripe for plucking; or that they should go and weed around the rice seedlings. When maple leaves drifted down, people knew that autumn had arrived and it would soon be bitterly cold. Over the years, the maple tree quietly oozed its sparkling syrup, like the teardrops of the villagers.

There was a steep mountain path winding past the ancient well and maple tree, leading to terraced fields cultivated by villagers on the mountain slopes. Beyond these were countless tall mountains married to deep valleys, covered in dense virgin forest which hid the sky from view. Among the trees, the only movement was that of birds, beasts and reptiles.

Left to ourselves, we enjoyed a quiet life in a tranquil environment, but we were not always left to ourselves. Intruders from other nationalities would come and plunder the village. Shouts of alarm would be raised, and everyone would flee to the mountains. Intruders would only follow as far as the hollow behind the village, before realising that they had no idea where to give chase. They could not simply keep going, for the mountain path had vanished. The people, too, had vanished into thick forest darkness and there was no way anyone could find their trail.

The lower slopes of the nearby mountains were decorated with vegetable gardens, one after another, with all kinds of vegetable throughout the year. Every morning, women would go and fetch whatever vegetables were needed for the day, wash and rinse them by the river or well and return home quickly to prepare a meal.

Above the vegetable gardens or on any flat land among the hills, one cotton field was strung onto another. While in spring, men ploughed or harrowed the fields, or sowed or transplanted rice seedlings, women turned over the soil to plant cotton. The women worked in pairs until the time of the autumn harvest. Generations of our ancestors had lived on this land, following these time-honoured patterns of cultivation. This is where they spent the sunrise to sunset of their lives.

Bamboo groves flourished on the untamed mountains around the village, with young shoots sprouting up everywhere. Tall trees and short, thick and thin, competed stubbornly for sky space. Otherwise, the land was covered by dense scrub. Some trees blossomed while others bore fruit; some were deciduous, others were evergreen. They provided the villagers with an inexhaustible supply of resources for building and tool-making, for fuel and food.

No one ever knew how many varieties of tree there were in the thick forest. We knew that in spring, you could pick cherries. In summer, there were jet-black bayberries, peaches, plums, apricots and pears. In autumn, the mountains were full of chestnuts. The whole year around, mushrooms and fungi carpeted the forest floor. Villagers helped themselves only to a small portion of the edible pickings. The lion's share was eaten by wild beasts or simply rotted where it grew.

How many breeds of bird and beast inhabited the primeval mountains and rivers, breathing the pure, fresh air? No one could say with any certainty. Such creatures might be seen at any time, encountered at any place. There were no hunters in the village. Come wind come weather, no one set traps or tried in other ways to catch the wildlife. There was no intrusion into their lives. As if in appreciation, birds and animals lived almost as if they had no fear of people. Only when someone passed by did they make way and leave, unflustered.

This was our Dong world. Dong people were happy to share their existence with the natural world, mountains and rivers. No one wanted to leave. It was beautiful and made a profound impression on my spirit as a child. Now, eight decades later, I still have a strong sense of nostalgia for that mountain habitat.

Farming

In Xiangye, survival was dependent on the fields and mountains. There was plenty of land, sparsely populated. No matter how widely people planted, they could never cultivate *all* the land.

In those days, farming meant rice, but rice could hardly be sold. Farming and rice did not seem to be worth anything at all, except to satisfy the basic need to eat.

Every Dong family native to Xiangye owned land and farmed it for food. True, some families had more land than others. Some had inherited land from childless couples in their clans. Others had taken it over during periods of famine in exchange for rice; or as payment for expelling sickness-inducing spirits, when someone was unwell.

As a child, I never observed villagers *buying* land. Later when the value of land had decreased, and decreased again, I witnessed paddy fields more than an acre being bought with copper coins.

I heard people say that certain shop owners in Langdong 'bought' Xiangye land by lending commodities such as salt, cotton, incense, money paper or firecrackers. When a Dong elder passed away, for example, and the family had no money to buy incense or fireworks for the funeral, a shop owner would 'generously' donate these. Later, however, the Dong family would end up surrendering land in exchange for release from debt.

Several families in Xiangye surrendered their land in this way to shop owners in the town. Most of the fields on either side of the path from Xiangye to Langdong, for more than two kilometres from Xiangye, belonged to one shop owner in Langdong. He never paid a penny, but owned most land in the village.

Former owners became the shop owner's tenant farmers. His agent lived in Big Village, supervising his grain. At the autumn harvest, his agent weighed the grain and collected the grain-rent, until it was piled high in several barns. People called that shop owner 'the Boss'.

Although that Han shop owner owned about a tenth of Xiangye's fields, there was still plenty of land to go around. People with plenty of land were referred to in Dong as *nyenc lis* (literally 'people who have', meaning 'rich people'). They could generally eat and dress well, and comprised around half the village population. The Dong language did not have the phrase 'tenant farmers', but used the term *nyenc hut* ('poor people') for people whose fields were few or non-existent.

Only Dong people who had migrated into Xiangye from outside did not have *any* fields. They would build a small one-storey house and live there, farming the fields of wealthier families. They would use water buffalo, farming implements and even rice seeds belonging to the field-owners, though they themselves cultivated the land. They would then share the harvest equally with the landlord. If the fields were further away, they would share on a ratio of six to four: six parts to the tenant and four to the landlord.

When I was a child, it felt like such practices were heaven-ordained, ensuring equity. In years of famine, the landlord would make sure the tenant had food to eat. The number of tenant households at the time was around eight per cent.

Poor people worked hard for themselves. None appeared to suffer just because they were 'renting' someone else's land. Everyone had food and clothing. As long as there was no famine and *some* grain was harvested, basically no one would go hungry. In those days, practically every household had surplus grain at the end of the year, used for rice wine or for feeding pigs and poultry.

Neighbouring Miao and Han farmers generally envied the living standards in Xiangye. They used to say that the lives of Dong people were easy.

It was traditional for men to plough the fields and for women to weave cloth. Anyone without a partner would 'need' to marry, and set up a traditional ploughing-plus-weaving household.

When I was a boy, several lonely young bachelors suffered depression and died. People were not surprised. How could they possibly survive without someone to stitch their clothes, to feed the poultry and pigs, and to wash their clothes or make rice?

Without ploughing or weaving, you could not raise a family, and people without a family would have difficulty surviving.

Men would say, "If you don't farm the land, what will you eat?"

Women would say, "If you don't farm the land, what will you wear?"

There was water in the fields all year around for raising fish. When the women fished up duckweed for pig food, they would simultaneously catch fish and shrimp.

Men cut grass beside the paddy fields for feeding the water buffaloes, and caught fish, shrimp and eels from the irrigation channels. After the rice harvest, the fields would be drained and a second bumper harvest would be gathered – of fish not grain.

At harvest time, women would gather cotton, gourds and beans. In autumn and winter, they would spin the cotton into thread, while in spring and summer they would weave and dye cloth in Dong style, making clothes for everyone in the household. Thread was spun from flax grown on the land. Only scissors and needles had to be bought. The same needle was often used for a lifetime.

Each family raised poultry and one or two pigs. Surplus grain was used to feed poultry, for eggs and meat.

During the farming season, men would collect firewood on their way home from the fields, and in the off season they would go out to chop wood. As long as there was a man in the family, the fire would be lit every day.

On their daily journey to the fields, men and women would carry a small bamboo basket around their waists for collecting fruit, chestnuts or kudzu vine (a vegetable) along the way. They never returned with an empty basket.

A sickle-shaped steel object was struck against a small white flint to create sparks, igniting dry velvet grass and pre-empting the need for matches.

There were no medicines for sale and no doctors. If you cut yourself, you would grab leaves from the nearest *mali* tree, chew them and apply to the wounded area to stop the bleeding. For headache or fever, you would steam maple tree paste on the back of an axe head, before applying it. Scraping a patient's forehead, neck, chest or back with a copper coin to release congestion in blood vessels and alleviate pain or inflammation was a popular folk treatment.

Pinching and massaging muscles along the spine was used to treat digestive disorders. Cupping was also common: a vacuum was created by lighting a flame in a glass, and the glass was applied to the skin. This therapy was used for arthritis, pneumonia and neuralgia.

Men were expert weavers. In the evenings by the fire, they wove sandals from glutinous rice straw. They peeled moist, fresh bamboo into thin strips for weaving all kinds of basket.

There were of course some essential commodities we could not produce ourselves. In summer and autumn, Miao people would come to sell clay jars and bowls. One jar or bowl could be exchanged for one item of old clothing. Young Han men sold needles, knives, axes, scissors, hoes and sickles. One needle, for example, could be obtained for five eggs.

As a child, I sometimes heard adults say, "This was passed down." I rarely saw anyone buying things such as the iron tripods in the kitchens, which only blacksmiths from other nationalities were able to make. No one could tell how old such items were, or where they had come from. People treated them as valued family heirlooms.

In those days, Dong people could hardly earn any money from the things they produced themselves. The price for 50 kg of rice was about one *yuan*. If you saw Han visitors carrying empty baskets into someone's house, you'd think that household was lucky. No one would dare to bargain over the price.

There were about 10 households in Big Village where the women made Dong cloth surplus to clothing requirements. Every market day they would go to Langdong to sell the surplus cloth, sitting in an obscure place at the side of the street, waiting for customers. Han people, however, generally didn't like the dark Dong cloth and women would often return disappointed.

One year, my mother sold cloth for two silver *yuan*. She took these and stitched them into the top of her skirt. For years, she wore the skirt by day and used it as a pillow by night.

My father earned some money from selling timber. He told us how one night he fumbled in the dark to find the main pillar of the house. There at the base of the pillar, he dug a small hole, where he put the money. He placed some wood on top and added some earth to flatten the ground out again, returning the area around the base of the pillar to its original state.

My parents often said in casual conversation that we Xiangye people had no money. We *did*, however, have some money that we put to one side, and my parents sternly told us we should never let anyone know about it. The small amount of hidden treasure would come in useful when we needed to save someone's life, or when an old person had died and needed money for buying water to drink on their journey in the afterlife.

When I was a child, my parents never gave me as much as a copper coin, so I never spent a penny. Occasionally, I would see copper or silver coins in the hands of adults, but I had no idea of their purchasing power and harboured no sense of need or greed.

We dressed warmly and had enough to eat. Our problem was that we were short of money for buying the things we couldn't make ourselves. It was, on the whole, an innocent poverty, without avarice. There was not much stealing or cheating.

Community Relations

We lived together according to surname, in multi-storey homes called *ganlan* ('hanging buildings', later synonymous with buildings with animals on the ground floor and people on the first and higher floors). Extended families shared the same veranda, each nuclear family residing in one or two, or perhaps three or four, rooms.

If a man needed to build a new house, each household from his clan would donate a few trees, and relatives would help with raising the wooden frame.

Originally, the Dong had no surnames, only clans. Han officials gave us surnames, according to clan.

People with the same surname could not marry. People with different surnames could become related through marriage and would then be considered 'family members' in a broader sense. Every individual was welded into the community through a complex network of family relationships.

In those days, it was difficult to distinguish the hard work of daily life from life itself. People worked hard, as dictated by tradition and necessity. No one needed to pester anyone else to work.

Once I went with an 'uncle' who was a tenant of my father's land, to harvest rice. His wife and children were cutting glutinous rice, and I helped by delivering the rice to him for threshing. The grain was threshed into barrels. My uncle praised me for delivering the rice so quickly, joking he was unable to keep up. This was the most exhausting work of the agricultural year.

In 1957 at the time of opposing the rightists, when asked to describe the household of my birth, I related this story. It drew mockery from some and fierce criticism from activists, who said I was painting things as praiseworthy from the perspective of a bourgeois landlord.

They misunderstood, however. The working environment was our world of freedom. We worked voluntarily. Of course, men would enjoy their rest during the slack farming season, but they were strongly self-motivated to engage in subsistence farming. If there was exploitation of farm-labourers, it was rare and small-scale.

No matter the time of year, there was no culture of staying home all day to rest. If someone stayed at home, then it would have been a Han person, a student or one of the wealthier *nyenc lis* 'rich people'.

When midwinter arrived, some would still go out to work all day, but most would spend their time huddling around the fire and chatting. The slack farming season was the time for the men to have a rest.

The women kept busy spinning thread. By day, they would prepare fodder, and in the evening, boil it and feed the pigs. They also looked after poultry, brewed rice wine, pickled fish, prepared meals and did other kinds of housework. There was no slack season for women. While the men were enjoying a rest, the women were working harder than ever. But there was no urgency. It was still in one sense a relaxed way of living.

There was no hierarchy among villagers with regard to work. So-called 'oppression' was what we felt when dealing with government officials or other outsiders.

There was mutual sharing. If a family had no vegetables, their neighbours would provide. If there was a bachelor on his own, someone would provide him with rice. If there was a widow, a sick or a handicapped person, people of their clan would take responsibility. People would join forces to help at weddings or funerals, and take turns to host guests. Han people called us 'Dong family'.

In the evenings, men and women, young and old would congregate in each house. Pigs, cattle and poultry would force their way back into their assigned places. As the curtain of night fell, the clear, cold daytime would seethe into a different kind of life. People would warm themselves and rest around the fire. The fire would flourish and people would come and go, lighting small fir-wood lights throughout the evening. When the weather was hot and sultry, they would enjoy the cool air outside on the veranda. Women would chat and laugh, preparing food for the pigs or spinning cotton.

Men liked to drop by with pipe in hand. When a guest arrived, the host would stand up and offer his seat. The host's wife would offer a handful of leaf-tobacco. Around 10 pm, guests would rise and retire for the night. Before leaving, they would tell us ghost stories. As the most terrifying parts approached, I would crouch behind my mother and watch with wide eyes. Or, if the stories were less exciting, I would already have fallen asleep.

Young unmarried men roamed the dark shadows, carrying *pipa* or *erhu* (musical instruments), scurrying around the houses where young women were. The men liked to play music as loudly as possible, to make the hearts of the young women race. The young women in turn fastened small bamboo tubes on their spinning wheels to emit a shrill sound, a siren call.

Men would wander in twos or threes, trying to catch a glimpse of the young women, up until the midnight hour. The women would end up engaging in romantic conversation, whispering to the men through the shutters.

The Xiangye of my youth had few bandits or beggars. Our language did not even have the words for 'bandit' or 'beggar'. These two nouns depicted people from other nationalities. Moreover, there were few thieves.

I remember, as a child, often seeing an old Han woman, who would come and beg for food after Dong New Year. People would compete to give her something – preserved meat or glutinous rice – and she would leave well laden. The word for 'beggar' was 'Han person begging for food'.

Those who violated village rules, and whose behaviour was discovered by village elders, knew they would have to leave. They did not have the nerve to face fellow-villagers, and usually left quietly to live elsewhere; until after Liberation that is, when some dared to return.

Such traditions seemed as solid as stone. Thus, everything seen and heard in a day was just the action replay of what had been seen and heard during the past thousand years.

Xiangye people were basically home birds, but sometimes had no choice but to enter the Han towns. When they did, they would feel fearful and flustered, without much 'face' or status.

When they returned home safely, neighbours would feel relieved and would sit around the fire listening to their story. Everyone would be wide-eyed, alternately surprised, pleased or alarmed.

Some spoke of the brick-built Han buildings, streets paved in cobblestone, and clothing different from our own. As a child, such things seemed impossible to fathom and left me with a deep sense of apprehension.

Negative Outside Influences

In the late 1930s, local Miao people rebelled against the Han government and were duly suppressed. All weapons were seized. Even meat-cleavers had to be surrendered. Afterwards, we used women's scissors to substitute for cleavers, and cut meat.

After air guns were surrendered, my father was somehow able to purchase a rifle, though I have no idea where from. It could load and shoot one bullet at a time. It was the only rifle in the village and was normally laid beside his bed. If there were any threat around the village, he would go and shoot a bullet in the air.

Generations of villagers never saw a death by shooting, but discussed how fearsome it might be.

There was another weapon the villagers really feared, namely a dagger that my father's younger brother brought back from a Han town. It had a copper handle and a blade 15 centimetres long. Villagers referred to it as the Small Stabber.

Occasionally, my uncle drew the dagger for inspection. Many would clamour to catch a clear view and that view created a sense of awe. Some said the dagger was razor-sharp from the fire. It could stab right into the bone. Its tip was poisoned so its victim would surely die. Descriptions of its deadliness were ever increasing in blood-curdling conviction.

Actually, it was just an ordinary dagger, not as functional as the daggers for killing pigs. Since, however, it was in principle to be used to kill people and not pigs, it created a terrific curiosity.

The isolated Xiangye villagers had never witnessed townspeople fighting, never mind killing each other. Such horrendous events had hardly been heard or spoken of at that time.

Yet things changed. Outsiders began to trickle in. The words and deeds of people from other nationalities began to permeate our society. While I was a child, people began to perpetrate actions intended to shock and terrify others.

Before I was 10 years old, my second uncle's Han friend, Mr Luo, took a concubine from Xiangye and moved to live in the village. Xiangye people treated him well, supplying him with food, and often inviting him for meals. Despite the warm welcome, within six months Mr Luo had created a fearful disturbance.

Mr Wu was the caretaker for the barns of the main landlord from Langdong. Wu wanted to curry favour with Luo, who had come from Langdong, so at New Year he invited him for a meal. Wu proposed many toasts, but Luo was already showing signs of being drunk, and had begun work with his chopsticks. The host, according to Dong custom, reiterated his welcome by proposing more toasts and reached out to restrain his guest from eating.

16

This, however, caused Luo to fly into a rage. He smashed his bowl, full of fish and meat, into smithereens and abused his host loudly. Wu tried to calm his guest, but Luo only became more indignant. He dashed to the fire and grabbed the vegetable knife, making as if to stab his host. Wu fled outside, his guest wielding the knife in pursuit, yelling, "Strike the Miao after eating Miao food! Kill the Miao after eating his food!" (*Miao* was a pejorative term encompassing all minority people at the time.)

Wu ran to our home, calling to my father for help. My father was not there, however, and Wu darted into a neighbour's house and bolted the door. From there, he opened the shutters, leapt on to the lower roof of the adjacent house and fled for his life.

Luo meanwhile slashed at the neighbour's door with the vegetable knife, until it was full of holes. Several people were urging him to stop, but none dared to intervene. In the end, he gave up and went home still brandishing the knife, and cursing Wu's mother. After this incident, Wu kept a low profile. Only after Luo had left Xiangye sometime later could Wu relax in his own home again.

After Luo moved away, my second uncle's other Chinese friend, Ni, came to live in Xiangye. Like Luo, this friend was from Langdong and had a wild disposition.

Xiangye people welcomed Ni generously. There was, however, always a dagger tied to his waist belt. This was the second dagger-for-people I had ever seen.

One day, a Han man Mr Zhang from Liuluo came to my home to buy a pig. After killing the pig and while we were still eating entrails hotpot, Ni and Yang (a Dong man), hopelessly drunk, came over to see Zhang. As Zhang accompanied them down the stairs, they grabbed him by the arm. Then Ni unsheathed the dagger and stabbed Zhang in the shoulder. Zhang struggled free, jumped from the stairs and fled, pursued by Ni and Yang. The two eventually gave up their murderous pursuit. I have no idea why they had been intent on killing Zhang.

No one dared to arrest Ni. Yang left the village of his own accord. Ni went home and took out a horse knife, intending to attack the home of my second uncle. Brandishing the knife, Ni made an almighty disturbance, apparently intent on blood.

Onlookers just sighed, apart from one massive man who came walking out stiff and straight. He grabbed Ni's arm and held on tight. The two men twisted and turned. Exhausted, Ni dropped the knife. He was ordered to go home and rest. After sobering up, he left the village and never returned. Neither did Yang.

That night, Zhang returned to my house wounded. Members of my extended family had fled, along with many other villagers. The next day, officials arrived from Liuluo. They killed a pig and drank rice wine belonging to my family, while treating Zhang's wounds. There was no sign of the culprits and three days later, they left.

We had never seen such things before and they destroyed the harmonious environment in Xiangye. No one could explain why such changes were occurring. We only knew there was a growing sense of foreboding.

Chapter 2
Harbouring Ambitions
(Childhood, 1930-43)

Parental Guidance

Dong nationality tradition shaped my childhood world. My parents were scrupulous in omitting nothing of that tradition from my informal education. Though now in my ninth decade of life, I still recall many of their tutorials.

At mealtimes, our family would sit together, my father facing the entrance to the house, with his back to the family altar. If we were eating fish, he would select a tail and pass it to me. If we were eating poultry, he would pass me a leg. If we were having pork, he'd give me a piece of lean meat. The rest was for the adults. Whatever we were eating, my father would first give me my portion. I was not permitted to help myself. Whatever I received was my ration for that meal, even if it didn't seem like enough. I was strictly forbidden to ask for more.

My parents used to quip that rice was for eating, but fried food was for show. You should eat lots of rice, but just a little meat and vegetables; an important part of the etiquette to be learned by any child.

I was expected to eat quickly then leave the table. Doing so would earn my parents' praise. If instead I dallied, this made me a glutton and invoked criticism. After finishing my food, I should politely say to guests, "Please take your time," and then leave.

As soon as I could feed myself, my parents insisted that if so much as a grain of rice fell to the ground, I should pick it up and eat it. I was never allowed to leave food in my bowl. Such rules became life-long habits.

From the time I began to talk, I was taught to use special kinship terms for addressing members of the wider family circle. This practice was the most assiduous of all. Wherever we met an adult acquaintance, my parents would first teach me to use the polite form of address for that person; then the adults would start to converse.

I was only ever taught the form of address, never the names of the people I met. There was a strict taboo against younger people addressing their elders by name. Violation was met by approbation of a kind that others might reserve for vandalism.

We should surrender our seats to anyone senior in age, and should not cross our legs in company. We were not to walk past just in front of others; if necessary, we should walk behind them. If there was really no space behind, we could cross in front, but only after saying 'sorry'.

Before going out to play, my parents would warn me I wasn't to quarrel or fight and I shouldn't get my clothes dirty. Throughout my childhood, I rarely saw children fighting.

My mother would chatter away day and night, often instructing and scolding, but never beating. My father was different; very strict. He used mealtimes to admonish, often knocking me on the head with the knuckle of his forefinger, or twisting my ear. When he was really angry, he hit me on the head with his tobacco pipe. I feared him and even hated him at times. When my father disciplined, my mother would be trying to protect me, dragging me away and consoling me afterwards with something nice to eat. I loved my mother deeply as long as she lived.

The memory of my father's knuckles cannot be purged, and my parents' cajoling 'home education' also left an indelible impression. Whole generations of Dong children grew up timid, feeling oppressed and guilty, with the result that they in turn oppressed and criticised their children.

In the company of relatives and friends, my parents sometimes commended me for correct application of terms of address. Otherwise, they had nothing good to say of me. Instead, they said I was stupid. I had grown so big, but still didn't grasp a thing. I still didn't know how to address the husband of my paternal aunt! I had no way with words. I was clumsy in manual labour. When carrying firewood on a pole, I scrunched up my neck. There was hardly half a sentence of commendation; only an accumulation of dispiriting and destructive criticism.

It was as if the more my parents spoke like this, the more praiseworthy it was. It may have reflected well on them, but it all made me blush with shame. Having been verbally attacked, I would retreat and leave the adults to themselves.

People in my village typically treated their children like this. This so-called training included beating and insulting children in front of outsiders, resulting in loss of self-esteem. The point was to inculcate in children a spirit that did not dare to defy; a spirit that swallowed up screams of pain and submitted to humiliation. The result was that children could not raise their heads in the presence of visitors, but were often timid and reserved.

Paradoxically, in my absence, sometimes even after I had been beaten and had scarpered, my parents would praise me to others, saying how clever and competent I was, how I had a good way with words, was ever courteous, and how I could even speak Chinese. They would sing my praises, but on no account (knowingly) in my hearing. This was everyone's custom.

Village taboos were part of the daily parental syllabus. Before I was old enough for manual work, my parents taught me not to breach the paddy-field embankments or drain water, not to throw stones into the fields, nor carelessly strike the oxen that ploughed the fields. From the 15th day of the 8th month (of the lunar calendar) onwards, it was permissible to pick gourds or fruit, beans or eggplants that others had planted, but otherwise, you must never touch anything in other people's vegetable gardens. My parents denounced anyone who broke such taboos, and fearing my father's painful retribution I never dared to do so.

My parents sent me to school earlier than most other children. Thus, when I was only seven years old, I had a special haircut and my clothing changed.

One sun-sparkling morning, mother invited an old man to come and shave my head in the area in front of the house. Family and neighbours had gathered to witness the event. The old man shaved off the rectangular block of hair on my forehead, until I was bareheaded just like all the other young men who had come of age.

A few days later, after Dong New Year, my mother roused me earlier than usual. A warm fire was already burning and other family members were sitting around the fire. Mother dressed me in a new jacket with five buttons and two pockets. After doing up the buttons, she produced a new pair of trousers, sewn up where the legs meet (unlike the split trousers worn by small children). She had me take off my split trousers and quickly put on the new pair. Afterwards, she pulled and patted the new clothes into shape, lightly tapped me a few times and then sat me down. From then on, I dressed as if I were an adult man.

Villagers recognised that if a boy's head had been shaved, and he wore a jacket with five buttons and two pockets, along with stitched-up trousers, then he had already embarked on adult life.

Afterwards, such 'young men' would no longer sleep in the same bed as their mother. By day, they would accompany their fathers outdoors and begin to learn all kinds of practical skills, such as chopping firewood and felling trees, ploughing, tilling and weeding the fields, transplanting rice seedlings, threshing grain and cutting glutinous rice, grazing cattle and cutting grass for them, slaughtering pigs and killing chickens, knotting nets and catching fish. By the time they were ready to marry, they should have mastered their father's skills, in order to set up a household capable of producing and subsisting independently.

Han people believed that courtesy was a defence against criticism; Dong people believed that courtesy was a sign of wisdom. During childhood, my parents hammered a code of courtesy into me. I should stand up and offer my seat to visitors, offer a cigarette, speak as politely as possible, and use respectful terms of address such as 'father' or 'mother'. When out walking, I should allow older people go first and follow behind. If my hands were free, I should volunteer to help an older person with any heavy load. I should become used to burning money paper [used when offering sacrifices], lighting incense, kowtowing and bowing, for making offerings to ancestors or gods. I should kowtow to the most respected elder in the family.

My parents harboured high ambitions for me, often saying, "If you are to gain the respect of others, you must be polite and learned. Then you will have some natural dignity and when you speak, others will listen."

My Father

My paternal grandparents arranged for my father to marry a woman from Small Village with the surname Wu. She gave birth to a son who died before he was a year old and soon afterwards, she too passed away.

After that, my father went with a few young men to Sebian village, now in County Rongjiang, to do some wife-hunting. He found another young woman with the surname Wu and brought her back to Xiangye, where he married her.

At the time he married, his father's family owned only a few paddy fields, and he and my mother farmed the land themselves. At first, there was no grain surplus, but gradually my father started to use surplus grain to buy land from people without heirs. In the end, he owned much fertile land.

It was probably around the mid-1920s that my father was ordered to lead a group of 25 young men from Xiangye to a garrison in Zhaisong, County Rongjiang, to maintain public order there. Some of the family land was then rented out to others. When my father returned, he was addicted to opium, and he never reverted to farming. Instead, he made some successful investments, purchasing more land at a time when it was relatively cheap.

It was probably in the second year after my father returned from Zhaisong, that he bought a plot of pine trees near the River Qingshui. He employed woodsmen to fell the trees and float the logs in rafts to Jinping town, where they were sold. This earned him a handsome profit.

At that time, Miao people in Zhanmo were abandoning their fields and homes. With an eye for a good investment, my father bought some fields there and a three-storey, tile-roofed house with five rooms, along with a plot of pine-wooded land. He employed a landless Miao farmer to take care of the house, grain and timber.

After my father returned from Zhaisong, it was natural for him to become a village elder. There was no election or ceremony to mark his promotion. People just naturally sought his advice on village affairs and he tried to respond to every request.

When officials came to the village, they would stay in our house, which they called the Big House. In fact, my family lived in just two sections of the house, a smaller space than available to many other families. These two sections were divided into five separate spaces: a living room/kitchen, three bedrooms and a guest room. Upstairs, there was storage area for grain, while downstairs there were pens for pigs, horses and water buffaloes. This was practically the same set-up as any other house in the village, but in the minds of the people, the Big House was the prestigious centre of the village.

Houses were built in rows according to surname. People from the same clan would live in one row, 15 or 25 metres long, sometimes housing two or three families, sometimes four or five. Our 25-metre row was shared with four other families from our clan. We shared the same spacious veranda.

Other villagers depended on the Big House for their well-being. When we hosted guests, or celebrated New Year or some other festival, people followed activities around our house with special interest. Villagers often popped by to ask about news from outside. Conversation would develop and quickly turn to local affairs in Big Village and Small Village.

Soon after he returned from Zhaisong, my father bought a tall, white horse. At the time, some Xiangye people had never seen a horse before and even the Dong word for 'horse' was borrowed from Chinese. People reacted towards the horse with apprehension and even fear.

If an outsider rode into the village, people assumed he was some leading official and he would be treated with great respect. Men and boys would crowd around, excitedly discussing the horse, but wary in case it kicked out. Women typically had horse-phobia. Upon seeing one, they would cry out in dismay and run off.

Xiangye villagers' horse-circumspection was only sharpened by the animals' aura of mystery. Beside the village of Zhanmo, there was a tall, steep mountain. People used to insist there was silver treasure on the mountain, guarded by a white horse. You could sometimes catch a glimpse of the horse, sleek and swift, magnificent beyond comparison. Then it would disappear in a whirlwind of fog halfway up the mountain. When I was young, I often heard my father relate this story.

A man was employed to care for our horse and he often tended it the whole day long. My father usually stayed inside and never rode it, nor was it used to carry loads. It would just walk majestically in and out of the sheltered area under the house. Only our horse-hand occasionally rode it, whereupon villagers would gather around to watch, showering him with admiration.

After several years of addiction, my father tried to quit smoking opium, whereupon he became seriously ill. Outsiders came to pay him a quarter-pound of opium in exchange for the horse. My family, never mind our horse-hand, could hardly bear to watch. As the horse was being led away, it too objected. Its keeper wept, but the women in the village were all relieved.

By the time I was 12, my personal contact with my father was still fairly minimal. I do remember that when he was feeling well, he would carry a book around. He would read for a while then rest a while. Sometimes he would talk to me about Sun Wukong (the Monkey King) and Zhubajie (Pigsy), and tell me stories from the Tang dynasty (618–907 AD). Only after growing up did I realise that he had been reading the Chinese classic *Journey to the West*.

I really have no idea where my father ever studied, for how long, or to what level. I don't remember him ever teaching or counselling me in any way, except via painful physical discipline. He rarely smiled, but lived in dignified and introverted silence.

My father preferred not to meddle in other people's personal affairs. He didn't bother about the families of his two younger brothers, or venture to judge them in any way. He was, nevertheless, held in high esteem and whatever he said stood. Other villagers trusted him and felt rather in awe of him.

Any time military personnel visited Xiangye, they came directly to our home. My father treated them as personal guests, hosting them generously. He spoke politely, constantly reasoning, making it difficult for them to take any offence. In this way, he averted much trouble from Xiangye.

I often heard my uncles tell a story from 1942. In that year, the Miao commander Li Zhifu led a large brigade of Miao men to fight against the Chinese in Langdong. In the middle of the night, their bamboo torches lit up the night sky as they passed Xiangye. After their defeat, they retreated along the same path, but neither coming nor going did anyone enter the village. It transpired that my father had gone out to meet Li Zhifu, to beg the Miao men not to enter. Others had been terrified and praised my father for his courage. Trouble had been averted.

One year, intruders came by night to drain paddy fields of water and steal fish. My father rose the following night, shouldered his rifle and walked over to the fields, where he shot into the sky before returning home to bed. He followed this routine for several nights and the night-time stealing of fish from paddies never recurred.

In those years, leopards occasionally emerged from the forest to raid poultry. My father sat on the veranda, watching, calling me now and then to pound his back. Once, he managed to raise the alarm and a leopard was frightened away.

My father's opium addiction gradually worsened and his health deteriorated. He hardly left the house. Sometimes he even seemed to lack the strength to talk. During the day, he would lie on his bed and not even get up. It was painful for him to eat or drink and he became thin as a rake. In 1940, the government prohibited opium and no more was openly available for purchase. My father became ever thinner, until he was just a skeleton. He gritted his teeth and wrinkled his face, but I don't remember him complaining.

One freezing night in the winter of 1942/43, we were staying in temporary mountain shelters having fled from bandits, when my father's heart faltered and quietly gave up. At the time, I was only 12 and thought he was just resting as he always did. My mother, however, shook his motionless frame before letting out a heart-rending cry of desolation. My uncle's family and others in nearby shelters woke up with a start and came around. The men wailed and the women wept. They carried my father's body home that night as everyone returned to the village.

The next morning, elder Luo, as he climbed the steps to our home, cried out bitterly, "Older brother Xi has left; this village is done for!" Many stood by the coffin, weeping and complaining, "Xi, you've gone and left us behind. What will we do now?" Men full of melancholy drew out leaves to smoke. Everyone was disconsolate and no one knew what the future might hold.

After my father died, it was unclear who would succeed him as the main elder in Xiangye. The leadership role was first given to someone named Yang, then transferred to my second uncle Ou Zhenghe, and soon afterwards transferred for a few days to a man named Luo. Then one of the Tians, from Small Village, was given the job. The position was passed from one to another, with the result that villagers could hardly keep track.

Subsequent leaders failed to enjoy the same kind of prestige my father had. They were not trusted to settle disputes. Instead, their duties became minimal:

collecting taxes and organising conscription. They even came to be regarded as outsiders. Some villagers clung to my father's memory, saying, "If only older brother Xi were still here…"

My Mother

My mother, from the Dong village of Sebian, often remarked that life had been tough for her parental family. They had been quite poor.

The language and dress of Sebian were slightly different from Xiangye. By the time I was a child, however, mother was speaking Dong like others in Xiangye and wearing dress that was the same. She still easily and often gave a lively and authentic rendition of the Sebian Dong accent, causing everyone to burst out laughing.

Mother's skirts were clean, and her face was fair and clear. She'd walk around bare-footed, though her feet usually seemed clean. The bun on her head was jet-black and shiny. Other villagers praised her neatness.

Mother was polite and friendly, generally on good terms with everyone. She rarely argued and never swore.

When my father was weak and ill, household affairs were overseen by my mother. She tended the pigs and the vegetable garden, carried water and washed clothes.

Mother arranged for two orphans to join our family. They were distantly related and were treated as if they were family members. When my mother gave us new clothes, she'd also give a set to the two adopted children. They helped with collecting firewood, making the fire and feeding the horse. My father never beat or swore at them. My sister, brother and I always addressed them as 'uncle' and 'aunt' in keeping with the formal differences in our generations.

Mother helped the 'uncle' who took care of the horse to find a good wife and to choose an auspicious day for his wedding. He didn't really want to leave for his own home, however, and only left upon mother's earnest appeal. Sadly, he died young without children, and his family line ended abruptly.

Mother also helped the other adopted child, our 'aunt', to find a husband, and helped the new couple find a house. This aunt, however, also died young and left no descendants.

Mother later remembered the two orphans with sadness, regretting the tragedies in their lives. Other villagers praised her kindness and warm-heartedness.

Mother was hard working. I rarely noticed her relaxing. If she ever did sit down, she would promptly fall asleep.

Having belonged to a poor family, mother always seemed ready to use her possessions to help the poor. My father was unable to eat meat, but my mother still raised two pigs, generating food for guests and for gifts all year around. Father could not drink alcohol, but mother still brewed rice wine for guests or temporary workers.

We had one young uncle who drank lots of rice wine each breakfast and dinnertime. His family hardly managed to brew half of his daily requirements.

He used to catch fish, then stare and scowl at the feast of fresh fish in his bowl. When mother noticed he was out of rice wine, she would call him over and fill a pot for him, enough for two meals. In return, he would give us one or two fish.

During the spring ploughing season and autumn harvest, we often employed people to work in the fields. Mother fed our temporary workers handsomely. At harvest, both meals would be replete with fish, meat and rice wine. At other times, the better meal would be in the evening, with more meat and fish than could possibly be consumed, and no fixed ration of rice wine. Mother would sit to one side and encourage the workers to drink more. They loved working for my family. In addition to these meals, my mother paid generously with grain.

Visitors to our home were invariably recipients of room and board. They only had to mention the name of some mutual acquaintance and they would be accorded the status of honoured guests. As they left, we'd present them with gifts of preserved meat and glutinous rice.

Each month, nuns from the Buddhist temple in Liujin would come to buy grain and mother would treat them as guests. She would sell half and donate half, and prepare a special vegetarian meal for them.

Mother often visited the market in Langdong, making friends with people on the street. Such friends often came to visit for a few days at a time. They would be kindly wined and dined, and when they left, they would take with them gifts of preserved meat, pickled fish and glutinous rice. It was odd, however, that my mother never went on reciprocal visits, nor did she even know where those friends lived. She didn't really know them well.

Why then was she so generous and hospitable, making friends with Han people far and wide? In the past, no one bothered to think about such things. After Liberation, Party cadres explained to Dong villagers that such hospitality was the means whereby landlords would rope people into friendships for their own personal advantage.

Often mother took up the cases of young unmarried men. Whenever she identified a suitable young woman, she would volunteer to the young man in question to go on his behalf and arrange for the woman to be his wife. If the young man hung his head and smiled, this would be the signal for mother to pay a visit to the woman's home.

The woman's parents might have reservations but would often agree, saying, "We can see from older sister's face that we should agree. The girl is very stupid, however, so we hope her new family will take good care of her."

Even if the young woman herself was reluctant, she might nevertheless submit, "Okay then, Auntie…" Usually things worked out well.

Many families in the village were at some time or other beneficiaries of mother's matchmaking prowess. She never accepted a penny for such services; not a chicken, a chunk of preserved meat, pickled fish or even a few eggs. She rushed around serving as matchmaker completely without remuneration, sometimes using our own possessions as gifts to consolidate arrangements.

Mother believed that every man ought to have a wife and every woman ought to have a husband. Everyone should have a family and raise children. This had been the tradition in Dong communities from time immemorial.

When people married, mother felt absolved of her matchmaking duties. She did not usually participate in the weddings or go to congratulate the couple. Above all, she made no demands on new couples. They would feel deeply obliged to her. This kind of affection was strong and steady, holding good in Xiangye right up until Liberation.

The Ou Family

My mother gave birth to three children. The first was my sister, whose Dong name was Mao and written name was Ou Chaojin. She never went to school. As a result of our general timidity towards those with power and influence, she became the concubine of a Han Chinese official.

The second-born was my brother, with Dong name Deng and written name Ou Chaoxi. He studied at primary and middle schools in Counties Jianhe and Rongjiang respectively. Before the end of the War of Resistance against Japan (1937-45), he studied at the Military Police Academy in Sichuan Province. After graduation, he served in the army until victory in the War. Then he returned to live in Xiangye.

I was the youngest. My Dong given name was Red, a popular colour among the Dong people as well as the Han Chinese. In Dong and Han culture, red is associated with joy and good fortune.

In my childhood, I used various Chinese given names: Tongming 'understanding things well', Tonghan 'communicating widely' and Chaoquan 'with ruling authority'; this would not have appealed to me after Liberation in 1949. In the end, I settled for Chaoquan with a different *quan*, meaning 'a spring bursting forth'.

After my birth, our nuclear family consisted of five people. As mentioned above, while I was still a child our family adopted two orphans with the surname Ou, after which there were seven people in the family.

When I was four or five years old, my paternal grandfather would take me by the hand and go for a walk to the rice fields, sometimes catching one or two carp there. He'd have me carry the fish back to his home and keep me there for a meal, presenting me with the fish tails which were easier to eat – less bony – than the heads. He was tall and strong. My father and his two younger brothers inherited this physique from my grandfather.

As a child, I often heard relatives say that our family history originated in Tianzhu (a county in Guizhou Province). Variously attacked by people of other nationalities and pursued by government troops, our ancestors fled upstream to Xiaoguang (in Guizhou). They lived there for generations; but it eventually became difficult to eke out a living. When they again met with persecution from government forces, they fled to the southwest, ending up in Xiangye.

As they were leaving Xiaoguang, our ancestors feared their family graves would be desecrated by people of other nationalities, so they brought with them the remains of buried relatives. They re-buried everything on the mountain behind Xiangye, building a great tomb and setting up a stone tablet there, complete with sculpted epitaphs. From the time I was seven or so, I accompanied my family to the graves at the time of the Qingming festival in spring. The dates on the tablet were from the Qing dynasty (1644–1912 AD), covering five or six generations of people.

Zhengcha, a village about five kilometres from Xiangye, now consists of around 10 households. At the time of Liberation, residents were all Dong people with the surname Ou. The story goes that when our ancestors left Xiaoguang in search of a new home, some stopped there in Zhengcha, while the rest kept going until Xiangye.

It was an arduous trail, with tall mountains and deep valleys, precipitous and dangerous mountain paths, through virgin forest which bore little or no trace of human occupation. The early Ous waded through rapidly flowing streams and rivers, and passed through Han nationality and Miao nationality villages.

The Ous in Xiangye were assumed to be related through one common ancestor, though they divided naturally into many clans according to grandfather. My paternal grandfather had three sons and one daughter. He lived into his eighties, being at that time the oldest person in the village.

My father's Dong name was Xi and his Chinese name was Ou Zhengxian (Zhengxian means a 'worthy and virtuous person'). He was the eldest son. When he first left his father's home, he built a house on the untouched land at the western end of the public square in the village. The public square was called Da Sa Lao; Sa Lao was the ancestral female goddess, revered by Dong people everywhere.

My father could speak Chinese and read some Chinese characters. Nearby Han officials had him serve as their village representative, until he passed away. In those days, there were not many meetings to attend. My father rarely went to the local or regional government offices.

The second child in my grandfather's family was my aunt. She was given the Dong name Song. Before she was 10, she was betrothed to the eldest son of one of the other village elders. The young man was well educated and worked as a private school teacher.

A man named Long from Liujin, however, much older than my aunt, took a fancy to her and asked to have her as his concubine. The town of Liujin four kilometres away had been an army garrison, and the region's villagers feared the Han people there.

My aunt's family felt obliged to agree, despite her earlier engagement. So she duly became the third concubine of Granddad Long, who in turn became a son-in-law in my grandfather's family circle. Long's influence extended throughout three counties in that neighbourhood and Xiangye was thereby rendered a safer place to be.

My first uncle was the third child in the family. His Dong name was Shi. He probably never learned to read. My grandfather arranged for him to live just outside the village. There were five in his family, including three children. He

28

often related to my father various things he had seen and heard, loudly and with much animation. He'd be speaking one moment, laughing the next. While still talking, he'd get up and leave; talking and laughing until his shadow disappeared into the distance.

Every day around 10 am, after the morning meal, under the home of the Yang family at one end of the village, the village men would congregate for a chat. They'd talk for up to an hour before dispersing in different directions to work in the mountains.

Without fail, my first uncle would be there. He would move about among the others conversing loudly and laughing. He'd speak so that others could overhear, and if anyone ventured to contradict him, he would carry on an argument. He'd argue until flushed to the ears, as though it were a serious altercation. Then he'd leave, still quarrelling on one hand but laughing on the other. He didn't drink and was physically healthy.

My second uncle had the Dong name Fa. He had five children, but the second died young of a sudden and aggressive illness. He himself was tall and robust. He often went to visit his sister, my aunt, stopping with her for months at a time. When he returned, he'd be dressed in Han clothing, speaking Mandarin mixed with Dong, as if he had been serving as some kind of Chinese official.

Fa was best friends with two Han men, Luo and Ni, whom he had first met in Langdong. He often went to stay with one of them. Thereafter, the two men reciprocated, taking turns to come and live in Da Sa Lao of Xiangye. The whole extended family had to share the responsibility of hosting them for as long as they stayed.

Once when Fa was about twenty, he returned to the village smoking opium from a crystal-glass pipe. At first, we all dashed over to stare at that pipe, since we'd never set eyes on such a splendid item before.

The same uncle liked to play around with knives and rifles, much feared by other villagers. He behaved as though he were a cut above everyone else in Xiangye. My father was the only person he respected, the only one he did not dare to boss around. For his part, my father was not worried about Fa, saying he was just uneducated and ignorant. Fa often railed at others, and hardly anyone in the whole village had not experienced the sharp end of his tongue.

Fa had taken a Dong woman from the village as a concubine, but within two days, she had run away. After my father's death, people in the local government appointed him village leader, having observed his aggression and propensity for cursing. He held this position for several months, but since he was far from conscientious in collecting taxes or attending meetings, they soon replaced him.

My father and his siblings died relatively early. Judging by numbers alone, however, my father's descendants have flourished, as have those of my two uncles and aunt. All, however, are scattered to the winds. Part of the devastating legacy of long-term class struggle is that they hardly relate to one another at all. Some are not even acquainted. They are related only by blood, not by affection or loyalty.

Four-Plus Years of Primary School in Xiangye

Not long after I donned men's clothing at the age of seven, the biggest change for me was starting school. I studied in Xiangye from 1938 to 1942. First, I was in a private class, then in the newly founded Nationalist Primary School. Really, it was just an initiation, an introduction to Chinese characters and language.

At the beginning, there was no school building, only a teacher employed to give children a basic education based on the *Four Books and Five Classics* of Confucianism.

My older brother and his peers had already studied in this way. His teacher was an elderly man named Yang, who lived in Big Village together with his wife and large family. He spoke neither Dong nor standard Chinese and hardly anyone understood what he said. Perhaps he spoke the Fujian dialect of Chinese. Only after he came to work as a teacher did he marry and have children. His children thus became Dong, but he himself did not change and still spoke a language that most Xiangye people could not understand.

My teacher was a different Han person from outside, one who was also unable to speak Dong. He taught under the grain barn at the eastern end of the village.

On the morning of my first day, the teacher was sitting beside a square table. On the table was a memorial tablet to Confucius. My father led me in and I knelt and bowed three times before the sage Confucius, who was revered like a god, while the teacher looked on.

The teacher did not know that the generational names for our surname Ou went as follows: 'Jun, Da, Zheng, Chao…' He only knew the names for the Yang surname were: 'Zai, Zheng, Tong, Guang…' He gave me the name Ou Tongming, according to the Yang names. I was ready to embark on my student career.

The first text the teacher taught was the *Hundred Family Surnames*, listing 504 Chinese surnames, compiled in the early northern Song dynasty (960–1127 AD). Then he taught the *Three Character Classic*, which was a 13th century text with triplets of characters for easy memorisation. His intention was to teach many common characters, grammatical structures and elements of Chinese history, together with the basics of Confucian morality.

Pointing with a writing brush at characters on the blackboard, the teacher taught us how to read. Students took turns going to the blackboard, one by one. None of us could understand Chinese. We would stare wide-eyed at the character indicated by the brush and read it out after the teacher. Once we knew pronunciation of a character, it was assumed we had mastered it. We generally had no idea what the characters meant and the teacher did not explain them. We studied every morning and afternoon, about eight hours a day. There were no holidays. In one year, the teacher only taught those two books. Though we didn't know what any of it meant, we could repeat it all by heart.

The teacher was usually serious and consistently discreet, lodging alone under the barn and never conversing with women. Each day, we brought food for him, supplying all that he needed to eat and drink. At Chinese New Year, every student brought him a gift: glutinous rice cakes, glutinous rice, preserved meat and pickled fish. Someone was appointed to carry these gifts for him to his home outside the village, where he was to celebrate New Year. If we paid school fees, the amount was small, and I don't remember my parents mentioning it.

My second teacher in the private school, after the first left, was a Dong man from Xiangye named Yang. He taught in the same way as the first, though he added a textbook entitled *University* and taught using some Dong. Since he himself did not know the meanings of the words in the book, he was unable to explain them to us. At the time, people described this as 'moonlight teaching'. Each Chinese pictograph in the book was like the moon in the sky; you could see but not understand it.

We focused on learning to pronounce and write the characters. We practised every day using tissue paper to copy over a sheet produced by Mr Yang, copying the shape of each individual character. Some students wrote nicely, just like the teacher, even after taking the copy sheet away.

Each morning, we had to learn by heart the book text. If we had difficulties, we had to kneel in front of the memorial to Confucius and recite it until we knew it. Those who *could* recite it could leave for lunch. Some had to kneel for a long time after others were dismissed, and *still* could not memorise it. Mr Yang would use a brush to paint red rings around their eyes. We called it 'wearing glasses'. The rings could not be scrubbed off during the lunch break at home, for they had to be worn back to school in the afternoon. Otherwise, the subsequent punishment would be to wear them overnight, until the next day.

My father often taught me a word or two of Chinese. He then forced me to practise what I had learned with any Han visitors. If I spoke well, there would be some praise. If not, there would be a burst of laughter and I would feel stressed and humiliated.

I think it was 1940 when the government ordered each *bao* (or village) to set up a Nationalist Primary School with six year levels, and to abolish private schools. Our village commandeered an empty house as a school building, and established the Liukai Nationalist Primary School.

At first, Mr Yang from the private school was engaged to teach in this new school. Textbooks were printed and distributed by the government. In addition to reading and writing, we were supposed to learn singing and physical training. Mr Yang could only teach recognition of Chinese characters, absolutely nothing else, so other subjects on the syllabus remained untaught. Yang was probably rather opposed to the New Study System. He did not understand Chinese culture at all.

On the first day of the new regime, Mr Yang changed my name from Ou Tongming to Ou Tonghan (*han* meaning 'broad and wide'), using Dong to explain to everyone that I was good at the Chinese language and could communicate well – part of the meaning of *tong* – with Han people. He wrote this new name on my book and I used it as long as he was teacher.

I have one more lasting memory of Mr Yang. He discovered that three phrases from the old private school system had been omitted from the new textbook. He wrote those very phrases on the classroom walls, as a motto to stimulate students: Study to Death [*du si shu* 'study very hard'], Die to Study [*si du shu* 'try hard to be able to study'], Die Studying [*du shu si* 'keep studying until you die']. He often used Dong to explain this, and urged everyone to live according to this celebrated slogan. Having been deeply impressed by this, I spent my whole life studying, and ultimately became a *bona fide* bookworm.

Within a year of establishing the New Study system, the Nanshao government appointed a new teacher for us, a Han man named Wang. He had graduated in New Study. He did not know Dong, but used the educational approach of the Han, and the Chinese language to explain. So for the first time, we had the opportunity to study Chinese in a Chinese-speaking school environment.

Mr Wang noticed that other students sometimes sniggered at my name 'Tonghan' (because it sounded like 'communicating with Han people'). He was irritated by such distraction, so he restored my old name, Ou Tongming. About a year later, another Han teacher was sent to replace Mr Wang.

During my two and a half years in the Nationalist Primary School, we studied from textbooks with modern Chinese (rather than ancient Chinese). Every morning, we raised the national flag and sang the national anthem. After Wang arrived, we did physical training and were taught to stand in line like soldiers, to run in line, to march in step, and do right, left and about turns. We were taught to sing military songs from the War of Resistance against Japan.

At last, there was a much wider curriculum. We did not have to read *moonlight* any more or to recite texts to death, from memory. Thinking and studying were livelier and freer. We could understand some of the Chinese we were hearing and our fear of Han people and culture began to diminish.

My teachers and parents alike were pleased with my progress and reckoned I had potential to do well in Han schools in future. Most villagers, however, on observing my progress, shook their heads and sighed. They felt ambivalent, as I was showing signs of changing beyond recognition.

Chapter 3
Bridling the Horse
(Langdong, 1943-45)

As a child in Xiangye, I occasionally caught sight of Han visitors, but I was completely unfamiliar with Han towns, which in my mind's eye represented an entirely different world from my native village. They filled my heart with dread and under no circumstances did I want to venture into the Han world. To me, it was safest and best if I didn't set eyes on any more Han people.

I was not, however, at liberty to defy my parents, who wanted to send me to a Han town to study, and I was forced to leave the village I loved so much.

My First Two Visits to Langdong

From the beginning, my parents had planned to send me to study in Han schools, forcing me to speak to Han visitors in Chinese. One day, a government official came to the village to assess the 'taxable land', and was hosted by my parents, as usual for such guests.

After a meal, my father introduced me as Ou Tongming and our guest casually remarked that this name was inauspicious. If I was going to study outside, he would give me the name Ou Chaoquan, for the bearer of *that* name would be identified as having good heritage, and would be less vulnerable to bullying. My father repeatedly agreed and from that time onwards, he adopted this new name for me.

My brother had formerly been known as Ou Tongben, but on hearing about my name change, his teacher changed his name to Ou Chaoxi, saying that *xi* was the auspicious light of the Kangxi Emperor [who ruled China from 1661 to 1722, becoming in the process the longest-reigning Chinese emperor in history].

At that time, my brother was at primary school in the town of Langdong, 10 kilometres away. During winter and summer holidays, and on Sundays, he would often bring one or two Han friends from school to play at our home and I would tag along, listening to the visitors and watching them have fun. Everything about them seemed more interesting than the children from our village. I envied them with their smart uniforms and peaked caps, but I was afraid to join in.

Han guests would sometimes reach out and stroke my hair, asking what class I was in at school, who was my teacher, or had I eaten yet. I'd reply bashfully and hesitantly, using the few words and phrases of Chinese I had learned, before running off.

33

When I was four years old, a distant aunt married a Han man from Langdong with the surname Wang, and thereafter lived in his brick-built house, surrounded by walls. To all outward appearances, she became a street-wise Han person. On market days, my mother would visit her. At that time, she was our only relative in town and while my brother was at primary school in Langdong, he lodged in her home.

On one occasion, my brother invited me to Langdong for a holiday and I plucked up courage to go. I had never left the mountains before, and when I first entered my aunt's home, my heart was beating like a drum. Everything about the town was different from home and I recoiled from it all, not daring to embrace what seemed so new and strange. Whether I was walking in the streets, talking to people in my aunt's household, or even eating a meal with them, I did everything in a hurry and finished as quickly as possible.

Once as I was hurrying along outside, a slightly older boy started to chase me armed with stones, yelling that he was going to get me. I dashed back to my aunt's house and my brother's intervention, scouting around outside, deterred the boy from following me in. Afterwards, someone in my aunt's family told me the boy was a well-known troublemaker, bent on intimidating village children, and I was warned to beware of him in future. This terrifying encounter soon after I had arrived in the Han world shocked me deeply and cast a shadow over my whole childhood.

Around that time, a man named Yu was appointed leader in Langdong and one day he rode into Xiangye, along with a group of soldiers. Without a word, he marched into Big House and as usual, my parents were captive hosts, playing the friendly landlord, killing poultry and catching fish to feed the guests. In the evening, Yu stood beside the well, watching the young women fetch water, while by day he wandered in the fields and hillsides, as if looking for something. On the second day, he went home.

A few days later, a man came to my home selling opium and announced that Mr Yu wanted to marry my sister, Yunyun. My parents were appalled, but dared not demur, tactfully replying with a few pleasantries, using the kind of courtesy normally reserved for relatives.

At only a few years of age, my sister had been betrothed to the son of one of the richest men around, named Li, from the nearby village of Zhanmo. The eldest son of the Li family and my sister were roughly the same age, and my parents reckoned that our two families were well matched in social and economic status.

Years later, the Li family sent someone to finalise the match and my parents promptly agreed, though my sister disliked Li's eldest son, for he was short and seemed incompetent. She quarrelled with the matchmaker, seized the engagement chicken and released it. The killing of the chicken to settle the engagement [ensuring that after cooking both eyes were either open or closed] was cancelled. Both sets of parents, however, still gave tacit consent to the match.

My 18-year-old sister remained adamantly opposed, fussing and swearing any time the issue was raised, but she had never been able to extricate herself from the proposal. There was no good match for her in either Big Village or

Small Village, so for days on end she was out of sorts. She'd pick up a basket and wander far away to gather chestnuts or wild vegetables.

While gathering vegetables in the mountains about two weeks after Yu's matchmaker had visited, my sister was kidnapped by three soldiers. She was taken to Yu's home and promptly became his wife, at 19 years of age embarking upon her short and inauspicious first marriage.

Afterwards, the matchmaker came to inform my parents that my sister was now living in the Yu residence at the southern gate of Langdong. My mother wept softly to herself for several days, and the whole family felt sad and sorry for my sister. My father sighed, remarking ruefully how fierce were the Gejia (Han) of Langdong; better never to offend them.

Although Yu was from a higher social class, he really wanted to marry my sister, Mao. If we had refused, he might very well have organised people from Langdong to take possession of our village and drive us all away. With Yu as a relative, we were more secure; my family's relationship with him helped all the other village families. So there seemed to be no other way of resolving my sister's situation.

Not long afterwards, Ni and Yang stabbed Zhang outside our home (see Chapter 1) and ran off. Convalescing beside the fire in my house, Zhang intended to investigate whether my family was in any way responsible for his injury. At this, my father trembled with fear and sent someone to Langdong to notify my sister. That same night, Yu sent 10 soldiers to search for the culprits, while arranging for someone to accompany my father and me to take refuge in Langdong. We stayed at my sister's house until the storm subsided, while mother stayed at home alone, in the expectation that no one would bother her.

While my father and I were staying at my sister's home, our minds were ill at ease, imagining the household property and livestock might be stolen and my mother evicted. At the same time, we were afraid of the Han people all around; even of Yu's domestic servants and farm labourers. We did not converse with any of them and only went to eat when my sister called. We would hurriedly finish our meal before going back upstairs to cower in the bedroom, not daring to venture outside.

One day, my sister disappeared. Yu searched everywhere, yelling and screaming her name. This was the cue for my father to leave, and we stealthily returned home. That trip to Langdong had not been to visit my sister but to seek asylum, and I was even more confused than during my first visit. My father's stubborn self-respect made him seem arrogant to people in Yu's household. For my part, I never felt at home, just estranged, basically afraid of the Han people.

I was plagued by the memory of my first visit to Langdong, when I had suffered the ignominy of being pursued by that boy threatening to blast me with rocks. On my second visit, I spent whole days cringing by my father's side, longing for the familiarity of home, urging my father to return there.

Sometime later, a Han person from Langdong with the surname Ou came to our home addressing my mother as 'auntie'. He was generally easy-going, wore an open smile towards everyone and was modest in all he said, just like a Dong person. When I observed his amiable disposition, my usual fear of Han people dissolved. He went around with me, listening to and conversing simply with me, answering my questions. I addressed him as 'older brother'.

This Ou was the first Han person I had encountered who made such a good impression. There was no sense of estrangement or intimidation when I was with him. This was a major development and emboldened me to return later to Langdong to study. The home of this 'big brother' was the first place I lodged there, and starting from his home, I stepped over the threshold into the Han world and began generally to accept Han culture.

Two and a Half Years at Primary School in Langdong

The difference between my mother and other Xiangye women was that she had no special affection for the village. Many other women there were native to the village, but mother was not and simply never learned to love Xiangye, always hoping her children would leave, aspiring to a better position in society for them. Dong and local Han people alike accorded higher social status to someone the more he or she had travelled and accomplished in other places.

In 1943, my brother had long since graduated from primary school in Langdong and was attending junior middle school in Rongjiang, and my parents planned for me to follow in his footsteps to Langdong primary. One market day early in the year, a man was employed to accompany me to the home of big brother Ou in Langdong. The man carried gifts of rice, preserved meat and hot pepper on a pole and delivered them to Ou. The following day, he brought me to the primary school and I applied to attend the second semester of grade 4 there.

A boy named Yang from Xiangye, five years my senior, applied on the same day and we ended up in the same class. Yang lodged with a family at the north gate, along with two distantly related Dong cousins. There they enjoyed conversation and companionship, as though still living in the village. They did not feel so startled by the strangeness of everything, but I was staying alone in older brother Ou's house, unused to everything and inclined to feel homesick.

This was my first time away from the village for any extended time. There were three people in Ou's family: himself, his wife and his daughter. Since I was young and timid, big brother Ou kept me company upstairs and also slept upstairs. His wife slept downstairs with their daughter, who was in grade 3 and whom I accompanied to and from school every day. We two, however, did not talk; she never spoke to me and I never spoke to her. Even her mother rarely ever spoke to me. There seemed to be an invisible barrier between us, beyond which we didn't dare trespass.

We ate together for almost a year, but only Ou ever called me to the table to eat. He passed choice food to me with his chopsticks, often encouraging me to eat more. In the evenings, he chatted with me and on Sundays took me to his fields to pull up weeds, or do some other manual work with him. When he was with me, he always seemed to be smiling, more cordial even than my own brother. This was one fixed thing I could rely on at that time, and it enabled me to concentrate on learning at school.

In the evenings after school, I often went to the north gate to play with my schoolmates the Yangs. Together, we cheerfully forgot we were in town, and it was like being at home, free and unrestrained.

We went home every Saturday evening, arriving around dusk. My mother would often weep with joy, hurrying to kill a chicken and steam some glutinous rice, after which she'd sit beside me and urge me to eat more. She kept saying how sorry she was that I had to suffer so much in the town. We boys had a standing arrangement to meet the next afternoon at about five o'clock and return to school together. My mother would accompany me sadly to rendezvous with the Yangs.

After nearly 15 kilometres of mountain paths, I was always delighted to reach home, never tired, feet light and nimble, though it was nearly all uphill. When returning to school, however, my feet felt heavy and my heart heavier. None of us felt any pleasure. I'd be reluctant to leave mother and village, feeling deeply attached to both. Mother, too, found it difficult to accept my living at a school that subjected me to such discipline, depriving me of the village liberty I enjoyed to speak, laugh and do as I pleased; my meat-deprived diet, with its vegetables and tofu; and especially my loneliness, having no one really to turn to.

Each time I reached Mount Qingwang on the journey back to school, the shining white 'seals' – 'forts' occupied by Han people – in the distance would impress their contours on my vision, along with the dragon-like, zigzagging Langdong town wall. It would always strike me how bizarrely different this was from the Dong, Miao and Han villages with which I was familiar. This picture belonged to an entirely different world, standing in stark contrast to its environment and causing me to feel awe-struck and home-sick.

I hardly dared to go down and invade that scene, usually pausing on the hilltop for 10 or 15 minutes, observing the forts from a distance, and thinking about the Langdong people I knew. It felt like I was a wild horse being reined in, surrendering the unbridled freedom experienced at home. It took time to pluck up courage to re-enter the place where I would encounter all kinds of unwelcome restrictions.

During my first semester in Langdong, classes were convened in an empty Buddhist temple. We studied Mandarin, mathematics and art, along with geography, nature, physical education and physical work. Yang and I were the only two countryside children in my class, which otherwise consisted almost entirely of Han children from the town.

Being one of the eldest, Yang was the tallest in the class. The teacher appointed him class leader, to preside over weekly meetings, organise orderly lines when leaving school, and suchlike. No one dared to contradict him. I looked upon Yang as an older brother, speaking directly only to him, for I was shy towards the teacher and other classmates. If anyone spoke to me, I didn't know how to respond, but simply smiled.

In the afternoons after art class, the son and nephew of the headmaster, both in grade 6, often came to our classroom to play. Surprisingly, they would sit next to me, joking and chatting, in a disarmingly friendly way, but I still didn't dare to respond. After school, the headmaster's son was often just in front of me or behind me as we lined up, always laughing and talking. He never bullied me, so most others followed suit.

In my class, however, there were two students who bullied me a lot. One was Li, the boy who had chased me the first time I ever visited Langdong, who lived in the town with his father, an inveterate drinker. The other was a local Yang from the north gate. These two would often come over and create a disturbance; for example tearing my books away and throwing them on the floor, before running off.

Sometimes, I'd just be standing in the corridor when Li and Yang came to push me around, to swear at and humiliate me. I'd turn and move away, but they pursued me, until the teacher howled at them to stop.

My classmates realised what was going on and became accustomed to it. No one dared to say anything, for the two boys were widely feared. I studied in terror, perpetually fearful of seeing their dreaded shadows or hearing their mocking voices. This made me even more reserved than I would otherwise have been.

After one semester, the two bullies had to repeat a year because they failed their exams, but instead they never returned. I managed to pass every subject and made a smooth transition into grade 5. On the first morning of the new school year, after the teacher announced the fate of the two abusive students, I looked directly at each classmate for the first time, surveying them in their seats. I felt absolutely overjoyed, as though waking from a nightmare. My fellow Dong student, who was presiding over the class meeting that morning, leaned over and said in Dong, "Now you don't need to be afraid any longer."

One market day, the mother of a boy from Xiangye, who was two classes below me at Langdong primary, came into the school premises to visit him. With her Dong skirt, she soon became the object of curiosity, surrounded by students having a good look. The son lost face and privately scolded his mother, telling her to leave and not come back.

Each market day, my mother came to see me, engaging someone to carry a load of food and deliver it to the place where I was staying, while she carried a separate package of glutinous rice with chicken drumsticks and pickled fish, and gave it directly to me. I would take the precious package to a secluded place and enjoy the food, enough to constitute a full meal. Otherwise, I always felt famished, and I longed for my mother's visits, so I could enjoy some good food.

On market days, I often observed distressing scenes of peasants being victimised by townspeople. Red bayberries grew seasonally in the wild, big and juicy, jet-black and sweet, and were picked by Dong and Miao people. Villagers would rise early to collect as many as they could carry, filling bamboo baskets and carrying them to the market on a pole.

As soon as they entered through the town gate, townsmen would approach and casually grab a bunch to sample. If the fruit was sweet, the men would follow and grab more, but if it was sour, they would throw it away in disgust and swear, saying, "____ his mother; so sour!"

The baskets would be set down and people milling around would squat down and sample the fruit, while reaching for more. Some having just eaten their fill, would stand up and pronounce their verdict, 'Too sour!' smacking their hands on their thighs as they left. Kinder customers would buy one or two pounds, handing over a few copper coins. The bayberry sellers would behave as if they had just encountered an angel. Sometimes, however, a whole load of bayberries never met one such angel, the spoiled, leftover fruit after 'sampling' had to be thrown away, and villagers would return home empty-handed.

In the cold season, farmers carried loads of charcoal into the town. As soon as they appeared at the town gate, people living near the gate would seize some sticks for themselves. When the rest were placed at the crossroads for sale, government soldiers invariably helped themselves.

Vendors stood there waiting. If they were lucky, someone would come along and make a purchase, the income would be used to buy a little salt or money paper and they would go home contented. If, however, by dusk they had not been so lucky and had sold nothing, they would just give the leftover charcoal to the shop owner behind them, to lighten their load and get home quickly.

On market days, my mother went to town to sell Dong cloth, while my aunts and other relatives went to sell eggs and dried fish; but they experienced similar exploitation. Observing such things made my heart ache, and I wondered, "When shall we villagers, so weak and vulnerable, ever escape injustice at the hands of the townspeople?"

I had just become used to lodging in the home of big brother Ou when my mother decided I should lodge instead with my aunt, the one who was married to Mr Wang. Her husband owned one of the forts, was already old and had four wives, all over 30 years of age. None had any children, so the household consisted only of Wang and his four wives. Strange as it may seem, there were no arguments.

Like the others, my aunt spoke Mandarin – she had apparently forgotten most of her Dong – but she was fairly uncommunicative anyway. Each day, two meals were served at the square table in the central room, with three or four vegetable dishes and one or two slabs of tofu. Sometimes there would also be a plate of pork; mainly for the man of the house, who would distribute a small portion to each person individually.

In autumn and winter, a charcoal fire would burn in a metal basin supported by a square wooden frame in the main room, and the house door would be kept wide open. Adults huddled around the fire warming their hands, but I was still young and the women made no space for me, so I usually got nowhere near.

In the side room where I stayed, the door and windows were also kept wide open, and the table, chair and bed were icy cold. After lunch, it was too cold to sit there and I had to go out on the streets to walk about and keep warm, but being young, that felt like no problem.

After the evening meal, I had to sit quietly in someone else's bedroom, doing my homework and reading. As soon as the metal door of the fort was closed, everything fell silent and it felt gloomy and frightening. There were many long nights when I was unable to sleep, curled up under my quilt with a phobia about ghosts.

Whenever mother came to visit me in Langdong, she also went to see my sister in the Yu family home at the south gate. Eventually, she arranged for me to go and lodge there, rather than in my aunt's cold, gloomy house, reckoning that the Yu family was friendlier than Wang's.

My sister's house was a two-storey wooden building. People lived on the ground floor, with only one room above reserved for study. The other space upstairs was occupied by piles of grain. I lived alone upstairs, with a large window overlooking vegetable gardens, rice paddies and mountain paths at the back of the house. Often and for long periods, I gazed out the window at the beautiful scenery, daydreaming, but otherwise I would do homework and no one disturbed me. In the evenings, frogs began to croak and sounded busy, right up until midnight. Lying in bed, I frequently felt afraid, sleeping alone with the whole floor to myself.

There were two other students lodging there and each morning, my sister gave us hot rice for breakfast; the only time during my two-plus years at Langdong primary when I was able to eat breakfast. At lunch and dinner, there would be some meat; the best meals I had in those years.

Yu was the first ever regional leader in Langdong. During his term of office, a 'complete school' (for all six primary grades) was built in the west of the town, with tiled roof and wooden frame, all painted with tung-tree oil to prevent rotting. The primary school moved out of its temporary temple premises and convened in the new school, a two-storey building with four classrooms on each level, two on either side of the steps.

While Yu was regional leader, some teachers who had graduated from middle school and teacher's college were appointed to teach in Langdong primary. They improved standards and Langdong became the best complete primary school in the region. Primary school graduates became local 'scholars', progressed to study at a higher level, and eventually worked in government offices, or served as principals or teachers at junior primary schools in the countryside.

I moved into the new school building when I was in grade 5. My grade teacher had just graduated from the Dushan branch of the Central Military Academy. He insisted that all boys in the class should live at the school and assemble at the crack of dawn, when he would lead us in a jog down to the river to wash our faces in cold water, followed by a jog back to the school. Then he personally ran to the bell tower and rang the bell to summon everyone else out of bed, a resounding call that could be heard throughout the town. The townsfolk rose and organised their children for school.

The same man was our Chinese teacher. Occasionally, to add physical to mental exercise, he led us to the cotton fields on the mountain outside the town gate, and delivered his lessons there. We listened as he shouted various slogans, as if he were leading an army into battle, and afterwards there were exhortations about how we should conduct ourselves. I still remember two phrases always on his lips: 'Blessed are the soldiers in the War of Resistance' and 'Military matters are the most important'. He insisted that every boy should be ready at any moment to put down his writing brush and pick up a sword.

During my second year in town, Yu retired as district leader, took my sister and left Langdong; first to live in Rongjiang county town, but then to return to Zhaihao and run their own small store.

After my sister left, mother arranged for me to lodge with a Taoist priest named Gong, who had moved to Langdong from outside. He officiated at funerals, including my father's, convening memorial ceremonies for the dead and helping them to start their journey in the afterlife. Dressed in filial mourning clothes, I had followed behind Gong to worship on bended knee before my father's coffin.

Within a few days, Gong had formed a good impression of me, saying I was quick-witted, intelligent and polite. He had no sons, just one daughter who was still small, so he asked my mother if I could be his adopted son and mother agreed. I subsequently addressed Gong as 'step-dad' and his wife as 'step-mother', but stayed in their house only to eat and sleep. Actually, it was the worst living situation I experienced during my time in Langdong, for there was nowhere to read or do homework, so I had to spend as much time as possible in the classroom to complete my work.

In the second semester of grade 5, my former Chinese teacher's younger brother was appointed as our grade teacher. From any text we were about to study, he first taught us how to write any characters we did not yet know. Then he used the dictionary in his hand to look up each of these characters and teach us how to say it correctly, while explaining its meaning. Finally, he discussed the text, often assigning as homework the task of learning to recite it from memory. Those who failed to recite the text would be punished by having to stand for one whole class.

It was a school rule that if you failed any subject, you had to repeat the whole year's study. Many students gave up. When I was in grade 4, there were 40-plus students, but by grade 6, only 20 remained.

It felt like torture for me to persevere and finish grade 6. On the day I graduated, I left Langdong immediately for home, like a wild horse that had just been set free. This concluded for me a period of unbearable loneliness.

Chapter 4
Steering a Clear Path
(Rongjiang, 1946-47)

Testing the Waters

My mother's dream had always been for me to continue studying after primary school. *Where*, however, should I study?

Middle schools were only established in county towns. Our village was in County Jianhe, but only a few villagers had ever gone to live in Jianhe county town, and we had no close friends or relatives there. My mother and I had never set foot in the town, so it felt out of the question for me to go there.

While my brother had been doing teacher-training in Rongjiang, my parents had given money to my sister to invest in a store in the town of Zhaihao, County Rongjiang. Thus at that time, my sister was living in Zhaihao and the stage seemed set for me to apply to Rongjiang Middle School.

Mother often sighed wistfully, "Where can you study that's not too far from home?" She was caught between wanting me to have more education and not wanting me to go too far away, and faced with this dilemma, she seemed content to have me stay at home a little longer.

In 1944, the Japanese were attacking Guilin near the northern border of Guangxi, intending to invade Guizhou Province from there, and China was in crisis. Our village was located in the southeast of Guizhou, close to the border with Guangxi. Everyone in the region was perplexed, wondering what the future would hold and what to do for the best.

The programme of conscription intensified. Originally, one in every three able-bodied men had been called up, but this was increased to one in two; if there were two brothers in a family, one would be taken to serve in the army. In 1944, officials only had to set eyes on a young man for him to be tied up and dragged off to fight. They'd reason, "This is a national crisis. If you have money, we need your money. If you have manpower, we need your manpower."

Young Xiangye men (aged between 18 and 25) worked in the fields by day as usual. At dusk, some returned home stealthily to spend the night. Having boiled a day's supply of rice they would then leave again at the crack of dawn. Others slept in cattle sheds far from the village, only daring to go home once every couple of weeks.

Occasionally, two or three children would be sitting around the drum tower, when suddenly men armed with rifles would rush into the village. Not chancing upon conscription candidates, they would take out long metal tubes used for cleaning the rifles and chase the chickens and ducks instead, poking at them, and killing some. They'd leave in high spirits, with spoils on their gun barrels.

Villages seemed to be fair game, as if willing accomplices in such looting. Homeowners would hide in the mountains as their possessions were being pillaged, and the village would remain deathly still until evening. Then under cover of darkness, kitchen chimneys would resume puffing smoke, and fir-wood lights would dance on the open verandas, as if to announce to anyone who cared to know, that this village was inhabited after all.

When I graduated from primary school, there was no one at home apart from my mother, no one else with whom I could communicate. By day, I hid upstairs with the grain, reading or keeping a lookout over the desolate village. By night, I whiled away the time playing the *pipa*, though I could hardly play one complete tune, but simply enjoyed the tranquil tone. When mother observed me idle and bored, she became worried. One day, she announced I should go and look up my sister, and ask her what to do.

The Yu family now had a brick house in Zhaihao, with a cake store in the front two rooms. They hired a businessman from Hunan to run the store and two workers to make pastry. My sister lived there, keeping an eye on the financial side of the business. In autumn 1945, mother hired an old man from the village to accompany me to my sister's home. It was my first time going to such distant parts.

I walked downwards through the mountains with my elderly companion, along rugged paths through primeval forest. It was cold and gloomy, and we walked a whole day without meeting a single human being. Occasionally, we'd see smoke rising from chimneys in the middle distance, with 10 or more households packed closely together.

It was often difficult to steer a clear path through the mountains. After Langdong, each stretch of path seemed littered with a corpse lying to one side. In some places, there were many corpses, completely naked!

These people had been in the National Resistance Army fighting the Japanese, under the command of General Yang Sen. When Guilin fell, many soldiers retreated into Guizhou via mountain paths in the north of Guangxi and dispersed in the direction of Guiyang. Many died of starvation or cold along the way, as they trudged through uninhabited forests. Ammunition and clothing of those who succumbed were commandeered by mountain residents. The naked corpses scared me out of my wits. My elderly companion sternly instructed me to look the other way.

We arrived in Zhaihao as night was falling. I was so shocked from the journey, I did not talk the whole night. The old man related what we had seen on the journey and my sister urged him to return by another route. A detour via Sebian would avoid such macabre scenes.

The original inhabitants of Zhaihao had been Dong, but many Han Chinese people had moved to the region from 1911 onwards. The street where my sister lived was full of business people from Hunan. They were originally from the same area as my sister's husband Yu, running businesses selling salt, sugar, pastry, money paper and suchlike. Their customers were local Dong and Miao villagers.

During those days at my sister's home, I observed many Dong people walking around with shoulder poles carrying loads of firewood and charcoal. There were more women than men. The women made their own clothes and looked very attractive. Local residents and business people had learned to speak Dong. Many of them took Dong women as wives. At that time, most men in Zhaihao were Han, though more than half the women were Dong. Most of the Dong women, however, already dressed in the Han way and had no plans to return to the Dong villages.

My sister suggested I go to Rongjiang to investigate the middle school there, whereupon we rode a boat for a day to reach the county town. We stayed with a family also named Yu, people from Hunan, who were related to my sister's husband.

There were then two secondary schools in Rongjiang: the state-run Teacher Training School and the county-run Middle School. Because of the War of Resistance, staff and students from Guangxi University and the Han Middle School of Nanning had migrated to Rongjiang from Guangxi, and were temporarily staying in the county town.

The county guildhalls and temples were full of students. There was no standard uniform for these young men; they wore all kinds of traditional and modern attire. Rongjiang had practically become a student town.

On Sundays, you could see students flocking to church. I accompanied them respectfully to listen to the preaching and was presented with a few small gospel tracts. Later, I bought a Bible from a street vendor displaying books on the ground. I often read it and felt drawn to its message.

At around this time, I received a letter from my brother in Duyun, advising me to look up his former classmate Xia, to collect a parcel of books. He had given Xia several works of Soviet literature, including *And Quiet Flows the Don* (1934). Xia's home was in the town centre. He kindly invited me to stay there should I return to study in Rongjiang. Perusal of the books served as a wake-up call to the existence of The Soviet Union, a federation of Communist republics.

I stayed in Rongjiang almost a month and liked the town, returning to my sister's home only reluctantly. It was winter before I returned from Zhaihao to Xiangye. Since my last sojourn in the village, I had begun to experience the outside world. It was the first time I had seen a county town or a middle school, and the first time I had ever met university students. The trip served as good preparation for starting middle school.

Junior Middle School

Mother wanted to send me to school in Rongjiang, but for about half a year, she had prevaricated. She would resolve to send me, renege and then again decide to send me. One day in spring 1946, after spending the previous night in tears, she hired someone to accompany me to Rongjiang.

The day after I arrived, I registered to take the middle school entrance examination. The next day, I was in a classroom full of students taking the exam. There were many vacancies, so it was quite easy for me to pass and become a new first-year student at the school. Apart from my brother, no child from Xiangye had ever studied before at middle school.

No one in the school, however, knew I was a Dong boy. They all thought I was from an influential family in Langdong. I played along with this. So it transpired I was generally treated with courtesy and respect. For many years after Liberation (1949), none of my Rongjiang acquaintances realised I was a Dong person from Xiangye village, of County Jianhe.

In those days, Dong, Miao or other 'peasant' children would often be chased around the school playground, to guffaws of laughter and general amusement. They would be openly despised as 'Miao boys' or 'peasant kids'. The minority boys could hardly resist some rejoinder, but if they answered back, they would be beaten up. Academically weaker students were particularly vulnerable. Announcement of examination results became the occasion for insulting the Dong boys.

In the minds of many from Rongjiang, the people of Langdong were also peasants, and fair game. One night after end-of-term exams, several Rongjiang classmates were loitering outside my lodgings. They bawled out my name, swearing and calling me to come out. I knew they wanted to beat me up, so I hid in the vegetable garden behind the house and so avoided a thrashing.

There was a bridge in Rongjiang separating the town from the local Dong community. Two of my classmates were from that community, and wore traditional black Dong clothes, speaking to each other in Dong. They were often heckled, 'Miao language!' or, 'Miao boys!'

The bell at the end of the school day was the Dong boys' cue to make a dash for the bridge, often with several bullies in pursuit, shouting 'Yup! Yup!' as if driving animals away. In the mornings, they would often be obstructed at the school entrance. Only when the bell rang would they be allowed to enter the school and classroom. These two Dong classmates persevered for a year, but after the start of my second year, I never saw them again.

In 1943, all my father's profit from selling timber had been ploughed into the Yu family shop in Rongjiang, and there had never been any return from the investment. In the summer of 1945, Rongjiang town was submerged in a flood and due to flood damage, the Yus' business was bankrupted. All the investment capital was thus lost. My middle school studies could no longer be supported from the proceeds of that business, as previously hoped.

When I arrived in Rongjiang, a friend introduced me to Aunty Zhou, in her fifties, and I lodged with her near the middle school. Her daughter was a widow with two young children, a son and a daughter.

Zhou and her daughter lived in a small wooden house, with three rooms downstairs and an open attic upstairs. Some students from Hunan lodged upstairs. The beds were squeezed tight against each other. At the dining table downstairs, the seats were often full. Aunty Zhou and her daughter were busy all day preparing meals for the students.

One of the Hunan lodgers, in his third year at the teacher-training school, was named Wang. He respectfully addressed Aunty Zhou as his mother. She had no sons and was delighted to 'adopt' this young man, supplying him with food and drink, setting aside some of the best food for him. After graduation, Wang joined the army in Hunan and in 1949, he fled to Taiwan. After Liberation, Aunty Zhou would occasionally receive a letter from him. She became obsessed with the idea of his return. I was later told that on her deathbed, during the Cultural Revolution (1966-76), she often called out his name.

When I first went to stay in Aunty Zhou's home, it was packed. By the end of term, however, only two brothers named Zhou remained, along with Wang, who still turned up for meals, every lunch and dinner.

By the time the second semester began, I was the only lodger there. From then on, the house was quiet and peaceful. There was no breakfast, only lunch and evening meal. The main staple was rice, supplemented by vegetables and tofu, with a tiny saucer of hot pepper in soy sauce on the side. There was no meat, fish or eggs. Even the cooking oil was vegetable oil. So it was a strictly vegetarian diet. Every day was like this, until my belly felt hot with pepper. How I longed for a taste of meat!

Once Aunty Zhou won a prize in the lottery and splashed out to buy a pound of pork. That night, the five of us shared a feast, with fatty meat, and crisp, savoury skin, in sweet soy sauce from Guangdong; a fabulous memory of 1940s cuisine! That was the only time I tasted pork during one-and-a-half years with Aunty Zhou.

Perhaps because she was vegetarian, Zhou had strong friendships with monks and nuns from the temple on the mountain behind her house. When they came to town, they would stop at her home for a break. They talked about how cool and spacious it was in the temple, and how flowers bloomed on the mountains all year around. By contrast, the town was sultry and noisy, a place where malaria and cholera were easily contracted.

On one occasion, Aunty Zhou and her daughter spent two whole days preparing a vegetarian banquet, including beans and tofu, for temple guests. Three monks and two nuns turned up and shared the fare with the two hostesses and me. There were eight large dishes and four smaller dishes, with a big bowl of tofu and vegetable soup. It was a no-holds-barred feast: deep-fried, stir-fried and boiled; with pieces, strips, noodles, chunks and dumplings.

To outward appearances, it looked like a normal banquet with meat and fish, but actually, it was completely vegetarian and tasted insipid. Zhou and her daughter warmly encouraged the guests to eat more. The two nuns were so grateful they wept. They were so busy wiping away tears, they hardly had time to eat. The three monks were genteel to a fault, not conversing, only smiling and eating.

In my 18 months with Zhou, she twice put on vegetarian banquets like this, entertaining with magnificent largesse. Perhaps this was born of her faith in

Buddhism and the hope that her good works would earn her blessings in this life. The relationship between Zhou and those Buddhist friends was certainly extraordinary.

Zhou treated me very well, if not quite as awesomely as the Buddhist monks! Neighbours said she was even kinder to me than to her informally adopted son Wang.

Zhou's daughter was around 30 years of age. Raising a son and daughter without a husband was really difficult. I addressed her as 'big sister' and she treated me as if I were her own younger brother.

Zhou and her daughter felt just like family, and lodging with them in those 18 months felt just like living at home. There was, however, that secret I always kept from them, both then and later: I am a Dong person from Xiangye village in County Jianhe. I concealed my minority identity for fear of discrimination. This lack of honesty has left me with a guilty conscience today.

After the Japanese surrendered in September 1945, the Guangxi University and Han Middle School students returned to Nanning. Only the state-run Teacher Training School and the county-run Middle School remained in Rongjiang.

Compared to neighbouring counties, however, education in Rongjiang was still well developed. There were more than 1,000 trainees at the Teacher Training School. Its reputation was strong throughout the region, and it trained a whole generation of primary school teachers. Rongjiang Middle School was only established in 1944, opposite the Teacher Training School. In the mornings as the flag was raised and the national anthem sung, students from one school could hear those of the other.

There existed, however, an enormous virtual distance between the schools. Teacher-trainees nurtured the idea that Middle School students hailed from wealthy homes. Middle School students suspected the teacher-training was half-physical-work and only half-study. Such prejudices led to estrangement between the two school communities. The street between the schools was like a ravine. Teachers and students from the two communities generally did not mix. Feelings of pride and prejudice abounded.

Once when our school lost a basketball match to the teacher-trainees, and the trainees were celebrating with raucous cheering and banging of drums, some of our school's boys and girls burst out crying. Others were so angry they were ready to start a fight, but one of our teachers intervened saying, "Rongjiang Middle School has lost. Everyone return."

I was not caught up in mutual estrangement, however. On the one hand, my love for the Middle School was not as strong as that of many other students. On the other, the Teacher Training School was home to many of my 'older brothers', who had been classmates of my own brother and treated me as their younger brother. They helped me with any difficulties I encountered in life or study.

I went to see those older brothers two or three times a week and observed them studying hard, living simply, and submitting to strict discipline. Their teachers seemed to behave with dignity and respect, and the general atmosphere was one of conscientious compliance with the prevailing discipline. This all seemed in stark contrast to the Middle School and it seemed to me that the Middle School had a long way to go before it could attain such a positive atmosphere.

Staff at the Teacher Training School included some with good qualifications that the Middle School had declined to hire. Most of our teachers were from County Rongjiang. They came from mixed educational backgrounds and included university, senior middle school and junior middle school graduates. One had graduated only from a private primary school. He was actually the best language teacher. Our mathematics and science teachers were very experienced and had digested well the content of their classes. With a little application, it was possible to learn well.

Everyone approved of our Chinese teacher. There was general interest in his subject and it was one of my personal favourites. My private axe to grind was that the vocabulary of Dong seemed so limited. In Dong, we had to borrow many nouns from Chinese and many actions were also difficult to describe. Feelings of homesickness, for example, could hardly be expressed in Dong. To express sorrow, we mostly used 'sigh' or 'cry'; while to express pleasure, we mostly used 'laugh'.

After my studies in Rongjiang, the abundance and elegance of Chinese vocabulary seemed stunning. A rapid transformation of mind was underway, and language seemed much more versatile than before. Chinese could be used to express one's thoughts and feelings precisely, to articulate matters clearly. I was attracted by the boundless potential of expression in the written word. For me, Chinese was the easiest subject, as well as one of the most interesting.

Outside class time, I could hardly be found without a novel in hand. I devoured one book after another. Some impressed mainly because of their rich and elegant vocabulary; often I would not remember any story-content. Among those whose content impressed were the romantic novels *Opportunities to Laugh and Cry*, *The Woman in the Tower* and *Love in the Soviet Union*. In my diary, I wrote about the stirring of new feelings. Keeping a diary became a habit and this in turn improved my language ability.

After my first year, a writing competition was convened for all students at the school. The theme was: 'The perfect middle school student'. My essay won second prize. In addition to a certificate, I received a small financial prize. Of course, I was delighted. It was the only such prize I can remember from my time in Rongjiang.

Thus, I was fond of reading and perpetually hungry to read more. In addition to the set textbooks, I secretly read *And Quiet Flows the Don*. From that, I understood something of the circumstances surrounding the revolution in the Soviet Union. I always had to hide it beneath the wooden board on my bed, to prevent its discovery.

At that time, there were some 'progressive students' at the Teacher Training School, supporting Liberation. The county government sometimes dispatched army police onto the street between the two schools at 6 in the morning. They would enter students' rooms one by one and make a thorough search. They barged into my bedroom several times and flipped through the books on my desk, turning over my pillow for good measure. They were on the lookout for any trace of *The Little Red Book* by Mao Zedong. Thankfully, they never found *And Quiet Flows the Don*. If they *had* discovered it, my brains would have been blown out. No kidding.

There were very few 'rural students' at Rongjiang Middle. The overwhelming majority were youths from the county town. Thus, I was lonely, as before in Langdong. Boys from the higher grades often smiled in a friendly way, but never said a word. Most of the boys from my class did not talk to me either, and I never played with them. I was treated as a stranger and remained one. A few girls from my class stole furtive glances, smiling as they whispered to each other.

This all embarrassed me. In Rongjiang, I was always shy, only communicating with my desk-mate, a boy named Shi, with whom I formed a close attachment. He was from County Sandu, but I never ascertained his nationality, only surmising that he was Shui. He likewise could not figure out my background. We only talked about the present, not the past.

Most probably, Shi was concealing his minority identity from outsiders, just as I was. He was five years older, having only started middle school after turning 20. Thus, he was one of the oldest students in the class and appeared ill at ease in the classroom.

Shi was naturally friendly with me. We were both from outside town, seemingly incompatible with the townspeople in many respects, so the decision to sit at the same desk was an easy one. If one of us did not appear at class, the other would look him up to see what was wrong. Neither of us liked to sit alone. After class, we would leave the room together and at the end of the day, we would exit the school gate together.

At middle school, there was one other boy with whom I had a close friendship, named Hu, about the same age as Shi. His home was in County Sansui of Guizhou. His uncle had opened a shop and was doing business in Rongjiang town. He had been taken into his uncle's home as a child and had lived there ever since. When I knew him, he was in grade 3 of middle school. When he noticed my friendship with Shi, he gravitated towards us, and was soon coming to visit me at Aunty Zhou's.

We three often spent time together. Hu arranged for a walk in the eastern mountains one sunny and cloudless Sunday. He packed fish and steamed buns, and we shared a picnic at the edge of the forest, sitting in a three-person circle. We mostly just surveyed the placid and beautiful scene below, Chejiang's vast luxuriant fields. It seemed as though we could read each other's feelings.

Hu was an excellent landscape painter. One of the Hunan businessmen ran a poster shop and did a fine job of framing art. Hu drew 10 paintings and paid to frame them, giving the final products to me! I used these to adorn the walls in my bedroom. Everyone who saw them admired them.

One of Hu's classmates was the son of a county leader who was renowned for his wonderful calligraphy. Through his friendship with the son, Hu managed to obtain for me a couplet written in the revered hand of the county leader: 'We talk about history when holding a sword; we talk about heroes when making rice wine'. This too was framed into a wall-hanging and presented to me as a gift.

When the new term began in spring of 1947, Hu's uncle asked him to accompany a relative's wife to the city of Nanjing near the east coast. The relative was a major general and department head in the Nanjing military headquarters. Shi and I went to see Hu off, walking along together in silence. As he was about to board the boat, Hu presented me with a pocket watch. We stood on the bank watching the boat move off slowly, until it disappeared from view. I felt numb at the prospect of his moving to such a distant place.

One afternoon two months later, my two friends came looking for me at Aunty Zhou's. Hu was decked out in military uniform. There was joy upon our reunion. I took the pocket watch and returned it to Hu with thanks. This was an act of courtesy common among the Dong, and Hu was happy to accept my token of friendship and retake possession of the watch.

Hu had worked as assistant to the major general, managing appointments for the general's wife; something akin to a modern-day private secretary. Why did he have to be so busy just then, travelling from Rongjiang to Nanjing and then back to Rongjiang? Autumn of 1947 was just the time for electing delegates to the National Assembly of the Republic of China. Thus, Hu had accompanied the major general's wife back to Rongjiang, for her to represent her husband at election events.

One evening, I noticed Hu busy posting a stack of letters. He had written to solicit the support of local leaders for the major general, and included the major general's résumé with each letter. Letters were sent to all leaders at county, district, township and village levels.

At the start of the summer vacation, I went home, and found that my brother, who had just returned from military academy, was also busy distributing résumés on behalf of his wife's brother, Yang. Yang was a Dong man from Langdong, who had fought in Myanmar in the expeditionary force during the War of Resistance against Japan. After victory in the War, he retired from the army, and was appointed secretary general of the Youth League in Zunyi prefecture of Guizhou. My brother supported him in both Langdong and Zhaihao, distributing election leaflets.

Later, my brother explained that most people had supported the major general. When my brother distributed leaflets in Yang's support, some declined to take them, while others rolled them up for homemade cigarettes. My brother felt demoralised and gave up. Before the result was announced, he had resigned himself to failure. Two months later, the major general was indeed elected as the County Rongjiang delegate to the National Assembly.

After Hu left, Shi and I did not feel like continuing our studies in Rongjiang. Shi suggested we go to study in Guiyang. I agreed and said I'd follow Shi there. That was the summer of 1947, just after we had finished grade 2 of junior middle school.

That summer vacation, I walked home over the mountain paths alone. The journey lasted two whole days. I threaded my way through lofty mountain passes and hardly met a single soul. On the previous summer and winter vacations, journeys home had been in the company of teacher-trainee friends from Langdong who were students in Rongjiang. We had chatted and laughed all the way. When by chance we met an unsuspecting traveller on the way, bare-bottomed and attending innocently to nature's call, everyone burst out laughing.

When I returned to Xiangye in the summer of 1947, during the peaceful days after victory in the War of Resistance, one change was obvious. Young men no longer had to hide for fear of being conscripted. Instead, they were able to work in the fields and come home to rest as normal. As before, however, grain and money had to be sent as tax.

At that time, a 'Sinicization policy' had been implemented. On market days, the regional government had dispatched troops to the gates of Langdong. Women wearing skirts, with hair in a bun, were targeted. Soldiers grabbed any such women, cutting their skirts and hair with scissors and seizing any silver adornments. Market inspection tours were made and any women in minority clothing were similarly treated. Men who had accompanied their wives to market trailed behind, as the women turned tail in dismay and wailed their way homewards.

News spread quickly in the region and there was widespread shock. At first, no one dared return to the market. After a while, things relaxed and soldiers disappeared. Tentatively, people returned to sell eggs and buy salt, first men, then women. The women no longer dared to wear traditional clothing or jewellery, but wore trousers and plaited hair.

People just made the best of a bad job. The charming, beautiful minority women adopted a dark and swarthy appearance, sometimes nearly indistinguishable from men. Through that 'campaign for changing costumes', many Dong women near Langdong and Rongjiang lost their traditional outfits and adornments. My village was far from the towns and fortunately preserved minority dress. When I returned, however, in the summer of 1947, the atmosphere of intimidation experienced during the 'changing costumes' movement still persisted.

As a young student, my brother had laid down the pen to take up the sword. In spring of 1947, he left the military and returned home.

All our family affairs and finance were subsequently under my brother's management. He made a deal with a Han person from Langdong, exchanging a field for a horse, and often rode the horse to visit friends and relatives nearby. He enjoyed entertaining and there was a constant stream of satisfied guests. I was unable to work peacefully in the small room on the third floor and soon resolved to keep that appointment with Shi, busying myself with preparations to go and study in Guiyang.

Chapter 5
Drifting into the Open Seas
(Guiyang, 1947-49)

Going to Guiyang

The summer of 1947 was hotter than any I could remember. I felt like an ant in a hot pot. This lent all the more urgency to my plan to leave home and reach Guiyang for the start of the new term.

I had only ever heard tell of Guiyang. Was it in the direction of the sun's rising or of its setting? I wasn't sure. My mother and many other villagers did not even know the name 'Guiyang'. So I had no idea how to get there. Only one option seemed viable: I should go to County Jinping and look for my sister. She would know what to do.

After the demise of her husband Yu, my sister had moved to Liangzhaisi in County Jinping to stay with our paternal aunt. Our aunt had married the richest man in the region, who had good connections with government officials and rich people in the county.

Within days of arriving at my aunt's home, my sister was introduced to one Mr Wang, senior accountant in the county government. Wang also operated his own private timber business. My aunt arranged for my sister to become Wang's concubine, living at his business address in the county town Wangzhai (later called Jinping). After this, my sister became well connected with many people in Jinping.

My sister's eyes had been opened and she now realised the importance of schooling. She had written urging me to come, planning to send me to Guiyang to study. There was now a road joining Jinping with the outside world and you could reach Guiyang from there without walking.

Thus for the second time, my sister was prepared to clear the way for me to venture further afield. Though she did not know it at the time, she was the one who was mainly responsible for helping me to leave the depressed Dong village in the mountains, to follow a completely different life's journey from that of other Dong villagers.

In Xiangye, rice was about to be harvested. Those days were fine and clear. One morning, just after the roosters started to crow, mother was up making a fire. She woke me, then returned to her room and collected 20 *yuan* from beside her bed, wrapped in several layers of cloth. She opened the cloth slowly, her hands trembling. The coins inside were sticking to one another. As she prised them apart, she wept, saying that this money had been left over when father died. Years earlier, she had been worried my brother would use it all, and carefully buried it beside the water-buffalo pen. Today, she had dug it up and was giving it to support me as I left home to continue my studies. She urged me to use it carefully.

As I cupped my hands to receive the gift respectfully, I realised more clearly than before how poor my family really was, how tender and deep my mother's love, and how great the ambitions she cherished. I did not know what to say.

Just then, Uncle Qiao, from my mother's side of the family, arrived in a hurry. Mother handed him a bag for me, filled with a clean change of clothing and some glutinous rice. Then I left home, tagging along behind my uncle. Mother followed just behind, weeping and saying, "When will you be back this time, son?" She came to the edge of the village. "Go out and succeed!" she said, as she watched me leave. Thus, she expressed both her good wishes and her aspirations. She probably often wondered whether I was fulfilling her hopes and dreams.

Uncle Qiao had once accompanied my brother to Jinping and knew the path well. He chose various unlikely shortcuts through the canyon. Lower down, there was no wind and it seemed even more hot and humid. Before long, a raft appeared from nowhere on the rushing River Qingshui, alongside the path. Uncle Qiao boomed out a request to take us on. The raftsman agreed. He seemed to be local for his accent was like ours. We were both delighted to substitute a raft ride for a long, hard trek.

The raft passed through torrents and negotiated dangerous sandbanks. The saying goes that 'People ride the boat nonchalantly, while those on shore watch anxiously'. We didn't feel scared in the least. This was my first time on a raft, and I felt the novelty and excitement all the more for that. There was no time to calm down and enjoy the scenery on either side of the river before we had arrived in Jinping. As we disembarked and stood on dry ground, we just said a few words of thanks, in keeping with village etiquette. The raftsman accepted no money in exchange for his kindness.

When we arrived at my sister's house, everyone in her new family circle came around to say hello. My sister was delighted to see us. That evening she prepared a wonderful welcome feast, introducing me more formally to her family.

The next day, Uncle Qiao set off for home, carrying only a ball of glutinous rice rolled up in a facecloth. I saw him off to the end of the road. There, the smile on his face disappeared as he looked me up and down ruefully, as if he could not bear my leaving home. As I watched him disappear into the distance, my heart was filled with sadness.

My sister's house was brick-built with a tiled roof and a courtyard. Timber merchants lived upstairs. Some had lived there a whole year waiting for their timber to sell. The Wang family supplied them with two meals a day. My sister worked all day in the kitchen. I only caught glimpses of her coming and going. She had no time to take off her apron and rest. I stayed many days in her home, and she hardly ever gave me her full attention. She was too busy. I did not manage to see her husband, Wang. From her letters, I only knew he was an intellectual.

My sister told me every day a bus was about to arrive. I waited nearly two weeks before seeing a vehicle race along the mountain road. When my sister saw me off, she was still wearing her apron as usual. She gave me some money and said it was a year's supply. I was to study hard and not be homesick. As the van set off, she cried, then watched expressionless as it gathered speed up the mountain. It seemed for a moment as though there was something she had forgotten to say to her younger brother. It didn't occur to me then that I would never see her again.

The van had no canvas covering at the back. Sitting beside the driver was a tall middle-aged man in a grey overcoat. He hardly said a thing. The driver addressed him as Director Gu. As we left Sansui, the driver took a dozen Hunan people on board, each clasping a carrying pole, most with a bamboo basket on each end. The van had suddenly become overcrowded. People vied for space to crouch down and it was a difficult ride.

When we reached Machangping, we encountered a military police station. The police stopped the van and accused the driver of carrying people as if they were sardines. Everyone had to get off. After an hour's wrangling, Director Gu quietly uttered a few well-chosen words, the driver gave the police some money, and we were finally allowed to leave.

We reached Guiyang on an afternoon two days later. The van stopped in front of Nanming Hostel in Zhonghua Nan Street and Gu let me off. He pointed at the hostel signboard, advising me to stay there. Afterwards, they drove off northwards.

Thus, a junior middle school student from the mountain village of Xiangye was deposited in this completely unfamiliar provincial capital. He wasn't in the least afraid, only at a loss as to what to do next.

First Impressions

Nanming Hostel, with its guileless way of doing business, left good and lasting first impressions of Guiyang. In the 50 years following my first arrival, the hostel was always my first port of call if I needed to pass through the city. Then in 1995, the hostel disappeared when a comprehensive rebuilding project began there.

I don't remember the exact date when I first arrived in Guiyang, but I do remember there was already a chill in the air. Smartly dressed people were eating hotpot in the tripe restaurant beside Dashizi in the centre of the city. It was probably around the beginning of the ninth month of the lunar calendar. Schools had begun more than a month before, so I was late and had no prospect of starting school that semester.

Shi had passed the examination for first grade of the private Southwest Senior Middle School. After lodging a day or two in Nanming Hostel, I went to Daximen to look for him. I had just reached the school gate when I saw him approaching, wearing a dark yellow military uniform, with school emblems on either side of his collar, face covered in smiles. We revelled in that reunion. He kept asking, "Why were you so late?" He was annoyed we had missed the opportunity to study together in the same class.

I was more disappointed than Shi. My next possible starting point would only be in three or four months. My mind was blank. There was no plan B. Shi came with me to the hostel to collect my belongings and brought me back to his place at Daximen. He had rented a small room, with table and bed, above a restaurant. He insisted I stay there with him. With such a friend around, I did not feel any of the usual disorientation of being in a strange place and I was able to settle down smoothly.

As a child, I had heard neighbours remark how remote and remarkable the provincial capital was. Now that very city was right under my nose, and I soon began to explore.

Unlike other regions in Guizhou, Guiyang was not known for its timber. The timber regions were not yet connected by road to the city so it was difficult to transport wood there. Wooden homes were nevertheless the norm, with relatively few brick buildings, referred to by locals as 'foreign buildings'. Only banks and other official and public institutions were constructed in this 'foreign' style. Nanming Hall was one of them, along with a few other mansions on the bank of the River Nanming, lending the nickname 'mansion district' to that stretch of the river.

Rumour had it that a military commander had built one of the mansions there using bricks and glazed roof tiles which had been flown into Guiyang from India, along with carpets, sofas and other furniture. Engineers had been invited from Shanghai. The mansion certainly caught the eye. All comers extolled its wonderful architecture, right in the centre of Guiyang.

The inside story of the commander's wealth was uncovered by a journalist at one of Guiyang's tabloid newspapers. After touring the new building and conducting interviews about the construction process, he quizzed the commander about the funding, threatening to publish his findings. This was blackmail. The commander offered a huge bribe for him to keep quiet. After accepting the bribe, the reporter broke confidance and passed on an article for publication with the title 'Red Building of Nanming'.

The story created an instant sensation in Guiyang and the southwest. Word spread that the commander who owned the mansion had gained his fortune via the national purse. People fell over themselves to see the Red Building of Nanming, gasping at the awesome spectacle. Everyone judged it to be first among the foreign buildings in Guiyang.

In those days, the great shops and hotels in the other main streets of Guiyang usually had brick pillars, but wooden or bamboo walls, painted with white lime. These were known as 'second-class foreign buildings', still regarded as prestigious.

Other ordinary housing and small shops and hotels throughout the city were third-class, relatively shabby, wooden buildings. The main need of local people was for appropriate housing. Existing housing was congested and dilapidated.

Likewise, the main problem for outsiders who moved to Guiyang was not food or clothing, but accommodation. Many were only able to rent hotel rooms.

Students often lived in crowded rooms in small hotels; students upstairs, prostitutes down. You could see the women clearly, lying around lazily, through cracks in the floors. A constant kerfuffle of gossip and laughter spiralled upwards. Even snoring and breathing from below were clearly audible above. How could a youth remain calm and composed, never mind study, in such an environment?

In the evenings, streets and alleys were packed with prostitutes. They struck up conversations to intercept passers-by, stretching out an arm to draw customers to one side. Housing and prostitutes were my two worst early impressions of Guiyang, the two problems that most evoked apprehension.

The fact was that many students had no choice but to rent a room in one of those run-down hotels. The rooms were cramped and decrepit, but the rents were extortionate. Shi's room was not in a hotel but above a restaurant. Downstairs people stir-fried meat and vegetables. Pungent, spicy vapours floated upwards, and we choked uncontrollably. Then there was the cacophony of people eating and drinking together. All this was enough to make anyone feel sick and stressed out. Though the room was so Spartan, one month's rent was still equivalent to about three months' food expenses.

I huddled up in Shi's small room for about a month. I was often to be found standing at his window watching the vehicles coming and going. Military jeeps from the USA were most common and awe-inspiring; fast like the wind, strong as a hurricane. The smart green post office vehicles were shaped like a loaf of bread.

At that time, there were few public passenger vehicles – few buses or trains. Anyone who could hitch a ride in a post office vehicle was doing well. Occasionally, a convoy of American jeeps would drive by, full of officers in military uniform. Other transport consisted mainly of carts and rickshaws. A few pedestrians would be coming and going. This was all novel to me and I wouldn't have minded watching the world go by like this the whole day long.

Shi's room, however, was cramped and its air was polluted. It was okay to sleep in at night, but not so great to rest or study in during the day. So at the end of a school day, or on Sundays, Shi and I would stroll down the street to mingle among the crowds. We'd examine merchandise at vendors' stands and in the shops, watch a film or visit a teashop, especially if the shop was hosting a performance.

I gradually became familiar with the city. Shi introduced me to some of the students from County Rongjiang. In addition, I was introduced to a dozen students from towns in County Jianhe, not far from my village. While at home, we had already known each other's names, so when we met in Guiyang, we naturally struck up friendships more easily. So although I was living away from home, although everything was strange and had to be learned from scratch, I did not feel lonely or overawed.

In Guiyang at that time, only one road was laid with flagstones, about 300 metres long. It led to the provincial government building. On either side were 'foreign buildings' such as the Central Bank of China. This was the best street in the whole city. Nearly all the other streets and alleys were muddy dirt roads, full of potholes. Guiyang was, after all, reputed never to have three rain-free days in a row.

Rickshaws were the most common means of transportation. Passengers were jolted violently up and down, with always the risk of being flung off unexpectedly. The next most popular form of transport was the horse-drawn cart, typically equipped with four seats.

Pedestrians made slow progress, cautiously and solemnly picking a path through the mud. When carts or jeeps drove by, pedestrians had nowhere to hide, but stood still, watching the vehicles stoically and having their trousers drenched by dirty water. Pedestrians even inadvertently splashed the muddy water on each other.

One evening, as people flocked out of the cinema to make their way home, I observed a young man in military uniform squelching dirty water, with careless heavy steps, onto the lovely traditional gown worn by a young woman. Instinctively, the woman scolded him roundly. The soldier protested it had been an accident. When she complained again, swearing, he gave her a taste of her own medicine. Using the English word 'sorry', he replied, "I said sorry to you. Why do you still swear at me?" Persisting, he repeated this twice. In the end, she simply said 'sorry' in English. That stopped his nagging.

Each Sunday around mid-day, an American-style jeep drove slowly through the main streets. Carts and rickshaws hastily made way. A fierce-looking old man sat in the jeep, wearing a yellow woollen military uniform and a military cap. He wore stripes for the rank of lieutenant general and surveyed imperiously the pedestrians on either side. They in turn stopped, gazing at him in admiration and respect. Some muttered that this was the army commander Yang Sen.

Yang had been a leading warlord in Sichuan Province. During the War of Resistance against Japan, he had been head of the Nationalist army defending Guilin. When Guilin capitulated, the army scattered, retreating towards Guizhou. When Yang arrived in Guiyang, only a few officers still accompanied him. He was an army chief without an army.

The Nationalist government appointed Yang governor of Guizhou. Following his military instincts, he made a tour of the city every Sunday, inspecting the main streets in his jeep, as if he were inspecting the troops. This inspection happened rain, hail or shine. It was a source of entertainment to me on Zhongshan Street, every Sunday that year.

The people of Guiyang told many stories about Yang Sen. They said, for example, that wherever he went, he married a new wife. No one knew how many dozens of wives he had. He might easily fail to recognise his own sons in the street.

Within days of being appointed governor of Guiyang, Yang Sen married a university student from Guizhou. They said this was the first time a Han general had married a 'border child', a minority person, and he had done this in order to promote such marriages. Yang built a mansion for his new wife outside the city centre and stationed officers there to keep watch.

Zhongshan Street was an important commercial hub with old-fashioned houses on either side, mostly with two storeys; accommodation upstairs and business downstairs.

The shops always used to hang up banners advertising massive discounts. They would invite trumpeters to play popular songs, such as *Missing Relatives in Autumn* and *The Whole River is Red*, attracting customers until the place was bustling with noise and excitement. This enlivened the otherwise dismal atmosphere in gloomy Guiyang with its continuous autumn rain, and caused migrants like me to cease longing for their homes. I love those two songs to this day.

The city was home to three cinemas. The Guizhou Cinema and the Qunxin Cinema screened Chinese films. Their clientele were mostly soldiers or city residents. Guiyang Cinema focused on foreign, mostly American films, featuring English. Most spectators were students and intellectuals. Admission was twice the price of Chinese films, with screenings each evening and also Sunday afternoon. Usually there would be a new film every two weeks.

At the time, two teahouses were entertainment hubs. Each had a stage, with rows of seats for spectators. A teacup was placed on a board in front of each seat. Spectators bought entrance tickets, and would then drink tea and eat snacks as they watched Beijing opera, listened to music or were entertained by magicians. Waiters would circulate distributing facecloths and looking for tips. One performance lasted about two hours, and Sunday performances attracted large crowds.

People said the population of Guiyang was about 300,000, mostly farmers and manual workers. Many who lived in the main streets were business people with family registrations in Hunan or Sichuan. In addition, there were many military and government personnel.

Most of Guiyang's students were from Guizhou Province. Nearly all were from wealthy families, most being children of leaders at regional, county or township level. Their behaviour and bearing seemed refined.

People who met in Guiyang were often strangers meeting by chance. Outwardly, everyone seemed friendly and well disposed; I can't remember ever seeing any fistfights or serious arguments.

Thus, Guiyang when I first arrived seemed pleasantly different from the county towns, where I had often felt intimidated by objectionable characters. The residents of Guiyang reminded me of my home village. You could relate naturally to them and there was no sense of estrangement. There was no bullying. On the contrary, there was mutual deference, and public sympathy was extended towards anyone in straitened circumstances, especially anyone who had met with sudden misfortune.

The city lacked commodities, the homes were simple and coarse and the residents were mainly poor. Most people, however, seemed to live within the law.

Life in Guiyang was peaceful and calm, except for the stress of poor housing. It was still difficult, for I had no money; but I was not homesick.

I knew a middle school student named Yang, also from County Jianhe, who lived at the Young Men's Christian Association (YMCA). He told me the rooms there were good and inexpensive. Food was half the price of food outside and it had an English cramming class. Hearing all this, I was enticed to move in there.

So one sunny afternoon, Yang led me to the YMCA office, to help me join, for you had to be a member in order to lodge there. Yang had already lived there over a year and was well acquainted with the office staff. He introduced me and I joined up on the spot. Part of the application was to complete a form in which I declared I was a Christian – my faith had been born at the time of my first visit to Rongjiang county town. Registering and fee-paying were handled efficiently.

Yang then led me to a two-storey building where I was to live in a two-person room. My roommate was another person named Yang, from a town not far from Xiangye. He was at Dade Senior Middle School. When I had been at Rongjiang Middle School, he had been at the Rongjiang Teacher Training School and we had often spent Sundays together. Unexpectedly, we now found ourselves sharing a room together in Guiyang! Meeting an old friend far from home was a wonderful encouragement and we were both well pleased.

The Yang who had introduced me was living next door. He was a little deaf and not very talkative, but had a ready smile. He often came to sit in our room, though I never found out much about him.

The western-style building had been purpose-built to provide lodging for YMCA members. All residents were students. Most had come from outside the city to study in senior middle schools, while a few were university students. Someone, probably a music student, used to rise at first light and practise playing an instrument. In the evenings, there was another private music practice. At other times, however, everything was quiet. Even the sound of loud voices was conspicuous by its absence.

One staff member was responsible for cleaning rooms and supplying boiled water. Everyone called him 'Old Xu'. The YMCA paid his wages, and he was honest, considerate, guileless and hardworking, never accepting any money from students. He arrived and left with a smile on his face.

The dining hall was in front of our building, spacious and bright, and equipped with new, clean tables and benches. Members ate there; a large bowl of rice, a plate of meat and fried vegetables, and a bowl of soup, referred to as a 'standard meal'. It was tasty and satisfying, cooked with special attention to hygiene. The church subsidised both food and housing. Many people wondered why it carried on this charity business.

The teachers at the YMCA English cramming courses were young Chinese Christians who spoke fluent English with good pronunciation. They went to great lengths to teach well. The day after I moved in, I registered for evening classes, from 7 to 9 pm, with up to 20 students in a large, brightly lit classroom. The textbook, including revision exercises, was intended for junior middle school students.

Since I joined the class partway through, I didn't understand much at first. By day, I stood in my room, learning vocabulary line by line, so I could remember the text for the class that evening. The problem was I couldn't pronounce the words!

In the evenings, I would listen carefully, ignoring the writing, as the teacher read the individual words and then the text. I annotated some of the difficult words, using Chinese characters. For example: 'building' became *biao ding*, 'strong' became *si te lang* and 'prize' became *bu ai shi*. At the start of every class, there would be two or three minutes of dictation. When I couldn't remember the English letters, I just wrote in Chinese, resulting in much amusement when later reviewed.

It was difficult enough for Dong people to learn Chinese, but English was doubly difficult. I could never pronounce the words correctly and couldn't remember the vocabulary. As for the grammar, it seemed unfathomable. Trying at once to acquire a working knowledge of English grammar, while simultaneously taming the mediating language of instruction (Chinese), simply seemed beyond me, no matter *how* well the teacher taught! It was just mind-boggling.

From the time I started English at junior middle school in Rongjiang, I reckoned it was the hardest subject. As the English teacher entered the classroom, my heart would be pounding. When the bell rang for the end of class, I'd heave a sigh of relief. When I later skipped one-and-a-half years to study at senior middle school in Guiyang, the relative difficulty of English seemed even greater. I was apprehensive, but still threw myself body and soul into English study.

Every evening at the YMCA, I braced myself for English, persevering with determination until the Christmas holiday. It was just over a month and I felt progress had been quite good. I had learned the meanings of many words and could speak a few sentences of everyday English.

After Christmas, I left the YMCA, for I was short of money. Shi introduced me to a teacher and I went to stay for some weeks in his home in Qianlingxi Street. There was a sign on the door, announcing: 'Yunmeng English Cramming Class' (Yunmeng is a county in Hubei Province), but inside there was actually no cramming class. Any notions of taking extra English lessons proved misplaced.

There were a few students from County Jinping lodging there, eating two meals a day and sleeping on the floor. We all came from poor homes. One of the others failed to pay for his lodging that month. At dinner one evening, our host's wife reminded him of this. He blushed, for he had no money, but promised he would pay. That night, he did not sleep on the floor as usual and the next day at lunchtime, he was nowhere to be seen. Our hostess asked where he had gone and no one knew. She simply smiled, saying, "He's run away."

A few days later, he returned and paid the overdue lodging fees. "Sorry Madam," he said. "My family ran out of money and told me to go home immediately. I'm no longer able to study in Guiyang. We borrowed this from people in our village. Here it is; my lodging payment. Sorry it's so late." So saying, he turned and left.

Within a few weeks, I also left, for I, too, was still short of money. Winter vacation was almost upon us and I had no alternative but to return and stay with Shi. After schools closed for the holiday, I went to stay with some Rongjiang students in their school dormitory.

Once, I tried renting a room in a tattered tavern in Taiciqiao. The windows on one side had no glass or shelter from the winter wind, which wailed fiercely through the room, and it was freezing. My bed was a straw mat on the floor, my covering a shabby quilt. In spite of everything, I would sleep soundly until daybreak.

In the end, more than half of that winter vacation was spent at Shi's place. His kindness to me in Guiyang exceeded that of my own brother. I'll never forget his generosity.

I spent evenings reading at the provincial library in Kexue Street. Later during senior middle school, the library became my favourite bolthole.

Senior Middle School

In the early autumn of 1947, our old classmate Hu came to visit Shi and me, and stayed with us for over a week. He hardly left Shi's room over the restaurant, except to stroll around with us.

While Shi was at school, I was at the library, and Hu sat silently in the room forging a couple of diplomas for me, supposedly from Meitan Middle School, which was affiliated with Zhejiang University (Meitan is a county in Guizhou). One was a certificate of graduation from junior middle school, the other a certificate of completion of the first semester of 1st grade of senior middle school. They seemed really authentic.

Documents in hand, I went to register for the entrance examination to the private Dade Senior Middle School. Fewer than 100 people sat the exam and afterwards it was announced that everyone had passed. So, it transpired that I enrolled into the second semester of 1st grade without any problem.

Tuition fees were low: for one four-month semester, about equivalent to half a month's food and lodging. So, no one worried much about the fees. Classes were convened in a huge ancient temple which later, in 2004, was converted into an opera theatre.

Dade had a long history. By the time I arrived, however, its reputation had been sullied. Its students, generally children of rich people, with mixed educational backgrounds, were said to be easy-going and under-achieving.

In Guiyang, or among any students from Guizhou, Dade was better known by far than the provincially established senior middle schools, even than Guiyang Middle School or Qinghua Middle School – but for the wrong reasons. Sometimes people would simply sneer at the mention of its name.

The teaching at Dade followed national standards, each subject with its own specialist teachers. An old man taught Chinese, with glasses balanced on the bridge of his nose. As he read, he would take on roles of characters in the stories, sometimes weeping uncontrollably. He would wipe away tears with his hanky, telling the story through voiceless sobs, so that everyone felt moved. Some female students joined in with their own hankies.

Our English teacher was part-time, an ex-university-student, otherwise keeping his young wife company at home, often playing mah-jong. He would rush into the classroom as the bell rang, just on cue. Sometimes his first words were from mah-jong, 'Out millions!' but everyone would just look blank. Then he would come to himself, realise he was teaching, and say in English, "Good morning, class..."

He would read aloud some English vocabulary, then translate the English text and teach us to read it. As soon as the bell rang for the end of the lesson, he would turn tail and leave in the same haste with which he had arrived. He never assigned homework or classroom exercises. Student attendance declined, but it was some time before he noticed and asked, "How many students are there in your class anyway?"

Each semester, he invigilated a surprise test in which one of the texts had to be written from memory. There would be biting of pens and leaning over desks, but no one would be able to write a thing. The 'test' would then be suspended, with instructions to go and memorise the text before returning to re-sit the exam.

Our maths and science teacher never missed a class. He taught loudly and earnestly. He knew that students were mixed ability and examination results were generally poor. Students in turn knew that the teacher had to try and improve standards in order to collect his salary. In his case, teacher and students tried to cooperate.

Each week, two periods of military practice were led by a high-ranking military officer, working as a full-time teacher. He and his family, six people in all, lived in a solitary small room on the right of the school entrance. He was responsible for both senior and junior school military practice. He always wore uniform and required students to do likewise for his classes. If your jacket was not buttoned up properly or your collar did not have the requisite school badges, he promptly delivered a stern rebuke.

He was tall and fat. He would stand in the middle and order everyone to march around him, kicking anyone who fell out of step. Anyone not standing straight or turning in the wrong direction was upbraided, "What's going on in your head?" This was often reinforced by a punch in the stomach or a twist of the ear.

The officer spoke with an accent, and one student, misinterpreting, memorably replied, "My father is like his older brother!" The instructor stamped his feet in rage and delivered two punches in lieu of the usual one.

On 10th October, the anniversary of the 1911 Wuchang uprising, all primary and middle school students in the city gathered for inspection at the Liuguangmen public square. Dade boasted the most disciplined student soldiers, with good marching and smart attire. We also had an accomplished brass band commanded by our own large military instructor. The band played and marched ahead of all the school groups, and had done so at the annual event for years. It maintained its good reputation even after Liberation in 1949.

In 1955, when I returned to Guiyang after field surveys in Yunnan, I went to observe the 1st May celebrations at Liuguangmen. Our fat military instructor was still leading the band, still clad in the military uniform of yesteryear. There was, however, no longer any sign of military rank on his shoulder. The spirit and pride exuded in former years was completely gone. I pointed him out to my companion. "That man used to be my military instructor at Dade." My friend reminded me curtly that a purge of counter-revolutionary elements had begun. How could I still dare to recognise him? This was my last memory of Dade Middle School. Not long afterwards it folded, merging with another school.

In my student days, one of the rear classrooms was normally unused, but had a complete set of tables and chairs. After class one afternoon in 1948, when the War of Liberation had almost been won, a classmate dragged me over to that classroom, to listen to a lecture.

At the door was a small blackboard announcing the lecture title: *Two Worlds*. About 20 or 30 people were seated inside, with more chairs empty than occupied. A middle-aged man in a long traditional gown was standing on the platform, delivering a speech in undemonstrative tones. He explained that China consisted of two worlds. The liberated one was light and the other, not yet liberated, was dark.

As we entered, the lecture was reaching its conclusion. Suddenly, the speaker raised his voice, declaring, "Every Chinese person is anticipating the arrival of the light. The future China will be wonderfully bright." There was no applause and the audience left surreptitiously, as if worried about strangers breathing down their necks.

I heard that such lectures were convened only occasionally. They were not advertised, except by word of mouth. Most people, however, knew nothing about them. Having only heard the climax, I didn't really understand what the lecture was about and never asked my classmate.

After Liberation, I realised that Dade had been a centre for underground activities of the Chinese Communist Party. Party leaders such as Wang Ruofei were former students of the school. Authorities did not exercise direct control over private schools, and especially after victory over Japan, Dade was not rigorously inspected. It was easy for members of the underground Communist Party to operate there, joining the underground revolution. A number of young revolutionary martyrs were reported to have been killed in pre-Liberation Guiyang, including both teachers and students from Dade. Today, the former location of Dade Middle School has been marked by the government to commemorate its revolutionary history.

Dade was near the YMCA and I returned to live at the YMCA, with the same roommate as before. Our settled routine was to walk to school together in the morning and return together in the afternoon. For three months, however, I did not receive any money, either from home or from my sister. So, there was not enough money for food and I was unable to pay the YMCA fees. My former problem had again raised its ugly head.

Out of the blue I received a phone call from Yang, the Dong older brother of my brother's wife, who had earlier stood unsuccessfully for election in County Rongjiang. He asked how I was doing and I answered honestly that my main challenge was paying for accommodation. He said that Dade was near the Young Soldiers' Friendship Association where he had a room, and invited me to go and live there. I wouldn't need to worry about rent, for it would be rent-free, one of the perks of his job. The problem with which I'd been preoccupied 24/7 thus seemed to be resolved, and that night I was so happy I couldn't sleep!

The next day I left the YMCA and moved to Yang's compound, where he was serving as director of the newly established Young Soldiers' Friendship Association. The Association occupied a row of two-storey buildings, with offices downstairs and living quarters upstairs. My living space was a table and bed in the corner of one of the upstairs rooms. Two office staff lived on the other side of the room, separated by a large empty space in the middle. It seemed spacious and quiet.

My two roommates never talked to me and I never spoke to them, as if we were strangers on the street. Although there were several work units on the compound, there was often no one to be seen. In the evenings, however, lights in the adjacent rooms proved that they were indeed inhabited.

One Sunday morning, I went to listen to a speech at the compound auditorium, though I only arrived after the guest of honour had been speaking for over an hour. There were perhaps 200 people in the audience. I remember some indignant criticism of unscrupulous businessmen who had been profiteering by stockpiling salt, causing hardship to impoverished Guizhou farmers!

The speaker observed how public security had deteriorated. He had just returned from the USA, where he had never been robbed. Two days earlier, he had arrived in Guiyang and checked into a small hotel. He forgot to close the window of his hotel room, with the result that someone stole one of his western-style suits.

At this, a dispute arose between two listeners. They stood up and engaged in a tussle, while those nearby scattered for fear of injury. There was a sudden rush to the exits and the meeting adjourned, before the speech had officially concluded.

Afterwards, I discovered that the speaker had been Professor Li Dongfang. During the War of Resistance, he had been well known for his lectures on *Romance of the Three Kingdoms*.

Normally, my new residence was relatively quiet and good for study. It was great to have a settled place. I left the room early for school and returned late, and time passed quickly. At the beginning of summer vacation, I stayed there, planning to finish senior middle school at Dade before going to university or military academy.

Two things happened while I was savouring these pleasant dreams. Firstly, my brother Ou Chaoxi arrived to ask Yang for help in finding a job, squeezing in with me for about 10 days, just as the holidays began. I showed him the sights as we strolled around Guiyang together.

One evening, Yang invited us for red-bayberry juice in the cold-drinks shop at Hebin Park, the only time he treated us, and my first time having any real interaction with him. He was well disposed but hardly said a thing, never asking about my studies or my brother's job search. As we broke up, he was still just smiling; he didn't say a thing.

Having run out of money, my brother had to go home. Before leaving, he warned me solemnly that we could no longer count on any income from rice. Even at the bargain price of one *yuan* per 100 kg, no one was buying. No one was buying timber either, and there wasn't a penny left at home. Ou Chaoxi had borrowed money for his trip to Guiyang. He recommended I take the examination for military academy, where fees would be paid, for there was really no money to support me further at senior middle school. He overlooked the fact that admission to military academy was contingent upon graduation from senior middle school, and I was still not quite 18 years old. My sweet dreams of completing senior middle school were fading.

To salvage control over my own destiny, I appealed to my sister for help. She wrote back promptly to say she would send money for tuition and food, and to recommend that I finish senior middle school. In addition, she enclosed a letter of introduction, written by her husband Wang, and addressed to one of the school inspectors at the Provincial Education Department, asking him to help me. In this way, my dreams were resurrected.

The other significant episode involved a fellow native of County Rongjiang, who came to Yang looking for a job. He wore a smart military uniform and pretended to be from the Chongqing Nationalist regiment. Yang was duly deceived and arranged for the new guy to serve in the accountancy office of the Friendship Association. Before long, Yang entrusted him with a large sum of money to deposit in the bank, but by evening, the newcomer was nowhere to be seen.

Yang came to my room, perspiring heavily, to ask if I had any idea where the man had gone. He marched to and fro in agitation, wiping the sweat from his brow with a towel, and deploring his own gullibility. It transpired that the fraudster had indeed been from Rongjiang county town, but everything else he had said was untrue. With hindsight, Yang repeatedly insisted that he should never have trusted him. It felt like he was desperate for sympathy. This was the only thing he had ever talked to me about since I first moved to stay at the compound.

Since public money had been stolen, Yang forfeited the confidence of his superiors. His staff no longer welcomed visitors with a smile, but seemed evasive. Yang's earlier smiling countenance was nowhere to be seen. Whenever he chanced upon me, it felt as if I was a stranger. Before long, my roommates said that Yang was to be transferred to another job. It seemed inappropriate for me to stay there, so just a few days before the new term, I moved back to the YMCA.

I had signed up for an English cramming class at the Guiyang Teachers' College and I attended class each morning during summer vacation. At first, I spent afternoons with my brother and had no time to revise or prepare for the next morning's class. After over a month, my progress remained slow.

Some classmates at the crammer spoke highly of Boqun Middle School. Canteen food there was much cheaper than outside and accommodation was free. This sounded good to me, possibly the dawn of a new era in my schooling.

Most schools recruited new students during summer vacation and I decided to take the entrance examination for Boqun. Given my family's financial circumstances, repeating grade 1 seemed impossible. My friend Shi urged me to enter grade 2, "There's nothing too difficult about it. Anyway, you have a letter of introduction."

After I had taken the examination to carry on into grade 2, I took the letter my brother-in-law had written and went in search of the school inspector, a man named Yi. Having read the letter, Mr Yi asked me which school I'd like to attend and which grade. I answered precisely and he wrote me a letter of introduction, instructing me to deliver it in person to the school principal.

One afternoon towards the end of the summer holiday in 1948, I made my way to Boqun Middle School. I found the principal outside a small western-style building located halfway up a mountain wilderness. He spoke with a strong rural Guizhou accent. There seemed to be something wrong with his neck for his head sat permanently at an angle. After reading the letter, he told me to go and enrol. He pointed out his house, and said if I had any problems I should look him up. A woman in the house, wearing Chinese-style dress, was peering out at us, but otherwise there was no one around. It was quiet and seemed a little desolate. I found the office and completed the enrolment procedures for grade 2 without any hitches.

The school was built on an otherwise desolate mountain. Classrooms were brick-built single-storey rooms, forming lines across the mountain, painted yellow and screaming for attention. You could see them from a distance. During the War of Resistance, the buildings had hosted the government-established Third Middle School.

The dark-green zigzagging River Nanming was at the foot of the mountain. On the other side of the river was the Guiyang Electric Power Plant, where the rumbling noise of machinery which belched out white vapour could be heard day and night. At the time, it was the only modern factory in Guiyang, possibly the whole of Guizhou, and was symbolic of Guiyang's modernisation.

The Nanming residential area was on the west side of the Power Plant, while the Shuikou Temple was on the east side. You could take a cart from Guiyang city to the Shuikou Temple Bridge, from where you could walk up to Boqun.

The government-established Third Middle School had erected a flagpole on the mountain summit. Two students would run up the mountain to raise a flag, which could be seen from a distance of some kilometres. Later, however, Boqun conducted flag-raising ceremonies on the sports field lower down the mountain.

There was no one else living near the school. The main road from Guizhou to Hunan ran behind the mountain, passing the provincial Agricultural Research Institute. An Institute agricultural experiments centre was located beside our school. It consisted of a wide expanse of seedbeds, meticulously arranged, like a public park. There was normally no sign of anyone there, only birds flying around chirping. Located as it was on a mountainside near the riverbank, the school's environment was beautiful and secluded. It was a pleasant place to study.

Wang Boqun had been a leading public figure in Guizhou Province, one of the chief figures in the Xinhai Revolution [of 1911, which ended the Qing dynasty]. His prestige was comparable to that of a provincial governor. In later years, he took an interest in establishing schools and supporting talented but poor students from the countryside. He was pleased to set up Boqun Middle School, serving as chairman of the school board.

It was a private school, but fees were minimal and no one was excluded on financial grounds. As in public schools, however, you needed to pass an examination to be accepted.

Private schools were like charities and in the case of Boqun, expenses were covered from property belonging to the chairman of the board. No applications for funding were made to the government, and no plans were made to extract funds from the students.

Boqun, however, was often hard pressed for money. The principal once explained that the empty petrol barrels that could be seen alongside the airport belonged to the school. After they had been sold, there would be funds to buy new tables, benches and blackboards, not to mention a few new basketballs. This encouraged everyone, but the new benches and balls never materialised.

The Boqun teachers were dedicated and professional, rarely late and rarely leaving early. One morning, our English teacher was still running up the hill as the bell rang for class. He arrived moments later, wearing a western suit and standing tall and erect. As he entered, he announced in English, 'Sorry I'm late', whereupon he stepped onto the platform, loosened his tie, placed it on the table and promptly began to teach. Shortly afterwards, a gust of autumn wind blew through the open windows, swishing the tie to a corner of the classroom. Only at the end of the lesson did he go and retrieve it, saying simply, "I didn't notice it blowing away."

That teacher was an engineer at the Power Plant opposite, teaching part-time. He would walk from the Power Plant to the Temple Bridge before turning around and coming up the mountain, a walk something over half an hour, after which his leather shoes would often be covered in brown mud. The walk was quite strenuous and before starting to teach, he would take out a hand towel and wipe the sweat from his face and neck. Come wind come weather, he never missed a class and was always – or nearly always – on time.

Our Chinese teacher was an old man in a long Chinese gown whose only teaching aid was a piece of chalk. Once in a while, he would glance at the textbooks of the students in the front row. Some classmates reckoned he had taught this class for decades. He would explain the texts as if he were telling a story, talking non-stop. He was everyone's favourite teacher and the examination results for Chinese were generally good.

According to school rules, if anyone failed any of the three main subjects Chinese, mathematics or English, he or she would have to repeat the year. This was intimidating to me for I had jumped classes twice and felt weak in some subjects. With algebra, for example, I would still be figuring out the meaning of the teacher's first sentence, when he would be on to the second and third. I simply couldn't understand and soon lost confidence, wondering how many times I might have to repeat grade 2.

The daily assembly for raising the school flag was the most nerve-wracking part of the day. The principal would stand to attention on stage and invariably select two or three students to recite from memory their current English text. Failure to do so would result first in a verbal warning; then in a note on your school records; and the third time, in a more serious mark beside your name. If you failed a fourth time, you would be expelled.

As the flag was being raised, anxiety saturated the student body. At each assembly, I contrived to hide behind taller students. I figured that if I were unable to see the principal, he would be unable to see me. This didn't prevent my heart beating hard and fast, but I was never singled out. Although I never saw a notice on the bulletin board confirming the ultimate punishment – expulsion – for poor recitation, the tense atmosphere at assemblies caused some students to be constantly nervous, fearing the sudden, potentially debilitating, demand to recite English.

A few students from rich families rode to school by carriage every day and went home every evening. The overwhelming majority, however, lived at school, in the large bungalows that served as dormitories, with windows arranged just as in the classrooms. The windows, however, had long since been broken, and nothing had been substituted to counter the wind.

Each dormitory was just one big room, with no divisions apart from the double bunk beds arranged in rows. One dormitory housed around 100 students. During the late-autumn nights, cold winds blew in and it felt freezing. By climbing into bed, however, and pulling the quilt over you, you promptly entered your own land of dreams; and the sound of the wind was soon competing with the sound of 100 students breathing deeply.

Long after the wake-up bell had begun to sound, some students still did not rise or stir. Every morning, our military instructor, smartly dressed in uniform, came dashing into the dorm blowing his whistle, his right hand busy pulling the duvets off those students starving for more sleep.

School food was cheap. Students took turns to buy supplies from the city, including oil, salt and vegetables. At the end of each month, a detailed list of expenditures was published. The main staple was brown rice, which was just what soldiers ate. Grain and chaff had not been separated and the rice was coarse; so the other term for 'brown rice' was 'coarse rice'.

In addition, we ate chard (a kind of beet, with edible, white stalks and green leaves) every day at lunch and dinner. It was an inferior vegetable, its only commendation its price. There was not much oil, but at least the chard was fried. The food was the same every day and we tasted no meat or fish for months on end. Today if I ever see coarse rice or chard on the table, it makes me feel like vomiting!

As the saying goes, 'Life at home is good, but as soon as you leave home you meet with difficulty'. This was apt for me, a Dong student from a remote mountainous region. My crowded accommodation in Guiyang and my own room at home were as different as night and day. Meals were also different, for at school I usually felt hungry while at home I could always eat my fill. Formerly, I never even knew the taste of 'coarse rice' and chard; now I ate them every day. Clothes too were different: I spent two cold, gloomy winters in Guiyang wearing only unlined shirts and trousers, whereas I was better equipped for the extremes of weather at home.

Although life was so difficult, I never felt ill or out of sorts and was able to persevere with study. From beginning to end, I felt cheerful and energetic, and there was never any thought in my mind of 'turning back'. I'm not sure where my strength and good spirits came from.

On the banks of the River Nanming, everything was quiet, except for all kinds of harsh noise from the Power Plant. By the time winter arrived, leaves had turned yellow and the grass had withered, rendering the environment bleak and desolate. In the winter of 1948, the 'Battle of Xuzhou' in the Huaihai Campaign (November 1948 to January 1949) was on everyone's lips and people kept saying the Communist Party had already liberated northern China. Nothing could prevent the ultimate liberation of the vast southern region of China, but no one knew when liberation would reach Guiyang.

Gradually, children of officials dropped out of school and teachers began to miss class. Our Chinese teacher no longer taught from the textbooks, but taught about the current political situation. At flag-raising assemblies, the principal no longer pounced upon students to recite texts. Psychologically, everyone was rattled. The serenity of ordinary people going about their business was replaced by anxiety.

One morning, the newspapers announced major currency reform. A new currency named *jinyuanjuan* was to be used, and for a set time, there would be limits set on currency exchange. Commodity prices rose rapidly and the price of a meal was soon four or five times higher than before. Students were no longer dispatched to buy food for school meals, this job being reserved for school officials.

We still ate brown rice and chard, but there only seemed to be the taste of salt. The flavour of oil had disappeared, as the chard was boiled rather than fried. I wrote home asking for food-money, but no money came, nor letters in response. My sister had earlier sent money intended to last half a year, but after 'currency reform', it was just enough for half a month.

69

Price rises made us feel like flood victims, or as if we were being attacked by wild beasts rather than the vagaries of civil war, and tension rose by the day. Students from distant counties began to leave for home and general alarm swept through Guiyang. My student friends from Rongjiang and Jianhe were wondering what to do for the best. Some wanted to persevere and finish the winter semester, unwilling to waste money they had already invested in the school year. Everyone was in a state of uncertainty.

My own dilemma seemed acute, and in my confusion I agonised about what to do for the best. Change was charging towards us and it would almost certainly be impossible to study much longer. One freezing morning, I rode a carriage from Shuikou Temple into the city, having decided to leave school. It felt like drifting on a sampan into the open seas. I had no means to be independent and no place to stay. I rushed through city streets and alleys, with no definite plan, hardly noticing a thing. By evening, all I felt was hunger.

Three days later, I didn't dare to return to school, having left without giving any clear explanation. I could only eat my pride and go in search of Shi again, to relate my predicament of the previous three days. He was about to break for winter vacation and invited me for a meal, suggesting I squeeze in with him for a few days. As soon as the vacation started, I could go back home with other students from Jianhe and Rongjiang.

It was early 1949, the coldest time of year, and Guiyang was constantly overcast and rainy. Wearing my unlined shirts and trousers, I walked around the streets to keep warm. Day and night, I experienced the scarcely endurable torment of hunger. The cold of Guiyang and callousness on strangers' faces cut to the heart.

On the first evening of the holiday, Shi gave me two penguin-brand cigarettes, as my fare for the trip home, and went with me to sell them at a tobacco store. Then reluctantly, we said goodbye. Taking my fare money, I went to find Zhen, a friend who had been studying at the Technical School, who was the same age as, but even kinder to me than, my brother. The next day, Zhen accompanied me back to County Jianhe and we reached home without any problem.

Chapter 6
Teaching and Marriage
(Pre-Liberation, 1949-50)

Upon seeing me home in the winter vacation at the beginning of 1949, my mother's first reaction was, "You've returned. Don't ever leave again!"

My brother said there was upheaval everywhere and we had no cash in hand. Later when the situation had improved, we would sell timber to support my future studies.

My sister who had sent me to school in Guiyang and posted money to support me there, had lost contact with relatives in the village and did not know I had dropped out of school. Over the next 10 years, she had no contact with the rest of the family and no one received any news of her.

Our village was remote and villagers were generally unconcerned with affairs outside a five-kilometre radius. When people realised, however, that I was not returning to school after the winter vacation, they caught a whiff of the significance of developments outside. Some were pleased to see me staying longer, but others harboured misgivings.

Life in Xiangye carried on much as ever. Bonds of mutual affection and support made the village seem like one large family. Nothing had changed this. It seemed I had returned to the immutable Xiangye of my childhood. The half-year after dropping out of school passed quickly for me among old village friends.

Having failed to find work outside, my brother was still at home with his two wives.

There were several ex-students of Langdong Primary in the village. One was the same age as my brother. When I returned, these ex-students came to see me one after another, but they never talked about school or study. In fact, they hardly said a thing, but just smiled. They were pleased to see me and it seemed as if they were using smiles to substitute for speech, to express their welcome and good cheer. They were similar to other young men in the village, except that their parents were richer and they themselves did not work in the fields or chop firewood. They were just biding their time waiting for marriage, children and family life. None of them, however, had a fiancée and they seemed bored.

My brother was also bored and generally idle. He often invited guests for meals; two or three student friends from the village and some Han Chinese friends from neighbouring towns. They took turns hosting each other. They would toast one another playing the finger-guessing game, until they were totally drunk. [Two drinkers would each extend a number of fingers and announce a number at the same time. The man whose number tallied with the sum of fingers extended by both men would be declared the winner and the loser would have to drink his bowl of rice wine.] Occasionally, I kept them company. They'd burst into fits of raucous laughter, but rarely talked about anything.

At one meal, we'd begun to drink when the host's father remarked that the newly appointed township leader Yang Rui was more fearsome than his predecessor. Yang was constantly complaining and the host's father felt this was ominous for us, for Yang viewed Xiangye as a rich village, perfect for exploitation.

On the day he took office, Yang Rui had sent a team of young men to Xiangye to collect a 'hearth tax' (from each fireplace). The young men demanded additional payment of a 'straw sandals tax', to cover the cost of wear and tear on their sandals. Those who couldn't pay were tied up and forced to sell livestock until they had paid in full. In addition, they then had to pay a 'hands-on tax' for the extra service of being tied up. The straw sandals tax and hands-on tax together were about equivalent to the so-called hearth tax, and were retained by the young tax collectors. Dong people feared this hearth tax. They were basically paying to have people come and blackmail, bind and beat them.

Yang Rui had actually been my brother's classmate at Jianhe Middle School. His examination marks had been bottom of the class. When he became township leader, he promptly failed to recognise the people he had known before. At first, he himself came to Xiangye to perform his duties, beating up some people and tying up others. All felt terrified as he extorted the few *yuan* of money they had carefully hidden away, until they were penniless. Now everyone in the village knew the name Yang Rui.

My brother joined in, "Yang Rui's evil! Wicked!" A few days after my brother had been elected village leader, Yang had been appointed township leader, whereupon my brother had resigned. Yang tried to force him to serve, but he refused, so Yang despised him. When I heard all this, I feared Yang Rui might arrange to have our family murdered.

Sometimes my brother invited our second uncle to meals, but he could be extremely rude, insulting both host and guests. After a bowl of rice wine, uncle would find fault with our guests, scoffing at their appearance. He would fly into a rage, cursing my brother, me and the guests in turn. He cursed in a mixture of Chinese and Dong, full of obscene language, but empty of content, without rhyme or reason, and often no one understood exactly what he was saying! He found it particularly irritating if anyone was slobbering or snivelling, though I don't know why.

Our uncle's short temper was common knowledge in the village. When it flared up, most paid no attention, but kept on drinking. Some sighed sympathetically and tried consoling him. Such melodrama invariably dampened the spirits of host and guests, and often caused the party to break up prematurely. After a while, my brother no longer dared to invite our second uncle when other guests were also involved.

My brother did, however, sometimes invite one particular old farmer and one other relative to drink along with our uncle, drinking and listening to his mixture of Chinese and Dong curses. When cursed, these guests did not lose their tempers, but only nodded their heads sympathetically. When our uncle was so upset and angry that he shed tears, these guests offered advice, staying until his anger had dissipated, before taking their leave. Otherwise, when my uncle was mentioned, other peers shook their heads helplessly.

During this period, my capacity for liquor increased, as I joined in with the drinking, encouraged by my brother's hospitality. The taste I had originally experienced as bitter became instead the precursor to merriment, and I cultivated my own liking for liquor. Throughout my life, there have been many times when I have abstained, then drunk again, then again tended towards abstinence. At home, it was just customary to drink, though I could easily go without drinking, and fortunately, I have never been addicted.

While studying, I would abstain completely for half a year, or even some years on end. If conditions permitted, however, I could enjoy a good drink, able to down a quarter of a litre of white spirits without side effects. People often assumed I was teetotal and though this was untrue, it was convenient at times, for I was usually not pressurised to join others in over-drinking at meal times.

During my first months back home, I was closest to two 'uncles' about my own age. Since both their family circumstances were poor, neither had found a wife and they still lived as bachelors.

While I'd been just a boy, my parents had organised my engagement to a girl from the village. Now, prior to marriage, I was living on my own surrounded by grain on the third floor of the house, a floor that served alternately as my study and bedroom.

After dinner in the evenings, my two buddies would come and look for me. I didn't have the heart to ignore them and keep on studying. Instead, the three of us would keep each other company, mostly in silence. Each was lost in his own thoughts, though it sometimes seemed as if we were thinking over the same thing. We would sit together until around 11 pm before retiring for the night. Before long, my mother had set up a couple of mats outside the door of the small study, to allow them to sleep there and keep me company.

'Keeping each other company' was what young men did in the evenings; going together into the village, searching out and visiting young women. The men would later sleep in the same room somewhere, but split up at daybreak to work in their respective fields. Only after marrying would this kind of companionship come to an end. This Dong tradition resulted in our keeping each other company in our own way for over half a year.

Sometimes my two 'uncles' would listen while I played the *pipa*. Sometimes they would retire early and sleep at around 10 pm. We never ventured into the village together, however, and didn't have the courage to talk about girls. From their general demeanour, those two seemed to have lost hope with regard to life's major event, marriage. Not having a girlfriend at their age marked them out as different, and when they observed others courting or married, they seemed embarrassed, and reluctant to talk.

The same applied to me. When I sat with my brother and his wining and dining friends, I didn't have much to say either. I was just a spectator, a silent witness to the excitement of others. I had never seen the girl to whom I was engaged; in fact, it seemed as if she didn't even exist. I couldn't begin to anticipate what lay in store for me and during those months, I felt a depression and loneliness I had never experienced before. So, we three were happy to keep each other company. When we were together, at least there was some warmth and peace of mind.

Once I went with one of these two friends, along with a young student from the village, to look for girls in Zhanmo seven kilometres away. At about 9 pm, we navigated our way through the darkness to a house where there were some girls. We climbed steps onto an open veranda, where we could see three rooms sharing the light from a single fire. Parents and brothers seemed to have withdrawn, in deference to us, the young male visitors, and everything seemed quiet except for the noise of a spinning wheel.

As it happened, the light was coming from the 'young women's room'. We entered and saw two girls, studiously oblivious to us. The older girl was sitting beside the fire, resting a moment. On observing our arrival, the flicker of a smile creased her face, along with a trace of alarm. She returned to her work. The younger girl was also spinning cotton.

We sat around the fire on low heaps of wood, watching the movements and expressions of the girls. We were not good singers, so we couldn't sing as per normal courtship practice, and we didn't say a word but just watched. They in turn busied themselves with spinning. Only when thread broke did they take the opportunity to snatch a glance at us; but only as if we were not really there at all.

It was already late when the older girl began to talk to us, with the utmost modesty. We told each other how our families were poor, we were foolish, not well matched and so on, repeating such things over and over. This was part of the formula to earn mutual affection, as the girls kept working their spinning wheels. They were weary, however, and eventually gave up and sat beside the fire, burying their heads between their arms. They said they were just shy, but they were still alert and listening attentively to anything we might say.

At last, my student-companion lazily picked up a small wooden stick and flicked it around, among the ashes of the fire. The two girls, who had been pretending to doze, seemed startled, looking up and declaring in alarm: "Oh! You're writing characters to make fun of us!" It felt as though something detestable had happened and the atmosphere suddenly soured. The girls seemed paranoid and stood up to leave. We stood, too, and followed them through the door.

We walked down the steps into the pitch darkness at the bottom of the building, where there were pillars but no walls. The girls were no longer walking away and we stopped there very close to them. I did not notice exactly who reached out first, but before long we had taken each of the girls by the hand, two boys to each girl, and the girls acquiesced.

We quietly stood there a long time holding hands, none of us wishing to leave. Then suddenly, we heard a door opening upstairs and the voice of a woman calling the girls, who dutifully pulled away and beat a retreat, up the stairs and into the house. As reluctantly we left, we noticed the gentle stirrings of light on the horizon, the sky faintly resembling the belly of a fish, and realised it was nearly daybreak. We had been immersed in thoughts of love, and were loath to abandon such emotions.

On another occasion after a meal of *bianmi* [fried, freshly harvested glutinous rice] with some young women in a relative's house, I went to the home of my maternal uncle Duan. When Duan heard how the young women had behaved, he insisted I must have made a good impression on them. He was eager to bring me to talk through the shutters with them and get to know them better. It was already nearly midnight, but I agreed and we set off immediately.

Duan was in front, I in the middle, and a friend carrying a ladder at our heels. We arrived beside the young women's bedroom and propped the ladder up outside tightly closed shutters. Duan nimbly climbed the ladder and stood beside the shutters while we two stood at the bottom anxiously awaiting developments. We watched while Duan called softly through the chinks in the shutters, saying, "You, you…" and then imploring the women, "Don't despise us."

After a while, we heard movement inside, followed by some derisory calls to leave them alone. Duan hastily climbed down and urged me up the ladder, saying the women had started to swear at him because they hadn't recognised his voice. They would surely open the shutters for me, for they knew me. So, he urged me to go and call them.

It was the first time I had done this and my heart was beating fast and furious. Before I reached anywhere near the top, however, I could hear a torrent of non-stop abuse coming from inside the room, causing me to give up and beat a hasty retreat down the ladder. Duan called me a coward and said I had forfeited a good opportunity.

Listening to Duan excited my yearning, but my first attempt resulted in such complete failure that I was never able to experience for myself the mystery of love bubbling up during night-time shutter conversations. We turned tail and went home, but this time the friend carrying the ladder led the way; of the three of us, he had been most alarmed by the girls' swearing.

During the blistering hot weather, I often went with friends to swim in the River Langdong, three kilometres away. There were deep, dark green 'pools' there, where you could swim and play to your heart's content. Slipping down naked into the clean cool water felt wonderfully exhilarating.

Once I overdid it, swimming backwards and forwards too many times. When I was practically sapped of energy, I was surprised and trapped by a whirlpool, unable to struggle free. As I was about to succumb and go under, my brother and uncle took a hand each and pulled me into shallower waters, from where I was able to reach the bank safely. For a few minutes, I could not speak with shock.

Later, however, I remained undeterred, retaining a passion for swimming in hot weather, deeming it one of the great joys of life.

There were shoals of fish and shrimp in the river. After each swim, we caught fish in the shallows near the bank, groping among the cracks between stones and pebbles. We'd soon feel the soft slippery skin of the fish and while some slipped away, others were captured. Within an hour or two, I'd often have a haul of between 500 g and one kg of fresh fish, of all colours.

On the way home, we occasionally encountered four or five girls swimming naked. On observing our approach, they'd cover their faces with both hands and submerge their bodies in the water. We reluctantly turned our backs until we'd passed, then we'd hear them shouting behind our backs, "We caught some too, more than you!" They came to the river mainly to fish, not to swim, but used their fishing expeditions as an excuse for a wash.

Teaching in Langdong

In the six months that I was home, village relationships warmed my heart and renewed in me a reluctance to leave. There was in me a deep settled affection for the village. After studying for years in Han towns, however, my head was full to the brim with Han culture and thoughts of modernity. In each place I had been, I still had friends who seemed as close as relatives, and my best friends were former schoolmates, 'outsiders'.

Whether relaxing among relatives or experiencing the camaraderie of drunken celebration, whether forgetting my worries in the company of friends or enjoying the ecstasy of swimming during the sizzling summer heat, it was impossible to forget the world outside that had left such profound impressions. Everyone at home could perceive this and they often remarked how different I was from them. Although we were relatives, they would say, it was difficult for me and them to get on well together. After all was said and done, they predicted I would leave.

Indeed, I was never reconciled to the idea of amicably muddling along, letting events take their course, like my companions in the village. Instead, I became determined to leave and return to the 'outside' stage upon which I had once lived.

Yang, in whose Guiyang office building I had lodged for a few months, was now in charge of the Nationalist government in Rongjiang county town. It occurred to me that I could ask him for a reference for a job at Rongjiang Middle School; possibly doing miscellaneous work such as transcribing or making wax prints to be copied.

Yang himself had studied at Rongjiang Middle School, so if I obtained his recommendation, I would have high hopes of being accepted. My mother and brother agreed whole-heartedly. My brother wrote a warm letter to Yang and instructed me to deliver it in person. It was summer 1949 and Guiyang was still quietly awaiting Liberation. After Liberation, I could return to Guiyang to finish senior middle school.

After I arrived in Rongjiang, however, I only saw Yang twice, and true to form, he only smiled, not speaking to me either time. The new school year at Rongjiang Middle School had been underway for almost a month, but there were only a few students and I saw no trace of any teachers. The school had not yet closed, but it looked as though closure was imminent. There was no way my plan to work at Rongjiang Middle School could materialise.

Then a message arrived from my brother. Our mother had taken seriously ill and may not survive. She might soon be speaking her last words, so I should go home quickly.

I arrived home the next day, anxious and in low spirits. On seeing me, mother wept, saying she had feared she would never see me again. She was still feverish and devoid of appetite. In the village, lack of appetite was one of the most reliable heralds of impending death, so other villagers had feared the worst. In fact, mother was ill with malaria, which was often rampant at harvest time, and there was no known cure. You could only drink the water scooped from boiling rice. The illness sapped strength and every year caused one or two villagers to die. Within a few days of my return, however, mother had recovered.

My trip to Rongjiang had nevertheless failed and I had lost hope with regard to work outside the village, so I resigned myself to staying at home awaiting the day when I could resume my studies.

One evening soon after my return, however, a fellow villager handed me a letter with an invitation from the headmaster of Langdong Primary School to teach there. This headmaster was another Yang, an *older* brother of my sister-in-law.

Langdong Primary had been established at the start of the War of Resistance (1937-45). It was widely praised as one of the three best primary schools in County Rongjiang. As an ex-pupil, I knew it well, and felt a measure of affection for it. Being invited to teach there was not what I had been hoping for, but it was too good an offer to refuse.

When I reported for duty, I discovered that fellow teachers' qualifications were much better than before. A group of teachers had transferred from Rongjiang Teacher Training Auxiliary Primary School, which had closed. Many of these were Teacher Training School graduates. Most of my former teachers had left. The new staff had more teaching experience than the old, and the school seemed set for even better results than before.

This news spread and there was a rush of applications to study at Langdong Primary. Some graduates even wanted to return and re-take grade 6.

On my first day, I taught citizenship to grade 6. I remember the theme was local autonomy and how citizens' rights could be used in a democracy. A female student rather older than many of the others was sitting in the front row. It dawned on me that she had previously been my classmate in primary 5 and 6 in Rongjiang. We had graduated there at the same time a number of years before. By some curious sequence of events, she had returned that year to study in Langdong. When I saw her in my class, I felt embarrassed. As a result, I spoke frenetically and found it a strain to keep going until the bell. Afterwards, I asked the director of teaching to arrange for me to teach grade 5 rather than grade 6, and he duly agreed.

It was late autumn and the People's Liberation Army (PLA) was moving into southern regions. Rumour had it that Hubei and Hunan Provinces had already been liberated. The people of Langdong knew the Liberation Army would soon arrive and realised we were on the cusp of an entirely new society. You could see men and women in twos and threes, standing around chatting quietly. Eating in the canteen, we were forever discussing the political situation, and one of the teachers from Hunan declared many times his expectation of going home soon.

In those days, people were unsettled and it was difficult to concentrate on the life and work before one's eyes. Since the start of the new semester, teachers had only been issued with one month's salary. The second month had nearly passed and the headmaster had been several times to regional headquarters to ask for salaries, but each time had returned empty-handed. Canteen staff said there was no money for cooking oil or salt, and meals were becoming increasingly insubstantial. Our diet soon comprised coarse rice and vegetables, fried with insufficient oil, flippantly referred to by some as 'soldiers' food'.

Funding had been severed, no one could concentrate on teaching and everyone just wanted to leave. Students from the surrounding villages left in a continuous stream, without first asking permission, and thus student numbers were depleted by the day. Only a few children from the town remained, spread among the different classes.

My old classmate, the young woman who had attended my first citizenship class, was nowhere to be seen. Why had she, at approximately 20 years of age, wanted to study grade 6 again? It still seemed so strange.

One afternoon, teachers and grade 6 students assembled for a lecture by a Miao nationality teacher, with the theme: 'The new economic policies of the Soviet Union'. In fact, his whole lecture was actually about the Great October Socialist Revolution in Russia. He spoke at high tempo, with surging passion, in a non-stop flood that lasted around an hour. Everyone sat quietly and listened respectfully, not really understanding, but certainly finding it novel. It was the first time I'd heard such a lecture, aiming to elucidate the current state of affairs in Russia and by extension China, so it held a kind of magnetic attraction and concentrated the mind.

Expressions on people's faces were strained and I couldn't spot any trace of a smile or of recognition. I surmised that no one really understood what was being said, though what follows is the gist of what I think I understood.

In the Soviet Revolution, workers and peasants overthrew capitalists, landlords and rich peasants, in a response to cruel oppression and exploitation. We in turn should respond *en masse*. Even soldiers sent to suppress the masses should reconsider their actions and change direction to side with the masses, to earn the title of revolutionary pioneers, overthrowing the ruling regime. The new regime in the Soviet Union was run by workers and peasants. Formerly, they had been powerless, the oppressed and exploited classes, but now factories were owned by the workers and land was divided among the peasants. Everyone was equal and where there was food, everyone shared it.

There was not a single student who would not have loved and longed for such a scenario. To me, a young intellectual who had been born into an oppressed minority, it was especially stunning. In my imagination, it evoked massive waves that would transform society. It generated a strong and silent respect for this Miao teacher. The dark underbelly of society, involved in blackmail and extortion, must be quaking in its boots.

Teacher Long

A teacher by the name of Long, from Hunan, whom I gathered was a staunch intellectual, shared a room with me. Just after he moved from Rongjiang to Langdong, however, he became seriously ill, causing him to stoop as if hunchbacked. It must have been some kind of lung disease for at night he coughed incessantly.

Long had no appetite for the coarse rice or boiled green vegetables in the canteen. He'd take one look at the cuisine, shake his head, and turn around and leave, without saying a word; with the result that he often didn't eat at all. With no access to doctors or medical care, he just lay on his bed. There was not much I could do except bring hot water for washing his face and feet. He gradually became thinner and weaker, but never complained. Nor indeed did he speak to me about any personal matters.

The school director of teaching was also from Hunan and spoke with the same accent as Long. They had probably not known each other before, however, for the director never came to visit and never expressed concern for Long. Indeed, no one came to talk to him except Mr Liu, a teacher from Langdong, who came once a day. Liu was the one who had originally introduced Long to the school. He would always ask Long if he had eaten or not. It seemed as if Liu was his only friend; at that time and in that place, only Liu knew him well. No one else paid much attention to him.

When I wasn't teaching, I would sit by Long's bed and keep him company, silently keeping an eye on him. In fact, however, I didn't really know how to care for or console him. He never spoke about his own family or his own experiences and never asked about mine, but simply lay still, suffering the torment of his illness in silence.

Long once asked if I had read *Flowing Iron* [a Soviet novel about revolution] and said that the stories in *The August Countryside* and *Flowing Iron* were identical. I should look for one of the books and read it.

Sometimes he would softly hum the tune of a song and when I remarked it was pleasant to the ear, he advised me it was called 'Be as Enduring as the Universe'. Its words had been written by Tian Han [1898–1968, the author of the words of the Chinese national anthem, 'March of the Volunteer Army']. The song was popular in Hong Kong and Long said he'd like to teach it to me. I sang it after him line by line a few times and then we sang it together. That left a lasting impression. Later when reminiscing about Long, I would often sing that song; and I still remember it today.

It seemed incongruous, but from time to time Long would sit on the edge of the bed and knit. His handiwork did not resemble any kind of clothing, but I think he was just trying to take his mind off the unbearable pain of his illness. I asked him to teach me and he did so willingly, taking my hands in his until I had mastered the art. I still remember how to knit, and if prevailed upon I could still knit a scarf or socks.

I shared a room with Long for just over two months. We seemed to share the same values and he made a deep impression on me. We each only knew that the other was a teacher; that was all.

A branch of the PLA had marched southwards through Guizhou towards Guangxi and Guangdong. At all levels in County Rongjiang, the Nationalist government was vanquished and vanished. All funding for schools in the county had been suspended and inevitably, the headmaster announced one morning that our school was closing down. Teachers immediately packed their bags and left in haste, like convicted criminals making good their escape. There was no time for goodbyes and by mid-day, only Mr Long and I were left.

Long's health had shown no sign of improvement and he found it difficult to walk. His friend, Liu, came to bring him back to stay at Liu's own house, saying he could go home later, after he had recovered.

After leaving Langdong Primary for home, I never heard of any of my former teaching colleagues, involved in that sudden exodus, except Long and Liu. After Liberation, an old man from Xiangye went to sell some things in the market at Langdong. Liu bumped into him and passed on the news that Long had succumbed to his illness at Liu's home in the winter of that year (1949). Despite everything, I had not really expected this, and felt special sympathy for Long, who had died far from home. Did his family ever find out what happened?

Marriage

Within a few days of my return to Xiangye, we celebrated Dong New Year, the first day of the 11th month of the lunar calendar. The village was no longer haunted by soldiers appearing suddenly from nowhere to extort grain, money and conscripts.

It was no longer customary, however, for men to meet for banter after breakfast under one of the houses. The noisy clamour of the finger-guessing drinking game could no longer be heard at the evening meals. Children who used to chase and play in the alleys and fields could no longer be seen. People would come and go in a hurry and the village seemed different, desolate. Some fundamental change had apparently taken place. The same kind of atmosphere prevailed in the streets of Langdong, when I left the primary school.

One evening, my mother, brother and I were sitting warming ourselves around the fire. After a long silence, mother announced that at Chinese New Year, they would organise my wedding, and my brother chipped in to say that my fiancée and I were both old enough and we should go ahead and marry. The current political climate was chaotic and it would be a mistake to delay any further. Who knew *what* might happen next year?

I disagreed. Marrying would surely disrupt my plans to continue studies. Mother, however, was adamant. Everything had been agreed with the girl's parents and arrangements could not be cancelled now. My brother added that he had arranged to purchase a pig, and rice wine had already been brewed. It had been decided, and at the appointed time, we would do it.

It felt futile to argue and I retreated upstairs to ponder my predicament. If I left home, there was nowhere to go. I had no option but to comply with the marriage arrangements, which seemed to be part of my destiny.

On the morning of the wedding, according to custom, I lay low in another house warming myself by the fire. I heard the noise of fireworks and the din of the wedding party's arrival, but did not dare to go out and see for myself. The bride, accompanied by a younger sister and sister-in-law, was welcomed into my home by several of my close relatives. The three visitors stayed for three nights, before returning home.

During those three days of wedding celebrations, our family provided food for relatives and friends. My brother made a point of inviting his two Han friends, one being his pal Zhen, and the other his old friend Wang. They had been his classmates at junior middle school.

When these two friends had been in Guiyang at vocational secondary school and senior middle school, respectively, they often came to visit me, providing encouragement and support. Back then, seeing their familiar faces in a strange place had helped me ward off loneliness and fear. I regarded them as brothers and they in turn treated me as their younger brother. So, they were friends both to me and my brother, and it was natural for them to join in the wedding celebrations.

At the reception, my brother proposed a toast, saying, "We two," indicating himself and his friend Zhen, "are special buddies. You two," indicating Wang and me, "should also become special buddies!"

He was drunk, but that did not stop everyone approving unanimously. Wang laughed heartily. He was clearly older than me, so could only really be regarded as my older brother. How could we possibly be special buddies? I just laughed, saying, "Not really, not really…" Everyone was in high spirits, however, due to the rice wine, and no one paid any attention to my disclaimers. They just cheered and considered it a done deal. As it transpired, my subsequent friendship with Wang was limited…but before long, he did turn up unexpectedly and play a significant positive role in my life.

One evening, a month later, my mother sent my sister-in-law to bring the bride back to our home. My new wife arrived carrying a wicker basket containing a change of clothes, and walking slowly behind my sister-in-law. She came onto the veranda and put down the basket. Immediately, she took the carrying pole and buckets and went to the well to draw and bring back two buckets of water. Afterwards, she helped my mother prepare a large wok of pigs' food, as well as wash dishes and do other housework.

About 10 pm, my mother and sister-in-law and others left the fire to go to bed, whereupon the bride entered our bedroom. That evening, I had gone elsewhere, deliberately avoiding her, but towards midnight, I finally returned. This was the first time I had seen her figure, slim and slightly shorter than me. Her facial features were fine, quite pretty. She was sitting on the bed awaiting my return, dressed as she had been for the wedding. We didn't say anything, but turned the lights out and got into bed. This was the newlyweds' first night. I was 19. She was 17.

From then on, we were actually, as well as formally, man and wife. There were no tables or chairs in our bedroom, only a roughly made but stable double bed which had never been painted, sawn from pinewood; and a rectangular dressing mirror. The four walls were covered by my favourite calligraphy and Chinese art, presented to me by friends as gifts. Anyone with a school background said it looked great. One item was my own transcription of Chairman Mao's poem 'Snow on the Pattern of Qinyuanchun' (1936).

My wife seldom said anything; villagers believed this was a sign of submissiveness. She was not used to laughing or smiling; when conversing, there would be no trace of a smile on her face. She was always calm and quiet, and was never involved in disputes; as if everything was heaven-ordained and could not be altered. Her life seemed to consist of constantly following the same old routine, complying with the wishes of others.

During the year we lived together as man and wife, I rarely noticed any sign of worry, anger or sadness on my wife's face. Wherever she was, outside or in, she hardly made a sound – unless it was, for example, the sound of spinning cotton. The house was quiet as if there was no one else at home. Whether in private or in company, we never conversed; not because we didn't dare or were too embarrassed, but because we had already seen into each other's heart and knew that actions or facial expressions would be enough. There was no need for language.

My wife knew that after things settled down post-Liberation, I was planning to go far away to study, and I was not sure if I would ever be able to return. She often stood beside the fire gazing at me and when she saw me going out, she quietly leaned on the veranda rails watching me. She didn't say a thing and never cried, but I knew she was contemplating our imminent separation, dreading the future changes as yet unimaginable.

We passed that year in silence. Perhaps this feature of Dong marriages was after all a source of happiness, for in the end we were true to each other and understood each other, having become interdependent. I was not satisfied, however, with this kind of happiness. I was always thinking about study and yearned for the diversity of life in other places; meeting up with old friends and making new ones. Life only seemed to take on significance through striving together towards some shared future goals.

Chapter 7
Imprisonment and Release
(Liberation, 1949-50)

Waiting Dejectedly

In those days, news frequently arrived of liberation in other parts of the country, but I was still trapped in this remote Dong village. My thoughts were jumping all around and no one else was going in the same direction. Actually, I didn't have the courage to stride on alone. As the Chinese saying goes, I was 'lamenting my own inadequacy in the face of a great task', yearning for something, but incapable of reaching out for it. Just like a frog in a pot of water getting hotter by the minute, I was anxious to leave but unable to make the break. My depression of indecision before marriage had been replaced by a depression of fear after.

In the first six months after marriage, I spent most days in the study on the third floor of our house. By night, I would sit by the fire downstairs and chat to family members and villagers who would drop by.

In the study I read, with intense interest, *And Quiet Flows the Don* by Mikhail Sholokhov, and *Mother,* and *My University* by Maxim Gorky. Such reading opened my eyes to the world outside, helping me discover what was meant by 'class oppression' and 'class struggle'. I learned, too, about the state of society in the Soviet Union at the time of the 1917 October Revolution, when the old system of governance was overthrown and replaced by a regime led by workers and peasants.

I read books about socialist revolution, causing me to feel that every detail of the revolution was new and strange. The way China was being turned upside down in those days made me feel both excited and alarmed. Such transformations were based on intense and mind-blowing ideological changes.

These books helped me understand why there had been a revolution in China, together with the basic reasons for the sweeping victory of the communists and the rapid liberation of the whole country. The revolution happened in order to abolish injustice in society, a goal which enjoyed the unanimous endorsement of the people.

In our village and probably even throughout our whole region, I was the only person to have read books like this about socialist revolution. I was the only one who had a basic understanding of what was happening, superficial though it was.

Evenings found me chatting and gossiping around the fire. Relatives would often drop by for a chat. They would smile a lot and gaze at me for long periods, as if to ask, 'Do you have any good news?' in an attempt to discover my attitude to the current political situation. I was familiar with village customs, but like them, I knew only a little about class struggle in the Han areas. True, I had studied in a few places and had accumulated some qualifications, speaking Mandarin quite fluently and knowing many people. At least it was clear to me that the Han regions were very different from our village.

Of course, there were also social problems in the village, with land unevenly distributed. This is how I explained things to our visitors, according to my superficial understanding of the books I'd been reading. Our village society was an ancient one, unfair and needing change. Families with more land than average should share land with those that had none, or less than average, so that everyone had their own land to cultivate. Everyone would then be equal and no one would pay rent, or work as farm labourers for others. No one would have to pay grain levies and everyone would be able to stand on their own feet, with enough food to eat and enough clothes to wear. In future, we would be building the kind of society in which there would be no difference between rich and poor.

At that time, I was thinking: the situation in the Dong villages is very different from the Han regions and even more different from Russia at the time of the October Revolution. I imagined that peaceful means would surely be used to implement land reform in the villages, ensuring that everyone would become self-sufficient.

Some of my fellow-villagers around the fire, on hearing me say such things, would simply sigh. The tenant renting my family's land listened with a steady smile, culminating in a happy announcement, "So that's how it's going to be! If it turns out like that, everything's going to be just fine!" Obviously, he was sceptical, but content to pretend that it wasn't all just wishful thinking.

After people dispersed, I would feel dejected again, at a loss. I'd go upstairs into the dark grain-storage area to meditate and play the *pipa*, to search for a more tranquil frame of mind.

Summer of Imprisonment

The leader of the 1942/43 Miao rebellion (known as the Eastern Guizhou Incident) in our locality was Li Zhifu, from Baidao village. The rebellion involved people from three counties and the Nationalist Party dispatched a huge army to quell it. They tracked down and killed several dozen Miao leaders, but since Baidao was in a remote area of high mountains covered in dense forest, Li Zhifu was able to hide, and he survived. After the army left, he stayed at home undisturbed for many years.

In 1949, local Nationalist leaders stepped up their campaign to round up opponents. Chen Kaiming, the leader in County Jianhe, and Yang Rui, the leader in the township of Taiyong called Li to a meeting in Taiyong and arrested him there. The next day, Li was sent under escort towards Jianhe county town. As the escort was descending Mount Jiuyi, there was a fork in the road leading to Baidao and there the escort opened fire and shot Li in the back. Afterwards, they spread the rumour that he had been shot trying to escape in the direction of Baidao. His body was never found.

Miao people were appalled by the murder of Li Zhifu, and Han and Dong people in the region also heard of the incident. A Miao intellectual by the name of Yang Shi, who had served as a soldier in the war against Japan, lived in Li's home area. After victory, he left the army and went home, staying mostly in the village for several years. He and Li Zhifu had been relatives, both local Miao leaders, well known also to Han and Dong neighbours in the region.

Chen Kaiming and Yang Rui believed Yang Shi was supporting Liberation, and he became a thorn in their flesh. Within a month of Li's murder, troops were sent to arrest Yang Shi. He was imprisoned in Jianhe county town and never returned home. Everyone believed he was secretly murdered, drowned in the River Qingshui and his body fed to the fish. Again, no one ever saw his body.

On the day Yang Shi was arrested, fellow clansmen fled for their lives. The murders of Li and Yang terrorised the region, students in particular. No one dared to talk about the murders in public, but everyone, even women and children, knew the names of the victims.

The Dong people of my village knew hardly a thing about Chen Kaiming or Yang Rui. Most were illiterate and some referred to Chen as Chen Haimin (*haimin* means 'killing the people') and to Yang Rui as Yang Lei (*lei* means 'thunder'). They were terrified of these two leaders with reputations like tigers, but at the time, I was still a youth and had yet to experience anything really terrifying. Armed with life and breath, and a sense of right and wrong acquired at school, I sympathised with the relatives of Li Zhifu and Yang Shi, and publicly resented the murderers.

To those who dropped by our home, I often denounced Yang Rui. What kind of township leader was he? All he did was arrest people, collect taxes and extort money. He had connived with Chen Kaiming to murder innocent local leaders, killing people as if they were chickens, casually dragging them away and secretly having them executed. Afterwards, he never said a word about such executions and no one even knew where the corpses could be found. This was all too horrible for words. Whom would they kill next? My fireside farming audience applauded my bold ranting and resonated with my outrage.

In the winter of 1949, Chen Kaiming and Yang Rui conscripted young men into an army to oppose the communists. My brother was appointed deputy commander of a battalion and practically everyone who had studied with me in Guiyang was given some important position, forming the backbone of this makeshift army. Nearly all the young men of the whole region who had attended primary or middle school were incorporated into the Jianhe branch of the Anti-Communist Army – all except me.

I was the exception. With a vengeance, I detested the corruption of greedy officials such as Chen and Yang. I was unwilling to pledge my life or loyalty to them, but in my heart supported Liberation instead. Allowing those who *work* the land to *own* the land; equality, harmony and happiness without oppression;

these were traditions of our own Dong people. Who wouldn't admire and aspire to such a society?

With my admittedly shallow understanding of the revolutions in the Soviet Union and other lands, I was a keen supporter of the new movement. I was wholeheartedly looking forward to Liberation and to continuing my studies to honour my ancestors, an idea I had absorbed from my Han Chinese schooling. This was my settled goal and was also the desire of my family for me.

My brother, the head of the household, understood what was going on in my head. He had begun to resign himself to the general downward spiral of events, from a Nationalist perspective. Already committed to the Nationalist cause, however, he had no way of turning back. Instead, he invested his hope in me.

Mother did not understand what was going on. On observing all the educated people from the village going to serve in the Anti-Communist Army, she urged me also to 'go and do something'. She disapproved of my reasons for not joining them, though my brother scolded her, saying she didn't understand. He opposed my joining the army, pointing out there had been no choice for anyone else. When everything was done and dusted, he would come home to work the land, hire people to fell timber and send it to Jinping to earn money for sending me to university. Mother was uneasy about all this.

I hid upstairs among the grain, studying books and playing the *pipa*, rarely going down. The two relatives who had earlier kept me company still slept up there at night and this reduced the sense of loneliness they otherwise felt, while calming my lonesome fear.

The Anti-Communist Army organised by Chen and Yang established its main base at Mount Jiuyi, in the hope that the high ground there was easier to defend. That army base, however, did not last even two months. At the beginning of 1950, news of the liberation of Jianhe county town by the People's Liberation Army (PLA) filtered through, and the Anti-Communist Army at Jiuyi scattered to the winds.

My brother led our village battalion, with only one rifle among them all, in retreat. On the way to Nanshao, they encountered PLA soldiers approaching rapidly from the mountain path opposite. The PLA opened fire, and my brother's group was terrified, turning tail and fleeing back to Xiangye. The PLA didn't bother to give chase.

My brother's troops assembled the next day at the former bullfighting arena. Their commander, a Han person from outside the region, sadly announced they should disband, each to his own home. Then he turned and left in haste. My brother had not even served a month as deputy commander of the battalion. From then on, he relinquished any military involvement and stayed at home with his wife.

The PLA established a 'People's Government' in Jianhe county town, but did not establish offices at district, township or village levels. Instead, they instructed 'maintenance committees' to replace the former corrupt district and township regimes.

A former township leader in Taiyong was appointed director of the Taiyong maintenance committee. He did not arrest or kill anyone and refrained from launching any new projects in the area. Xiangye residents returned from the market in Taiyong saying they had heard that Yang Rui had fled and everyone was celebrating. During this transition period, however, there was general apprehension about what might happen next. Most villagers stayed within the village boundaries. Still, there was no sign of PLA or Communist Party personnel.

People were suspended in this kind of limbo for only a month or so, talking about Liberation but not sure if it had actually happened. We heard that the PLA had withdrawn completely from Jianhe county town and that former county and township leaders had returned. By then, however, it was too late to reorganise the Anti-Communist Army to Save the Nation, which had been thoroughly routed. There was a temporary break in communication with higher authorities at provincial or national level, and local news was conveyed by wireless transmitters. County security forces and township self-defence forces were improvised from the vestiges of earlier personnel.

Those who reassumed government leadership were like birds startled by an arrow, like badgers caught in headlights, constantly living in fear. They concentrated on the conversation going on around them, sending men on sentry duty to strategic road junctions at the borders of their regions. Such sentries interrogated travellers and pillaged people's belongings. If they intercepted anyone coming from places where the PLA were stationed, they arrested them on suspicion of spying. They also arrested any 'suspicious' public figures in the region and had them secretly executed.

My village was one of the furthest from Jianhe county town and from Taiyong, but being relatively prosperous it felt more vulnerable in the prevailing atmosphere of intimidation. There was no direct passage out of Xiangye into the liberated region, no easy way of escaping 'the Nationalist trap' and we experienced great psychological pressure.

I often sat with friends around the fire, verbally attacking the perverse continuing rebellion of former township leader Yang and former county leader Chen, who had reinstated themselves. Yang and Chen, however, soon got wind of our opposition and became furious, after which trouble became inevitable.

At the time Jianhe county town was liberated, a leader in the county government took two rifles from the office and escaped to the Han village of Liuluo, only a few kilometres from Xiangye. He was addicted to opium but had no money to pay for it. When the urge to smoke overtook him, he was smitten by unbearable suffering. In the end, he sent someone to ask my brother if he could help sell the two rifles.

My brother went to see him and found it impossible to reject his desperate appeals, paying something over 10 *yuan* to purchase the rifles and placing them in our home. He justified his actions by saying there wasn't another rifle in the village. Sometimes outsiders armed with only a club or a wood-chopping knife dared to come and rob us, when one shot in the air would be enough to dissuade them. At such a low price, the rifles were a bargain for they would guard against theft and ease people's anxiety.

After Chen Kaiming was reinstated, he researched the missing rifles, which had disappeared when everyone was fleeing in panic. He discovered my brother had bought them and sent orders for them to be returned, without compensation. Since my brother had paid for the rifles and was not going to be reimbursed, he ignored Chen's demand, but fearing reprisal, he stayed away from home. The reinstated township leader Yang Rui informed us that Chen was absolutely livid.

In summer 1950, Chen dispatched a large company of public security guards to our village, some of whom burst into our home early one morning in search of the missing rifles. With guns on their backs, they searched the village hoping to find and arrest my brother. When they realised he had left long before, the 'company commander' ordered my arrest. He himself tied my arms behind my back with a rope of palm fibre and sent me under escort to the home of the leader of Small Village. I could be released only on payment of 20 *yuan*. Otherwise, he would tighten the rope and hang me up by the arms, still tied behind my back.

There was no money in our family but my wife's mother could not bear to see me suffering. She fetched her life's savings and gave them to the blackmailing commander. This resulted in a loosening of the ropes, though I was still taken prisoner under escort to Jianhe county town.

When I was first tied up, the young men of the village ran to the mountains to hide, while elders, women and children were dismayed and protested against my arrest. The elders proposed using the names of all villagers to write a 'guarantors' certificate', to persuade the public security leaders to release me on bail. I urged them not to do so for even if they did, I would still not be released and such a certificate would implicate them all, as if they were all guilty of the same charge. So, they dropped the idea.

The guards dragged me away, as if they were bandits stealing some property. My relatives feared I would be murdered along the road, so one of the 'uncles' who kept me company in the evenings volunteered to follow me into Jianhe and stay in a guest house there, awaiting my release, delivering food morning and evening. He would accompany me home after I was released.

It was a large procession to Jianhe, my friend and I walking in the middle. In the villages we passed through, no one dared to come out and see for themselves. I only noticed a few people hiding behind shrubbery, stealthily stealing a glimpse. We reached the county town by late afternoon and saw a few older people standing at the entrances to their homes, observing. Someone asked in a startled voice where this student prisoner came from.

The soldiers first led me to their camp and just then, my special buddy Wang from the wedding reception hurried up to see me. He was a teacher at Jianhe Middle School. He did not seem at all perturbed, but just said I shouldn't worry: he would think of a way to have me released. By the time I was escorted to the county prison, it was already dusk. The former county leader Chen came, swivelled me around to size me up, and then announced loudly, "You've arrested the wrong person!" He ordered me to be locked up and they would talk about it later.

I was pushed into a small cell and the door was locked, with a team of prison guards outside. I heard the *huo-huo* scraping of a machete being sharpened and was terrified, for I thought they were about to kill me.

The next morning, my friend delivered breakfast, but I couldn't eat and had him take it back. As he was leaving, my special buddy Wang arrived and handed me *The Book of One Thousand and One Nights*. He reiterated that I shouldn't worry, but should read, relax and while away the time.

I saw soldiers wearing all kinds and colours of clothing, coming and going. There was the incessant *huo-huo* grinding of machetes being sharpened, enough to scare anyone to death. During those few days in the cell, I constantly feared I might be dragged out and beheaded. How could I be in the mood to read, relax and while away the time? After one or two mouthfuls at mealtimes, I had no appetite for more.

On my last morning there, I became aware of another prisoner in an inside cell, behind a firmly closed wooden door. He was a middle-aged man, who spoke to me through the door, asking, "Where do you come from? Why have you been arrested?"

Then in a fluent local accent, he told me he was from Taijiang. A week before, he had come to Jianhe to buy some things. Public security guards had suspected he was a communist soldier, working as a spy, so he had been arrested and locked up. He said someone had been dragged out of his cell and executed the previous week, assumed to be a spy from Taijiang, and he was afraid the same would happen to him today, market day. Despite all this, he spoke steadily; I couldn't detect any anxiety in his voice. He told me that Yang Shi had been locked up here, but after being dragged out for interrogation one night, he never returned.

This all seemed authentic at the time and I was so frightened I could hardly speak. In retrospect many days later, I suspected my fellow prisoner had been lying. He said he had been arrested a week before, but Yang Shi had been murdered six months before. That fellow may have been planted to prompt me to supply information that could be used against me. I never saw his next door room or 'my fellow-prisoner', and now I doubt whether he was really a prisoner at all.

Just after mid-day that day, a middle-aged man in grey uniform called me to go with him, and I was led into a spacious county government office. The former county leader Chen Kaiming, sitting alongside another official, addressed me as I stood in the middle of the room, "You're a student. Chairman Zheng and I are now releasing you to go home. You're not to cause any trouble, okay? After you get home, you should tell your brother to come home as well. I'm appointing him leader of Taiyong township."

With this, he released me and I left the office, noticing instantly how unusually blue the sky seemed. Walking along the sun-soaked streets, it felt as though I had returned from death to life. I was experiencing the relief and joy of survival and freedom.

When I entered the guesthouse and saw my friend face to face, he was so pleasantly surprised he was lost for words. There were no smiles, however, for we had to move quickly. We first paid lodging fees to the female proprietor. Then an uncle who had been forced to join the public security guards came rushing in, "Quickly, quickly. You have to go quickly!" It seemed as though someone was already pursuing us.

The three of us rushed out of the county town, not pausing to speak. By the time we had reached the foot of Mount Jiuyi, it was already nearly dark. We were still afraid that Yang Rui might intercept and murder us, so my 'uncle' took the lead and waded across the River Taiyong to the opposite bank. In this way, we avoided Taiyong town and thwarted anyone who might have been waiting there to arrest us. We arrived home around 11 pm.

The whole family was still on the veranda and they greeted us with exclamations of surprise and pity, "You poor children!" My mother-in-law pushed to the front using both hands to place a red cloth around me, then taking two or three mouthfuls of rice wine and spraying me with it, to drive away evil spirits and avert any future calamities.

That night, no one slept, but sat around the fire. My brother had just come home that very night and was sitting in the group along with the others. They speculated one by one on how the former leaders could possibly have freed me; all of them had been convinced I would never be freed. At first, I also did not understand, but simply related what had happened.

Later, I thought of three possible reasons for my unexpected release. One was that my special buddy Wang had influenced the headmaster of Jianhe Middle School, who was in fact Chairman Zheng. After Liberation, I discovered what none of us in the village had previously known, that Wang had been a Nationalist agent.

The second possible reason was related to the fact that Chen and Yang had been killing people to try to eliminate the danger they perceived to themselves. Li Zhifu and Yang Shi had been close relatives, so they were both killed. Chen and Yang had sent guards to apprehend my brother Ou Chaoxi, but they arrested me instead. If they had killed me, they were afraid Ou Chaoxi would take revenge. Releasing me and casting the bait of appointing Ou Chaoxi as township leader, as a trap to capture us both, would eradicate any future threat. This was perhaps Chen Kaiming's strategy; loosening the reins only to grasp them more firmly.

The last possible reason may simply have been that they viewed me as an innocent student, not a Party member, nor a soldier, nor a member of any organisation. Indeed, I had never been formally affiliated with any of their enemies. Although I had opposed Chen and Yang verbally, I had never been involved in any real action against them. Releasing me might benefit them in future, while killing me would possibly do them more harm than good.

My relatives thought I was fortunate to escape against the odds. When my brother heard that Chen proposed to appoint him as township leader, he was sceptical and assured us he wouldn't be sticking his neck out to take up the appointment. Chen only wanted to kill him as he had killed Li Zhifu and Yang

Shi. My brother didn't dare to live at home any longer, and attempted thereafter to dissociate himself from relatives and friends, returning home only a few days every month.

Fearing Yang Rui would send guards to arrest his 'enemies', my family made me leave without delay. Before daybreak, my brother and a friend saw me off to a relative's place in Langdong. Officially, Jianhe authorities were unable to cross county borders to arrest anyone in Rongjiang, so our fears gradually diminished. A few days later, someone from Xiangye accompanied me to Zhaihao, after which I travelled alone by boat to Rongjiang. I was planning to look for my best friend Shi to accompany me from Rongjiang to a 'liberated' region, then on to Guiyang.

Shi was from County Sandu, but his family had opened a shop in Qianlingxi Street in Guiyang, and one in Rongjiang. They had always been willing to help me, so I was sure my plan was feasible.

Aunty Zhou had moved to a small wooden home in Rongjiang, and as soon as I arrived, I went to her new place to stop over. It had three rooms in total, with table and chairs arranged as they had been in her former home. They made up a bed for me in the living room. With Aunty Zhou, there was still a seamless family-like understanding. Although she realised I had come because of some emergency, she never asked me to explain. By nature, I was reticent anyway and we each remained uninformed of the general circumstances of the other.

On the day I reached Rongjiang, I bumped into my old school friend, Hu, at the pier on the road beside the river. He greeted me with the shocking news that Shi had recently died suddenly, having been ill with diarrhoea. My heart sank like a stone. Grieved and despairing, I accompanied Hu silently to his house, privately mulling over Shi's loss. At length, Hu related how on the day before Liberation in Guiyang, Shi had left the Southwest Middle School to go home to Sandu, and had later come to Rongjiang to wait for me there.

I went to Shi's family store where a young member of staff explained that Shi had suddenly taken ill and died upstairs, in a dismal room on the third floor. His body was only discovered later and the cause of death was unknown, for no one ever investigated in detail.

Shi's death changed everything. I could no longer rely on his family to support my study in Guiyang, and to make matters worse, the region's anti-communist forces were occupying Rongjiang at that time. There were Nationalist sentries all along the road out of Rongjiang and there were few pedestrians to be seen, for the sentries interrogated all travellers and arrested many strangers. I was not familiar either with the local people or the land. Even if I had been brave enough, there was no one to lead the way, and it would have been crazy to take the chance of going alone.

Hu knew that I wanted to go to Guiyang, but he said that without Shi, I'd certainly be captured and killed, so he warned me repeatedly not to go. There was no alternative but to stay in Rongjiang and await the right opportunity.

A few Nationalist leaders remained in Rongjiang, running the old county government. The primary and middle schools had long since closed, there were very few young men in the streets and the population had generally diminished. In the evenings, only two or three rice-noodle shops were open, with lanterns hanging inside and out. From time to time, gunshots were heard from the foot of the mountains to the west. The town was desolate and its citizens were fearful.

Circumstances detained me there for one or two months. I was constantly fearful. Aunty Zhou had a nephew about 10 years my senior who often visited her, and we became acquainted. When I had attended junior middle school, I had often seen him walking around, and I think he was a primary school teacher. He was tall and thin, also named Zhou, and behaved like a member of the family. Sometimes he would go for a walk with Aunty Zhou and invite me as well. Occasionally, we went together to visit Hu.

Once I accompanied Zhou to his room in the former Nationalist Party headquarters, surrounded by empty rooms. He was the only one who stayed there overnight. When we first entered, there was a large lounge with the door wide open, and I saw a young woman there wearing traditional Chinese-style dress, lying, relaxing on a canvas deck chair. Zhou informed me quietly that she and the former county leader had become friends over a game of mah-jong, she had been put in charge of the county seal, and was now still in a relationship with the former leader. At the time, she was the only employee in the county office. When I looked carefully, I recognised her as a former classmate from junior middle school. This startled me and before she had time to recognise me, I took Zhou by the arm and we left in a hurry.

I noticed that some people, perhaps soldiers, were living in the row of single-storey houses outside the county government complex. In the office area itself, however, there were only two inhabitants, Zhou and that female seal custodian. Zhou was there by night, while the woman worked there by day. I never found out what Zhou did (I did not usually ask about such things) but supposed it was some kind of office-work.

One night, my sleep was disturbed by Zhou's urgent knocks on the door. He burst in, declaring, "The Liberation Army has arrived and everyone has left. Let's go quickly!" Originally, I had been looking forward to Liberation in Rongjiang, but when I heard the PLA had arrived, I knew I would come under suspicion, as I was not a permanent resident of the town, but from a village far away. Disaster seemed imminent, so I immediately followed Zhou and left the room empty-handed. Aunty Zhou yelled after me, "Chaoquan, you left your suitcase behind!"

"I'll leave it for now," I called over my shoulder. "I'll be back later!"

Zhou led me groping through the darkness to his home in Zhongchengbao, where I had something to eat, slept two or three hours and woke before daybreak. Zhou and his wife were still fast asleep, but I didn't wait to say goodbye.

When I reached home, the village didn't feel as desolate as before. There was more pounding of rice in the mornings and a few young men were fetching grass to feed the water buffaloes. My brother, who had earlier fled from Chen Kaiming and Yang Rui, had been home for many days. He explained that the PLA had already reached Taijiang, Leishan, Sansui, Jinping and Liping, and would very soon reach Jianhe. The former leaders of Jianhe would not be causing any more trouble, for they had fled and were hiding in remote mountain locations.

One afternoon soon afterwards, a PLA reconnaissance troop stormed the village in search of enemies. When they realised I wasn't a typical farmer, they brought me to their leaders at one end of the village.

The soldiers had come to arrest my brother, but coincidentally, he had just gone to Zhanmo, seven kilometres away. They searched from house to house, while one of their leaders looked and asked me where Ou Chaoxi had gone. I told him the truth, and that I was Chaoxi's younger brother, for there was no sense in doing otherwise. Everyone else in the village had been similarly compliant and there was nowhere to hide. The leader hesitated, before ordering me to go home. Just as I reached home, I heard someone barking out my name, ordering me to return. Another leader was insisting they should take me to look for Ou Chaoxi.

Two villagers with the surname Yang were led away together with me. Early the next morning, the PLA surrounded and searched Zhanmo, but Ou Chaoxi had left the previous evening to return to Xiangye. Once again, they had been thwarted and my brother had escaped. They glared at me and eventually led the three of us to Taiyong.

That evening, a PLA political instructor told me, "Go back home and tell everyone the PLA has arrived, and this time won't be leaving again." He told me to prepare and display placards welcoming the PLA and to organise the villagers to welcome them as they entered.

The next morning, I left Taiyong for home, where fellow-villagers had again feared the worst and had been constantly fretting about me. They were delighted to see me, thronging around, beaming with happiness and asking all kinds of questions. I explained that the PLA had arrived and would not be leaving again. They would visit us within a few days and everyone should prepare to welcome them.

The Communist government for the southwest region identified as 'bandit territory' any places where the Nationalist Party still preserved a remnant of power or where Nationalists had restored themselves to power, along with any regions where anti-communist forces had formerly been stationed. Anyone who had belonged to an organisation which had been opposed to communism was labelled a 'bandit'. The PLA was instructed to conduct a methodical clean-up operation in bandit territory and liberate the people there.

The township of Taiyong was liberated in the early autumn of 1950. Shortly afterwards, anyone who had been a bandit, had joined a reactionary party, had worked as staff in the Nationalist government offices or served as a *bao* (namely village) leader, was instructed to report to the township government or to the working group in his village.

On the third day after the liberation of Taiyong, my brother was the first person to report to the township government, planning to turn over a new leaf. On the fourth day, he left home with a bundle of bedclothes to go to Jianhe county town, and meet with others for 'study'. Within a week of his departure, every villager who fell into one of the 'problem' categories had followed him, one after another, to report to the PLA for 'study'.

In this way, all my former student friends left. They all went to 'study', along with those who had served as *bao* leaders in the village. Some farmers said to me ironically, "Not long ago when the Nationalists called them, they all left and only you remained at home. Now that the Communists have called them, they have all left again and only you remain at home. You are the only one left who has ever 'studied'!"

They thought they were going to study but later they were sentenced to reform-through-labour. For many years after Liberation, villagers continued to confuse 'study' with 'reform-through-labour'. They maintained that those who had been sentenced to reform-through-labour had gone 'to study'.

After my brother left, home became cold and gloomy, though winter had not yet arrived. The fire continued to burn brightly, but only my mother and sister-in-law sat there. My sister-in-law had recently given birth to a baby boy and was still recuperating after the birth. My wife sat below the platform staring at the fire, always in silence. From early in the morning, I spent the time alone on the third floor, where the heat from the fire below warmed my room, and I only went to sleep very late.

At two or three o'clock one morning, my sister-in-law began to wail in distress, "My son is dead! My son is dead!" My mother and wife rose quickly to investigate and before long, they too were groaning, sighing and wailing, in grief and sympathy. I listened to the proceedings downstairs with blankets over my head, for it was too terrible for me, and I couldn't bear to get up.

Half an hour after the initial alarm, I heard timber being sawn and planks being nailed together, to make a little coffin for the deceased child. My mother lamented, "Deng" (my brother's childhood name) "has gone away to study. We don't know when he might return. His son is dead! What shall we do?" Whereupon she wept uncontrollably, inflicting stabs of pain on my innermost being.

Then there was the sound of feet descending the steps of the house. Our old relative Xin De was carrying the coffin down, taking the baby for burial under cover of darkness. His footsteps were followed by further distraught wailing from my sister-in-law and laments of my mother and others.

The baby had been born just a day before my brother had left to 'study'. He had been delighted to have a male heir, oblivious to the possibility he himself might be unable to return. Two weeks later, on a day when everyone in the household had been anxious about my brother's welfare, his heir the baby had suddenly died, and my brother had no way of knowing about the tragedy.

After the PLA had occupied Taiyong, a fellow student from Rongjiang days was appointed the first new township leader. When I had been at Rongjiang Middle School, he had been studying at the state-run Teacher Training School, but although we had known about each other, we had never met. The Miao men Li Zhifu and Yang Shi, who had been murdered, were his relatives. After their deaths, he fled to Zhenyuan, which had already been liberated. There he registered to study at the military and government cadre school.

Citizens of the township welcomed the appointment of this new leader and I quickly went to ask for an audience. Though we had never met, a smiling young cadre in grey uniform came over to meet me as soon as I entered the square at the government building. He grasped my hand and said, "Chaoquan, you've come. I'm Yang Zaichuan."

Yang behaved as if he were an old friend and asked me to fill him in on events after I had returned from Guiyang. He said the local government already needed staff urgently and he would arrange for me to further my studies. I shouldn't delay. How did that seem to me?

To me, it seemed like a dream come true and he seemed like an angel from heaven. I couldn't in my wildest dreams have imagined that this new leader would be so amiable, enthusiastic and sincere. Our meeting filled me with admiration for him. Now at last, through him I felt some support and peace of mind.

The newly established township government cooperated with the PLA to locate and annihilate bandits. Some registered to study after careful interrogation, while others stood trial in public for serious crimes. During this period, communist personnel were coming and going from all around, and all kinds of bulletin boards appeared.

Chen Kaiming was arrested in Hunan and brought back to face trial in Jianhe county town, where he was executed by firing squad. His execution marked the beginning in Jianhe of wide-scale public trials and executions of former Nationalists.

Regional-level officials had authority to execute first and report back later; they were not obliged to obtain approval for executions. In the towns around, there was hardly a public square where trials were not convened. News of executions came thick and fast, from every corner of the county.

Yang Rui, one of the most despised leaders in Taiyong, was shot by firing squad beside the river, after being tried publicly on a market day. He spent the night before his execution composing a letter to his wife and only stopped writing as they came to lead him out to trial. With a pistol in his hand, Yang Zaichuan, the new township leader, whose two relatives had been murdered by Yang Rui, examined Yang's corpse, then looked to the sky with a smile on his face. Township residents broadcast the news with elation born of long-term resentment.

A few days later, Yang Huanwen, the worst tyrant in the whole of Taiyong, was executed in Jianhe county town. The Miao people who had suffered under him were said to have demanded that his family line should be completely obliterated. His two sons were also executed by firing squad, in front of his home. This news spread quickly and was generally welcomed. Revenge seemed sweet. After this initial flurry of executions, public trials and executions came in fits and starts over the next year.

The outsiders' task force stationed in Xiangye occasionally interviewed people by day, but most work was done by night. Every night, a meeting was convened at the primary school. 'Poor peasants' investigated the activities of 'rich people' in the village. A judgemental spirit was stirred up among the farmers, and awareness of social class was taught, in preparation for land reform.

Just at this time, an aggressive sore grew on my right leg, inflamed and painful, making it difficult for me to move at all. For several days, I lay in bed groaning with pain, as the sore grew ever bigger. Mother poked it with pins to try and release the pus, but most was deep inside and only a little was released.

Our fellow clansman and old tenant farmer, Xin De, heard of my plight and came to have a look. He also used traditional methods, applying chewed up *mali* leaves on the affected area, but the inflammation continued and the pain intensified. Xin De felt alarmed as he watched me suffer unbearably. He said if only we could release the pus, I would be healed, concluding in desperation that he would suck it out. He was ladling out water to rinse his mouth, when I demurred, but he reiterated it could not be healed as long as the pus remained and insisted on sucking it out. Just as he bent over to begin, I jerked around quickly in dismay, insisting, "No! You can't!"

Xin De was forced to change tack. He now said that from the leg's appearance, it was likely the pus would discharge itself within the next couple of days. He suggested I should put up with the pain for two more days, after which it should improve.

The task force cadres had not set eyes on me for many days, but only heard that I was sick. Eventually, one of them came to my bedroom to examine my leg and was shocked by the sight. He asked when I would be better and I replied once the pus was completely drained. He advised me to rest well and take time to treat my problem. When I was fully recovered, he would come back and see me.

In fact, the pus did finally drain within a couple of days as anticipated, and I did recover completely. One afternoon, I went to look up the task force and a cadre asked if I was interested in continuing my studies. I happily replied, "Yes. I'd like to. I've been waiting for such an opportunity for over a year." He wrote a letter of introduction and instructed me to deliver it in person to the township leader Yang Zaichuan.

Dawn

The next morning at daybreak, mother rose to light the fire, carefully stacking plenty of wood, intending to create a brighter and warmer atmosphere than usual to mark my farewell. The wood was probably a little damp, however, and the fire never did light properly.

My sister-in-law went to the garden for some vegetables. My wife could not face the sadness of saying goodbye and disappeared somewhere, with our baby on her back. Mother and I were alone, sitting quietly by the fire. Her mood was heavy, to the point where she was unable to speak. We sat there staring blankly at the red flames and the smoke struggling through the wet wood in the fire.

Uncle He suddenly strode in, breaking the silence, "So Red, you really are leaving." His words were the cue for mother to break down in sobs, as he sat down stretching both hands towards the fire.

"How can the hearts of Han people be so wicked?" she protested, between choked sobs. "We Dong people are finished. Who knows what will happen now?" She had premonitions of disaster, and felt helpless, yet still uncertain exactly how everything would evolve.

Uncle He just sighed. "So what are we to do?" he exclaimed. My heart sank under the weight of such pain and despair and I didn't know what to say. Everything happened so quickly that morning.

Her face covered in tears, mother changed tone unexpectedly, "Son, go now. Go far, far away – the further the better. And don't ever come back!" Her words cut to the heart. During the succeeding 60-plus years, I have never forgotten a word of that short speech. She was simply overwhelmed with grief, warning me not to return for she wanted to save her son from being destroyed along with the rest of the family. She felt sure that everything and everyone she knew was on the verge of destruction.

On that overcast winter's day, it felt like a layer of lead was pressing down from the sky over Xiangye. Someone carried my luggage on ahead and we three followed: mother, Uncle He and I. As we reached the edge of the village, an uncle from the Ou clan came running up to reason with me, "Everyone who's capable of negotiating with the Han people has left to study, and we don't know when they'll be able to return. Now you are going too. How are we going to manage?" His face too was stained with tears and he couldn't bring himself to say more. He seemed as pitiful and inconsolable as a young orphan suddenly left alone to fend for himself. I tried to comfort him by saying I'd be back soon.

The four of us stood motionless, not knowing what to do next. Tears were streaming down mother's face, but none of us said a word. After a few moments' silence, I plucked up courage and started to bid goodbye. Mother interjected, wailing loudly and pronouncing her farewell, "Go well, son! May Heaven bless you!" Her plaintive cries and sense of desolation filled me with anguish. How would she be able to survive?

I also started to weep, wiping the tears on my sleeve as I walked away, unable to turn around for another look. Mother had lost both my brother and me in the space of these two months and we were the last of her immediate family. She was convinced this was the last time she would ever see me.

Chapter 8
Learning and Loss
(Landlords, 1950-51)

Before I had gone 500 metres, my second uncle rushed up behind, his face flushed crimson from a mixture of rice wine and exertion. He seemed sullen and dismayed. "They've ordered me to go and study, and I've no idea when I'll be able to return home," he exclaimed with a groan.

Someone had accused him of having been a *bao* leader for a few days. The village task force had subsequently ordered him to go to the township to register for 'study'. Afraid they would drag him off to build the railroad and that he wouldn't be able to cope with such hard labour, he had hidden for a few days. Upon hearing I was going to Jianhe, he finally relinquished his rice wine and determined to accompany me as far as Taiyong.

As soon as Yang Zaichuan, the Taiyong leader, saw me, his face creased into a smile. He read my letter of introduction, which said something to the effect that I was the only young intellectual left among the minority nationalities in the region. Yang already knew me, of course. Now he would send me to the county 'training class for intellectuals', urging me to study well and return as soon as possible.

So saying, he sat down and wrote a new letter of introduction in his own hand, instructing me to deliver it personally to the training class at the county offices. He also wrote a note for my second uncle, instructing him to make his way to the 'study-group' and join my brother in 'turning over a new leaf'. Early the next morning, we arrived in Jianhe county town and my uncle was led away to join the 'study-group', while I was taken to the training class for intellectuals.

That winter in Jianhe, the days seemed overcast until sunset, when you could finally catch a glimpse of the sun. The buildings and businesses seemed the same as they always had been, except that many people, nearly all men, had appeared in the streets wearing dark yellow military uniforms. They were mostly young cadres from government departments, each armed with a pistol, but nevertheless restrained, rather like students. While physically robust, they appeared mentally stressed out.

The Jianhe 'bandits', including former government staff and others 'with problems', were assembled in the county town, where the PLA organised their studies. Practically all of them were punished; some executed, others sent to prison. My brother, who was among them, was sentenced to life imprisonment, though I only discovered this some years later.

The alternative 'study-group' consisted of intellectuals who had never associated with the Nationalist Party or with other 'bandits'. The great majority of these later served as cadres or teachers.

These two categories of 'student' had never existed before. People came to differentiate them with the names 'reform-through-labour group' and 'teacher-training group', respectively.

I had left the village with my second uncle, but we were separated into different classes for study. We didn't realise we'd never see each other again.

Many years later, my uncle's daughter informed me that her father had joined the same class as my brother. After completing his sentence, he returned to live at home for a few days, but life in the village was then so difficult and there was so little food, that he loaded a bag on his back and set off to return to his reform-through-labour team.

In the event, however, he probably couldn't face going back to the team with its associated torment, so he drifted around aimlessly in the mountains and fields near the city of Kaili. He probably froze or starved to death, but no one ever discovered where his body finally lay. It was just one more personal tragedy that people preferred not to talk about.

My class was organised by the County Jianhe Communist Party committee. Several dozen students had registered, from all over the county. Most were graduates from different classes of primary or junior middle school. I was the only one who had ever studied in senior middle school and I was also one of only a few minority people.

County leaders took turns to teach from the book *On New Democracy*, by Chairman Mao. They said we would study for a month and then work as primary school teachers or village cadres. We studied hard, spurred on by a sense of optimism. At the end of each lecture, our faces were covered in smiles. Unprecedented hope was on the horizon.

Towards the end of the first training week, a cadre announced one evening that I had been recommended by the county government to go and study in Guiyang, adding that they wanted only minority people, and 'the rest of us don't qualify'. There was a ripple of knowing laughter. After Liberation, it was a standing joke for some Han people to say, "The rest of us don't qualify." Still, everyone glanced admiringly in my direction: I was going to study in Guiyang.

It had been less than a week since I joined the training class, but that evening I left the group without further ado, to prepare for the journey ahead. Instead of eating with other students, I was invited to the county offices for a meal, along with a Miao trainee Wang. When we entered, two cadres in military uniform were already there, along with Yang Zaichuan. We were seated and the kitchen staff served food and wine. Rarely before had I dined so luxuriously, savouring such delicious meat dishes and washing them down with rice wine. Everyone concentrated on eating and drinking, with little energy to spare on conversation.

At the end of the meal, one of the cadres announced that this had been a farewell dinner for Wang and me. He said we should study hard and return after graduation, for there would be much work to do upon our return. After thanking our hosts, I went outside clasping hands with Yang Zaichuan, who was assuring me repeatedly that he would be looking forward to my return.

The Provincial Minority Cadre Class

The next day, we travelled to Guiyang by van, arriving in Youzha Street by night. We passed a factory door with an illuminated sign, on which was written 'Celebrating New Year's Day'. It dawned on me that this was 31st December 1950, and the next day would be the first of 1951.

Otherwise, the street was pitch-black, shops were closed, and there were no people or vehicles to be seen. Perhaps everyone was celebrating New Year at home. The van stopped at the great south gate, and we two students entered the military and government university campus. A cadre led us to our accommodation. Classes were to begin the next day.

At breakfast, we ate with the other students, about 100 in all, young minority intellectuals from different parts of Guizhou. A few were wearing cadre uniforms, but most wore cotton-padded traditional Chinese jackets issued as emergency relief. That afternoon a cadre gave me one of the jackets, and thereafter I was warm enough, though I was still wearing unlined trousers.

The food was nutritious and plentiful. A couple of years before, I had studied in Guiyang for 18 months, but this was my first time on such a good diet. In addition, I lived in a nice room, shared with about 10 others. Such living conditions were better than at home and what's more, we didn't need to pay for them. This made me feel well pleased, the first thing about this new society that seemed clearly better than the old.

The Communist Party emphasised the equality of ethnic groups. Minority people would no longer be subjected to oppression or discrimination. Actually, this was the first I had heard the phrase 'minority nationality'. Strange to say, I still did not know to which official minority I belonged! In the column for 'nationality' in the class register, I first filled in 'Yi nationality'. Later I noticed that a cadre identified me in another register as 'Zhongjia'.

When after the course I went to the Southwest Institute for Nationalities, a cadre asked me my nationality identity and I used the 'Zhong' that I had seen on the form in Guizhou, but not long afterwards, I changed it to 'Dong'. In those days, few people distinguished between the minorities by using distinct names, but instead simply said 'minority nationality' or 'fraternal nationality'.

The minority cadre class was led by the well-known sociologist Fei Xiaotong. He was responsible for the schedule and he himself lectured on nationality policies in *The Common Programme*. This was the formal programme of the Communist Party after 1949, which served as the interim national plan. In addition, our teachers included the sociologists Wu Zelin and Liang Oudi, and the linguist Wang Fushi.

Our teachers were young, sincere and energetic. They were equipped with cadres' clothing, including cotton caps with ear-warmers. They analysed nationality questions from the perspective of social class, examining who was responsible for nationality oppression, repeatedly emphasising that Nationalist reactionaries were most guilty. Imperialism, feudalism and bureaucrat-capitalism, the 'three big mountains', were caused by Han bureaucrats and landlords, not by ordinary Han people.

Our first lessons were supposed to help everyone remove the scales from their eyes, to distinguish between enemies and friends, with many real-life case studies. Communist and Nationalist Party members mainly consisted of Han people; one party was revolutionary, the other counter-revolutionary, and they had been fighting for several decades. Poverty-stricken Han people had been oppressed and exploited by Han landlords. For example, the nobility of the Qing dynasty had oppressed Han and minority citizens for several centuries. The teachers never discussed, however, how minority landlords had oppressed and exploited minority people.

The theory of class struggle seemed reasonable and clear, and in principle, everyone was willing to accept it. When, however, we split into small groups to discuss everything from the perspective of personal experience, there were some dissenting voices. A Miao student pointed out that Nationalist soldiers were nearly all poor Han people who had been forced to go and fight. Those who had come to quell the Miao uprising of 1942-3 (the Eastern Guizhou Incident) had been such Han people, from poor backgrounds. They killed many Miao and burned their homes, so the Miao people hated those soldiers, and not their commanding officers, since the officers were not the ones who killed and burned.

Many students recalled their experiences in the market towns. Poor Han people on the streets swore at them, calling them 'Miao' or 'barbarians', shamelessly offending and intimidating. Everyone had similar stories to share, generating intense debate and agitated argument. Some stood up to gesticulate, subduing others by their volume and intensity. The discussion forum developed into an altercation forum.

The teacher summarised in a closing address. Oppressive policies towards minority nationalities had been pursued for generations, and had been implemented by landlords and bureaucrats who propagated ideology discriminating against minorities. The Han people had wrongly accepted the errors this ideological poison had created, and minority nationalities must not blame, but should make allowances for them. The teacher guaranteed that now, post-Liberation, no one would be yelling 'Miao' or 'barbarian' any more. No one would push minority people around any longer, for we were all brothers and we would certainly achieve unity among ethnic groups.

Another theme was nationality policy: implementing nationality equality and nationality cooperation. Regional autonomy for minorities would be implemented. Students were strongly supportive, excited by this fine blueprint for a new society. It was a wonderful plan, the like of which they had never dreamed of. Most were delighted, growing steadfastly in faith in the great future prospects unfolding before their very eyes.

Someone remarked, however, to a Miao student, that the Ama Photo Studio in Guiyang had used a photo of Li Ying, a young Miao woman, in an advertisement. Crowds of people were admiring it in the glass display window. Miao students became upset and there was great commotion at mealtime, as they argued heatedly among themselves. 'This is a form of bullying of the Miao people!', 'It's discrimination against the Miao!' The more they talked, the more animated they became. No one dared to venture an alternative opinion, and even the cadres just sat to one side, listening cautiously.

The Miao students reasoned that the studio should withdraw the photograph immediately. There was a self-conscious fuss about the issue for a couple of days, but no one dared to go to the studio to raise the question. In the end, cadres contacted the studio and the photograph was withdrawn. Those Miao students had no personal knowledge of Li, but only knew she was a graduate of a vocational medical school. She just happened to be the only minority nationality 'beauty queen' at the time, inadvertently fanning into flame intense nationality feelings.

On the day we graduated from the provincial minority cadre school, I was informed I had been nominated among 30 students to study at the Southwest Institute for Nationalities in Chengdu, Sichuan Province. Most of the 30 had graduated from senior middle school. We had been selected by Mr Fei and the other teachers. When they announced our selection, we were all very pleased.

Wang Wenmin, who had come to Guiyang with me from Jianhe, had decided to go back to the county to work there. He was pleased to hear my news and repeatedly congratulated me, proposing we go to a small restaurant to 'crash out there'. We shared a goodbye meal and toasted each other with white liquor. After that, I never saw him again, but later heard that he had served as vice-chairman of a political conference in County Jianhe.

My goodbye dinner with Wang Wenmin reminded me of my three good village friends who had kept me company during the months before Liberation, and I briefly described their circumstances to him, explaining my concern for them. Wang asked if they understood Mandarin Chinese. I replied that their Chinese was not bad and that they were quite well acquainted with local affairs. Wang said that as long as their family background was 'good', he would help them become land-reform cadres.

All three of my friends did indeed serve as cadres. Two were from my village and clan, and were named Ou. In keeping with clan traditions of seniority, I addressed one of them as Uncle Hu and the other as Uncle Cai. Neither had studied before and both were slightly older than me, but my good word for them turned out to be a help in their future careers. Uncle Hu became leader of a village group until his death, while Uncle Cai became the village party secretary until he retired.

My third close friend during my year at home was a Dong person from another village whom I addressed as Uncle Di. Like Cai, he had been my family's tenant farmer. He was about seven or eight years my senior, had studied two years in primary school, and was proficient in Chinese, magnanimous and shrewd. With my help, he also progressed, becoming a cadre in County Jianhe. He was quickly promoted to deputy leader of the county, which office he held until retirement. On my visits home, I always tried to meet up with these three friends.

The 30 students nominated to study in Chengdu lodged at the Provincial Nationalities Commission Guest House. Cadres at the Commission informed us we would celebrate Chinese New Year there and early in the New Year, they would find a vehicle to take us to Chengdu.

The Guest House meals were excellent. Every day, we rested and read. There were no organised studies or discussions, though three teachers often came to visit us.

A Miao cadre named A Yi was staying at the Guest House. He had just graduated from the Nanjing Border Institute. He was tall, energetic and spirited, well known to all the students. One evening after drinking some liquor, he came to our dormitory to look up a Miao friend from his region. They spoke warmly, and earnestly, to each other in Miao. A Yi alternately sat and stood, animated and apparently agitated.

We non-Miao students couldn't understand what they were talking about. As they were talking, someone went to report them to the teachers and Mr Wu and two cadres came to urge A Yi to go home. Wu's voice was trembling and the two cadres also seemed tense. A Yi said he had just been having a chat with his friend and refused to go, but the two cadres dragged him away, as the blood drained from his face.

It seemed as though something untoward was afoot and everyone was edgy. Afterwards, I heard that it had all been a storm in a teacup. Since they had been speaking animatedly to each other in Miao, someone had suspected them of hatching some sinister plot, while in actual fact, they had really just been chatting!

Sometimes some of us went for a walk, to visit the library or simply to have a look around, for otherwise it was fairly boring. During winter and summer vacations in Guiyang, I had studied in the library every day, so I was familiar with the area. There was a hostel near the library exit and as always, there were two or three women at the hostel entrance. They had cigarettes in their mouths and wore traditional Chinese dress, hoping to attract customers.

The streets seemed unchanged from 1947-49, except that now many shops were closed in the evenings and there were fewer people strolling around. Prostitutes no longer lingered beneath the street lamps, but only showed up at hostel entrances. Just after Liberation, no one knew what lay in the future. Everyone was wondering, quietly sitting at home waiting for tomorrow to arrive.

Disintegration of My Family

In the autumn of 1950, after my brother Ou Chaoxi turned himself in to 'study', he came to recognise that he was 'guilty' and sincerely wanted to help the people. He expressed his intentions to cadres who were leading the study:

that he was willing to surrender his land, forest and property to the people. He only requested that the government return to him a small portion of the land, so that he could do some subsistence farming, like everyone else. The cadres commended him for his enlightenment and escorted him to the village to announce his decision.

That day a general meeting was convened in Xiangye. My brother first criticised himself publicly, before announcing he was handing over all his land, forest and other property to the people. His manner was sincere and people said he expressed himself well; though his audience remained silent. In the end, the chairperson just said, "We'll talk about all this later." Chaoxi was escorted back to the 'study-group' in Jianhe.

Land reform began soon afterwards. Anyone who had rented out land, even just one or two fields, was listed among the landlords. My family was clearly 'guilty'. In Big Village, there were around 100 households and more than 10 of them were designated landlord-households.

Shop owners in the towns, who had opportunistically seized land in lieu of loan-repayments, owned about 10% of cultivable land in Xiangye. It was common knowledge that one Han man from Langdong was the biggest landlord of all. Since his small shop was designated a 'business venture', however, he only had to surrender the land, while his other property remained untouched. The Dong 'landlords' of Xiangye felt this was unfair, muttering under their breath, "They're pinching our noses – cheating us."

Land reform in Xiangye followed the methods used in Han regions, though villagers claimed it was more aggressive in the village. My brother's public act of conciliation before land reform had officially started was apparently unprecedented and passed virtually unnoticed. His month-long role as deputy commander of a Nationalist battalion identified him as a bandit, and he was given a life sentence of reform-through-labour. He forfeited all his possessions, and the eight members of his household were guilty by association: our elderly mother, his two wives, his two daughters two years and one year old respectively, my wife and daughter and myself. My circumstances were different from the others, for I had earlier joined the Revolution.

One small area of arable land was allocated to our extended family. The five-roomed three-storey house in Zhanmo was forfeited and donated to the village for public use, along with the water buffalo for ploughing the fields and the horse that was now too old and weak to ride. Other Dong villagers did not have the heart to take over the two-roomed three-storey house in Xiangye that my parents had painstakingly built and maintained. Instead, it was occupied by a Han family who had migrated into the village.

At first, my mother and six other members of the family remained in their home. During the month before their eviction, cadres from outside Xiangye and Xiangye activists entered every now and then, seizing household items at will. In the end had commandeered practically everything, stripping the house bare of the dozens of paintings and items of calligraphy, and of books and souvenirs. Even table and stools were taken, along with pots for cooking rice and most of the dishes and plates, carefully selected. A cadre also requisitioned the double bed in one of the bedrooms.

On the morning of the eviction, breakfast consisted of rice and a shared bowl of stewed vegetables, with some hot pepper sauce. Mother, her three daughters-in-law and three granddaughters, were sitting around the fire eating, when they heard the sound of footsteps on the stairs outside. Mr Xu from the Xiangye Farmers' Association was shouting, "Auntie, Auntie…" as he led several men onto the veranda. Mother hurried out with the others and stood there disconsolately.

"This house is no longer yours. The people have decided to give it to Mr Peng" (who had recently come into our area from outside) "and it now belongs to him. You must move out and live with your brother-in-law's family. There is a room set apart for you there. This house is no longer yours and you need to move today. Get out as fast as you can!"

Mother was stunned and just kept repeating in a faint voice, "How can this be?" It all seemed like a bolt from the blue. My sisters-in-law and wife stood motionless beside my mother, dumbstruck and terrified.

Our neighbour Uncle Fu and his family assembled and others also came to see what was going on, mostly relatives, people who had frequently been beneficiaries of my family's hospitality. Just then, however, it seemed as if they were total strangers. They just said, "Ah! So that's how it is! Oh! So that's what's going to happen!" Afterwards, they followed Mr Xu out of the house and dispersed.

As mother watched them leave, she broke into wails of dismay while the three younger women, along with their children, joined in, crying to heaven for help. These wretched appeals for help, where none was to be found, attracted the neighbours' attention. They stood at their railings and abjectly stared towards the commotion, just as they had often stood before, to observe the excitement when our family entertained guests.

When my mother and relatives left the house, still weeping, people watched as bedding, clothes, straw mats, two cooking pots, a tripod and two small stools went with them. Other furniture and possessions had already been looted. This was effectively the final day of my family's existence, the day it was conclusively destroyed.

Mother led the evicted family to the house of my second uncle, a legacy from my paternal grandparents, already old at the time of inheritance. There were four rooms, two on either side of the living room. Some parts of the veranda were already rotten. My uncle's family consisted of six people: my uncle, his wife, and four children aged between two and sixteen.

My uncle himself had left to join a 'study-group', after which he too had been designated a landlord and held back for hard labour, so my aunt was left alone to raise the four children, with no one to help work the fields. The grief of losing her husband was added to the stress of her responsibility and she became depressed and reluctant to talk, spending her days trying to hold back tears. When she encountered friends or relatives, she would just shake her head in despair.

After mother and company moved in – excluding my wife, who returned to live with her own mother – there were eleven people sharing those four old rooms. Mother and her entourage were allocated one normal room and one small box room, where by night they squeezed together on the floors to sleep. The 'two families' shared one iron tripod, with one family cooking first, then the other.

You only needed to stretch your legs in the narrow, old house for it to echo with creaks and groans. It was never so bad they felt it was about to collapse, it just felt full to the brim. These incomplete and inconsolable families of women and children had no food and no firewood. In the evenings, they had to attend public meetings where they were denounced, and by day, they were expected to farm the land, to pay grain tax.

Years later, relatives recalled for me the campaign for 'fighting the landlords', part of land reform in Xiangye, weeping as they did so. Before 'the fruit of victory' was divided, meetings were convened by cadres most evenings to 'fight the landlords', either at the school or in the home of the old *bao* leader. Pine lights would be burning and poor farmers, lower-middle-ranking farmers and activists would sit smoking homemade leaf-cigarettes.

Cadres called in the landlords, most of whom were old women whose husbands had been called away to 'study'. They were ordered to surrender any silver money that had been buried for safekeeping or any hidden property. Often they would reply that they couldn't even afford salt, so how could they have any money stashed away? The cotton cloth they had woven for clothes and their good quilts had already been seized and now they had nothing valuable left at all.

Among those who attended the meetings were activists who had formerly fled from the village, but recently moved back. They didn't feel family affection for the other villagers and they were fiercest in doling out punishment. Old Bao, who usually presided over the denunciation meetings, was one of these returnees. He often invited strangers who had just arrived in Small Village to accuse the denounced, in order to bolster his own position.

On hearing a woman pleading, "I don't have anything," Old Bao would pull out a rope and tie her arms behind her back. After slinging the other end of the rope over the beams, he would pull on that with all his might, raising the woman off the floor. She would be bawling and yelling, *unable* to confess to any hoarded treasure, while neighbours urged her through the smoke in their mouths to confess.

Leaf-smoking spectators issued words of warning and accusation, cursing terribly, but they were never involved in hanging anyone up. Their reluctance to do so was reflection of the last shreds of human kindness harboured in their hearts.

When a woman seemed about to breathe her last, Old Bao would release her, and she would fall into a paralyzed heap on the ground. After recovering a little, she might be hung up again, in another vain attempt to force her to surrender imaginary hidden possessions. The cadres called this process 'salvaging the hanging property'.

My mother was hung up like this several times, tortured until she almost died, but she had nothing to surrender. When she'd recovered her breath, she'd say frankly, "In the past this village was one big family. How have the hearts of people become so wicked in the space of just a few months? You are just too cruel! The people of Xiangye never really earned any money. Where did the money come from, that we are now being tortured for?"

Old Bao, who was mainly responsible for this hanging torture, would reply, "If you don't hand it over, I will wring water out of dry wood!" He hung people up over a period of several months, some of whom died, while others were horribly injured. From the water he wrung out of dry wood, there was not even as much as twenty *yuan*, along with some cloth and clothing.

All the 'landlords' in the village were hung up, more than 10 people. Once as Old Bao savagely pulled on the rope and hoisted a middle-aged woman into the air, the belt of her pleated skirt broke and the skirt fell to the ground, exposing her nakedness. One of the smoking spectators jumped up and snuffed out all the pine lights, creating pitch darkness, while Old Bao dropped her to the floor and she put on her skirt again. Some in the audience laughed and some swore, but the woman simply wailed, "Have mercy on us! Have mercy on us!"

The arms of all who suffered this hanging torture, male or female, were either broken or severely crippled. Victims were carried home, where they would lie on their beds complaining of unbearable pain. Sometimes their family members scattered to the winds in a frightened bid for survival, leaving the victims with no one to take care of them. Some died, whereupon those complicit in the hanging torture said they had 'fallen ill and died'.

An uncle of mine, tall, strong and robust, died after being hung up on a tree outside the school one night. Like several other women, a strong Miao woman who had married a 'landlord' from the village, also died after being hung up.

My mother and the wife of my father's younger brother fortuitously survived. Afterwards, their arms could no longer chop wood or carry any heavy weight. Mother often said, "Ever since the time heaven and earth were split apart, Dong people have never made other Dong people suffer like this. Such cruelty! This kind of life is worse than death!"

Some Dong villagers, under instructions from cadres but in violation of their own cultural norms, helped themselves to the property of 'landlords'. They led away water buffaloes, carried off rice and other food, moved into the landlords' homes and attended 'hanging meetings'. Such activities lasted about a year.

What followed were nightly rallies, to which all villagers were invited, continuing the 'fight against the landlords'. Landlords were no longer hung up, but forced to stand and submit to denunciation. This was not as horrifying as before, but mother still had no male to support her. There was no one to work the fields, chop firewood or transport the grain tax to the Han offices.

Now everything had to be done by my mother and my first sister-in-law (my brother's main wife). Mother said it was the first time in history that Dong women had gone out to do the work of men, but what choice was there? How could they survive otherwise? They struggled to survive, a day at a time.

My mother and sister-in-law broke with tradition by going to the mountains to chop and collect firewood. They also had to farm, but our buffalo had been commandeered and my brother's old horse had to serve as a substitute. Horses were for riding, not for ploughing the fields, but at that time, everything changed. After mother's eviction, there was no stable for the horse. Instead, it was tied up at night below my second uncle's home, where it could stand up or lie down as it pleased. By day, it grazed in the mountains, with no other food supply, and it gradually lost weight and even hair.

At the spring ploughing, my cousin Bei came to help, attracting a following of laughing children as he led the old horse to the fields. There the children gazed at the astonishing sight of a horse ploughing the fields, unseen in the previous 1,000 years. Soon afterwards, however, Bei was summoned to join a 'study-group', and for him this was also followed by reform-through-labour.

The following spring, my sister-in-law had to lead the horse to the fields herself. A woman driving a horse to plough was an even stranger sight, and the children were yet more amused, but adults called them back.

After harvest, my sister-in-law drove the old horse to carry rice to Nanshao and pay the grain tax. On the way home, she chopped and collected as much firewood as she could bundle on the horse's back, but there was no grain to spare for the horse to eat. Instead, when they rested, she released the horse to graze on any grass it could find. It had become emaciated, tears were suspended from its eyes, and it had long since stopped neighing.

On the night the horse returned from Nanshao after delivering the grain tax, it quietly lay down underneath the house and never got up again. It died with both eyes open, looking outwards, as if yearning for its mistress. The old horse had silently worked for the survival of my mother and sister-in-law, and its death, depleted of physical strength, added to their grief.

The women in the household had been suffering unbearable strain from the events swirling around them, and constantly warned, "We can't keep going." They were like birds sitting on a wall, flying away one by one as catastrophe loomed.

On the day they were driven out of mother's home, my wife Mei Yuan had said to mother that, since there was not much living space in the new place, she would go back to her parental home and live with her mother, awaiting my return. Thereupon, she handed our infant daughter to my mother, since the child 'belonged to' my family and Mei Yuan feared she'd not be able to care adequately for her.

Mei Yuan's own father had already been taken to 'study', for he had been a village leader and a 'landlord'. She left quietly, carrying a skirt in her left hand and a bundle of clothing in her right, just as she had arrived when she first came to share a bed with me. Her mother's home was also in Xiangye, so our daughter sometimes went to stay with her in the months that followed.

Mei Yuan and her mother had nothing left, not even the wherewithal to light a fire or cook a meal. They squeezed up together in the room they had been allocated. At that time, I was studying in Chengdu. Before long, in order to survive, my wife married a Dong farmer in Zhanmo, having informed my mother she could no longer wait for me. Eventually, news came that she had given birth to more children, but then committed suicide by jumping into a river. Her circumstances must have been overwhelming, and her demise was tragic.

My brother's second wife lived with my mother for a while, but it was overcrowded and could not be sustained. For the sake of survival she also left, with her two-year-old daughter, and married a farmer from Langdong.

My brother's wife, Lan, kept my mother company for nearly two years in those miserable early days. Lan was the one who harnessed the old horse to plough the fields, paid the grain tax, and chopped firewood, doing the heavy work of a man for my mother. A few days after the horse died, Lan's eldest brother was arrested and executed by firing squad, because he had served as party secretary in the Nationalist county government. Lan then took her daughter and left, marrying an old Han man in Langdong and moving with him to County Sansui.

In the end, only my weak old mother remained, along with her two-year-old granddaughter, my daughter. In sorrowful and inconsolable delusion, she yearned for her sons to return, even as she was being denounced at the evening meetings.

In the space of just two years, the large household of nine people thus disintegrated. Most of my clan, though formerly close, had now fallen out with my mother. Those who had not participated in mother's hanging and beating had nevertheless attended some of the meetings and now were like strangers to her. It was as if she had been whisked over into a barbaric foreign land, where you had to beg for survival, though there was no help on hand. After many sufferings, other family members disappeared.

Only the deep immutable affection of the age-old hills and the murmuring stream remained constant. As the grass waved in the breeze, however, and the water burbled its way eastwards, it seemed as if even they were saying goodbye to my family.

Chapter 9
Promoting Nationality Unity
(Chengdu, 1951-52)

In 1951, just after Chinese New Year, an open-backed van pulled up on Science Street, Guiyang, and 30-plus people were ushered on board. Some crouched, others sat on their luggage, while still others stood, holding firmly to rails of the van. There were no seats, so everyone just squeezed up together.

Thus, a crowd of cheerful and optimistic youth left Guiyang in the direction of Chongqing. On mountain roads several kilometres from County Qijiang, our slow-moving van was involved in a collision with a fast-moving military truck coming in the opposite direction. There was a violent jolt, followed by frantic screams, as passengers flipped on top of each other. The van screeched to a halt, the driver with blood streaming from his forehead. The van owner and truck driver descended to assess the damage. Each blamed the other. The front of the van was badly damaged, but the truck seemed unscathed.

The van owner suggested we make the rest of the journey to Qijiang by foot. He was in no mood to worry about us and we were thus abandoned halfway. No one bothered to reason with him, but we simply grumbled our way along the road towards Qijiang.

With the cold weather, each student had been issued with a set of cotton-padded clothes. Qijiang inhabitants seemed bewildered by this troop of 'uniformed' young people – peasants who were not real peasants, refugees who were not real refugees – arriving as from nowhere.

A campaign was underway for 'Purging Bandits and Opposing Tyrants'. People's militia were standing guard at every corner primed to interrogate passers-by. It was common to see people tied up and walking at gunpoint through the streets, so the atmosphere was tense. As we arrived, militiamen, guns slung on their shoulders, rushed up, surrounded, and interrogated us. After checking our letters of introduction, they led us to a small village beside the river, recommending we board a boat from there to Chongqing.

The Yi students, however, wanted to drive, while the Miao students preferred to go by boat. There was a loud argument, as militia stood to one side, guns at the ready. Both sides were serious and there was no easy way to settle their differences.

In view of the impasse, I suggested we decide via a democratic show of hands, whereupon there was a hush. The majority then expressed their preference to go by boat. Early the next morning, we boarded a wooden boat, squeezing up and crouching down, as if we were pigs or ducks. We arrived in Chongqing as night fell.

We were treated grandly for a week at the Southwest Nationality Affairs Guesthouse, as if we were a minority leaders' tour group. We visited factories by day, and read, or were entertained by various performances, by night.

One sunny morning, we boarded a comfortable coach and the next day arrived in Chengdu, at a mansion compound on Xinyusha Street. A cadre there announced, "This is the Southwest Institute for Nationalities."

Students at the Liu Estate

Chengdu lies in the biggest plain of the southwest region of China, with fertile land growing rich produce, earning the nickname 'land of plenty'. The city was built at the centre of the plain, said to be in a basin, but actually you can hardly see the edges. Its civilisation and accomplishments are described dramatically in the classic novel *Romance of the Three Kingdoms*.

Traditional civilisation in Chengdu remained relatively intact right up until the first half of the 20th century, when, before Liberation, many senior officials of Sichuan Province took concubines and built mansions there, living as if in imperial palaces. Concrete western-style mansions seemed to decorate every street, most with slanted roofs, but otherwise varying in shape and size.

From 1939 to 1950, Liu Wenhui was Governor of Xikang Province, in what is now western Sichuan. He had gained power as a local warlord. His mansion area in Chengdu was in the city centre, occupying ground surrounded by four streets, roughly square in shape, and one square kilometre in area. Its address was Xinyusha Street. At the time, this street was synonymous with the Liu Estate.

Within the estate, there were three large three-storey buildings, one one-storey building and one other building. All were 'foreign buildings', with rooms like classrooms, though these were partitioned, some serving as dormitories for officers, or bedrooms for guests.

Packed together along the perimeters of the four streets were many single-storey wooden houses, with iron-railed windows, like walls of the estate, keeping out the ordinary people. Each room in each of the houses served as a dormitory for around 10 people.

In the land behind, there were more wooden bungalows, homes for soldiers who guarded the mansions, with room for more than 1,000 people. Within the mansion complex, there was also a sports field, a fishpond, a rock garden, ancient trees and wells that for years had provided good drinking water. Even with 1,000 residents, it would have felt spacious and comfortable.

In the winter of 1949, Chengdu and Xikang were peacefully liberated, and Liu Wenhui became a high-ranking Party officer. He moved to Beijing to lead the Department of Agriculture and Forestry, whereupon his mansion compound in Chengdu was turned over to the general public. The People's Government designated it as the site for the newly established Southwest Institute for Nationalities.

We Guizhou students were the first to arrive at the Institute, sometime around February 1951. None of the staff had yet arrived, but three cadres took responsibility for arranging our food and accommodation. Sometimes they led us in cleaning the premises and flattening the sports field, as we waited for studies to begin.

In this new environment, with soldiers of the predominantly Han PLA standing guard at the entrance, some minority students felt trepidation. Metal bars in the windows of our bedrooms also generated a sense of foreboding. 'A perfect example of prison confines', quipped some students. Students whose families had been designated landlords or who had previously been affiliated with the Nationalist Party had a weight on their minds, fearing they might be bundled away to study-groups, hard labour, or even execution.

During those early days at the Institute, an ulcer developed on my back just above the waist, perhaps related to climate and humidity, and I became feverish. I was bedridden for days, with horrible pain, and was unable to share in the physical labour. Students from other dormitories were not notified of my illness, and after a few days, there was some conjecture I had been arrested. Later, when one of the students met me, he asked in astonishment, "When did you get back?" On learning of my convalescence, he corrected himself saying, "I was only pulling your leg."

The ulcer tormented me for 10 days or more, until Su, a female classmate from Chengdu, who had been coming to check up on me, was appointed to take me to The People's Hospital for an operation. The hard source of pus was cut out, about a fingertip-length in size. Su helped as I left the hospital, arranging for me to ride in the back of a three-wheeled pedal-taxi. She walked behind, until we arrived at the Institute together. Within three days, I had recovered completely.

Each new student arrived at the Institute with some measure of apprehension and after a while, we organised a group with waist drums to welcome students from the three other provinces. Cadres also arrived to serve as staff, demonstrating meticulous care and attention to students' well-being, so that classmates' misgivings gradually subsided.

By the beginning of March, the full quota of cadres and teachers had arrived. Students from each of four provinces had been sent to the new Institute, and apart from 10 Han students who had transferred from Yunnan University, all were minority students.

Communist Party policy emphasised the unity of nationalities, aiming to sweep away any impediments to liberating minority regions and to launch the new regime in those regions. Cadres resolutely implemented this policy, striving to unite wherever and whenever possible.

Students at the Institute included both children of landowners and those of hereditary leaders; a system of hereditary leadership had been prevalent between 1271 and 1911. A student in my small study-group was one such hereditary leader, from the Dai nationality of Yunnan, and there was a female Dai hereditary leader in another study-group. Many Yi students were Black Yi, the Yi nobility, and several Tibetan students were children of landlords.

The overwhelming majority of students, however, were children of farmers, albeit from different social classes within the farming community. Students would walk around beaming, in good spirits, as long as they were among their own minority peers. When, however, other nationality – especially Han – students mingled with them, they would become solemn and restrained. Educational levels were unevenly distributed and ideology was each to his own, with people from different provinces having their own peculiar provincial ways of viewing the world. Thus, there was great diversity.

In the two years after Liberation, higher education was reorganised. Some institutes were merged and some closed down, while many new institutes were established. The ideal length of study, and even the content of study, was still in doubt. New specialisations were set up; new systems for both enrolling and teaching students. Everything was in flux, under construction, and indeed each institute's situation was unique, without any recognised national standards.

At the time, many specialist subjects were not well endowed with teachers or were simply unavailable. In the southwest, there were no teachers of Russian language, for example, and no other foreign languages were taught. Politics, current affairs and Marxism-Leninism were core subjects, and these were linked with remoulding ideology in the campaign to resist the US and help North Korea, and in the whole land-reform movement.

The Southwest Institute showcased such trends, giving special emphasis to nationality issues. There were over 500 students, divided into four classes according to Mandarin ability and region of origin. The first and second classes were composed mostly of students from Sichuan, including Tibetan and Yi students. They focussed on improving competence in Mandarin and studying nationality theory and policy. The third and fourth classes consisted mostly of students from Yunnan and Guizhou; a few had been to university, but most had studied only at senior middle school, and some only at junior middle school. In addition to nationality theory and policy, we also studied Marxism-Leninism and current affairs. The intention was to reformulate our ideology.

Encouraging Nationality Unity

The Institute aimed to reinforce cooperation between nationalities. Even the appearance of disunity was not permitted. At that time, I was in the 'accelerated class', which focused on finishing quickly; not taking any summer or winter vacations, and resting only on Sundays. We who had arrived first actually studied for a full 15 months; those who entered last studied for only 12 months.

Everything was intense for us. The fourth-class director appointed a Han student named Wang, who had come from a physical education college, to serve as my study-group leader. I was in the seventh study-group of the class.

Wang was responsible for the studies, ideology and activities of everyone in the small group. He was always smiling, always fishing for a response from others, always proactive, the self-appointed proponent of all kinds of activities at the Institute and in the class. His energetic personality, and predisposition to be involved in everything, was different from most others in the group; and he was not too popular.

After two or three months, Wang was transferred to start up a physical education group; then Fang, another Han student, took over. Fang's temperament was much the same as Wang's; he, too, would smile politely and never lose his temper.

After Fang, a Tibetan named Wu, from Lijiang in Yunnan, was appointed group leader. Wu was a member of the Communist Party and had formerly engaged in guerrilla warfare for a few days, but his educational background was quite weak. He had serious difficulty reading or keeping written records, he often lost his temper, and his manner was abrupt. Others were reluctant even to converse with him, never mind submit to his leadership, so small group discussions were punctuated by pregnant pauses and awkward silences. He made us take turns to speak and when someone had nothing to say, he exerted pressure. He started to use verbal abuse, referring to 'ideological problems', thus increasing the misgivings of others. After a month or so, the Institute sent him to Beijing for further studies.

We were still 10 in the group and the class director allowed us to elect a new leader. I was elected, with another Dong student as assistant leader. Thereafter, studies, ideology and other activities finally felt well balanced and there was no longer much occasion for anyone to be in a bad mood.

Among the 10 students in my group, two were female – one Hui and the other Han. The group included students from seven nationalities of Yunnan, Guizhou and Sichuan: Dong, Bouyei, Miao, Yi, Dai, Hui and Han. The person in the bunk above me was a Dong person named Lai, from Rongjiang. Although we didn't use Dong to communicate, we were on good terms. After graduation, Lai was assigned to work at a trading company in Guiyang, promoting minority trade. When back in Guiyang, I often visited him and we reminisced.

Our two Han colleagues, one male and one female, were both from Sichuan. The male student Sui left a deep impression on me. He had earlier responded to a Nationalist appeal for '100,000 youths to join the army', but just as he joined, victory was proclaimed over Japan. He was returned to his hometown, where he taught in a primary school. He was one of the oldest in our group, content to sit with us during the small-group discussions, rarely speaking. Otherwise, he would always seem to have a book in hand, and kept himself to himself, as though he were a guest in a hotel. Only late in the evenings did he reappear, from who knows where, to go to bed.

Sleeping below Sui was a young Dai hereditary leader named Dao, about 20 years old, able to use the Dai script for correspondence and also fluent in Mandarin. His bearing was refined, and he spoke slowly and deliberately, like an archetypal intellectual. All the Dai students respected him and would often seek him out for conversation in Dai. Nothing in his behaviour towards them indicated any sense of superiority.

Dao's nationality sentiments, however, were exceptionally strong. Whether in public or private, he would always extol the Dai people, along with their language and literature, their clothing and personal adornments, their social customs and the geography of their region. To make matters worse, he never acknowledged the merits of other nationalities.

At dramatic performances of Tibetan or Uighur singing and dancing, or of musical comedy, there would be unanimous applause and acclaim…except from Dao, sitting beside me, who would remark, "Our elephants can dance better than that." Nothing compared favourably with the Dai, and Dao seemed indifferent to anything non-Dai.

A Bouyei student named Liao was disgusted with all this, and confronted Dao indignantly: "Is the noxious vapour in your region also good?" Dao replied that in actual fact that vapour was just a myth, created by the reflection of sunlight in pools of water! Reports of noxious vapour had been fabricated during the period of Greater Han nationalism, just slanderous propaganda against the Dai. So, he went on and on. After that, Dao and Liao barely spoke to each other. This did not reflect too well on nationality unity.

Our study-group also included the young Hui student Su, who had accompanied me to hospital for my operation. She was from a poor family in Chengdu and had worked for almost a year in a cotton mill before joining the Institute. By disposition, she was cheerful and optimistic, happy to converse with anyone. She seemed to attend every conceivable Institute activity and almost everyone at the Institute knew her by name.

Su had never been to school, but had attended evening classes while working at the cotton mill, so her educational background was weak, but she was always anxious to improve. Every morning at self-study, I helped her with Mandarin, teaching a few new characters and often explaining a text. All day long, Su would carry a textbook and notebook under her arm, studying in free moments. She worked very hard and within a year was able to read announcements in public and to take simple lecture notes.

During this whole process, Su and I were often to be found in each other's company and developed deep mutual affection. Su described with great enthusiasm the Communist Party Youth League, and urged me to join, for that would be a sign of maturity. Just as you simply *had* to travel as a youth, so you simply *had* to join the Party, to support the Revolution. She even ventured that if you didn't apply to join, this was tantamount to saying your family was from the exploiting classes or was somehow counter-revolutionary. No matter how well you argued otherwise, the Party would not believe you.

Su's encouragement reflected what we were being taught. Since she felt attracted to me, she repeated it all in private and in detail many times, earnestly urging me to join. After my family had been listed among the 'landowning classes', I had been identified as the family's odd-one-out. Naturally, I was unwilling to miss out on any opportunity to progress and I was even less willing to have others accuse me of being reactionary, stubbornly retaining membership of a landlord's family. As far as students in the Institute were concerned, not identifying with the Revolution was tantamount to being one step from the grave. Everyone knew this warped kind of reasoning was going on, but pretended it was none of their business, and looked the other way.

Winter arrived and Su noticed my clothes were thin and worn. I had no sweater and she suggested I buy some wool for her to knit one, but I had no money for this, so instead she tore off the sleeves from her own sweater. She then used the wool from the sleeves to knit me a pair of gloves and a false collar, like a scarf. Throughout the winter, I covered my neck with that makeshift scarf and it proved quite effective against the cold. Su was concerned for me in various ways, but her knitting moved me most.

I had never really experienced before what romantic love felt like. When I went to the Han areas for junior and senior middle school, some of my female classmates had dressed enticingly and spoken smooth, salacious words. At such times, I felt strongly attracted, but in my heart there was estrangement, caused by my covert minority identity.

Su was so generous in her affection that the huge impact on my spirit was unsurprising. In a kind of daze of first love, I was powerless to resist her advice. So under the circumstances, more pointedly under pressure from my girlfriend, I agreed to apply to join the Youth League. Su jumped for joy, saying she would give me an introduction to the Party, and within 10 days, my study-group and the local Party branch had processed and approved my application. Thus in July 1951, I became a member of the New Democracy Youth League.

Thereafter, Su also introduced two other members of our study-group to join the League, so in the end, our group included four League members.

As group leader, I only supervised the study side of our work, ignoring ideology and activities. I had a lot on my mind, speaking little and smiling less, feeling progressively less optimistic. On Saturdays, I participated half-heartedly in the League sessions, rarely divulging what I was really thinking, lacking conviction in whatever I said. I was one of the most backward League members, seeming to be head and shoulders beneath everyone else.

On the other hand, I spoke up enthusiastically during our study-group discussions, though there I didn't argue or criticise and the atmosphere was serene. In the study-group, each of us had his or her personal ideas, wrapped up in our own histories. We had different anxieties, though we shared an inability to control our prospects or destinies. Among us, there was no discrimination or bullying, strife or verbal abuse, and our shared study was amicable.

Most of us were concentrating on how we should adapt to the new society. As workers and peasants, we sincerely wanted to improve our education and knowledge, and with this in mind, we paid close attention to every aspect of our studies, transforming our own thinking in the process. No one, apart from our Dai nationality classmate Dao, dared to emphasise their own nationality traditions, but instead abandoned them. We made every effort to fit in with the new society, striving to make a decent future for ourselves.

At the time, the country was implementing a policy of special care for minority nationalities, so students attended the Nationalities' Institutes at public expense, with food and accommodation free of charge. In winter, free cotton clothing was distributed. In summer, our uniform included shirt, underpants and a pair of shorts. Students were given pocket money each month, and after buying toiletries, there was enough left over for cigarettes and for weekend tickets to the cinema.

On Saturday evenings, the pubs on Xinyusha Street were full, and the clientele included many Yi students. Inside, students would drink like heroes and later emerge pushing and pulling, howling and swaying their way home, some leaning on the arms of two companions. On observing the spectacle of drunken students with distinctive black Yi cloaks draped around their shoulders, women and children on the street would stop and circle around for a closer look. The students resented this and swore in Yi at those curious spectators.

We ate three good meals a day, beginning with rice porridge or steamed rolls, with pickled vegetables. For lunch and dinner, each table of eight shared four fried dishes and a soup, including fish and meat, vegetables and tofu. At Sunday lunch, we had bigger portions of fish and meat. At first, our main staple was wheat-based, with a basin of steamed rolls on each table, but students from Yunnan and Guizhou were not used to this and later rice was provided instead.

On the food front, life at the Institute was luxurious. When I recalled my time as a student before Liberation, eating only one meal a day – the sad fare of brown rice and chard at that – it felt like Institute life was simply a pleasure, full of unprecedented luxury. Other students probably felt likewise, for minority regions had been generally impoverished.

Politics classes were taught as a means of passing on pertinent information. Special prominence was given to nationality policies of the 'Common Programme', adopted by the Communist Party after 1949, emphasising the equality and unity of nationalities in China. Lecturers never tired of examining pre-Liberation examples of discrimination against, oppression of, and even massacre of minority people.

After lectures, we split into small discussion groups, during which minority students would be eager to contribute examples from their home areas and personal experiences. There were some who, after giving vent to their anger, actually sobbed and wept, as though relieved that grievances of the poor peasants were finally receiving a hearing.

The intention was clear: articulating earlier mistreatment of minority people would hopefully arouse enmity against the former Nationalist regime. We were repeatedly taught that practitioners of Greater Han nationalism were the perpetrators of nationality oppression. These were identified as landowners, compradors (native agents of foreign businesses) and capitalist officials of the Nationalist Party.

Han workers had been oppressed just the same as minority people; they were not practitioners of Greater Han nationalism. We were urged to differentiate clearly between workers and Nationalists. National unity had to be built upon the foundation of equality and our teachers emphasised this equality. Marxism-Leninism resolved nationality problems with this equality policy and the Chinese

Communist Party espoused the same policy. It would never change until nationalities had naturally died out, meaning until they had integrated.

All cadres had to implement this policy. Minority cadres would also be required to supervise its implementation, and should report any problems at any time to higher authorities.

On hearing all this, everyone was delighted. Like the rest, I was convinced the Communist Party meant what it said and there would be no reneging on such intentions.

Wang Weizhou, the Institute President, had studied in the Soviet Union as a youth and later joined the Red Army. He was a member of the Chinese Communist Party Central Committee and his speeches often drew from privileged insights. In public speaking, he was specific and focused, addressing problems directly, always without a script.

Wang told us that on the Long March, the Red Army had advanced through the meadows of northwest Sichuan, eating grass and leather belts when there was no more food. Local Tibetans had fled on the advice of the Army's enemies and couldn't be found to receive payment for requisitioned food. The Army only passed through that dangerous region to avoid starvation, only apologetically seizing grain and meat from empty homes.

Wang said that local residents who had remained had provided great assistance to the Red Army. Now, after Liberation, we should treat them with humility, atoning for past wrongs and guaranteeing nationality equality. We should help them purge themselves of bandits and develop production to improve their livelihoods. They had formerly experienced extreme deprivation, and now it was the responsibility of the Party to help them emancipate themselves.

Every time he lectured, Wang criticised certain cadres, one of whom was our class Director Xi, a Yi man from Guizhou. Xi had formerly been an underground Party member, and was a university graduate, poised and smart. He was admired by many Institute students and staff, and even by most public figures in society at large. He was a super-popular young cadre, because he was an intellectual and related well to students with good educational backgrounds, especially those from Yunnan.

On the other hand, Xi had less contact with students from worker or peasant backgrounds, or even with Yi students. It seemed as if he had separated himself from the masses. Such students harboured a growing grudge against this otherwise popular cadre, resenting his perceived distance.

A Yi student in our study-group remarked, "Director Xi is obstructing the sunshine of Chairman Mao's Communist Party, so we are unable to enjoy the warmth of the sun." This remark was reported to the Institute's President Wang.

Wang immediately investigated, demanding indignantly, "Does this kind of Party member really exist?" Thereafter, in President Wang's speeches, he often repeated the remark about blotting out the sunshine of the Party, thus indirectly criticising our class director in public.

This was obviously humiliating to Director Xi, and in his subsequent encounters with students, he often seemed embarrassed. Intending to deflect ridicule, he announced to a meeting of small-group leaders, "I feel it's glorious indeed to be able to receive this kind of criticism from a Central Committee member." Hearing this and seeing his wry smile, everyone burst into laughter.

President Wang was always anxious for the welfare of students, often inspecting the dining hall and the dormitories. He would try to fix any problems, or correct any mistakes, immediately. He emphasised nationality unity, but at the same time valued nationalities' distinct social customs.

Once there was a dispute between Yi and Tibetan students. President Wang was informed and the next day he called both sides together for a meeting.

To restore unity, a banquet was arranged. According to Yi and Tibetan custom, those involved in the dispute would toast one another and reconcile, while other Yi and Tibetan students drank the same toasts. In the event, the protagonists made short speeches saying that in future there would be no more disputes, then they drank. Everyone joined in the toast.

Before Liberation, Han people used many derogatory names for minority people. The Common Programme taught that such names were the product of the era of nationality oppression, and no one was permitted to use them any longer.

The old terms 'barbarian' or 'Miao' were still overheard, however, when students ventured onto the streets of Chengdu wearing nationality costume. President Wang summoned Sichuan leaders to a special meeting to discuss this, and afterwards all cadres were strictly forbidden to use such derogatory names.

Thereafter, Institute students would often be met by smiles from the city residents on the streets and alleys of Chengdu. This happened around the beginning of 1953.

Not only did the Communist Party not discriminate against minority people, it even treated us with special respect, making us feel warmth like the sunshine in March. President Wang, because of his kind treatment of minority students, enjoyed high prestige among them, and they referred to him as the 'Venerable Wang'. When in 2003 the Institute was upgraded to the status of Southwest University for Nationalities, a statue of President Wang was erected on campus, to honour his outstanding contribution and cherish his memory.

Apart from Vice Presidents Xia and Zhang, our teachers were all part-time, invited from off-campus. Vice President Xia Kangnong belonged to a non-communist party. As a youth, he had studied biology in France. He was an expert in nationality affairs and lectured us on Marxism and Nationality Issues.

My indelible impression of Xia was that when lecturing, he never stopped smoking, going through more than one packet of cigarettes per two-hour lecture. He'd be smoking and coughing, while spluttering out his lecture. The very act of speaking entailed a strenuous effort. Although he used standard Chinese, not many people understood what he was saying.

Vice President Zhang Tianwei had been on the Long March with the Red Army. He had served as head of the Education Department of the Southwest Revolutionary University, and people continued to call him Director of

Education. In actual fact, he was the leader of the Communist Party at the Institute and went by the nickname Old Bolshevik.

Zhang had most class time with us, teaching various politics classes. He was always smiling, and rarely verbose. Each sentence was invested with special substance. From his very posture, you could observe the dignity of the Party. When he taught, every student felt a sense of awe and the usual background noise of the lecture hall would be transformed into silence.

Once when Zhang mis-wrote a Chinese character on the blackboard, a classmate Wu stood up, pointed at the character and said, "That character is wrong." Zhang's face blushed from top to bottom, but without a word, he turned and corrected what he had written. The incident caused great indignation in the student body. After class, everyone stared at Wu, appalled, and someone asked, "How come were you so insolent?"

He simply replied, "I just forgot myself." Thereafter, Wu was branded as arrogant.

The Institute and Class Struggle

At the time, various campaigns were underway: Resisting the US and Helping North Korea, Purging Bandits and Land Reform.

The campaign to Resist the US and Help North Korea was ongoing in every corner of the country and the Institute arranged for every student and staff member to write a letter of support to the Chinese People's Volunteer Army, which in 1950 had been deployed to help North Korea. The editor of the Institute magazine also arranged for each student to write an original, non-plagiarised article about the war effort. Poorly written articles were revised by the editor, and the writer's name and minority nationality were added.

Whether in lectures or tutorials, the content of our studies was Resisting the US and Helping North Korea. Even our mathematics classes incorporated the theme; so, for example, we sometimes counted how many enemy planes had been shot down the day before.

A daily newspaper-discussion class led to a fraught atmosphere. At the time, counter-revolutionaries were being arrested all over the country. Early one morning, through the metal railings of our windows, we saw two middle-aged men emerging from a house opposite the Institute gates, with guns at their backs, and later heard they had been counter-revolutionaries. They had been arrested while in bed with their wives.

One lunchtime, a well-educated female Tibetan student committed suicide. She had been a star performer of the *guozhuang* (one of three major Tibetan dances). Perhaps her pre-Liberation activities had been suspect, for after she died, there was no evidence to incriminate her with any counter-revolutionary allegiance...such allegiance was commonly used at the time to explain suicides.

One day in one of our class study-groups, ideological discussions boiled over, and all of a sudden, students were shouting at each other. Most of them, including the study-group leader, were Yi from western Guizhou. Afterwards, the group leader reported to the class Director that an older Yi student, named Zhang, had just completely denied his previously acknowledged personal history. He had insisted he had had nothing to do with the Nationalist Party. The class Director asked, "How did that subject even come up? You shouldn't have been questioning him!" The next day, Zhang disappeared, and no one tried to find out where he had gone.

After such incidents, Shi, a student in my own group, became nervous, his complexion pale and actions hurried. It seemed he was going crazy with fear and he became detached and remote. During small-group discussions, he said nothing, then once on hearing the sound of a whistle, he just looked around and walked off. It seemed that psychologically he had snapped.

Our Bouyei fellow-student, Liao, talked a lot in his sleep at night and the rest of us often woke with a start from sweet dreams to the sound of his shouting and screaming. He must have been horrified by recent events, to be so terrified by his dreams.

Despite all this, our study-group remained tranquil. Shi and Liao were exceptions to the rule, but others were not unduly disturbed, so in our group we lived together in harmony.

A thread weaving all through our current-affairs classes was that we should understand the contemporary situation and reform our thinking. We should purge our thinking of any trace of 'Esteem the US, Fear the US, Support the US' and establish anti-American thinking in its place. We should support the leaders of the Communist Party and the people's democratic dictatorship, walking the way of the New Democracy. Our future prospects were bound up with these obligations; there was no leeway for personal choice.

The campaign to 'Purge Bandits and Oppose Tyrants' was still underway. As we had travelled from Chongqing to Chengdu, we had observed village rallies at the roadsides, for accusing and denouncing bandits and tyrants. From time to time, we also heard gunshots, which we assumed to be the sound of executions.

While at the Institute, I once travelled with a dozen fellow-students to the local countryside. We saw assemblies in village fields, with people tied up in front of makeshift platforms. Square placards dangled over their chests, stating their name and offence.

In one place, we saw a man thrusting a wooden cudgel roughly into the back of the accused, whereupon two others pushed the accused away. Shortly afterwards, a gunshot rang out. As he left the meeting for home, we heard a middle-aged farmer say, "We've made a mess of that clay pot," by which he meant they had shattered his skull. "Let's go home for some rice wine."

It was a Sunday when we made that trip and observed such things in various villages, causing us to hurry back to the Institute shaken, silent and subdued. Accusations were fierce and people were being killed.

The Institute did not organise such outings, nor did it prohibit our going. It seemed almost as though such events beyond the Institute's confines were illusory. In lectures, they were referred to in generality, so that everyone knew society was 'Purging Bandits and Opposing Tyrants', as well as promoting Land Reform. The peasants, it was reported, were wild with joy, but details of what was happening were not divulged or discussed. If you had not witnessed such things with your own eyes, you would naturally not understand them very well.

The Institute did not dwell on the aforementioned chaos and class struggle in society because it was striving to develop unity among minorities. Only after taking the first step of unity could we move towards developing the class struggle. Despite this, students did discover a little about events in society at large, and anyone born into a land-owning family was deeply anxious.

A Miao student from Guizhou confided in me that on hearing any radio broadcast he felt afraid, because the broadcasts always discussed 'fighting the landlords' and distributing the land. He was wondering how his family was faring.

Another Guizhou student named Li was generally popular, but never talked openly about his own experiences or family. On days off, he often invited me to eat at a restaurant, partly because of our common geographical origins. He generously paid for the food, with money sent from home. There was hardly anyone else in the Institute who went out with excess money in their pocket.

Li, however, said to me several times that his family was finished, and how would he get by without eating? In future, we'd just have to go without. I didn't know his family background or why he had to be so pessimistic. All I could do was listen sympathetically.

I too was very concerned for my family. My mother was old and had no male relatives at home to help her with physical labour. How could she possibly cope after Land Reform? For me, everything was better in Chengdu than at home, but I was never able to erase thoughts of family from the back of my mind, especially during this period of confusion when everything was being turned on its head.

According to ideological reform, however, we were not permitted to have such thoughts. On the contrary, we were supposed to draw a clear line between ourselves and our families. We should rather educate erring family members, regarding them as enemies until they amended their ways. In small group discussions, we had to say how our families had exploited others by leasing land to them or having them work as farm-labourers. Peasants had been forced to care for our land-owning families in the past and it was right and proper that now the land should be returned to them.

In small groups, such speeches were profound and detailed, and eventually a 'model speech' for the whole class was selected. One classmate confessed how everything his family owned had come from peasants; not only the family's food and clothing, but also its land, house, poultry and beasts of burden. Even a pair of leather shoes he had worn to the Institute belonged to the peasants! He indicated he would mail them back promptly to the villagers.

Students from worker and peasant backgrounds were duly impressed and thought this was brilliant. Between gritted teeth, our classmate was fuming with rage at his parents, accusing them of eating the flesh of the peasants and drinking their blood. They were like wolves, not people, and their guilt deserved 1,000 deaths. In Hades, they deserved the high-torment water prison and in the next life, they would certainly return as pigs or chickens to repay their debt to peasants.

He declared his determination to substitute his land-owning parents, who were not really his parents any longer, by peasant parents.

Our teacher and fellow students praised him for drawing boundaries so distinctly, thus reflecting great progress. When other Institute cadres heard of his speech, he was hailed as a 'very red' student. Cadres urged other students of land-owning parents to learn from his example, and disown their parents and families.

Later, however, I heard that when that student returned to his village after graduation, and saw his parents' changed circumstances, he broke down and wept. They were living in a small dilapidated house, labouring every day without enough money to buy even oil or salt, and still suffering public denunciation in the evenings. Since he had been forced to disown his parents, the son complained, why had he been sent back to their village, only to witness them enduring this pitiful state of affairs? His plight was awful. Local peasants viewed it as an alternative punishment to 'reform-through-labour'.

Although students from different minorities and provinces treated each other with respect, we were not really able to relate harmoniously. We simply didn't relate much at all, shunning any differences that may have led to conflict, and studiously avoiding disputes, in case such disputes might grow into some inter-nationality problem, exhibiting disunity. That would be unpardonable and everyone was wary of it. While everyone was cautious and timid, the atmosphere remained good. After all, we were the first big family of nationalities established by Party and government in the southwest region. From my perspective, we students fell into one of five categories.

The first consisted of those who were forlorn, living in dread of the new society; some of whom were ultimately overwhelmed by fear and took their own lives.

The second category, to which I myself belonged, consisted of students who studied hard and strove with all their energy to adapt to the emerging new world. We had mostly been born into the land-owning classes. We welcomed the arrival of the new society for it offered opportunities for further study and work, helping us realise our dreams. We were able to learn quickly new elements of the new society and these were easy to accept; apart from the great problem of untangling family relationships, which remained unresolved.

The third category was students who had been 'born well', into non-land-owning, non-prosperous homes. These were mostly Tibetan and Yi, but some were also Miao; activists who had been nominated from the grass-roots level. A few had been engaged for short periods in guerrilla warfare. Most had no education and some did not even understand Mandarin, so they needed someone to interpret the Institute reports and speeches. They were to be leaders of the new society, the ones who loved it most naturally and ardently. The Party was relying on them to develop the Revolution in their respective regions and their presence would help to eliminate estrangement among minorities. Night and day, they were happy and cheerful, without a worry in the world. After graduation, they returned to their regions and served as cadres, securing incredible positions and promotions. One of them, a Yi man, was later appointed deputy governor of Sichuan.

The fourth group stood out from everyone else. At the Institute, they were known as 'the inner circle'. They were the 10 students from a university in Yunnan, three of whom were minority nationals and seven Han. They had supported Liberation and the government had appointed them to do nationality work. Originally, they were told they were to go to the Southwest Institute for Nationalities to serve as cadres.

Once they arrived, it was decided they should rather study along with the rest of us, though there would be limits on how long they should study. They created their own clique, chatting and laughing together. They seemed indifferent towards other students, not communicating much with them, and tending to despise them.

Other students felt 'the inner circle' were indeed special, and denigrated themselves. For a time, relationships between others and the 'inner circle' were tense. Early on, Institute staff noticed this was affecting the spirit of cooperation between nationalities. One of the Institute leaders actually publicly criticised the inner circle's cliquish behaviour.

Our class teacher, however, and other Institute cadres paid special deference to the 'inner circle' and gave them special leeway, treating them almost as though they were equals. Most were appointed small group leaders and when we first established the students' union, the Institute appointed Wei from the 'inner circle' as chairperson.

When this was announced, it caused great commotion in the student body. The consensus quickly grew that Wei was too arrogant and disconnected from other students to be the student union chair. Some said he would only be able to represent members of 'the inner circle', not the rest of us. A student from a peasant/worker's background had some inside information about Wei's family, claiming they had been landowners, and his parents had committed suicide during land reform to escape punishment. Wei was clearly not eligible as chairperson, for basically no one supported him.

After the evening session of self-study that day, the first small group in our fourth class was the first to make a public protest. By the end of the evening, students in all four classes had been mobilised in the cause.

Everyone was upset at the prospect of Wei serving as students' union chairperson, and demanded instead that an election be convened. One Shui student took the lead in all this, carrying a notebook soliciting opinions, and intending to propose three candidates. He quietly told me, however, that they had decided to elect me.

The next morning, before there had been time to inform the class director of the previous night's proceedings, an Institute general assembly was announced, convened by a cadre who had been on the Long March. On taking the stage, he immediately began to criticise everyone for lacking organisation and discipline. Resisting the leaders' decision was precisely the same as confronting the Party. Moreover, confronting was the same as rebelling, equivalent to counter-revolutionary activity. In conclusion, he announced the decision from the day before: Wei would be chairperson of the students' union. Whoever disagreed should stand up and say so.

Heads drooped but otherwise no one moved. You could have heard a pin drop.

The upshot was that the idea of establishing a students' union was promptly abandoned. Not only were no student representatives elected, but no students' union meeting was ever convened. No one ever mentioned again the chairperson appointed by Institute leaders, for the union itself never transpired, at least not before my class had graduated.

Within two days, the whole matter had been dropped, having been played down and officially forgotten. Most students still regarded 'the inner circle' with respect and upon graduation, only one of the 10 'inner-circle' students left campus for a job elsewhere, to join her new husband. The other nine stayed and became the backbone of administration and the Party committee at the Institute. Leaders seemed to have special confidence in them.

Otherwise, in the fifth and final subgroup, there were two students who particularly impressed me. They were among those who could not adapt to the new society; one was a Miao person named Xu from Guizhou, and the other a Han person named Shen. They behaved in extraordinary ways and there was no person in the whole Institute who did not know them.

I got to know Xu on the way from Guiyang to Chengdu. He was more than 30 years old and wore a grey woollen uniform, better than the emergency-relief cotton-padded clothes worn by the rest of us. Since he was Miao and from the same province as me, we liked to spend time together. When people discovered that before Liberation he had been a student at a college in Nanjing and wrote Chinese characters beautifully, they respected him. No one ever accused him of saying or doing anything wrong.

In his small group, Xu never made a speech and behaved as though he didn't hear what others were saying. Instead, it seemed he was musing over other burdens on his mind. He tried to avoid cadres at all costs, but if a cadre was present, he was even more likely than usual to maintain silence and look gloomy. He'd pucker up his eyebrows and twist his face on one side. A cadre would say, "Xu, you're a university graduate, one of the most prominent Miao intellectuals. Why do you not say anything? If you have something heavy on your mind, it will help for you to articulate it."

Xu would reply, "No, I don't have anything on my mind." Despair, however, was wearing him down. After graduation, he returned to Guizhou and I heard no more news of him. Fifty years later, after I had returned to live in Guizhou, I heard a Miao friend say that Xu had died within a few years of returning, without ever having married.

Shen behaved in a different yet also eccentric way. He spoke standard Mandarin very well and most of us enjoyed just listening to his elegant pronunciation, while overlooking what he was actually saying. After graduating at the Southwest Revolutionary University, he had been sent to work on nationality affairs, before being registered as a student at the Institute. He viewed himself as a sheep among goats, superior to the rest of us, and we his classmates also realised he was different.

When Shen opened his mouth, out came Marxism-Leninism, a whole ream of theory. He felt he should be a teacher, not a student, but ironically, he lost esteem among fellow students. He became the butt of his group leader's criticism and discipline. Shen despised the class director, however, complaining that the director didn't understand a thing and was too proud and arrogant. The class director, in turn, did not think much of Shen and never appointed him to the position of small group leader.

Shen's small group disliked the uniform he always wore and disapproved of the glass tea jar he carried with him. During group meetings, he drank tea incessantly and chattered about political theory. He liked to sleep late in the mornings and if no one came to wake him, he wouldn't get up. He did not sweep the floor nor do any other kind of everyday work, instead having others do such chores for him – just like a cadre. At the small group leaders' evening meetings for reporting each day's events, his leader often reported Shen's words and actions, vividly and colourfully, causing everyone to laugh, setting Shen up as a general nuisance, too proud and troublesome.

After graduation, a jeep came to collect Shen, after most other graduates had already left. I never heard of him again.

One morning, as graduation evaluations were beginning, a general Institute assembly was called. After everyone was seated, three captives were pushed onto the front of the stage. My goodness! Was that young woman not the very one who had often performed on that same stage in the Uighur dance group? She was a slender, pretty Uighur woman from Xinjiang, who before Liberation had studied music in Chongqing. After Liberation, she had worked in nationality affairs and then arrived at the Institute to establish a cultural skills group. Her dance skills won particular acclaim. She had been all the rage there in Chengdu, the most popular of performers.

Her circumstances that day caused much astonishment. She wore a blue uniform, with two long ponytails trailing behind as always. She was pale and looked as though she had lost weight, standing there in blank terror, not daring to look around. Several Institute leaders were sitting on stage and one of them read an account of the 'counter-revolutionary crimes' of the three people.

We heard that the Uighur woman's problem originated in 1948 after she travelled from Xinjiang to Chongqing. While she was studying in Chongqing, she had made friends with a VIP from the Nationalist Party and now she was refusing to confess.

As soon as the accusations were announced, a few robust middle-aged men swiftly used some coarse flax rope to tie the three people up together, arms behind their backs and ropes looped around their necks. When one person pressed his right knee on her back and pulled the rope violently with both hands, you could only see two silent streams of tears running down her cheeks, her face contorted in pain and humiliation. Afterwards, she was pushed and pulled off-stage.

Several hundred students in the audience were scared stiff, like rabbits caught in headlights. The apprehension of most students, who had been born into families 'guilty of exploiting others', was greatly increased. When the meeting adjourned, a Yi student from Guizhou quietly remarked, "She suffered so much. Will it be the same for us in future?"

A Han student then observed that they generally wanted to catch people *before* they graduated. He was afraid there would probably be another such general meeting before too long.

Graduation

We had studied in the wonderfully elegant environment of the Liu Estate, without winter or summer vacation. Only Sundays interrupted the concerted and concentrated onslaught of learning during those months. On 1st May 1952, I graduated.

Apart from unspoken worries about family and future prospects, I'd have to say it was quite a happy time there. After graduation, other members of my group were assigned to work back in their home provinces. I was to stay at the Institute and immediately wrote to my mother, explaining I had been assigned to work there and would be unable to go home and look after her. I confessed how deeply I felt the weight of shame in not performing my duty as her son, because now I couldn't say when I might be free to visit her at home.

During the week before graduation, Su was beside me every day, in person and ideology. Abruptly, however, she was torn away; in spirit, far away. On hearing she was assigned to work elsewhere the following semester, she promptly left my company. She didn't look for me to explain, as if she had developed some objection to me; not at all like the classmate with whom I'd enjoyed a special relationship over the previous months.

I made an appointment to chat with her; she said she'd see me in the morning at the rock garden near the small pavilion. We kept our appointment, sitting side by side on a wooden bench. Her usual smiling countenance had been replaced by solemnity, as she explained that she was going to strive hard for Party membership. Only if I was also a member could we be on the best of terms.

I told Su I wasn't a good League member and I'd never dared to think about joining the Party. Then she bluntly retorted, "Forget it!" She asked how things were with my family. I told her there had been no letters from home and I had hardly written. Were they still alive and what was the general situation there? I didn't know. When she discovered I had a wife and child, and other close relatives, she mistakenly assumed I would go home after graduation. Her last kindness was to advise me to take good care of my wife when I returned home; it was good we were from the same nationality, and I shouldn't leave her in search of anyone else. Then she rose and left hurriedly. So, we split up.

Su was assigned to the Religious Affairs Department of the government in Chengdu. Although she wasn't far away and often came to the Institute, she never came to see me. When in 1956 I was a graduate student at the Central Institute for Nationalities in Beijing, a former classmate from the Southwest Institute informed me that Su had been transferred to another job. I never heard more news of her. Recalling that period of unfulfilled friendship, I composed the following poem:

> We were lucky enough to meet from far-flung fields,
> Different nationalities with disparate destinies.
> Short-lived affections struggle in the winding up,
> Now we say goodbye and will never meet again.

Chapter 10
Surveying the Stone Minority
(Qiang Nationality, 1952)

On the evening of 1st May 1952, Vice-President Xia Kangnong summoned me along with three other graduates from the same class, to appoint us to work in a new Nationalities Research Unit. The preface and epilogue of Chairman Mao's 'Report on Investigations in the Countryside' were read aloud. The importance of survey research was emphasised and arrangements were outlined for fulfilling the task of survey among the minorities of western Sichuan.

Three Research Unit members had already been appointed: Mr Li Zhichun and two others. Mr Li was over 50 and very experienced, having done survey in the border areas of Yunnan Province. The seven of us were to comprise a survey team, with Mr Li as team leader. Vice-President Xia was to be Director of the new Research Unit.

On 2nd May, I joined a sub-team to survey the Qiang nationality in the northwest of Sichuan.

Surveying County Blackwater

In 1952, not much of the Qiang Tibetan region in the northwest of Sichuan had been liberated. Many Nationalist leaders had taken refuge there. Planes from Taiwan frequently flew overhead dropping leaflets and occasionally even special agents. Most of the leaders of local minority people gave tacit support to such resistance.

To pave the way for thorough emancipation of minority people in the region, the new administration in western Sichuan decided to send a Visiting Team, to permeate the region with information about nationality policies of the Communist Party and to provide emergency relief.

Thus, the Institute had to send specialists to undertake survey, and to facilitate implementation of the policy of nationality cooperation. On the day after our graduation, a team of six people (five male and one female) under the leadership of Mr Li, accompanied by several hundred male and female cadres, set off from Chengdu in the direction of the Qiang Tibetan region.

On the first day, we took a bus to County Wenzhou, as far as the Qiang area. The bus could only go so far and thereafter we had to go by foot along the banks of the rushing River Min, on horse-tracks. The tracks were rough, uneven mountain paths. I was instructed to accompany Mr Li and help him as much as possible.

Li used a walking stick and occasionally needed an arm for support, or even to be pulled along. The slopes were steep and full of unexpected potholes, so we moved along with some apprehension. Occasionally, we needed to bend down and crawl before emerging at the other side of some low-hanging brush. A wrong step and you could end up in the raging torrents below. The path was so challenging that you could travel only 20 or 25 kilometres in a day.

The first night, we stayed in a Qiang village where everyone spoke Mandarin. If it hadn't been for the people's stone-built single-storey houses, their sleeveless sheepskin garments and thick sackcloth leg wrappings, you'd never have known they were Qiang.

The Visiting Team consisted mostly of former cadres from a county in Chengdu. Nearly all the males carried pistols. After we stopped that day at the village, they went into a cave and tested their firearms. On hearing the guns, the Qiang people working outside rushed home in panic, spreading the warning, "There's a gun-battle!" One of the cadres quickly explained they were just doing routine firearm testing, not fighting.

After two days, we reached Fengyi town in County Mao, where for five or six days we fine-tuned preparations for the trip ahead. Anxious to avoid enemy observation, we left Fengyi by night. After a day, we arrived at the site of regional offices, where we stayed a week or more.

On moving on, we reached an encampment named Chibusu. One or two kilometres outside the camp, there was a turbulent surging river with dark water, almost black. Porters carrying our supplies informed us, "That's the Blackwater." The bridge spanning the river had been destroyed.

The Visiting Team was stationed at Chibusu, near the river. Wabuliangzi, the towering mountain there, formed part of the boundary of the Blackwater region. The whole region was full of Qiang people, so it was a good place from which to launch our Qiang survey.

Three days later, Comrade Wen and I went with District Chief Wang Taichang to visit his home village of Qugu. We walked from Chibusu up a tall mountain, taking two hours to reach halfway. From there, you could see Qugu opposite, with many stone houses.

It was mid-day and smoke was spiralling from chimneys in the village. You could hear the sound of pigs oinking and dogs barking. District Chief Wang pointed and said, "That's my home. From here down to the stream and back up to the village will take another three or four hours."

This was the typical geography of a Qiang village. Mountains were tall and valleys were deep. Two villages would face each other across a valley. You could see people and horses moving around in the opposite village, and could even shout to one another, but to reach the other village, you'd need to trek a good half-day. Qiang people lived on mountaintops to defend themselves against invasion and plunder.

Wang said that in the past, Nationalists had sent soldiers to stamp out the opium trade. When they reached this point, the villagers opposite saw them very clearly, so by the time they reached the village, everyone had disappeared.

When we reached the mountaintop, we sat down for a rest. District Chief Wang eyed me up curiously and asked where I was from and how things were at my home. Our leaders had repeatedly emphasised that you had to be careful when you talked to minority leaders. Whatever I did, I shouldn't make any irresponsible remarks that might give rise to apprehension.

In answering his questions, I hummed and hawed, not actually commenting on the situation in my village. Wang asked to make sure, "So, you are also a minority person?" apparently more cordial now than when the interrogation had started. In the evening, we sat around a jar of local liquor. He often passed me the bamboo 'straw' for me to take my turn.

Before Liberation, District Chief Wang had attended the Central Military Academy in Chengdu and after graduation, he had returned to Qugu to work as township leader. After Liberation, the Communist Party made him undergo 'consolidation', namely united-front training, then entrusted him with the position of leading Chibusu.

When we returned to the Visiting Team, Comrade Wen reported that I had been chatting with District Leader Wang, who had appeared to have some misgivings about the future. Wen criticised me in front of other team members. I had conversed too casually to a minority leader and had been too intimate with him.

From then on, I was more circumspect, trying if possible to avoid contact with senior minority leaders. I had been reticent to begin with and after this, I was even less inclined to speak up. A loose tongue could cause a lot of trouble, so I tried to guard against it.

Every few days, Visiting Team leaders wanted us surveyors to go to Qiang villages to see what was going on. They decided that Mr Li should lead me, Luo, Li and Ms Wu to Weicheng, and sent a local primary teacher named Liu and a Qiang cadre to accompany us. We thus comprised a small team of seven people.

At the same time, another Wu from the Institute went to survey in Yadu with a different small team, led by a Qiang district leader named Chen.

We walked through Yadu and by the time we reached Weicheng, it was already evening. After we had eaten, it was already dark, and it was then that someone rushed up to announce, "As district leader Chen was on his way to Yadu with the other group, they were ambushed and Chen was shot dead. His body is still lying there."

On hearing this, we were scared to death, fearing that Blackwater people were already on their way to attack us. We should leave as soon as possible, but our natural escape route back through Yadu had already been cut off. The Qiang cadre lit a torch and set off to lead us to the lowest point of the valley. We groped about in the dark for three hours on a path as twisty as a sheep's intestines, until we reached a large stone cave and the cadre announced we had reached the end of the path.

Before us loomed the great Mount Snow, beyond which was the border of County Li. Our guide recommended we take shelter in the cave. He lit a bonfire and everyone sat around. From time to time, Mr Li or our female Comrade Wu would sigh and ask, "What's to be done?"

A mountain spring flowed beside the cave, so the next morning we were well supplied with water. The maize and wheat flour we had brought was enough for about 10 days. The cave could shelter us from rain and we could wait there until the Blackwater people had left.

The Qiang cadre roasted maize and wheat cakes, to be washed down by mountain spring water. On the second day, Mr Li invited suggestions on how best to extricate ourselves from our predicament.

The Qiang cadre thought our only option was to scale Mount Snow and return via County Li. But there was no path over the mountain and few people had ever climbed it. Would we really be able to do it? Everyone looked up at the steep snow-covered mountain and no one said a word.

After a while, Liu suggested we should return to Weicheng and find out more about the situation there. He volunteered to go if someone could accompany him; but no one was willing to do so. I volunteered. The Qiang cadre took the pistol from his side, and gave it to me. It still had a few bullets and could be used in self-defence. When we set off, our comrades observed us with a peculiar gaze, as if wondering whether or not we would return alive.

By mid-day, teacher Liu and I were stealthily entering a house in Weicheng, where only an old woman was at home. She knew Liu from his teaching and knew about our flight that evening. The Blackwater people had not entered Weicheng, she said, for they hadn't known that government cadres had come there.

Villagers in two other homes confirmed this intelligence, whereupon we returned and reported the news to our colleagues in the cave. They were overjoyed, and praised our courage.

The Qiang cadre recommended leading us along another path back to Chibusu, bypassing the place where our colleague had been killed. Thus on the third morning, he led us alongside a stream, difficult terrain as it passed through thickets and undergrowth, until at 3 or 4 pm we arrived at a log bridge. Cautiously, we crossed the bridge, and this marked the end of our danger.

The burdens on our hearts fell away and were replaced by smiles on our faces. Halfway up the mountain, we encountered armed soldiers on their way down, who asked, "Are you the comrades from the Visiting Team? We have come to escort you back."

By evening, we arrived at their camp on a mountaintop beside a Qiang village, with a view of Weicheng on the opposite mountain. On the other side of our mountain, at the bottom, you could see Chibusu. After our great escape, eating our fill, and sleeping peacefully through the night, the world seemed a much brighter place.

Before mid-day, we left the small army station and made our way back downhill to Chibusu, relaxed and cheerful. It was a bright, clear day, as if the heavens themselves were smiling at our escape. When we were halfway down, however, a plane rumbled overhead and soon paper leaflets were blotting out the sky and spilling onto the surrounding mountain and fields. It was a Nationalist plane from Taiwan and the leaflets announced that the Blackwater region was Nationalist territory. Our alarm returned us quickly to Chibusu.

County Blackwater had traditionally been ruled by hereditary headmen, but after their power waned, other local leaders governed. The county had 55 ravines, many tall mountains and deep valleys, which had never before been ruled by central government. Its inhabitants only knew about Blackwater, not China. After Liberation, some were still asking, "Which is bigger, China or Blackwater?"

At the time of Liberation, Blackwater's population was 24,000 and after Liberation, it was ascribed the status of a county.

After Liberation, packhorses were being shot dead by Nationalist guerrillas on the other side of the river, and the situation was grim.

In 1952, liberation of Blackwater and the neighbouring grass plains was the primary military goal in the southwest, and soldiers were stationed in Chibusu. The enemy on the other side of the river would shoot at people or horses on our side.

One night, our leaders organised for us to grope our way in the dark to the mouth of the river, so we could carry food from there back to Chibusu. It was so dark that when you held your hand out, you couldn't see your fingers. Everyone grasped the back of the clothing of the person in front. We weren't allowed to smoke, speak or cough, but had to carry the food back as quietly as possible.

The stinking dead carcass of a horse lay along our path and upon treading on the carcass, one comrade cried out in alarm. On hearing his cry, gunmen on the other side of the river opened fire in our direction, but fortunately for us, covered by a curtain of darkness, no one was hit.

After soldiers moved into Chibusu, we saw them daily make the arduous climb up Mount Wabuliangzi beside our settlement. We'd occasionally hear the sound of an explosion, followed by waves of gunshots. Such skirmishes, however, were not yet very intense.

Wabuliangzi was dotted with Qiang rock towers. Afterwards, I discovered that many of the towers had been defended to the death by armed bandits, firing outwards through tower embrasures. Ultimately, soldiers had to lay explosives to collapse the towers. These were the explosions we often heard from the foot of the mountain.

After about 10 days of such explosions, the PLA finally won over Wabuliangzi and established a presence there, awaiting the command to press on into Blackwater. Soldiers said that the towers had been occupied not only by Blackwater people but also by Nationalist agents, and the enemies had been tenacious. Towers had been blown up and the people inside buried alive. No one had emerged to surrender.

After the conquest of Wabuliangzi, there was calm in the region; the calm before the troops stormed into Blackwater itself. We all breathed a sigh of relief.

Just then, our Visiting Team leaders decided not to wait until troops advanced upon Blackwater.

Instead, Mr Li was instructed to take me, Ms Wu, Li and Comrade Wen back to Counties Mao and Wenchuan, to survey the Qiang people there.

Not long after we left Chibusu, the PLA advanced on three fronts into Blackwater. Planes were sent to bomb Seergu and Sidiaolou villages and the PLA used heavy bombardment and fierce gunfire. Many rock towers and most of the stone houses were destroyed. On the western front, planes had not been used before for bombing.

Through air bombing and ground artillery, many natives of Blackwater were killed. My fellow-student Wu, who stayed behind and fought in this campaign, seemed to the rest of us like a hero.

Surveying Counties Mao and Wenzhou

Mr Li led the four of us back to Counties Mao and Wenzhou to survey the Qiang people there. There was an endless stream of people with horses, carrying commodities along the narrow bridal paths beside the River Min.

Li warned that with the battle going on in Blackwater, we needed to be extra-cautious. We shouldn't make any irresponsible remarks and were not allowed to go around alone. We all followed his orders during the next month of survey.

Yanmen, Weimen and Shuixi were the three main survey points, situated along 50 kilometres of the path. Everyone spoke Mandarin, while only older people spoke the 'local language'. Local Han people referred contemptuously to this language as 'barbarian language', and to the speakers as 'barbarians'.

The speakers themselves said they were Tu, and lived in stone houses with stone roofs. There were no more stone towers, though you could find their ruined remnants. Older locals said that when the Qing [1644–1912 AD] army came to conquer the county, stone towers along the route had been demolished.

The Tu people wore woollen garments and flax leg-wrappings, and ate corn congee. On their housetops, they consecrated white stones for offering sacrifices. In these respects, they were similar to the Qiang people in the mountains.

I spent two days learning the International Phonetic Alphabet from Mr Li for use in writing down the local language. Tu tones, vocabulary and grammar were all similar to the Qiang spoken in the nearby mountains. The only difference was in the mixing in of more local Mandarin Chinese.

After collecting much good data, we returned to the guesthouse at Mao county town, where we compared results and convened research discussions.

The so-called Tu people had been relating closely with Han people. Young people used Mandarin and the Tu language was tending towards extinction. There had been discrimination against minorities before Liberation.

According to the findings of our survey, these 'Tu people' were actually Qiang, but tending towards assimilation with the local Han people. Those in leadership agreed with our analysis and henceforth regarded them as Qiang. They were no longer to be called Tu and it was forbidden in future to use 'barbarians' or any other such offensive name for them.

When he convened discussions in the guesthouse, however, Mr Li continued calling the local Qiang people 'barbarians'. On hearing this, my Han comrades grinned, especially our female comrade, who seemed most complicit, constantly looking askance at me.

I was the only minority person in the group, and on hearing the term 'barbarian', I felt insulted. My comrades' contemptuous behaviour added injury to insult. I felt isolated, and so angry my face turned bright red. Sometimes I was so agitated I just wanted to withdraw and hide.

I developed a chip on my shoulder against Mr Li, imagining he was deliberately annoying me and currying the favour of Han comrades. I felt estranged from my colleagues, most of all from the female comrade, whom I tried to avoid. She was, however, a small-group leader, and during group activities, she criticised me for having 'petty, narrow-minded, racist ideology'. The other comrades didn't agree, but at the same time they didn't object to what she said.

Within a few days, my relationship with Mr Li and other comrades had been mended. Strangely, however, Mr Li assigned Ms Wu and me to march together through ravines to survey Qiang villages on the mountains.

Wu and I set off with backpacks, Wu in front, our faces stony and serious. We didn't converse along the way and in the villages it was the same, even when eating with Qiang people. We conducted our survey work separately, but in the evenings, the Qiang led us to stay in unoccupied stone houses. She would sleep in an inner room while I slept in an outer one, as if guarding her; but we still didn't converse.

I don't know what she was thinking. She was older than me, for she had already graduated from university before Liberation and now seemed like a veteran. She later married her class director and continued doing research with me for four or five more years, but the estrangement between us persisted.

Qiang life on the mountains seemed the same as in the Chibusu region. The main food was maize, and maize flour was steamed to make corn bread, eaten as a staple much as Han people eat rice; or adding pickled vegetables to make porridge, like the rice porridge common in Han areas; or using hot ash to make maize pancakes.

The most precious non-staple food was pig fat. Villagers strangled pigs with ropes, and cut off pieces of meat, hair and all, hanging them on roof beams above the fire to smoke and dry out. The longer the fumigating period the yellower they would be. The meat would be roasted, scraped clean and boiled, before eating. Qiang villagers sometimes boiled pig fat for us as a special treat. It really did taste good; better than any preserved meat or pig fat cooked by neighbouring Han people.

Perhaps as a result of generations with maize as a staple, neither at that time in 1952, nor in 1960, did I discover any Qiang people suffering from illnesses of the arteries (of the brain or heart). Even the symptoms of such illness were unknown.

Qiang women carried water or firewood and worked the land. If you asked why, the reply came that most men smoked opium, which had been planted in the region before Liberation, so were unable to do heavy work. Other men had been conscripted into the army. There were few able-bodied men and consequently heavy work, both in and outside the home, was the domain of the women.

For this reason, the marriage age was higher for women than for men. Fourteen-year-old boys would sometimes marry women who were 20 or more. This would add to the labour-force of a family.

One local Han person told us that if young women were weeding a field together, they would stop when boys passed by. They would swarm around the boys, noisily urging them to have a rest, embracing and rolling around with them. If the young men noticed the women on time, they would normally take a detour. Naturally, there were also some who deliberately walked by, to engage in such adventures. When Han men ventured in, some were also attracted, later becoming Qiang.

Since there were not enough men to go around, and women could not always find husbands, the women sometimes had to suppress their natural physical instincts. Both men and women wore leg-wrappings, binding their trouser legs tightly around their lower legs. These wrappings were not easy to remove and may have helped to prevent 'sleeping around'. Notwithstanding, a doctor from the Health Department of Shaba said that half the adult Qiang men and women of the region had sexually transmitted diseases.

Research into hereditary leaders took Li and me across the rope bridge in Weizhou to the mountain opposite, where hereditary leaders had lived. This journey resulted in a bird's-eye view of the area within a 20-kilometre circumference of Weizhou.

We reached the summit only after a challenging trek up a steep mountain path. On the ridges before our eyes were arrayed around 100 stone houses, and our local guide explained that this was the official residence of the Wasi hereditary leaders.

According to our research, these leaders, whose titles had been bestowed during the Ming dynasty (1368–1644 AD), were Jiarong Tibetan. Many ordinary Jiarong Tibetans had come along with these hereditary leaders and most lived near the main village, which was called the 'leaders' residence'. Some served as housekeepers, some as guards. Others served as minor chiefs in the Qiang community, helping the hereditary leaders rule.

The official residence of hereditary leaders was separated from Weizhou by the torrential waters of the River Min. On the east bank of the river, Han settlements were connected with Qiang villages via bridal paths. The west bank, however, was mostly tall and precipitous mountain terrain, frequented not even by mountain goats.

The Wasi hereditary leaders depended for their power on such terrain. In that region, they were like little emperors, maintaining hereditary leadership for over 300 years.

The only links between the east and west banks of the River Min were rope-bridges, made using bamboo twisted into rope-like strands.

Along the 100-kilometre border of the two counties there were also about four or five places where *single-line* rope-bridges existed. These so-called sliding bridges consisted of two bamboo ropes. Holding on to the line above, you would walk along the rope below and so reach the other bank, but skill was needed to negotiate this slippery 'tight-rope'. I watched confident Qiang youths fly backwards and forwards over the river on these ropes, feeling so nervous I broke into a cold sweat!

The Qiang guarded their village strongholds with gunpowder, and bows and arrows, maintaining separation from the outside world. Their rock towers, stone houses, language and culture remained relatively well preserved. Most people spent their whole lives on one side of the river and never crossed over to the other side.

While in the Wasi leaders' village, Li and I stayed in spacious guest rooms at one side of the hereditary leader's house. At mealtimes, we were invited to the fireplace of the main room, where two middle-aged women and two 17- or 18-year-old girls sat to one side. The older women watched us eating and asked about our backgrounds and families, but as we spoke the younger women just smiled shyly, then went outside, making us feel embarrassed and even a little nervous.

Later we realised many households, including that of the hereditary leader, consisted only of females. The Qiang often invited sons-in-law from outside. These incomers would adopt their wives' family names to maintain the family lines. Prospective sons-in-law would sign a contract, pledging to climb the mountains to chop firewood, and go down the mountains to bring back water. If they tried to leave, they would be beaten to death.

Married men could take a wife from a second household, providing they took care of both households. The hereditary leader stipulated that Han husbands were not permitted, but in fact, many Han farmers from northern Sichuan had entered the Qiang communities. After taking their wives' surnames, they themselves simply became Qiang.

Qiang terrain was endowed with more stones than earth. The Qiang on those tall and inaccessible mountains collected stones locally, of all shapes and sizes, to construct their homes, and used clay to bind the stones together. Houses were two or three storeys high and had no pillars, only walls and beams. Animals were raised on the ground floor and people lived upstairs.

Qiang people used their masonry skills to construct stone towers, some of which were square, some with six sides and some even with eight sides. They were three or four, six or seven, or even 10 storeys tall, and from a distance, looked like chimneys. There were openings in the walls from which guns could be fired, and their doors were thick and sturdy.

Each village had three or four such towers, enough to accommodate all the village women and children. If outsiders invaded, local men would defend key points on the approach to the village with gunpowder, guns, bows and arrows, and stones, while women and children hid in the towers. If their resistance failed, men would retreat to the towers to defend themselves to the death. In times of peace, the towers stored rations, timber and other essential commodities.

The stone houses were robust, rarely collapsing or falling into disrepair. There had been many earthquakes, but the houses survived, and both towers and houses seemed in good condition. The locals assured us few of the buildings had been built recently; some of their houses and especially the towers were centuries old.

The technology of building with stones had been passed down through the Qiang generations and each male was an expert. Every autumn and winter, men went to Chengdu to earn money by digging wells; they would use stones to build the well interiors. Such wells were known for their longevity.

At the time, Qiang people were unable to speak Mandarin. Thus, they would walk the streets and alleys carrying wooden signs on their backs announcing 'well-digger'. Chengdu residents of old mostly drew their drinking water from wells, but most did not realise that these wells had been constructed by Qiang people.

Since their survival was intimately connected with stonemasonry, the Qiang worshipped the stonemason god. There was a small tower on the roof of each house, on which was placed white stone, an altar to the god. At the house-corners, offerings were made to the god and his wife, who was treated as a goddess, revered for having helped in the house-building.

Qiang women could plant corn and vegetables in cracks in the stony ground and they grew well. They did not treat stones as a hindrance. Men said, "One stone is worth three ounces of oil. Without stones you can't do anything." They are a 'stone minority'.

My colleague Mr Li was moved to write this poem:
The Min Mountain peak and forests reach for the sky,
while crashing river torrents drive deep sleep away.
Tall towers and rope-bridges were made by Qiang of old,
whose ancient tales with mixed liquor and *guozhuang* dance are told.
Qiang flutes pipe their way to unknown places,
while white stones attract worship of the Erma*.
*[Footnote: Erma is the self-appellation of the Qiang.]

We studied the Qiang people of Counties Mao and Wenchuan fairly thoroughly, including their Tu brothers. We collected much first-hand material about their socio-economic conditions and history, their language and culture.

We also corrected mistaken ideas about Blackwater people, clarifying their nationality heritage. Leaders there were Jiarong Tibetans, who had brought with them Tibetan Buddhism and the Tibetan script. Han people mistakenly thought the people of Blackwater were Jiarong Tibetan.

Blackwater people were, however, undoubtedly Qiang, and from then on, they were known as Qiang. At the time, County Blackwater had about 24,000 Qiang people; 94% of the county population. The other 6% were Jiarong Tibetan.

In 1952, the total Qiang population was 65,000. Before Liberation, since the mountains were tall and the valleys deep, only Professor Hu Jianmin from Sichuan University had gone to the Qiang regions to do short-term study, afterwards publishing several articles in various journals.

For several months, we had conducted the first comprehensive field research of the Qiang people. Upon our return, we arranged everything into two books *The Circumstances of the Qiang (Erma) Nationality* (Southwest Institute for Nationalities mimeograph, 1953) and *Qiang Survey Data* (printed only later by the Southwest Institute for Nationalities, 1984). These were groundbreaking materials in understanding the Qiang nationality.

Chapter 11
Grasslands and Slaves
(Tibetan and Yi Nationalities, 1952-54)

Towards the end of autumn 1952, Mr Li Zhichun led me from County Mao to County Songpan to prepare to enter the Tibetan grasslands. Mr Li, however, was not too robust, so it was inadvisable for him to explore the Tibetan plateau, where oxygen was relatively scarce. Instead Mr Wu, our heroic comrade who had fought in Blackwater, was transferred to take over from Li. I stayed in Songpan county town with Wu for almost a month, prior to our grasslands expedition.

Songpan was an ancient town, where in 637 AD, Chinese and Tibetan troops clashed. It subsequently became renowned among the Chinese as a strategic location for repelling Tibetans.

The town wall and steps up to the wall were still intact. The town's cobbled streets were uneven, but they were clean and on either side were shops managed by Hui and a few Han people. The vast majority of residents were Hui.

The area around the county town was inhabited by Tibetans who could speak Mandarin. Every day, many of them entered the town. Some sold animal products such as wool or leather and in return bought essential commodities such as tea or salt. Others seemed to be there just to enjoy themselves, sitting on mats at the side of the road.

Several dozen comrades had arrived from Chengdu to join the western Sichuan survey group assigned to Songpan. Most were single young men and women, and lived temporarily with us in the guesthouse while awaiting assignment. The county government often organised dances for them, to liven up their otherwise monotonous lives and provide opportunities to make friends.

Assembly halls, conference rooms, or dining halls were transformed into makeshift dance halls. A gramophone record would set everyone prancing, before pairing up and dancing together with more elegance. One startling difference between then and now was that most male and some female comrades were wearing pistols. My colleague Wu's revolver, hanging over his shoulder, kept swinging against his thigh. When I teased him, he quipped, "This is what a hero looks like."

Having left the big city of Chengdu to come to this remote region, most of the young men were anxious to find a partner and marry. Such aspirations were even more pronounced among the female comrades. During formal meetings, they were repeatedly encouraged to settle down there, and spend their whole

140

lives working in the Tibetan region. Their leaders hoped they would not endeavour to be transferred elsewhere.

Consequently, whenever young men and women met, they easily formed relationships, and many resolved to marry. After each ball, more made-for-marriage couples emerged.

One morning, everyone assembled for a routine meeting. Sitting next to me were a young man and woman, members of the survey group. Since they were from different work units, they hadn't known each other before. During the meeting, there was a 10-minute break and after returning to sit down, they started to talk. They didn't ask each other's names, but before long I heard the young man asking, "Will you marry me?"

The woman replied: "Why not?"

That night at the ball, they were together on the dance floor and a leader announced their marriage! I heard later that only after their first night together, they enquired about their respective family circumstances.

One day, Wu told me that one of the female comrades had given birth to a baby. The child's father had already gone to the grasslands and there was no one to take care of her; so a woman who had just turned 20 was left alone to look after her newborn baby. Wu felt sorry for her and we went to visit. She was sitting on a bed, breast-feeding the baby. When she saw us, she sobbed, "Lei has gone to the grasslands, leaving me here alone. Life is so difficult. What can I do?"

Wu tried to comfort her. On our way back, he confessed that he had strong and heartfelt feelings for this young woman. She was from Chengdu, recently graduated from junior middle school, with only her mother still alive. Lei, a Songpan party secretary, had met her by chance in Chengdu and taken a fancy to her. He arranged for her to join the southwest visiting team bound for the minority regions of southwest Sichuan.

After Lei insisted on marriage, they left Chengdu together; her mother, the same age as Lei, having agreed to the match. To any outside observer, it was a conspicuously sorry state of affairs. The husband was dark and coarse, poorly educated, with a voice like a horn. The wife was young, thin and weak, and her voice was feeble. Anyone who didn't know their background would have assumed they were father and daughter. Wu exuded indignation. He clearly judged all this to be absurd and felt contemptuous.

More than a year later, Lei's 45-year-old wife turned up to look for him. She had two children by him. There was no one left at home to do the farming and she was in dire straits. She had not guessed that Lei had found a new wife in Chengdu, much less that his new wife had given birth to a son. On hearing this, she couldn't help bawling out loud. After she had created weeks of disturbance, some leaders stepped in, warned her she needed to do some 'ideological work', and gave her money for the journey home. So their divorce became 'official'.

Those who knew about all this felt aggrieved for the first wife, and sympathetic towards the second. Quite a few men in liberated Sichuan, however, ended up in such complicated relationships, especially among the older worker- and farmer-cadres at regional and township levels.

Wu and I had both been party to marriages arranged by our parents. My wife had been the daughter of a landlord and could not bear the struggle during the land reform era. Under daily duress of menacing circumstances, and with the sudden change from prosperity to poverty, she could no longer wait for me and felt compelled to remarry. There had never even been any letters between us and our former love had become mist in our eyes. In my heart, there was no longer any feeling of love towards her, and I just felt empty.

During that half-year, I witnessed many lightning-quick marriages between young men and women, and some senior worker- or farmer-cadres marrying young middle school graduates. The new environment obviously had a massive influence on the mentality of the young men who had been thrown together into this difficult region. To some, it was mind-blowing and marriage became irresistible, but unlike most others, I remained unmoved.

One reason was that feelings of love and emotion had already been drowned out, and the second was that future prospects were still obscure. I had the sense of simply drifting along and I was not in the mood to seek happiness in a relationship with the opposite sex. I observed the love-connections occurring in those days with a detached eye, without developing any personal desire.

Perhaps Wu's arranged marriage had been even more unreasonable than mine, for the conflicts engendered in him were much greater. He was more shocked by the aforementioned quick-fire, sometimes poorly balanced, partnerships, so he often raised them in discussions, good for a laugh; revealing a deep sense of unease.

Surveying Aba Tibetan Qiang Autonomous Prefecture

By midwinter, in the twelfth lunar month of 1952, Wu and I set off for the grasslands with two doctors from the central health team. Two Tibetan men serving as guides drove before them a herd of yaks and invited each of us to mount a yak. Other yaks carried the doctors' medicine boxes, but the Tibetans themselves rode horses and shouted instructions to the yaks at the top of their voices. We slowly made progress in the right direction.

Eventually, we came to the source of the River Min, at Huangsheng Pass. Historically, this was where government troops had been stationed, to guard against attack on Songpan by Tibetans from the grasslands.

After Huangsheng Pass, we came to wide open meadows, where swamps had already frozen over. The Tibetan guides directed the yaks in a straight line and that day we travelled 25 or 30 kilometres, before erecting tents in which to rest. At daybreak the next morning, we drank tea and ate breakfast before setting off again, observing no sign of human habitation or of herdsmen the whole way. After five days, we finally arrived at our intended destination: Zhongaba, also known as Aba, where the new People's Government had established a working base.

In 1952/53, Aba was temporarily governed by a task force of the new government. Our research was overseen by the task force and we met with its leader practically every day.

That leader wore a thick pair of glasses and spoke with a thick accent. The first thing he said to us was, "There are often air-drops by night and many enemy agents have been airdropped here. You should take care." His primary objective was to join forces with the local Tibetan leader Huaergongchenglie. Since he was so focused on this central mission, he didn't have much interest in anthropological research. We asked if we could go among the tribes to investigate, but he replied that although Aba was more than half-liberated, without Huaergongchenglie's guarantee of safety, that would be too risky.

Improving health services was undoubtedly the best way to help Chinese leaders have a positive point of contact with local Tibetans. In the autumn of 1952, the Central Health Department had sent a group of 60 or 70 to the grasslands, mostly people who had just graduated from medical college, highly skilled and themselves in robust health, and Wu and I went along to join them.

We met them first in Aba and lived with them for about half a year. Wherever they stayed, they set up an outpatient service, treating people free of charge, without exception. Every day, there was an endless stream of Tibetans coming for treatment, mostly women, with more than half suffering from sexually transmitted diseases. We were told that Buddhist monks also had such diseases, but usually didn't come for treatment. The second major source of illness was the digestive system.

Sexually transmitted diseases were caused by sleeping around. In the course of investigation, I discovered that a few households were openly practising a system of one wife to several husbands. If the eldest brother in a family took a wife, she would nominally be his wife, but in practice, all the brothers would have sexual relations with her; a system described in earlier literature as 'brothers sharing a wife'.

According to local Han people, as the curtain of darkness fell, friends who stayed in Tibetans' homes were often able to have sex with the woman of the house. Although the husband knew what was happening, he pretended that he didn't, and was unlikely to try and prevent it. Supposedly, this was carried out in secret; earlier literature had referred to this as 'entertaining guests' or 'friends sharing a wife'.

Although such sleeping around was common for those living near the monasteries, others 'from outside' usually turned a blind eye. 'Good people' never went to 'disturb the happy couples'. Moreover, there was usually no interest in discussing such issues, but they were treated as confidential.

Huaergongchenglie, or Hua for short, was the grasslands' highest local official. His Tibetan title, Jiaerwo, meant 'king' and Tibetan people treated him just like a king. They were sometimes oblivious to the fact that there were even greater officials ruling the whole country, and even less aware of national issues.

The 'king' lived splendidly in a spacious, bright and clean, three-storey home, with glass windows, and Tibetan rugs spread over the floors. He sat on a woven mat to one side of a small table, issuing a steady stream of instructions in Tibetan to officials several feet away. When he noticed Tongsi our interpreter leading us in, he instructed his officials to make way, and proceeded to converse with us in Tibetan.

Hua was under the mistaken impression we were there to invite him to go on a tour somewhere, greeting us with, "I'm not going to Mao County, and I'm not going to Chengdu. Thanks anyway for coming to invite me." He asked when we'd be leaving Aba, or would we be staying after all. When he realised I was a minority person, he stared at me in disbelief, appearing puzzled.

We articulated to Hua the policy of ethnic equality and unity, and expressed the hope that he would support the work of the People's Government. Not only had the government sent people to cure the illnesses suffered by Tibetans, it also wanted to help with poverty relief, to help develop production and to improve the lives of locals. The plan was for Tibetan people to take charge of Tibetan affairs.

Hua said this was all very good, then paused and asked Tongsi, "Is it really true?" Tongsi only explained this to us on the way home, saying that Hua still had major misgivings. Hua was used to dealing with many visitors and did not conceal the fact that he was basically just giving us some 'face', but did not really want to discuss anything substantial. In keeping with etiquette, he agreed to have a photograph taken with Tongsi, Wu and me in front of his official residence.

Later in 1958 when I was being denounced as a 'false expert', Wu who had been with me back then, accused me of displaying a warm and friendly attitude towards this senior public figure, Hua; and ultimately surrendering my dignity as a revolutionary cadre and having a souvenir photograph taken with Hua. That photograph, however, also included Wu himself. Wu only shot that arrow of accusation to manifest his own revolutionary fervour.

During the nearly half-a-year that we worked in Aba, we visited Hua many times and with his consent – a strict requirement – we were able to enter various Tibetan villages and do field survey. Every time we met him, I left with the impression he still had misgivings about life after Liberation, and still felt estranged from the Han people.

Since Tibetan leaders had such misgivings, some always tried to avoid the cadres. The People's Government still strove patiently for unity, assigning special government jobs to such Tibetan leaders.

For example, Hua was appointed vice-chairman of the Sichuan Province Tibetan Autonomous Region (later re-named the Aba Tibetan Autonomous Prefecture). At the time we visited him in winter of 1952/53, he still did not know he was vice-chairman of the 'autonomous region'. He asked me, "Am I vice-chairman? What's a vice-chairman?"

With Hua's permission, we entered the Geerdi monastery district to conduct investigations. Beside the monastery were several dozen dilapidated cowhide tents, one tent per household. We only observed women and children, no men; each clad only in one tattered sheepskin garment. Inside each tent was a smoky cow-manure fire, while outside were scattered wooden casks containing water or dried cow-manure, making the place look a shambles. Outside some of the tents there was also an emaciated Tibetan dog tied to a wooden stake, barking madly. Apart from these basic things, there was almost nothing.

We asked if we could enter one of the tents to observe and interview, but our interpreter Tongsi advised otherwise, "There is nothing more to see. If you go in, you can't stand up [it was too low], and you can't sit down [it was too small]." We just had to drop it.

The people were abysmally poor. They supplied cow-manure to the nearby temple, cleared the snow and carried water in there. As reward, they inherited any leftover noodle soup from the Buddhist monks and lamas. They were 80% women and children; not beggars, for they supplied the temple with cow-manure and water.

Tongsi told me that most of the couples in the tents were not husband and wife. After collecting cow-manure together during the day, they simply slept together in the evening. On subsequent days, a man was likely to collect cow-manure with another woman, drink milk tea and eat *zanba* [tsamba, a basic Tibetan dish consisting of ground roasted barley made into a paste with butter, tea and other ingredients, and formed into balls] with her, then sleep in that woman's tent.

Young men fit for heavy labour often left the monastery area to become herdsmen with other clans. In these monastery communities, the fixed population consisted of women and children. I asked Tongsi whether children stayed with their fathers or mothers, to which he replied they didn't have fathers. When I asked their mothers, they merely smiled.

Tongsi explained that Buddhist monks and lamas often came by and, though they didn't talk to the women, they furtively slept around. Most of the children here were fathered by them, and on growing up, most of the boys would enter the temple and become monks themselves. Only the girls stayed with their mothers, some eventually marrying herdsmen of local clans.

Since those living in this monastery area were the poorest of the poor, and most were women and children, unable to grow the food they needed for survival, they were among the first to receive emergency aid from the People's Government.

Once we accompanied local cadres and Tongsi to Geerdi monastery to distribute emergency relief, and Tongsi called everyone together for a meeting; about 100 people in all, including children. We had planned to distribute assistance according to household, but at registration, it was extremely difficult to ascertain the members of a given household, and in the end, we simply used tents as the main unit for relief.

Each tent was given 25 kilogrammes of emergency grain, two-and-a-half kilogrammes of Tibetan tea, and some money (about the equivalent of 100 *yuan* today). Adults and children alike were delighted, holding up their thumbs in approval, saying "Thank you" (in Tibetan) with great appreciation. But this drop in the ocean was only able to satisfy their needs for one or two months of life, and they still had to ask at the monastery for any scraps of leftover food.

We reached the Aba grasslands in the winter of 1952/53, when they had not long been liberated. Defeated remnants of the Nationalist Party and some special agents, who had been airdropped in, were hiding among the minority people. Local minority leaders loved lightweight portable automatic carbine rifles and if the Nationalists presented a leader with such a gun, he would guarantee their safety in return.

Such rebels, however, kept a safe distance from the People's Government. We surveyed in Aba for almost six months and were always restricted to central Aba, where Hua lived and where the grasslands' only market was convened.

The leader of a nearby village had a pretty good relationship with us and was able to speak a little Chinese. Once he secretly, without Hua's authorisation, led us to his home and helped us examine the housing situation of his fellow-Tibetans. He also allowed me to draw a plan of the layout of his house, though he was perplexed, asking repeatedly, "What's the use of drawing this?"

After repeated requests from our working group, the central authorities finally agreed for us to go and visit Chali monastery of the Anqu tribe. The monastery manager let us stay for two days in the bright, clean room where the Living Buddhas [lamas from the 17th century] had stayed.

We were treated to *zanba* and butter, but our interpreter Tongsi was not there, so because of the language barrier we were unable to carry out much real work. We were, however, able to view various halls and sacred writings in the temple, to see where the lamas now lived and to enjoy the surrounding scenery.

Nationalist Party fugitives wore Tibetan clothing. Some could even speak Tibetan and slung guns around their shoulders as they rode on horseback. We were very different. One glance would reveal that we were cadres from the People's Government. In this environment, with gunshots from time to time in the distance, it all felt rather unsafe.

Each cadre was issued with his or her own pistol. Only the health staff and I were without one. Local people often mistakenly assumed I was a doctor and welcomed me with a broad smile. When I went on survey with gun-carrying colleagues, I just had to tighten my belt and be prepared for the worst, not knowing at what instant I might find myself in the after-world.

One mid-day, Wu and I were on the road back to our living quarters when someone on the mountain opened fire and shot twice at us. Thank goodness, neither of us was hit and we reached home safely. A few days later, a young student who had just begun working was shot dead by a hidden gunman on the way back from Chali monastery to Aba.

In spring 1953, just as the PLA was preparing to take control of the grasslands, Wu and I had to go to the Ngawa Tibetan area. After a dinner of *zanba* and butter, we spread felt mats on the grass, with leather coats as blankets and saddles as pillows.

In the middle of the night, we heard horses' galloping and two men alighting. A hand reached down to grasp the leather jacket covering me, but whoever it was released his grasp, mounted his horse and left. I had been feigning sleep and felt terrified, but didn't dare make a sound. Although Wu had a gun, he also didn't dare to move, and our Tibetan companion was also silent. When in the morning we asked who had passed by, our guide just shook his head and said he didn't know.

"That was a close call," Wu remarked. Local people later said that the 'uninvited guests' had been robbers. Perhaps because they had observed our Tibetan guide, they had chosen not to kill us. The People's Government called such people bandits, not simply robbers.

Tibetans of County Zoige

When Wu and I arrived in Zoige in late spring of 1953, there was still ice and snow on the ground, and it was freezing because of the high altitude. Although we wore leather overcoats, fox-skin caps and long tube-shaped leather boots, they seemed powerless to protect against the cold. There were 12 Tibetan tribes in Zoige, with plenty of pasture, and all lived in cowhide tents. There was not a house to be seen.

The western Sichuan survey team followed the PLA from County Songpan into Zoige. When we arrived to join them from Aba, and they saw I wasn't carrying a gun, they were astonished, saying there had been many airdrops and armed Nationalists had scattered in all directions.

There was continued alienation between Tibetans and Han. If we encountered enemy forces, we might simply have to fight, and even female comrades had been issued with firearms. It was simply too dangerous without a gun. With such alarming warnings, they issued me with a multi-firing revolver. Day and night, I kept it on me; but from beginning to end, I never fired a shot. No one ever taught me how to use the gun, nor did I ever experiment. So, I never found out whether it was good or bad, or whether it could even shoot. There were just two reasons for carrying it: it helped embolden me and it served to scare others.

The central party had attached great importance to the liberation of the grasslands. They had been preparing for a great battle, but made progress with lightning speed, for there was no resistance.

It was said that when the cavalry had first crossed the Tangke-tribes border, Tibetans in distant circles of tents had fled. They scattered frantically across the grasslands, some riding horses or cows, others running or walking. The cavalry regarded them as 'bandits' and charged, indiscriminately brandishing sabres, and ruthlessly slashing people down. Not a single shot was fired. Later, this was referred to as the 'Tangke military campaign'.

There had been about 300 households of herdsmen in Tangke, with around 1,000 people. After the Tangke massacre, we visited a ring of tents there and asked how many people were left in the tribe, but most just shook their heads in silence. Only one old herdsman said under his breath, "Many were killed. There used to be more than 60 people in our circle of tents; now only 30 or so remain." Afterwards, the population grew quickly and the 12 tribes in Zoige became the core population of County Zoige; around 30,000 in 1958.

The clean-up operation in Sichuan and Gansu Provinces had originally been assigned to foot soldiers but was later passed on to cavalry. In rare clashes, fighting was intense, involving carbine rifles and submachine guns, and some women who had been airdropped into the regions.

Army officers from Gansu were stationed beside the Yellow River, where soldiers often fished for carp. One day, the commanding officer cordially invited Wu and me to his tent for a fishmeal. As we were eating, a soldier rushed in, saluted, and said, "An important matter to report."

The officer went outside to receive the report, and returned beaming, announcing, "Ma Liang has been captured alive!"

Wu and I rose and asked if we could go and see, but he replied, "You can't see him now; he's being interrogated. I'll let you see him later." Ma Liang was a Nationalist commander from Qinghai Province, who had fled to the grasslands of Zoige after the liberation of Qinghai. He was the 'bandit leader', the Nationalist officer of highest military rank in the region. Upon his arrest, the military operation in Zoige was basically over. Subsequent work would consist of mobilising the masses to expose leaders and religious figures among Tibetans who had participated in armed rebellion.

In June, winter vanished and comrades in the survey team replaced their leather coats with cotton uniforms. County Zoige welcomed its first *post-liberation* migrating warblers. The Aba grasslands had been liberated!

At this time, Wu and I received orders to return to the Institute in Chengdu. We arrived at Namo Temple from the grasslands and stayed two or three days, after which soldiers arranged to drive us on in one of their military vehicles. On the morning we boarded their truck, we discovered a short man tied up there, wearing a traditional black jacket. Soldiers were standing on either side, with rifles at the ready. A soldier with a pistol around his waist told me quietly, "That man in your truck is Ma Liang."

We felt nervous and awkward. We each sat on our rucksack, as usual, but didn't dare to converse. After Ma Liang had been arrested, we'd asked to see him, but now that we could see him close up, we didn't want to look twice. After a few hours' drive, we arrived at Xiahe and disembarked, but the truck escorted Ma Liang on to Lanzhou.

We stayed two days in Xiahe, and on the third day took a public bus to Lanzhou. We stayed a night in Linxia and after dinner, Wu and I strolled around. The Han lived inside the town and the Hui outside.

Han people in Linxia told us that before Liberation, the city gate had normally been locked and there had been no dealings between Han and Hui, only armed confrontations. In winter 1949, after the PLA arrived, the city gates were opened wide. The new nationality policy was publicised and disputes were mediated. A general meeting for the cooperation of nationalities was convened and after that, people dared to venture across borders to talk to each other. Before long, the Linxia Hui Autonomous Prefecture was established in Gansu, with Hui and Han cadres working together. A new atmosphere of cooperation emerged.

A car set off from Linxia and took us to Lanzhou before mid-day. We rested for two days, before taking a bus towards northern Sichuan. The weather became warmer and the pile of cast-off clothes grew higher. It was midsummer when we reached Chengdu, and it felt unbearably hot.

Just after we returned from the grasslands, a Minority Research Unit office was established. Two experts in Tibetan and Yi cultures respectively, Yu and Chen, had transferred from Western China University, and they shared the office with Wu and me.

The former director of Anthropology in Beijing's Qinghua University, Wu Zelin, was in the office next to ours. He had just been transferred and had presented many minority cultural relics as gifts to the Southwest Institute. He was the most senior expert in the Unit, specialising in minorities of Guizhou Province. He became Director of the Cultural Artefacts team, responsible for exhibitions, with the goal of creating a museum.

Wu Zelin often dropped by our office, providing a good opportunity for us to ask his guidance. Our first goal was to write a report on recent investigations in the Tibetan grasslands. I wrote about marriage, social customs and religious beliefs. Wu and Yu, along with Mr Li, asked me first to read aloud relevant writings from earlier scholars. They said we should first see how others understood the Tibetan situation, before putting pen to paper.

We began in the summer of 1953 and by spring the following year, we had finished the report, about 150,000 characters in length. It was printed and distributed as reference material for staff in other departments.

For the first time, leaders in those departments noted my name, for they valued highly such first-hand field-survey materials, helping them understand Tibetan culture. In 1985, the book was published by the Sichuan Social Sciences Press as *Survey of Tibetan Society and History in Aba of Sichuan Province*. It is still the only publication to date specialising in that subject.

Yi of Greater Liangshan

By 1954, vast rural areas in the Greater and Lesser Liangshan regions of Sichuan had not yet been liberated and were operating as before, still as a slave-owning society.

One afternoon in the early summer of 1954, a man in his thirties wearing army uniform arrived at our office. He had come to request specialist research personnel to participate in a survey of the Yi situation in the Greater and Lesser Liangshan regions.

Within a few days, a notice came from the Personnel Department announcing that three people had been selected to participate. Two would go to the Greater Liangshan area, and one to the Lesser Liangshan. A car would be sent to drop Wu and me off at the bus station, where we'd meet the rest of the survey team.

The study was organised and led by the Sichuan military, and there were over 10 people in the group investigating Greater Liangshan. Apart from the two of us from the Institute, dressed in blue, others were all army officers, wearing yellow military uniforms and carrying pistols. University leaders said Liangshan had not yet been liberated, and guns must be carried in self-defence, so they issued Wu and me with pistols, too. Again, we received no training in how to shoot them, and their main function was to frighten others.

We boarded a public vehicle and drove west and then south, eventually reaching Xichang, where we stayed for a week, preparing for survey. We listened to Yi cadres introducing the situation in Greater Liangshan and Xichang, but most of our time was dedicated to examining materials in various scripts, and strolling around the streets observing the customs of local people.

Xichang seemed ancient, and full of Hui and Han people involved in small business. Occasionally, we saw people with their heads wrapped in Buddhist turbans, men with capes (*caerhua*) draped over their shoulders, and women wearing long colourful robes.

Xichang was a strategic entry-point for Greater Liangshan, and thus historically a strategic place for defending the Yi people. Nearby was Lake Qiong, with many houses beside the lake.

Towards the end of the war with the Japanese, there had been a dire shortage of food in Chongqing city. Nationalists prepared to move government from Chongqing to Xichang and to use the Kham Tibetan region in Yunnan as a base for operations to continue the war. Many houses were built in Xichang, but just as they were completed, the War of Resistance was won. Afterwards, officials from Western Kham Province lived there, setting up a technical college for professional training, the only such college in the whole province.

There were all kinds of fish in the lake, and boats were equipped not only for catching but also for cooking the fish. Tourists rode in the boats and swam in the lake, while fishermen cooked the fish, preparing delicious fare. Unfortunately, there were not many tourists at the time.

Each year in summer and autumn, students from the nearby technical college would swim in the lake. Yi people sometimes hid in the mountains looking for an opportunity to capture the swimmers and enslave them.

Once before Liberation, a female student was captured and taken to Liangshan, where she was sold and subsequently passed through many hands and places. After Liberation when she encountered some Han people, she merely wept uncontrollably. When asked where she was from and where she had been captured, she replied, "The technical college at Lake Qiong."

We walked from Xichang to Zhaojue, a town created for the People's Government of the Greater Liangshan autonomous region. Apart from government offices, there were small shops on both sides of the main street. Every day, Yi people went there to shop, sell or stroll. You could often see black-cloaked people leaning against the walls, obviously drunk, clutching nearly empty bottles. Just before dusk, men would buy another bottle for the road, drinking as they walked. Drunkenness seemed to be the panacea for life's multitudinous problems. Prostrate figures of inebriated men littered the roadside.

Six of us walked northwards until we arrived at Yuexi county town and stayed several days there. Escorted by a platoon of PLA soldiers, we descended from Yuexi to Puxiong, observing Han villages along the road with houses all built in the same style. I took some photographs along the way. Later, when I mentioned the Yi people of Puxiong to some long-term Han residents of Yuexi, their complexion changed!

Before Liberation, these Han people had been terrorised by Yi raiders, especially at night. Small groups of Yi men with rifles would enter the town, grabbing anyone who happened to be around. Sometimes they would burst through the door of a house and kidnap the inhabitants, except for the old, sick and infirm.

If local people caught sight of Yi marauders, they'd raise the alarm, "The slave-snatchers are here!" The raiders would tie the hands of their captives together, slinging ropes around the captives' necks. One person clutching the neck ropes would lead the way, while another with a rifle escorted from behind. Anyone unwilling to walk was forced to run, or risk being shot.

After a while, soldiers slept inside the town walls, so Yi people snatched slaves *outside* the town, and there was hardly a household outside that hadn't been plundered. Many houses there were empty. No one waited for night to fall before stopping work and making their way home. They lived on the upper storey of two-storey buildings and pulled the ladders up behind them.

By day, soldiers patrolled the town, arresting Yi men at will and demanding ransoms from their relatives. The Yi were terrified of this, saying that some whose family failed to pay simply died in prison. They blamed the soldiers and the Han people of Yuexi, saying, "They tar us all with the same brush and treat us as though we were all bandits." Estrangement developed into outright hostility, so that encounters between Han and Yi often led to fighting and shooting. The centre of Yuexi became a battle zone.

Yi of Puxiong

When we entered Puxiong, a People's Government had already been established there. There was a dirt road and on either side were government buildings and small shops, which had been built within the previous two years. Formerly, the road had been part of the arable land farmed by Yi people.

Otherwise, the region was full of Yi villages. The famous Ahou household was on the opposite bank of the river, looking across at the government buildings. Government staff first had to gain permission of the leader of the Ahou household for work or travel in the surrounding countryside.

We visited the Ahou home, a long line of wooden houses, with two perpendicular lines of low wooden houses on either side, like the courtyard (*hutong*) houses in the north of China. In the biggest residence, we were received by the lady of the house and some young people. The owner, they said, had gone to the fields; but in reality, he was exercising his prerogative and simply declining to see us. Our plans to engender more unity came to nothing. No grass-roots political system had yet been established, so Puxiong had not really been liberated.

One day, we went for a walk and noticed some Yi people gathered about a kilometre away from the government buildings, some crouching, some standing and some with rifles slung around their shoulders. On approaching, we discovered the two crouching men had hands tied behind their backs, and one had an iron ring around his neck. A man with a gun was standing over them, holding their ropes in his spare hand, while others whispered to each other. Our approach caused uncertainty, but we did nothing to disturb the assembly.

We had no interpreter, so we could not communicate. On inquiring later, we ascertained that the two men had indeed been 'slaves' at auction.

Anyone who needed a slave would first have to examine those for sale and then negotiate a price. The highest price was for men aged between twenty and thirty, approximately equivalent to the price of four cows. People from far away were more expensive than those from nearby, although recently captured slaves were cheaper. Apart from age and sex, the price depended on how difficult it might be for a particular slave to run away.

People captured by the Black Yi, whatever their nationality, had to put on the tattered clothes of slaves. Their hair would be cut in the Buddhist style, leaving a square portion on the front of the head, and a flax cloak would be draped over their shoulders. Every day, they'd be fed with boiled potatoes and led to manual labour by more experienced slaves.

The Black Yi captured and dealt in slaves. There were three classes of Black Yi in the Greater and Lesser Liangshan regions. In their own language, they called the first of these the 'Black Community' or 'Black Bones', reflecting the idea that their bones were good and their parentage pure. Their skin colour was the darkest and they were relatively tall. These were the tough slave-owners.

Beneath these in status were people with relatively paler skin colour, of mixed Yi-Han or other parentage. In Mandarin, these were called the 'White Yi' or 'White Bones'. Their bones were regarded as inferior, rendering them physically weaker. The White Yi were the ordinary people, most prolific.

Slaves themselves were the third class, divided into those who were married and those who were single.

The Yi married strictly within social class. If a Black Bones man were to marry a White Yi woman, he would be expelled from his clan and lose the nobility associated with Black Bones. People known as the Yellow Yi, descendants of Black Bones who had broken the marriage taboos, lived in County Leibo of Lesser Liangshan.

The Black Bones did not do manual labour, but passed their days sunbathing, grooming their beards, searching for lice, practising with guns, fighting enemies and catching slaves. They were proud and arrogant, supreme in their opinions. They would fight over trifling matters, with the result that one generation after another spent its days intent on revenge.

After Liberation, the Black Bones society discontinued. Very few people retained skin colour as dark as the Black Bones Yi.

Han people from Puxiong told us that in 1943 an American plane had been performing a mission in the Allied cause one night when it lost direction and dropped, with a loud explosion, to paddy fields in the Puxiong valley. Black Yi men with rifles were first to the scene, eager to plunder any spoils.

Two uniformed Americans emerged from the wreckage. Though their hands were full of gestures, no one understood them. One Black Bones youth forced his way into the wreckage, followed by other Black Bones and White Yi. A scramble for booty ensued. By daybreak, people were still trying to salvage whatever they could.

The Americans were led away by gun-wielding Black Bones', who announced, "We've got two strong slaves. We'll not sell them for less than 500 silver coins each!" The Americans were forced to discard their clothes in exchange for the standard slave rags, had sackcloth draped over their shoulders, and hair cut in the slave-standard way. Each day they were fed boiled potatoes and forced to live an inhumane existence.

Two Han men related the story with some mirth, but I felt sympathy for the two young men who had met with such injustice while opposing fascism.

After the plane crashed, Nationalists sent out search parties, but the Yi in Puxiong imposed a strict blackout on news. Only after the army moved in was the wreckage discovered, whereupon a ransom was paid for the two American soldiers. Han men conveyed them by sedan chair back to Yuexi county town.

The Black Yi regarded youth as a form of wealth and any youths from outside their community were vulnerable to being seized. Escaped slaves were considered fair game. Outsiders didn't usually dare to enter the Liangshan region. Previous research was scarce and generally confined to the borders.

Anyone who went in had to ask a clan head for protection, and to pay with silver coins. As they moved on, they would have to pay the next clan head, and so on. A trip right through the Greater Liangshan area may have needed 10 or more such agreements.

The Black Yi were sometimes fickle. Having received the protection money some secretly colluded with other clans, and arranged for travellers to be captured by those clans. So some travellers were after all reduced to the status of slaves. Such double-dealing was rightly feared.

We ourselves entered Puxiong under armed escort, causing Black Bones and White Yi alike to vanish. A Han cadre working in the area said to me, half-jokingly, "These days, the Black Bones only rarely come to buy anything; they are afraid of so many soldiers, so they are all in hiding. But they are so tempted, they can't get to sleep at night. Seeing the young soldiers, they yearn to take them as slaves and plunder their guns." He repeatedly warned us not to go out alone and always to be on the alert.

Yi of Tianba and Indirect Survey of Xialuo

After we had finished work in Puxiong, we transferred to Tianba in County Yuexi, to investigate the Yi hereditary leaders and governance there.

We stayed in the public guesthouses, but since the buildings were small, we split up to live in three different places. The ordinary soldiers in our escort lived in one place, a few officers lived in another place and I lived in a room upstairs on my own. It had a bed and a table and privacy, but lots of noise came up from the ground floor, with little or no soundproofing.

Since we had many meetings, however, I didn't spend much time upstairs. According to Yi custom, everyone was drinking at the meetings. Alcohol substituted for tea and we drank and discussed simultaneously. After two gulps, it was easier to converse.

Since leaving home in 1950, I had not had much acquaintance with alcohol, but in Tianba I never gave it a moment's thought. The working style there meant that I spent most of that month under the influence, apart from when I was in bed at night.

Our work was multi-faceted and I was responsible for surveying the social situation; for example, social classes, relationships between social classes, vendettas, relationships between nationalities and social customs.

Our target destination, Xialuo, was in a most inaccessible region, at the boundary of the Greater and Lesser Liangshan areas. Slaves were sold into the region as if they were entering their coffins, without any hope of emerging again. Other Yi people rarely entered Xialuo unless they had Black Yi relatives, and Han people were even less likely to be there. The name Xialuo, however, was known by all – probably because of its mystery and terror.

We also felt fearful of Xialuo because of the Black Yi there. But when you added to the Black Yi the bandit hegemony, land-reform fugitives, scattered Nationalist survivors and assorted rogues who had fled there, our survey group was even more interested in the region.

While we already had a good understanding of some other areas, Xialuo was a completely blank space. It could not even be found on any map, but Yi people had told us it was in a fertile river valley, with a population of several tens of thousands. Our leader was always dreaming of going to Xialuo, and would often ask for information about it, but usually ended up empty-handed.

One day, our leader asked me what I thought about taking a team into Xialuo. It would probably be very risky, for we had no contacts there. I replied that it was probably worth it, but he should decide who should go. He smiled and asked, "I'll send a Black Yi guide with you, who can serve as your guarantor. Is that okay with you?"

Without a second thought, I agreed and went back to write a research plan: 'Keys to understanding the Xialuo situation'. I pondered the fact that 'nine out of every 10 don't return', but I was youthful and naïve and didn't feel afraid, waiting with anticipation for the day of departure. Two days later, however, our leader notified me that superiors had not approved the plan, but preferred us to conduct *indirect* study from Tianba.

One afternoon, the leader brought a Black Yi woman in her early 20s to see me. She had studied in the cadre training class in Xichang, and had relatives in Xialuo. She'd even been to Xialuo two or three times in her early teens, as well as having lived there for over a month in 1950, the year the region was liberated.

I asked her all about the people of Xialuo. What clans were there, and whose influence was greatest among the Black Yi leaders? What were relationships like between the leaders? What was their attitude towards Han people? To what extent would they oppose, resist, evade or welcome government leaders? Were there still military arms among the Black Yi? She was unable to answer such questions. Instead, she just talked about seizing slaves, selling slaves, the labour done by slaves, and the other customs of local people. She couldn't be too specific about the geography either. In short, her knowledge was not what was required.

So, I prepared several tables for surveying the clans and passed mimeographed copies to her, explaining how to fill in each section. She set off towards Xialuo in Black Yi clothing, with the tables tucked inside her long skirt (in a pouch specially sewn for the purpose). Yi people did not suspect that a woman could do anything subversive. You could say they rather respected women, not permitting them to do or say anything construed as 'bad'. Our 'special agent' carried the tables confidently, and reassured me she'd be back in five or six days.

Ten days later, she returned, smiling contentedly as she handed over a belt full of tables. There was hardly any information missing, and after it was all sorted, it gave a rough understanding of Xialuo and its population, its clan leaders, the clans' distribution and their relative strengths.

There were hardly any Han people there, apart from slaves and people who had fled and hidden there. Most slaves had been captured from the Han district of Lesser Liangshan. It was curious that there seemed to be no feuding among the clans in Xialuo. Elsewhere in the Greater and Lesser Liangshan areas, inter-clan feuding was widespread.

Having understood all this, our small research group withdrew from Tianba and returned to Zhaojue.

Back the Way We Came

After we returned to the government headquarters at Zhaojue, we often went to the prefectural public security bureau [police station] to borrow books and other reading materials about minorities, or to ask for advice, and we discovered a lot in this way.

During the time there, I stumbled across a series about *The Yi Nationality Situation* written by hand, altogether 10 volumes. Authors' names were not given and there was no Introduction. The series content, however, was thorough, discussing the situation from before 221 BC to 1949; including population, social class, exploitation and oppression, nationality relationships and social customs.

It was probably July 1954 when we retreated from Greater Liangshan to the military district of Chengdu. The survey group disbanded, leaving Wu and me to sort out materials we had collected about social life. Downstairs in our living quarters were a few officers in their 50s and 60s, living with their young wives. Although they wore the usual yellow uniform, they were not quite the same as other officers. They stayed at home every day with their wives, rarely attended meetings and never sat down to write.

People said they had been senior officers in the Nationalist army; some had been captured, while others had rebelled, and now all had been entrusted with positions as high-ranking officers. Their 'young wives' were actually their concubines.

When I heard about their Nationalist past, I was apprehensive. Were they not possibly wondering day and night when the opportunity might arise for them to return and serve the Nationalist cause?

Around this time, Wu was afflicted by terrible toothache, making those few days more monotonous than usual for me, and magnifying feelings of loneliness.

After about a month, when the Yi-survey write-up was finished, we were instructed to return to the Institute. Our study of the Yi people of Greater Liangshan had lasted more than three months. The work had been difficult, but there was no great reward, just some satisfaction from summarising our findings.

When the new term began on 1st September 1954, Mr Wu Zelin invited me to help at the Nationality Cultural Artefacts room, which had two exhibitions. One highlighted the development of minorities after Liberation, while the other focused on the material culture, especially clothing and jewellery, of southwest minorities (particularly the Miao, Bouyei and Dong of Guizhou).

Mr Wu outlined my job, how I should write captions for each individual item, choose photographs for the exhibitions, commission clay figures to be modelled and draft maps featuring nationality autonomous regions. I spent more than one semester doing this work.

Chapter 12
Accelerating into the Sun
(Dai and Aini Nationalities, 1955-56)

On the Road to Yunnan

According to informal surveys, Yunnan Province had 260 different nationalities at the time of Liberation, but in reality, there were not so many. In 1952, nationwide survey work to distinguish different nationalities was launched, and by 1954, that work was basically finished. In order to understand and build on that survey data, our Research Institute sent a survey team to Yunnan Province, under the leadership of Mr Li Zhichun.

In March 1955, Li set off with me and four other researchers for Kunming, via Guiyang in Guizhou. The greatest impression I retain from that bus journey was the magnificent sight of Huangguoshu Waterfall, guarded by a wilderness of assorted trees and undergrowth on either side. We couldn't find the right road for approaching the scenic area, so ended up standing at the roadside and admiring from a distance. Even from there, you could hear the powerful rumble of cascading water.

At Zhenning county town, we were met by many girls holding up baskets of boiled eggs. There were said to be many hens there, so eggs were cheap: about 50 boiled eggs for one *yuan*. One *yuan* was also enough to buy a large cockerel.

I retain two other memories from that journey, the first of a road called the '72 bends': from the bottom of the mountain, you had to negotiate 72 bends before you reached the top. Our vehicle crawled up at snail's speed, tackling one bend after another. We heard the rumble of vehicles up ahead, some of which had to stop to be fixed. Other vehicles lay abandoned at the side of the road, having been involved in accidents. The Tang dynasty poet Liu Yuxi (772–842 AD) came to mind: 'The capsized ship lists over the shore on 1,000 journeys; the diseased tree anticipates 10,000 years of spring'.

We sat without a word, preoccupied with the thrilling motion picture outside, enveloped in the booming, terrifying atmosphere created by the vehicle. No one knew how much further we had to climb and no one dared to ask. Finally, the driver exclaimed, "We've passed the gates of hell!" The bus began to coast downhill. We had successfully scaled the 72 bends and it felt as if we'd survived some great calamity.

No one who travelled the road failed to gasp at the difficulty of the drive. No wonder the driver compared it to the gates of hell. The frightening atmosphere

157

and heavy blackness of the mountains and clouds left their mark. Throughout the journey, I felt gloomy and depressed, like the weather.

As the bus began to accelerate downhill, however, we caught a glimpse of the red soil of mountain slopes ahead, with short bushes blooming with safflowers. The sky became cloudless and sunny, we seemed about to enter a beautiful new world, and glum silence was replaced by happy chat. Someone announced, "That's the border of Yunnan, we're about to enter Yunnan!" The geography and climate seemed to change, as if Yunnan and Guizhou were two different worlds. That impression was profound and abides with me today as if it were yesterday.

Kunming

We were hosted by the Yunnan Provincial Nationality Affairs Commission, which arranged for us to stay in the Lu Han mansion beside Green Lake. Before Liberation, Lu Han had been the governor of Yunnan, and he built two mansions beside the lake. One was massive, capable of accommodating up to 1,000 people. The other was relatively small, with only two storeys, but still big enough to accommodate several dozen people. After Liberation, both buildings were passed on to the Commission to be used as guesthouses.

We stayed in the two-storey mansion, where all kinds of flowers, plants and trees flourished in the courtyard. The door and windows faced southeast, with a view of the lovely Green Lake. Sunshine was abundant, and the air was fresh and cool. We stayed there when we first arrived in Kunming and returned there after trips to the borders of Yunnan, altogether a month or more.

My time in the guesthouse made me realise the high priority Yunnan authorities placed on nationality work. A stay in the Lu Han mansion made us minority people feel the difference between pre- and post-Liberation. Formerly, most of us would not even have dared to peek into the beautiful mansion grounds. How could anyone not be grateful for this sea-change?

The guesthouse provided three sumptuous meals a day, as if serving honoured guests. Most minority people had never enjoyed such hospitality. The young guesthouse staff served with a smile, trying their best to satisfy. They accompanied guests for a stroll or for sightseeing; introducing, chatting and laughing as they went, as if entertaining their own family members.

During speeches, leaders addressed us politely as 'brotherly nationalities'. The cordial, kind and selfless help of cadres made us feel indeed that we were all members of the same clan.

The Commission appointed a Bai cadre to help us, a graduate of nationality studies at Yunnan University. He explained how Yunnan was differentiating nationalities according to Joseph Stalin's four theories of nationality.

The Place Where I First Ate Bananas

Our main job in Kunming was to examine materials relating to differentiation of Yunnan nationalities. Each nationality had one report, written according to

Stalin's four theories referred to above. Each report articulated the opinions of ordinary people and analysed from a historical perspective, in the end postulating how the nationality should be regarded.

We spent a couple of weeks reading these reports. Afterwards, we were most interested in the Dai people and prepared plans to survey the Dai region. The Commission approved, emphasising that the central features of border work were to improve nationality cooperation and to facilitate development. We could only research the nationality situation through attending to these main emphases. It was inappropriate to conduct any other investigations, for they wanted to avoid, at all costs, raising doubts or suspicions among the minority people.

So we made plans for about a month of survey, dividing into two small groups. Mr Li, two others and I were to go to the Xishuangbanna Dai Autonomous Prefecture in southern Yunnan, while the other group went to Dehong in western Yunnan.

It was probably in April that four of us took a bus south. Our first stop was at an office in Pu'er Prefecture. We hadn't anticipated that an alumnus of the Southwest Institute would be in charge of the office's Nationalities Department. She had been born into the Dao family, hereditary leaders among the Dai, and was kind and helpful, as if she were hosting old friends. After arranging our accommodation, she supplied many resources about the local minority situation, and came to see us every day, to offer whatever help we needed. Work went smoothly and pleasantly.

Dao had been divorced before arriving to study at the Southwest Institute, and when she saw us, she was still single. She said that if she married a Han husband, he would disregard her opinions, and she couldn't put up with that. A Dai man would listen to her, but suitable men had already long since married. She had no choice but to carry on alone.

She asked about one of our former teachers, who had also been born into a hereditary leader's family. She had earlier been interested in him, though she hadn't dared to say so, instead sinking secretly into the river of love, not expecting then that she would *still* be thinking about him now. We informed her that he had married and had a child. She blushed ever so slightly and fell silent, tears welling up involuntarily. She continued to visit us daily, though she wasn't as cheerful and chatty as she had been before.

May in Pu'er was scorching hot. In the early mornings, ponds in surrounding fields and valleys were enveloped in mist, which gradually dissipated, until by around 10 am you could see clearly. Earlier researchers had referred to this as malaria mist, for it was said to induce malaria and other diseases.

We were told that one summer about eight years before Liberation, malaria had been rife in the town of Simao, not far from Pu'er. Several dozen people died each day for a couple of weeks – at its worst, up to 100 people a day. On the first few days, people carried dead bodies outside the city, dug holes and buried them, but later the bodies were left on beds at home. There had been an overwhelming stench.

During the war against Japan, an airport had been built in Simao and it used to be prosperous. Since the malaria attack, however, few people had moved into the region and the airport had been quiet.

From the moment we reached Pu'er, I lost all appetite for rice or fried food, and only wanted to eat bananas. I'd never tasted them before; they seemed so sweet and delicious! For about 10 days, they were the main ingredient of my diet, for I could no longer stomach a cooked meal, though during this time my physical strength and spirit didn't waver.

On the streets of Pu'er, we often encountered Dai men wearing clothes indistinguishable from other minority men, such as Hani or Yi, but the skirts worn by Dai women were unique, so you could identify a Dai woman without hesitation. Those Dai were mostly able to speak Mandarin, more Sinicized than the Dai in Xishuangbanna.

Survey Difficulties in Jinghong

From Pu'er, it took more than a day to drive to Jinghong, the seat of government for Xishuangbanna Prefecture. Jinghong was in a great plain beside the River Lancang, with banana, coconut and tropical broad-leafed trees everywhere. In the early mornings, you couldn't see far, for it was misty.

At the centre of the plain was a mud road, with a few new, low buildings on either side: wooden houses, wooden sheds and straw dwellings. These were the shops and homes of Han people, but contrary to expectations, we didn't see any Dai homes. Apart from some Dai cadres, the people there were outsiders, mostly from Yunnan or Sichuan Province. We stayed in single-storey government buildings, with earth floors, wooden beds and small wooden tables and stools.

There was not much breeze, and windows and doors were left wide open day and night. The cadres there assured us, "Don't worry. There are no thieves here."

One morning, one of the Han prefectural leaders granted us audience, listening while Mr Li outlined our proposed survey plans, before replying briefly. His main concern was that we should pay attention to nationality policy; stressing that nationality unity was the primary goal and prerequisite of any and all work.

He was anxious too that we should not cross national boundaries. If you weren't careful and strayed a few steps across the border, someone might take a photograph and then protest to the Ministry for Foreign Affairs.

As to how we should conduct our survey into minority lives and production, he gave us no specific guidance. We proposed visiting the Dai governor, only to be informed that he had left for a meeting in Beijing. No other Dai cadres were available for interview and we weren't able to get hold of any materials about the local minority situation. In those few days, we just observed the general situation in Jinghong.

We visited other places in the prefecture, but these were much the same. It was difficult to learn much from the Dai people themselves, for they seemed shy of outsiders. Whatever the question, there would be an embarrassed laugh in reply. Then it would seem pointless investigating any further.

160

Before leaving Chengdu, we had made a note of the names of minority students from the Southwest Institute who had returned to Xishuangbanna. They were scattered in different towns and were respected local cadres.

After we arrived in Xishuangbanna, however, hoping to receive their help, we were disappointed. They always seemed to be absent on a trip, or attending a meeting. We only managed to connect with one former student, a woman from Kunming who had recently married a cadre, and was living in Jinghong. When she wasn't at work in the office, she'd be at home, waiting to give birth to a baby. Our team-member Li (not the team-leader) was also from Kunming, and together they had transferred from a university in Kunming to the Southwest Institute. They had formerly been intimately acquainted.

One evening Li went to see her, but he soon returned, remarking to me coolly, "She's married, sitting at home alone, as if she's on the point of giving birth. She doesn't know a thing about the nationality situation here and has nothing to say. I'm sorry I went to see her."

I met many recent settlers in Xishuangbanna who were totally absorbed in their new location. They'd decided to put down roots and set up a family. The climate and lifestyle were comfortable and easy, and they were content. It seemed as though everyone who arrived at this new place to start afresh lost interest in everything outside.

The whole day after 10 am, the main street in Jinghong was extremely quiet and there wasn't a soul in sight. Every morning at 5 am, however, Dai women hurried through the morning mist towards the main street, carrying goods in their arms or on shoulder poles. Some spread out plantain leaves to set up shop on the ground, while others propped up three stones to light a fire, preparing to cook.

At the crack of dawn, the plain woke up with noise and activity, full of young women selling things. Children were left at home in care of the men, so there was no obstruction to hand or foot. Bananas, melons and all kinds of fruit were for sale, along with rice, fish and shrimps.

Rice-noodles were good business, with a continuous stream of customers eating at small wooden tables. Some ate noodles with one hand while drinking a large bowl of rice wine with the other.

It was misty and you couldn't see more than a few feet ahead; you could only hear the din of the women. Around 8 am, people began to disperse, and by 9 am, the plain was quiet again, and the tranquillity of daytime was reinstated. This way of doing business was followed all year around, apart from when it rained.

There were one or two cadres, hygiene-school graduates, in each of the bigger villages on the Jinghong plain. Each carried a medicine box and went from door to door, providing free medical treatment to Dai people.

One day, a Han medical cadre led us into a Dai village to conduct some interviews. Women were collecting water from the river at one end of the village, while others were squatting or standing up in the river, with long cloths wound through their hair. They were steeping their bodies in the water and bathed like this practically every day. When collecting water, you would wash at the same time.

Villagers who lived far from the river would fill buckets with well water and wash directly from the buckets, standing beside the well. Some would be naked from head to toe and there was no shelter, but they weren't afraid of being seen. If men approached, the women would splash them with water to drive them away.

Once as we passed a well in the distance, we saw some naked women having a shower. They noticed us, but calmly continued to pour water over their bodies as though we were not there, then covered up with their aprons and carried water back home on shoulder poles. It seemed strange that I never saw any men, normally at home with the children, bathing in the river.

Carrying a medicine box on her back, Dr Chen led me into that Dai village. She was from Chengdu, had arrived in Jinghong two years before and already spoke Dai fluently. If she hadn't been wearing cadre uniform, you'd have supposed she was Dai. Upon seeing someone, she'd often burst into Dai conversation, usually buoyed by laughter. When she heard I was from Chengdu and heard my Chengdu accent, Chen treated me like an old friend, uninhibited in conversation, and taking it upon herself to serve as my interpreter.

I followed her into a bamboo house, climbing a ladder onto the open veranda. A few young women came to shake her hand, chatting warmly, but leaving me marooned on one side. A man was lying asleep on the bamboo-covered floor, undisturbed by all the commotion.

I asked Dr Chen what they were talking about and she replied that they thought we two were friends and were making fun of us. She had told them I had come to investigate Dai social customs, but they didn't believe her. They were joking non-stop and I had no chance to say anything.

Dr Chen said Dai girls and women were all like this. There would be no way of asking anything serious. So eventually, I tried instead to glean information from her, but wasn't able to extract much. She was more eager to talk about her former classmates, who had also been assigned to the border areas. I asked if she missed home and she replied that earlier she had missed home very much, but she had not been able to go back, and with time, she didn't miss it so much.

Coconut, Banana and Olive Plains

From Jinghong, Mr Li and I rode on a bamboo raft against the flow of the River Lancang to visit people in an olive grove beside the river. We travelled slowly and only arrived in the evening. The settlement could only be reached by water or via a mountain path, so in those days, it had very little contact with the outside. It was occupied exclusively by Dai people.

Just after Liberation, a government office had been established there. Cadres had been assigned to live in a new log house, serving as regional leaders. We stayed in their house for three nights. By day, one of the cadres led us around as if we were tourists.

It was a wonderful location, full of banana trees and coconut groves, heavy with fruit. Bamboo houses seemed so secluded in the coconut groves, yet women and children were coming and going, up and down, constantly calling and laughing in our direction. The cadre said they were welcoming us, inviting us to go and sit in their homes.

Occasionally, pigs turned up beside the houses, chomping bananas. They were fat, with smooth, reddish skin, reared on bananas rather than fodder. By day, they foraged in the open fields and at night were called home to their shelters. In the mornings, they charged out again. After six months, they could be slaughtered for meat.

A young man in bare feet climbed up an 80-foot-tall coconut tree, via branches on the trunk. He picked several coconuts at the top and threw them down to us as presents. At the time, this was the best gift a Dai person could give to outsiders.

The morning mist had not yet dissipated when some Aini [a less-numerous group related to the Hani minority] women descended the mountains, bearing planks on their shoulders, with bags of grain dangling from the ends. The planks were rounded in the middle, shaped like a wooden collar, but otherwise rested on the shoulders. The women were carrying grain to the government office to pay the local grain tax.

They never stopped chewing and occasionally spat out purple juice, which dyed both lips purple. Their teeth were black. I discovered they were chewing betel nuts, a lifelong habit acquired during childhood. The habit resulted in jet-black teeth that could never be brushed clean.

Most Aini people were tenant farmers in the Dai plains, and suffered much hardship. After Liberation, Dai people continued to employ them to carry grain and do manual labour.

My impressions of the region were generally positive: the beautiful banana plantations and tall coconut palms pointing to the skies, the bamboo houses near the coconut trees, the mountain paths plied by people and animals alike, all in the spring climate, with the fresh fragrance of fruit and flowers. Everything seemed so clean, soft and sweet-smelling, serving as a natural balm to busy stressed people, an intoxicating cure. No wonder outsiders who landed up in this remote region forgot about the world outside and surrendered any residual homesickness.

From Fohai to Mount Nannuo

We rode from Jinghong towards Myanmar, travelling west about half a day, until we reached Fohai. After Liberation, this had been established as the government capital for the Xishuangbanna region.

There was one street in the town laid in cobblestones. The small houses on either side were homes to Han people who had recently moved there. They didn't do any farming, and business was not good at first, so I don't know how they survived.

After the war with Japan, when an expeditionary force was fighting on the borders of Myanmar and India, Fohai had been a strategic town on the road to Myanmar. Military equipment was stationed there and it was awash with soldiers and trucks.

Most people in the mountains around Fohai were Aini. Mr Li and I went up to a government compound on Mount Nannuo to find out more about the Aini. All the cadres there were busy, and no one was prepared even to answer our questions, much less accompany us on a village visit.

When you left the compound, you immediately had to go either up or down the mountain. We were not familiar with either the people or the layout of the area and did not know our way to any village. We were just confronted by the hillside, with trees and bamboo everywhere.

The mountain range, with its lingering clouds and mist, was certainly beautiful, casting its spell. We could not see anyone, however, or any movement anywhere. It felt as if we were mysteriously hidden among the mountains, as if we were really just one with nature.

After a night at the compound, Mr Li wanted to return to Fohai. I preferred to go on another five kilometres to a tea plantation and factory on Mount Nannuo, to research a bit more. There were some Han staff at the factory and they would be able to help us.

We could not resolve our disagreement. Mr Li decided to return to Fohai alone, while I went on to Mount Nannuo, also alone. Local cadres supported Mr Li and were weary of my persistence.

I left the compound with Li, before parting ways. He walked down towards Fohai, while I walked up a mountain path, camera slung on my back. Before reaching the factory, I encountered an Aini man, a member of the people's militia, with a rifle on his back. He examined me carefully, alert for any sign of threat. He was able to speak Mandarin, and when he discovered I was going up to the factory, he volunteered to lead the way.

That day he had been hunting, but had been unlucky, and was returning empty-handed. He would usually have been able to catch a few pheasants or other wild birds. On the way, we chanced upon two young Aini women, twirling thread in their fingers as they walked. The militiaman chatted with them. We reached the factory area near nightfall and my guide led me to the workers' accommodation there. After introducing me, he went back home.

The tea factory was in a hollow in the mountain, alongside a Han-Chinese-style house. There was an Aini village on either side of the hollow, about two kilometres away by mountain path. From the factory, you could see smoke spiralling from village chimneys to the sky. The Fohai authorities had sent some cadres to live in the new wooden home next to the factory. After inspecting my letter of introduction, they seemed still to view me with suspicion, but hosted me anyway, coolly and grudgingly.

The next day, the cadres produced some documents for me to peruse, summarising the factory's history. I discovered it had been established before Liberation, but there was no mention of the local minority people. At that time, there were not many factory workers, and most of the tea was exported to Myanmar and India.

The tea had earned a reputation for high quality. After Liberation, Han people from down-river had come to the mountain to develop tea processing, and had employed several dozen workers from outside the area. Aini women plucked the tender green tea leaves one by one and delivered them to the factory. The resulting tea was particularly popular in India; fragrant and tasty.

I toured the tea-growing area with a cadre, and photographed the Aini people plucking leaves. They said something I still remember, "Here we have tea-leaves galore, more than we can pick."

I asked why they didn't roast and sell the tea themselves, and they replied they didn't know how. The tea mountain was 'theirs', and if they could have mastered the technology, picking and processing would have been obvious partners. As the market developed, Aini people would surely have become prosperous, and quickly. What a pity they were not really entrepreneurs, and had simply to continue as tea pickers and farmers.

When I returned to Fohai, I was reunited with Mr Li, three days after we had separated. He asked, with a smile, "Are you back?" Then he announced we were returning to Jinghong the next day and I should prepare to leave. He didn't ask anything about my trip to the factory.

Later I wrote up my impressions, including excerpts from the materials I had read. Mr Li then praised my endeavours and said they had been worth it. My short report was published in the Guangming Daily in Beijing. Much was edited out, but it was the first time anything I'd written had ever made it into a newspaper.

Honghe Hani and Yi Autonomous Prefecture

When we returned to Jinghong, none of the officials there met or debriefed us. The next day, we said goodbye to Xishuangbanna and took a bus to Yuanjiang. Mr Li and I took a little wooden boat from there to Honghe, to research the Hani people of the Honghe Hani and Yi Autonomous Prefecture. [The Hani are unrelated to the majority Han people.] This was to be the last station on our research trip.

We followed the flow of the river, with tall mountains keeping watch on either side. It was early summer and the weather was sultry. That evening, we pulled up on a bank and the two boatmen made a bonfire. From the nearby foliage, they cut some bamboo stems and cut these into sections, slitting along their circumference. They placed rice inside the stems along with fresh water, and used leaves to bind the bamboo tightly together again. Then they threw them into the fire, along with wood and straw.

The boatmen then walked along the riverbank and caught some fish with line and fishhook. They were back within half-an-hour and rescued the bamboo tubes from the bonfire. Splitting them open, they placed some pickled vegetables and red chili pepper on large leaves on the ground, and instructed us to eat up.

The boatmen didn't say much, but answered our questions in the local Mandarin, which was difficult to understand. By the time we finished eating, it was already dark. Our companions sat beside the bonfire, smoking incessantly, with pipes made from bamboo tubes. We finally withdrew, pulled extra clothes over us and slept soundly. It was cooler by night and there were still no night-mosquitoes.

At dawn, the boatmen stirred and went to investigate. Smiling, they returned with several small fish and summoned us to board the boat. At mid-day, Li and I disembarked at the foot of a mountain and set off up the mountain path aiming for the town of Honghe.

It was hard work for Mr Li to get up the mountain. Every now and then, he stopped for a swig of water and a rest. Local people flew past, nimble and sure-footed, in both directions. They cast sympathetic glances as we stopped and started, huffing and puffing; probably amused by our physical ineptitude. We finally reached Honghe not long before sunset.

During the Qing dynasty (1644–1912), a government official was stationed in Honghe along with a troop of soldiers, to govern the region. As a result, Honghe became the first place in the region where Han people really settled. We stayed in the government headquarters, in an old, spacious, beautiful building, a two-storey wooden structure. Its floors consisted of bright, clean flagstones, and it was surrounded by a brick wall. The house faced southwards, so caught the sun.

Such exquisite houses were often to be found at the far-flung borders of China. This had surely been the residence of the local ruler. The mountaintop town was crowded with Han people, but there was no river and there were no wells. People had dug a large pond in the middle of the town to collect rainwater, and this supplied water to residents and animals there year-round. We saw our reflections in the pond's yellow water. People constantly went there to fill buckets, and the cadre confirmed, "Everyone in Honghe depends on this water."

On the third day, we hired a horse to carry our luggage, as we walked on to stay at government offices in Yuanyang. We observed some Yao people as we walked; as well as some Kucong people, who roamed the mountains, hunting and gathering for a living, and using plantain leaves to build temporary dwellings. When the leaves dried up, they relocated to other mountain locations. They'd sometimes move twice in the space of a month. At the time, scholars had not determined clearly whether they constituted a nationality in their own right or were part of another nationality.

We found a middle-aged Kucong person who could speak basic Mandarin and whom we could interview. We recorded some of his language and Mr Li deduced from this that the Kucong couldn't belong to the Miao-Yao family. Maybe they were a branch of the Lahu nationality of Yunnan.

Ten years later, scholars in Yunnan did indeed identify the Kucong as members of the Lahu; but they were forced to leave the mountains and work as farmers in settled communities.

A Chance Encounter in Mali Village

Prefectural leaders wanted us to visit Mali village to survey the Hani nationality. Mali was a Hani village where people had no worries about food or

166

clothing, because the whole region from the bottom of the mountains to the top was brimming with layer upon layer of rice terrace, all well irrigated.

After absorbing the wonderful spectacle of terraced fields, we wanted to see how the village houses were built. Several Hani girls were sitting in front of a house at one end of the village, chatting and laughing, while doing some needlework. A Han girl was sitting among them, enjoying their company. We strolled over to ask a few questions and discovered they were all smiles, but gave no coherent replies.

I ended up chatting with the Han girl, a health worker sent from the county hospital to treat patients in Mali. She was from the city of Chongqing and when she heard my accent, she thought I must be from Sichuan. She was anything but reticent, not only answering my questions about the Hani, but also talking to me about many of her classmates who had been assigned to work in the border areas.

When I mentioned Dr Chen from Jinghong, she perked up excitedly and told me that Chen had been her classmate and they had been assigned together to Yunnan. They had split up in Kunming and she had never found out where Chen had been assigned.

The distance between us suddenly seemed to shrink. She called me Ou Yang and I called her Xiao Bai. She asked when I would return to Chengdu. When I answered that I would be going soon, she became listless and uncommunicative for a while. Finally, she announced that she would go back with us the next day to Yuanyang. There was something she needed to do back at the hospital there.

In the morning, when Li and I set off back to Yuanyang, Xiao Bai was waiting for us at the side of the road. She carried nothing, not even an umbrella, and followed quietly behind. Half-way down the mountain, we stopped for a rest. Xiao Bai sat on a rock, delicate and innocent, and I remarked that she looked very pretty. Could I take her photo? She agreed, and after I had returned to Kunming and developed the photo, I realised that she had indeed been very pretty. I enlarged it and posted it to her. She sent back a long reply thanking me profusely, beginning a year's correspondence.

During the next few days in Yuanyang, we met a few times, but only briefly and without much opportunity for conversation. Consequently, we didn't really get to know each other. In the end, she entrusted me with the job of passing on a watch to her cousin in Chongqing.

I was able to fulfil Xiao Bai's commission to her satisfaction. Again, she thanked me profusely in writing. During our brief association, I sensed her affections were simple and honest. She wasn't in the least moody, or inclined to deception or foolishness. She was serious and conscientious. If she was going to do something, she would say what. She always seemed so level-headed. She seemed to me like an old friend.

For more than a year after I returned to Chengdu, I received long letters from Xiao Bai practically every week and I always replied. We often exchanged photographs, sharing different facets of our daily lives. In the letters, we discussed each other's work, relationships, former classmates and friends. We wrote about some of the insignificant details of our lives, reflections on the approach of spring or the onset of cool autumn weather. She enclosed an autumn leaf with her letter. I asked if there were any differences between the Honghe of this year compared with last.

We never directly wrote 'I love you', nor openly admitted any romance. Thus the deepest impression I had of that friendship, blossoming through correspondence, was of steadiness and trust. There were no deep feelings of affection or romance.

The survey in Honghe mostly consisted of on-site observations. We saw many high mountains and deep valleys. The Hani and Yi people lived in the mountains, managing terraced fields and growing rice. The mountains were endowed with innumerable trees and bamboo groves, plants and animals, flora and fauna, providing tremendous natural resources. There was a harmony there, so that the Hani and Yi seemed to live lives that were free and unrestrained.

The Dai people, in contrast, chose to live in the river valleys, where the climate was hot and sultry. Their villages seemed to consist only of wooden houses. Apart from those who passed through early or late in the day, you could hardly catch sight of people, poultry or livestock. People stayed at home to dodge the blistering heat. Some poultry and livestock slipped into shady places in the forest, but otherwise they didn't leave their pens.

Travellers regarded the deep Dai-inhabited valleys as danger zones and usually passed through hurriedly without much conversation. They'd climb halfway up a mountain before daring to look around, then heave a sigh of relief, and begin chatting and laughing.

There was a sense of estrangement between local minority people and outsiders, locals were reluctant to talk, and our findings from direct questioning were relatively few. I took several hundred photographs, which represented a major part of my findings from the trip. After returning to the Institute, I sorted out the most useful photos and passed them on to the collection of cultural artefacts.

The Journey Back to Kunming

My work at the Research Institute was supervised by Mr Li, who was nearly 60 and not very strong physically. That trip to the border regions was certainly a difficult assignment for him. Except for the few days when I went alone to Mount Nannuo, I hardly left Li's side. In return, I was rewarded with much I learned from and cherished about him.

After graduation from university, Li had served as an English interpreter for the Chinese army in India. Because of his English background, he later attracted distrust from leaders and suspicion from ordinary people. This caused him distress, but he still worked energetically.

During our struggles up and down the mountain paths, Li never asked to ride a horse or sedan, and never complained. He drank cold water and ate pickled vegetables or hot pepper to help swallow cold rice. Li often said that if he had no other food, a couple of cloves of garlic would suffice. Sure enough, he always kept garlic in his pocket and often chewed on it. No one who knew him failed to praise the spirit with which he bore hardship.

Li demanded progress, including from himself. During our time in County Honghe it often rained, and the rain prevented us from going out for days on end. He couldn't be idle, however, and would sit on his bed reading a Russian book about political economy. Since he had never studied Russian before, he often consulted a dictionary and mulled over the meaning. When we returned to Kunming, he told me he had finished more than half the book. For someone around 60, to begin the study of Russian required extraordinary determination and I admire his spirit to this day.

Li and I walked from Yuanyang to Gejiu and stayed there three days. Gejiu was called the Tin Capital: the soles of our feet were literally treading on tin ore. We observed many Han people digging. The income from tin was enough to sustain a family of three or four.

Grasping letters of introduction from the prefecture, we toured the local tin ore factory, observing its massive ropes and pulleys. Tin ore was loaded into metal baskets in the mountains and passed down to the factory using the pulley ropes. Empty baskets were sent back into the mountains by the same ropes.

The factory had been set up by experts from the Soviet Union. Since it was part of the defence industry, it was a confidential work unit. Thus, we only saw the general scale of the factory, but were not at liberty to find out even the size of the workforce.

From Gejiu we walked to Mengzi. Mengzi was much cooler, with more beautiful scenery. Tradition has it that Mongolian soldiers of the Yuan dynasty (1279–1368 AD) who entered Vietnam were completely decimated by malaria. Only a remnant, those who were stationed in Mengzi, survived and later became Han.

There was a village near Mengzi with distinct language and customs, with over 100 households of people referred to locally as 'Tu'. We discovered that they had borrowed the Yi language while retaining some Mongolian vocabulary. The story was told locally of how their ancestors were Mongolians from the north.

Mr Li and I took a small train from Mengzi back to Kunming. The railway had been designed and built by French engineers during the war against Japan. Seats on the train were set against both sides, and travellers would sit with their backs to the sides of the train. Two rows of people sat face to face, knee touching knee, with no space for passing through between.

The train drove at a speed never exceeding 40 or 50 kilometres per hour and we were able to look around and admire the beautiful scenery outside.

En route from Mengzi to Kunming, we visited the Yi town of Eshan, spending four or five nights there. There were various summary documents at the government offices, describing local movements for cooperation and production. Mr Li and I thumbed through these and abstracted some details, gaining a general understanding.

After returning to the Institute, I wrote a long summary of the Eshan situation and sent it to the Eshan government for approval, but the summary was like a stone sinking in the ocean, and I never found out what became of it.

Back at the Institute

On the way from Kunming to Chengdu, we passed through Guizhou. In the summer of 1955, a national campaign was underway to purge counter-revolutionary elements. As we travelled through Guiyang, each work unit was busy convening meetings, and when we tried to contact the provincial Nationality Affairs Commission, no one was there to see us.

By chance, a cadre came walking briskly towards us, his whole demeanour screaming sobriety. He paid no attention to us. In the common dining hall where people generally met up, soldiers were huddled together devouring their meals in two and threes, with submachine guns on their backs. There were fewer guests than usual. It all reflected the tense atmosphere at the time of the counter-revolutionary purge.

Chengdu in June was already blisteringly hot and everyone had changed into white shirts. Within a week or two of our return, classes came to an end. Each department left only one or two people on duty, while everyone else engaged in joint studies. No one was permitted to go home. This was part of the movement to purge counter-revolutionary elements.

According to the policy in Sichuan, minority cadres who were not Communist Party members did not need to attend the classes for purging counter-revolutionaries. Mr Yang (Yi nationality), Professor Yu (Mongolian) and I did not have to attend, and were left to pursue our daily routines. I was delegated to keep the keys of the cultural artefacts room. I should take care of any visitors, and take responsibility for any arrangements in relation to the artefacts themselves.

In the evenings, the three of us studied the newspapers and any documents that had arrived at the office. Since Yang had to care for five children, however, he was often unable to come in the evenings. Yu remarked, "Mr Yang is not coming. I'll take the newspaper and read it in the teahouse."

One was busy with family matters, the other preferred to go to the teahouse. I was left alone in the office and all was quiet. I might as well read and write. During the half-year colleagues were meeting for study, I arranged all the materials from the recent survey trip to Yunnan into 10 parts. Afterwards, I passed them on to Mr Li for him to polish off.

Almost every day, and occasionally even in the evenings, there were visitors at the Cultural Artefacts room. Hosting them, explaining the exhibition, opening up and closing down, became part of my daily routine. Only when there were unusually many visitors did I ask Yu to help out.

When Mr Wu Zelin returned after the joint studies, I returned the keys to him. On the third day, he commended me for taking such good care of things.

Wu was erudite and renowned in the anthropological field in China. Ever since his youth, he had been interested in minority culture and he was always collecting materials.

After inviting me to work with him, Mr Wu advised me many times to sit the graduate-student entrance exam. This would be necessary if I wanted to succeed in research. Without further studies, I'd have to settle for administrative work.

Wu helped me to understand much about research, exhibitions and the distinctive features of minority cultures. He recommended anthropological classics for me to read, which helped me attain a firm foundation in the field. His kind and honest encouragement and his rigorous academic standards left a lifelong impression.

Chapter 13
Identifying Rightists
(Beijing, 1956-58)

Life as a Research Student

Before Liberation, sociology was studied at universities in China, as well as anthropology and ethnology. Many experts were nurtured in those fields and many articles were published.

At first after Liberation, anthropology was viewed as 'racism' and rejected. Proponents of the subject were given short shrift and peremptorily accused of being 'imperialist'. Sociology was regarded as a 'pseudoscience of the capitalist classes', and was also rejected. Since these two academic disciplines were suppressed, ethnology seemed guilty by association.

In 1956, when the country formulated a new 12-year national study plan incorporating sociology, ethnology was also in the plan. An Ethnology Department was established in the Central Institute for Nationalities in Beijing, to train undergraduate and graduate students. The country invited experts from the Soviet Union to come and lecture, to help establish and develop the subject.

I remember Mr Wu Zelin reading the 12-year plan at a meeting of staff in the Chengdu Research Institute. Everyone was beaming. Even Li Zhichun and other older staff were cheerfully chipping in, 'Good, good...', and sighing, 'We finally have some standing. The country has at last acknowledged our subject!'

On the way home, Mr Wu tapped me on the shoulder and observed with a smile, "Your opportunity has come. Strive to take it and don't let it slip away!"

News of the 12-year plan quickly spread through the Institute. It was mind-blowing to young people there, promoting the popular notion of 'marching towards science'.

At that time, however, I had been planning to leave the Research Institute and register for the medical school entrance exam, to study medicine. As a doctor, I could work among people of my own nationality, who otherwise experienced a dire shortage of medical help. It would be worth going back to university for a few years to be able to do this.

Now, instead, leaders at the Personnel Department decided to send me off as a research student, to study at the Central Institute in Beijing towards a semi-doctoral degree, slightly lower than a doctorate. I should prepare to leave. At the time, my only thought was to conform. There was no question of objecting, for research study was actually a notch higher up the scale. I felt pleased and excited at this unexpected turn of events.

Ten people were appointed from the Southwest Institute to study in Beijing. We travelled first to Chongqing, before taking a boat to Wuhan. From Wuhan, we continued to Beijing by train.

When studies began in September, our class, with the long-winded name of the Central Institute for Nationalities History Department Nationality Studies Research Student Class, consisted of 34 students, 20 of whom were graduates from the previous academic year's study, having been selected to stay on. The remaining students, including me, were cadres from provincial nationality institutes. Not long after term started, the Institute convened a meeting of student representatives. My classmates unanimously elected me as a research-student representative. I would never have dreamt of being honoured in this way and felt very pleased.

Teaching was led by Professor HH Qieboke Saluofu, assisted by Professor Lin Yaohua. Qieboke was Director of Nationality Research at Moscow University. He was a famous ethnologist, having published widely. Many accomplished local scholars were also involved in teaching the course, including Fu Lehuan, Wu Rukang and Pan Guangdan.

Government departments at the national level viewed this new training as strategic and paid special attention to the teachers and students involved.

Professor Qieboke personified the prestige associated with ethnology in the Soviet Union, referred to respectfully as 'Marxist-Leninist ethnology'. Left-leaning classmates believed in him heart and soul. Privately, they were rather disparaging of other teachers, especially during the anti-rightist period.

Mr Fu Lehuan lectured in history. There was hardly an era of Chinese history with which he was not familiar. Once started, he was off, and the content of what he said was brilliant. There was a tremendous kick to be had from sitting in on a year of his lectures.

The hardest lessons for me were on Russian language. Before Liberation, schools only taught English, and post-Liberation, I had not studied even a day of Russian. I hadn't even set eyes on the Russian alphabet. Three or four other provincial students were in the same boat.

Russian was nevertheless compulsory. We used two Renmin University graduate textbooks. The 20 students who had recently graduated in Beijing had already studied Russian and now we were stuck in classes along with them. It was really impossible to teach even-handedly when students had such disparate backgrounds.

Our Russian teacher, however, Mr Yi Lifu was patient, diligent and conscientious, popular with all his students. At the start of term, he used two afternoons to teach late-beginners how to pronounce the Russian letters. During normal class, he often stopped for questions, and when he corrected homework, he indicated mistakes clearly.

We beginners became primary beneficiaries of his teaching. After class, he often asked whether we had understood. His kindness as a teacher is engraved on my memory and ultimately I was able to gain a good grasp of Russian from him. Notwithstanding, Russian study caused me the greatest stress during my time in Beijing.

My pockets were stuffed with slips of paper containing Russian vocabulary. In any spare moments, whether outside walking, going to the toilet, waiting for a meeting or film to begin, I'd take a slip or two in hand to memorise. There was not a moment to lose.

I was 26 years old and felt embarrassed if I couldn't answer in class. All day every day during my one-and-a-half years of Russian study, I tried to squeeze in time for Russian. I spent winter and summer vacations, as well as festival holidays, at the Institute. When he saw how hard I was striving to learn Russian, a friend once teased me by writing the Russian text 'борьба', sounding like the Chinese word for 'struggle', above my dormitory bed.

Whenever we had a Russian exam, I only just passed. After graduation, however, having pushed myself, I ended up with a strong grasp of Russian reading and translated some anthropology books from Russian into Chinese, to help with academic research.

Otherwise, physical anthropology gave me the biggest headache. Our minority nationalities didn't know much about people's physical anatomy, having a word for bones, but little to distinguish between different bones or other body parts. We generally weren't concerned about such things and I was no exception.

Mr Wu Rukang taught the course, very well and in great detail. He warned that if you hadn't graduated in the sciences then you had better prepare for some difficulties. We had to remember the names and locations of all the body parts, and try as I might, I couldn't seem to do it. I found it difficult to generate the interest needed to learn everything, and only just passed the exam.

I was curious about the connection between human anatomy and race, often raised in Professor Qieboke's ethnology classes. I studied physical anthropology principally to research the racial origin of different nationalities. After graduation, I became absorbed in that topic, even translating a book by a Soviet scholar entitled *Many Races of Mankind*. Gradually, I understood better the physical anthropology I had previously studied.

Professor Qieboke taught ethnology eight hours a week for one-and-a-half years. A class of undergraduate history students joined our class of research students for the course. Teachers also came to listen, with Professor Lin taking the lead. The senior undergraduate class and research students from the History Department of Beijing University came by bus and also attended those lectures. The large classroom was filled and extra seats had to be brought in from outside.

In the first semester, this was always the case. Qieboke's lectures reflected the newest discoveries in Soviet ethnology and their scope ranged worldwide. His course was regarded as the first systematic teaching of Marxist-Leninist ethnology, 'completely different' from pre-Liberation ethnology. Party members were especially committed to attending the lectures, and it sometimes felt as if people like me in the 'backward [non-Party] group' did not deserve to be there.

I did not have much serious difficulty with any of the studies, except for Russian. Although ethnology was complicated and involved lots of information, my research work and practical field investigations gave me a good foundation, an advantage. I'd hurriedly skim over the material just before exams and still gain good grades. Classmates observed my struggle with Russian, and ease with other courses.

Under guidance from staff, I wrote two articles: one on the Tibetan people of County Songpan and the other on Khirghiz [a minority in the Soviet Union] collective farming. I distributed these, convening two small-scale seminars, during which I answered many and various questions from the floor. This helped me establish a routine for writing future papers.

Apart from the compulsory courses, I also attended two undergraduate courses: archaeology and the history of primitive society. I didn't miss a class. Their content was closely related to ethnology and they were helpful in my subsequent research and teaching.

The department often invited well-known visiting lecturers. I was most impressed by Mr Pan Guangdan, who presented a lecture on the history of migration of ancient Chinese nationalities. He didn't use a manuscript, nor did he write on the blackboard. He just sat on the stage and started to talk, revealing a succession of fascinating details.

Pan's book *The Ancient Ba People* attracted much praise not only for its content but also for its research method. He planned to lecture us later on the history of the Ba people (of the Zhou dynasty, 1046 to 256 BC), but before long, he was caught up in the maelstrom of the anti-rightist struggle. Since he had been researching such things and writing academic papers of a high standard, he was declared a 'rightist', and accused of 'inciting ethnic groups towards an ideology of national self-determination'.

Pan was denounced at a general meeting of the Institute. He arrived to face criticism leaning on a walking stick. No matter how cruelly the activists accused and slandered him, he just sat there, bent over with age. It was as if no one had ever seen or known him before, and he was treated without respect. He declined to say even a word in his own defence. As I observed his humiliation, I felt deeply sympathetic.

I was still highly motivated to study, with such an outstanding opportunity to learn from teachers renowned at home and abroad. In the afternoons, I read in the departmental study room, while in the evenings, I did homework or read in the classrooms or library. Saturday evenings were the same. I rarely watched a film or joined in the students' union parties. In the winter and summer vacations, I stayed at the Institute and organised my study schedule as if it was term-time. Apart from going into the city occasionally on Sundays to buy books, I spent my free time studying.

This habit of not relaxing outside normal school hours had been cultivated during my years of study before Liberation. At that time, there was simply not much entertainment available. During class, we listened to the teacher and after class, we studied. There was little else to do and the spectre of boredom compelled us to study.

Afterwards, it seemed as though I had been compelled by these study habits to walk the way of learning my whole life long. In the midst of such single-hearted devotion to study, whether serene or strained, a previously unimagined thing rushed through the open door of my heart.

One afternoon, soon after school started, I was in the departmental reading room thumbing through the *History of the Qing Dynasty*, when to my surprise I heard a voice outside the door calling my name. When I looked up, I saw two female students from the Southwest Nationalities Institute waiting outside. They had been among the 10 students selected from the Institute to go and study in Beijing. One of them was Chen Ying, and she asked if I could borrow a copy of the New Youth magazine for her.

Ying came from Zhejiang Province, but during the War of Resistance against Japan, her family had moved to Kunming. She had originally transferred from Yunnan University to work at the Southwest Nationalities Institute in compliance with government instructions. She was Han, a few months my senior. During our time at the Institute, we had fallen in love. We had been seeing each other for several years, but neither wanted to be first to admit being smitten.

After I arrived in Beijing, I assumed that since Ying was in the Politics Department studying Party History and I was in the History Department studying Ethnology, I'd not see much of her and my former love for her would gradually diminish. This seemed a propitious way to wind up the romance. I'd not anticipated that she would have the pluck to look me up, with the pretext of asking me to help her borrow a magazine. This was an eventuality I could only have dreamed of.

A few days later, one Saturday afternoon, Ying came looking for me again, to return the magazine. This second visit wasn't a surprise. I was mentally prepared and actually not at all nervous, accompanying her back to her dormitory. We sat down for a while, after which she accompanied me back to my place. While we had been traversing the campus twice, it had become nearly dark, and we'd contrived to miss the meal in the campus dining hall.

Instead, we ate dinner at a restaurant in the streets outside, and on the way back, we became boyfriend and girlfriend. Any feelings of misgiving from before seemed to have evaporated. She agreed for me to see her later that evening. That was when our more serious love affair began.

Thereafter, our silhouettes could often be seen on Saturday or Sunday evenings at one of two local parks, Weigongcun or Zizhuyuan. At the time, we were both busy with our respective studies and each week we only had these one or two opportunities to meet, but they were blissful interludes. They never seemed like unwarranted or unwelcome interruptions to our studies.

Our love in Beijing continued through the winter of 1956/57, and on 1st May 1957, we travelled together to Tianjin and married there. Ying graduated soon afterwards and returned to Chengdu, while I stayed in Beijing and continued my research course. Later, Ying went ahead of me to support the border region of Qinghai, and at the end of 1960, I followed her there.

Anti-Rightist Tides

For about half a year after the 1957 summer vacation, we research students attended classes during the day and many small and large anti-rightist assemblies during the evenings. The idea was to purge the Party of alleged 'rightists', mostly those intellectuals who appeared to favour capitalism and to oppose collectivisation.

Small meetings were convened for confessions and for informing on others. Before the meetings, the convenor would mobilise and organise participants. When all was ready, he would call a 'rightist' to join the meeting, for self-criticism or self-defence. In the large meetings, activists would take the stage to articulate public denunciations of others.

The struggle was extraordinarily intense. I always looked for an inconspicuous corner, as if to dodge the cutting edge of the verbal atrocities. Ding, a Manchu classmate, usually sat beside me. It was as if we were hiding there, subdued from start to finish, not breathing a word to each other. When the meetings adjourned and as we left, Ding would whisper to me, "Unbearable! That kind of punishment is intolerable!" I didn't dare to respond, but just glanced at him coolly and returned to the dorm.

Ding usually went from the anti-rightist assemblies directly to the library and read a Russian anthropology book, in Russian. He was eccentric at the best of times and normally didn't converse with anyone. After class or after a meeting, he just went to the library. On encountering anyone, he never so much as greeted them. When he sat beside me during the general meetings, we were like two dumb men.

At the 'weasel informant' meetings, we didn't offer any accusations or opinions, and at the denunciation meetings we didn't say a word. This attracted the undesired attention of some of our classmates. As we walked out of the main exit of the literature and art building, Ding would often repeat his verdict to me, "Unbearable!"

On one such occasion, the Youth League Party Secretary happened to be behind us and overheard Ding, whereupon he overtook us with much agitation. As he passed, he looked around ferociously at Ding, but Ding was short-sighted and possibly did not notice. I clearly observed, however, and understood precisely what had happened. I couldn't help being alarmed and concerned.

One evening in the later stages of the campaign, a meeting was convened at short notice to which Ding was summoned to explain his position on the anti-rightist struggle. He behaved true to form, only saying stiffly, "I don't have any position." A succession of activists interrogated him, but he didn't offer a single word of clarification. In the end, the Youth League Secretary asked him, "What do you mean by saying 'Unbearable!' after the meetings for denouncing rightists?"

Ding still refused to reply and the meeting was adjourned. The next evening, another meeting was convened, with Ding again in the spotlight. He was ordered to make a self-criticism, but remained mute, as before. The League Secretary convening the meeting declared that since the beginning of the anti-rightist campaign Ding had never made any statement and had had a negative attitude towards the whole anti-rightist struggle. Privately in ideology, he was standing together with the 'rightist elements', a covert rightist, who described the anti-rightist struggle meetings as 'unbearable'.

Ding was thus expediently identified as a 'rightist element', the sixth classmate of mine to be so denounced. Afterwards, he drifted completely away from me. I understood his behaviour, for he could see I was bound to try to avoid calamity and he was reluctant to implicate me in his 'crime'.

One Party-member classmate had been driven right to the forefront of the 'rightists without a public opinion' debate. One evening during a meeting, he disappeared. The convenor then announced he was to be criticised, saying his personality had changed. He no longer resembled a Party member but had metamorphosed into a lone wolf, not smiling at comrades, not communicating, and drifting ever further apart. Ever since the beginning of the campaign, he had made no supportive speeches and written no big-character posters. [These were posters using large handwritten Chinese characters, mounted on the walls. They had been used in China since imperial times, often as a means of propaganda or protest.]

Finally, the convenor chose one thing in particular to highlight. My classmate had been dating a young woman working in the Chinese Academy of Sciences. He'd often been seen with her, strolling around the streets and parks. That woman had been born into a capitalist household. In the context of the anti-rightist struggle, his behaviour was an ideological paradox. Since he had gone so far as to find that kind of person to date, he must be opposing the struggle in his thinking. He had been intoxicated by this love affair. We were convening this meeting for him to explain himself.

The classmate was called in. He was holding a piece of paper, on which was written his self-criticism. It took less than two minutes to read. Afterwards, only two or three people spoke, all describing him as a rightist element, but not saying much besides.

At the end of this short meeting, the convenor also publicly castigated him as a rightist element. Most people did not really understand why. One classmate joked under his breath, "He's a rightist because he is dating."

After the event, I asked him why they had attacked him, and he replied, "I don't know why. They just don't want me." In my mind, he was a good guy, who had formerly been very approachable, with a smile for everyone. He had been caught head-on in the process of falling in love. How could love become 'rightist'?

When this precedent emerged, I felt yet more apprehension, for I had married my sweetheart just before the anti-rightist campaign. I feared the cudgel of romance might be used to beat me over the head. What happened next proved my fear was not so fantastic or ill-founded.

Beijing leaders at the time had stipulated that no more than 10% of people in the universities and colleges should be classified as 'rightist'. Of the 34 ethnology research students, six had been so classified. That was almost 18%. Of these, four were Han and two were minority students. This already exceeded the stipulated percentage. Though some were insisting there were yet more rightists to be identified, Institute leaders reminded everyone that the required percentage had already been exceeded and we couldn't identify more. Thus, I had had a lucky escape.

Since the number of rightists uncovered in my class was relatively high, we had a good reputation as 'rightist pacesetters'. Institute leaders regarded our class leaders and activists with respect, often praising and consulting them.

In the winter vacation of 1957/58, just after the anti-rightist campaign, Professors Qieboke Saluofu and Lin Yaohua led us research students to survey a Yao village in Guangdong Province. We conducted more than a month of ethnological fieldwork. Our rightist-element classmates, however, were not permitted to participate, and had to remain at the Institute.

The rightist-accusers knew most clearly that I had not been classified as a rightist only because we were already over the limit. They kept their distance, viewing me with disdain, unwilling to talk to me and even less willing to work with me. Everyone knew what was going on.

When we divided up, I was placed in the 'experts' group', to provide assistance to teachers in surveying the relationship between the lives of the people and their family names, in different rows of houses. People with the same family name generally lived in the same row.

The 'experts' group' consisted of two teachers and three students. We visited all the households and recorded detailed information, drawing up a chart showing clearly the distribution of homes and the relationships between households.

In addition, Professor Qieboke spent two evenings taking the villagers' body measurements. Based on these physical characteristics, he told us that ancestors of these Yao people had come from the south, with a different origin from the Mongolians of the north. During those days, we received a kind of personal tuition. Having been pushed to one side by classmates, a bad thing had turned into a good thing, and I had learned a lot.

After we returned to the Institute, I drew on the experience to write an essay entitled 'Seen and Heard in Nangang', but this aroused jealousy among classmates. One classmate jumped to conclusions, without having read the article, and spread the rumour that it had been written by 'a Soviet expert'. I declared my innocence, bringing the hand-written article with me to the veranda of the literature and art building, where everyone could see. That settled the dispute, but my accusers promptly seized the article, and it was never returned.

Although this disturbance subsided, envy deepened. I had become a thorn in the flesh of some classmates.

It was spring of 1958 when we returned to the Institute after fieldwork. I wrote two articles: 'The system of appointing national minority hereditary headmen among the Yi nationality in the greater and lesser Liangshan regions of Sichuan Province', and 'Families and marriage among the Tibetan people of the grasslands of Songpan County in Sichuan'. These were published in Renmin University's journal Education and Research, in the third and fourth issues of 1958, respectively. They were my first publications in any academic journal.

Unfortunately, this was the time of the anti-rightist campaign, when the air seemed heavy with ill will, and you could unexpectedly be beaten to death by blows from the extreme left. The two articles did indeed attract unwarranted trouble, though they later served as testimonial, for they stood the test of time. In 1979, I was granted political rehabilitation, and the two articles received positive evaluations, and were published along with the rest of my collected works.

When the articles were first published, however, the Institute was just launching its campaign to 'Pull up the white flags and stick in the red flags' (namely to criticise the 'empty experts'). I became one of the first focal points of this campaign. Two or three of the extreme left-wing members of the Youth League abused me as 'an acute case of a delinquent who lived only for fame and profit', and 'an archetypal capitalist intellectual'.

Several meetings were convened to mobilise Youth League members to write big-character posters exposing and criticising me. These were pasted all over the literature and art building. I was furious at the patent dishonesty and slanderous nature of the posters. I wrote two big-character posters refuting the allegations, but that only led to more accusatory posters. During the day, they pasted posters and at night I tore them down.

Two far-left 'pioneers' wrote a letter in the name of the Youth League to editors of Education and Research, demanding publication of their anonymous 'article' slandering me. As a result, in the fifth edition of the journal in 1958, a big-character poster was published containing a personal attack on me, wanton disparagement and vulgar accusation, lacking any foundation.

They accused me of sympathising with rightist elements. Since I had previously studied under Wu Zelin and Li Zhichun, they said I was wearing a 'capitalist intellectual cap'. I was the archetypal capitalist, living just for fame and profit. I was opposed to Soviet ethnology, a cheat who defied Marxism-Leninism.

They tried to use the articles I had published from my own survey data to frame me as having 'stolen state data', and 'plagiarised'. Subsequently, their vituperative big-character poster appeared all over the Institute, setting in motion several days of crazy loud abuse from all quarters. Afterwards, there was a meeting to denounce me.

I submitted a request to resign from the Youth League, but its secretary said I wasn't allowed to resign. Instead, the League would expel me, and then I would be stripped of any relationship with League or Party. I would be notified once this was accomplished.

So at last, I was classified as a 'Party rightist'. Actually, the plight of such people was more wretched than that of the ordinary rightists. No copyright could be attributed to me. During subsequent fieldwork, I was not permitted to go to the countryside to survey. Instead, I was instructed to write an article for the journal Nationality Research and to sign everyone else's name. Authors' remuneration belonged to the others, while I was just the worker clutching the pen.

I still graduated as planned in 1959 and was awarded a graduate diploma. Ten years of national upheaval had witnessed all kinds of change. In 1980, twenty-two years after the criticism and slander endured during the anti-rightist period, I was retrospectively re-issued with an ethnology research student's graduate diploma.

Later I posted this diploma back to the Institute. Today it should still be in the administrative department of the Central University for Nationalities. I was politically rehabilitated by the Central Institute and reinstated in the records. They posted me a retrospective, then already outdated, certificate of membership of the Youth League.

Chapter 14
Screaming and Splitting
(Xining, 1958-64)

Getting Together and Splitting Apart

The fieldwork for my research course commenced in the autumn of 1958 and was to last a year. Originally, I had planned to do fieldwork in Guizhou, since I had grown up there. The director of research students, however, was sympathetic, and said that since my wife was working in Chengdu, it would be best for me to do my fieldwork in Sichuan.

I was to join the Sichuan Nationalities Investigative Group. In September, I left Beijing for Chengdu, to be with Ying, my wife of one-and-a-half years. I was given a teaching post at the Southwest Institute for Nationalities in the southern suburbs of Chengdu.

My daughter was just over six months old, and lived with her mother in a one-storey building owned by the Institute. Several families shared a kitchen, with a gas stove for cooking. The bedroom was narrow, simple and rustic, not at all homely. When I first looked around, I couldn't help feeling it was too cold and basic. On seeing the one I loved, however, who also reciprocated my love, along with my daughter, I could only feel happy, and delighted at the prospect of living with them.

In that first week, we rose daily at 6:30 am. After washing face and hands, we each went our separate way to work, having entrusted our daughter to a baby-sitter. My wife went to teach while I went to the old Institute site, at Xinyusha Street. We only returned home after eating dinner separately in the evenings.

On our first Sunday, Ying bought a chicken and cooked it along with some rice, and we shared a meal together. She said it was to welcome me back, like washing away the dust for me. It was the first meal we had eaten together since I re-joined the family. During those few days, I felt unspeakably happy to be re-united with my wife, able to chat freely with her.

The day after our celebratory meal, I was unable to return home at the usual time, for there was an evening meeting to discuss fieldwork plans. At dusk, Ying cycled over to look for me. Upon setting eyes on me, she burst out breathlessly, "The Institute is transferring me to Qinghai!"

The news was like a thunderbolt on a sunny day. We stood face to face, unable to utter a word. After she had caught her breath, she explained, "Qinghai is establishing a university and support is being sought from all the universities and colleges in Chengdu. Our Institute is donating an administrator and several teachers, of whom I am one." She said no more. There were too many questions. She had only worked a year since returning from Beijing and had only been re-united with her husband for one week.

How could this have happened to me? I was totally shattered, and could only ask, "What shall we do?"

"We need to do what we're told. What else can we do?" The Institute had said she should go first and I could follow later. Just then, the Research Group leader stuck his head out of an upstairs window and called me to the meeting. Ying turned around, mounted her bike and rode off towards the gate.

When I reached home, the baby was sound asleep. Ying was busily folding up clothes and told me coolly that the Institute had already bought tickets, and she would leave the day after tomorrow, in the afternoon. She didn't even look up and it felt as though I didn't exist. She just quietly immersed herself in preparations to leave and I tried to help where I could. For fear of riling her, I said nothing, for I felt conscience-stricken.

I was thinking: *If I hadn't been labelled a bourgeois intellectual and a right-wing informer during the anti-rightist movement, officials would not now be so anxious to send her away to Qinghai.*

Ying had become a respected cadre in the Youth Regiment, trusted by the Party. She understood everything more clearly than I, but she did not betray the slightest trace of reproach towards me.

There was no use my trying to remonstrate, to apologise or to beg for forgiveness. She did not want just then to express openly her feelings of love, for fear they would get the better of her and she would lose her composure. Silently, our hearts communicated, so that without speaking we could understand.

At length she broke the silence. "I've written a letter to tell my parents about the transfer. Have a look; it's there on the table. I'll be on the way to Qinghai when the letter arrives in Kunming." Her parents in Kunming would certainly be shocked and worried. They would never have dreamt of such a move.

On the afternoon of Ying's departure, I accompanied her and our daughter to the railway station. She queued up along with others from the Institute who were going as families – father, mother and children. Only my wife was alone, baby on back. She sat on a suitcase, as I squatted opposite, both silent. Thousands of words filled our minds, but only one feeling defined our mood, 'Broken-hearted'. At that moment, there was no person in the whole wide world who felt more devastatingly sick at heart than the two of us.

At college, before marriage, we had been passionately in love for nearly a year. Only at weekends during the daytime were we able to see each other, to stroll around, to eat dinner together then separate. After a three-day honeymoon, we'd lived together for less than four weeks before parting again.

Ying had graduated and returned to Chengdu, while I remained in Beijing. We had been separated by a great distance and could only communicate by letter. When our baby had been born, I could not be there by her side. I don't know how she managed during that difficult time. When I had joined her at last in Chengdu,

I had never imagined that we would be separated again after only a week, or that she would be transferred to Qinghai, totally unknown territory to her. All this was flashing through my mind.

Ying's heart was full of apprehension, for Qinghai seemed like a cold, strange wilderness. She felt afraid, despondent and heavy-hearted, though we could not discuss such feelings. She presented a veneer of strength, as if she were telling me, "I'm not afraid and can master whatever comes my way." Among her peers, she was always the most competent woman I knew, from the very first day I knew her. She was never inclined to depression or melancholy, never stumped by anything, but steadfastly optimistic.

No one could predict, however, the difficulties and dangers she might face carrying a six-month-old baby to Qinghai. She could surely overcome, no matter what, but I could not erase a sense of bitterness about our misfortunes, nor could I dispel the love and pity I felt for Ying.

Those in the queue rose one after another and we slowly followed to the appointed carriage. At the metal steps into the train, Ying stood to one side and temporarily left the queue. She lingered for 10 seconds, as if wanting to say something. "Better board," I said.

Then she turned and said to the baby on her back, "Better say bye-bye to your Daddy."

The baby stretched her head around to look at me, then promptly twisted back around, as if hiding. It seemed as if she was saying, "Why doesn't Daddy just go with us?"

After they'd boarded, I peered in through the window, repeatedly waving goodbye. Within a minute or two, the whistle sounded and I followed the train as the wheels chugged into motion, at first slowly then more quickly. I couldn't keep up and yelled twice at the top of my voice. There was no response.

As the train raced off, I could not refrain from screaming a cry of pain, my face covered in tears, standing stupefied staring into the distance, until it had disappeared from my line of vision. It was not until much later that my spirit finally revived.

The Remaining Time in Sichuan

A few days before we left for fieldwork, the group leader who had come with us, Professor Xia Kangnong, was appointed deputy head of the Central Institute for Nationalities in Beijing. He was replaced by a Mr Liu, who had transferred from his post as Deputy Director of the Southwest Institute for Nationalities.

Before returning to Beijing, Professor Xia looked me up. He felt sorry that Ying had had to leave for Qinghai, while I had had to stay in Chengdu. He tried to encourage me by talking about a stiff upper lip and finding contentment in my work, telling me that this group of research students, taught by experts from the Soviet Union, had practically already graduated. After one year of fieldwork, I could go directly to Qinghai, for it wouldn't be right to separate me from my wife any longer.

On his first day as group leader, Mr Liu also called me in for a chat. He showered me with praise, saying I was the group's only student with special expertise in nationality studies. He was kind and well disposed, according me special respect. In coming to lead the research group, he needed my help, especially in the field of nationality studies. He spoke non-stop, brimming with enthusiasm. Mainly, he wanted to emphasise that the Research Group needed me and he also needed me.

I was assigned to the Aba Prefecture Group. Other group members were mainly students of Tibetan language from the Central Institute. They were to do Tibetan language fieldwork. We were joined by a few teachers from other colleges and universities. We travelled on a Liberation bus, along rugged mountain paths, arriving at Aba's Maerkang station and staying in the government guesthouse. Several cadres from the prefecture were assigned to work with us.

The Group leader would not allow me to go to the countryside for fieldwork, but had me stay in the guesthouse with a professor and a history teacher, to organise research results. A working day consisted of 10 hours' work: four in the morning, four in the afternoon and two in the evening. There was no rest on Sundays. Many materials were already available at Maerkang and two weeks later, fresh reports arrived in quick succession from each small fieldwork team.

Our job was to organise the reports into summary materials according to content and region. We engrossed ourselves in writing and summarising, and passed the documents onto our superiors.

Afterwards, I was asked to work on written records from Jinzhou prefecture about Emperor Qianlong (1736–1796). My job was to extract everything that demonstrated benefaction towards the Tibetan people, for example, the provision of farm implements and seeds, the passing on of technology, encouragement to migrate, and so on. After I produced a one-volume summary, the group spent a morning listening as I read it aloud.

During Chinese New Year 1959, we in the guesthouse, along with colleagues in the Tibetan villages, continued work as usual. The only difference was that food was better, with red-roasted pork and beef stew.

After New Year, leaders appointed me and a teacher Mr Zhao, and a local cadre, to help the prefecture write a *Survey of the Tibetan People's Autonomy in Aba Prefecture*. Together we researched and wrote, and after a little over two months, produced a draft *Survey* which was typed and printed.

While we were writing the book, my superiors asked me to write an article describing the development of Aba prefecture since Liberation. Within five days, I had written 'The radiant path of progress of the Aba Tibetan Autonomous Prefecture'. This brought kudos to our working group. It was published in the Beijing journal Nationality Research, 1959, volume 9. Authors' royalties were shared by members of our group.

The manuscript of the *Survey* book was produced in early summer of 1959 and with that, my work with the Aba Group came to an end. Zhao and I were sent to help the Maowen Qiang group write *A Concise History of and*

Introduction to the Qiang Nationality and *A Survey of the Maowen Qiang Nationality Autonomous Region*.

We left Maerkang and travelled to Weizhou, to live with members of the Maowen Group for a month or more. We perused a huge pile of research results, summaries and manuscripts they had written and did the groundwork for the aforementioned two books.

When summoned during the summer holiday, we returned to Chengdu for a meeting to discuss the writing of three new series of books. On my first evening back, I went to post a letter to my wife Ying, when unexpectedly I saw her there at the post office in the act of writing a telegram to me! I gently tapped her shoulder and she looked around.

We were both so delighted at this heaven-ordained meeting, we could only laugh. Ying told me she had left our daughter with her (Ying's) mother in Kunming and had only just returned to Chengdu.

I went with Ying to the small guesthouse where she was staying. It was already 8 or 9 pm. Her train ticket to Xining was for early the next morning, and there was no time to go out and eat, so we just shared some *baozi*. She told me how she had taken a plane to Kunming and how the baby could not bear to part with her, crying at the top of her voice when Ying left. She also said how cold the winter was in Qinghai and how the people there ate highland barley noodles and steamed buns. She asked if I'd be able to endure such hardship. I reminded her I had already endured much hardship, and it should be no problem.

I explained that I was desperate to go and join her in Qinghai. The cold and hardship were nothing to me. Day and night over the past year, I had only thought of being with her, and I was eagerly looking forward to it. Each day had seemed like a year. I told her that our fieldwork phase was finished and as soon as the meetings in Chengdu were over, I would probably be allowed to leave Sichuan. The day of our reunion was already on the horizon.

We were both overjoyed at this prospect and it seemed almost as if we were already back together again. We refused to think about the next morning, when we would have to separate. I do not remember her goodbyes that day, her boarding a train and leaving Chengdu. The sadness of goodbye was overwhelmed by joy at the prospect of imminent reunion.

The summer vacation ended and our Research Group meetings in Chengdu also finished. I had assumed that this would be the time I would leave the Group to go and work in Qinghai. Leaders in Chengdu, however, informed me I would have to remain with the Research Group to research and write the two Qiang books. I could not join my wife in Qinghai. A letter had been sent to the Qinghai Institute to have me transferred, to be paid instead from Sichuan. They were just attending to the details and I should relax and remain in Sichuan.

The sunshine in my world had suddenly become a thunderstorm. I was sick at heart and confused, and my mood swung low.

The next day, I went to see my old boss Mr Liu to plead with him. I explained how since Ying and I had married, we had almost always had to endure the bitterness of separation. The Southwest Institute and the Central Institute had agreed that I should transfer to Qinghai. I had already fulfilled my Sichuan fieldwork responsibilities, and I asked him to help me to leave the Research Group for Qinghai.

Liu listened attentively and seemed crystal-clear about what to do. "You stay here," he said, "I'll transfer your wife back here to work with you." He told me to write to her and ask if she would be willing to return. He understood that under the circumstances it was nearly impossible for me to stay. Although he had authority to transfer me, he was unwilling to do so, instead suggesting this compromise.

Within a few days, Ying's letter arrived with her response. None of those who had been transferred to work in Qinghai was at liberty to leave. Qinghai's development had to be supported, for this was a key Party policy and whoever defied it would be treated as a deserter. She had no intention of deserting, nor would she ask anyone to intervene on her behalf. Whether or not I could go to Qinghai, she would remain there, and would die before she would ask for a transfer back.

Regarding the request from Sichuan to transfer me to Sichuan, several letters were sent to Qinghai and each received the same reply: I could not be transferred but should go to the Qinghai Institute without delay. No one else at the Institute could teach Nationality History.

Sichuan, however, overruled. Mr Liu's proposal to transfer Ying back to Chengdu had been simply intended to soften my resolve and secure my loyalty, but it failed on both fronts, for it failed to bring Ying back.

In the blink of an eye, it was Spring Festival 1960. During the holiday, Ying came to Chengdu to visit, and we were together for two weeks before she returned to Qinghai. I yearned for the impossible and my discontent grew ever stronger.

For work reasons, however, I had to remain in Sichuan for over a year as a member of the Qiang Research Group. Most days were spent in County Maowen, either at the County Committee's Office compiling the Survey book, or visiting Qiang villages to supplement existing materials by investigation and interview.

Returning to the Qiang mountains, rivers and villages, brought back vivid memories from before. During those days, however, my sense of wonder at the surrounding beauty was paralysed by my underlying discontent. I was no longer really interested in the work. The spirit that had earlier moved me to investigate all kinds of cultural phenomena had deserted me. I only wanted to do the bare minimum and report back quickly.

In the autumn of 1960, the Qiang Research Group was summoned back to Chengdu. There we continued to research and write the two books about the Qiang. At that time, there was a famine and each meal consisted only of a small bowl of steamed rice and a bowl of vegetable soup. Fortuitously, in the midst of suffering, Sichuan implemented a policy of reducing the pressure from over-population by promoting transfers elsewhere.

By winter, my departure for Qinghai was approved. The poor autumn harvest was followed by a harsh and cold midwinter. I didn't feel cold, however, for my aspiration had been realised. With great delight, I sorted out my luggage and set off on the journey.

The Days Just After Arriving in Qinghai

At the end of 1960 I left Chengdu, going north by train. At Baiji, I changed to a westbound train full of strangers. At dusk, we arrived in Lanzhou, where it felt absolutely freezing.

As we sped towards Qinghai, it was obvious that the thick cotton clothes I was wearing were not sufficient to repel the cold of that region. The temperatures simply could not be compared with those in Sichuan. No wonder people were reluctant to be transferred here.

The train reached Xining station at 2 or 3 am. Only about 100 passengers were still on board and everyone disembarked. Most trooped wearily through the station to the waiting room to warm themselves by the fire and wait for daylight. I followed and sat for a while beside a gas stove, wondering what to do. Maybe I should go home immediately, burning as I was with impatience. I left the waiting room and asked for the general direction of the Qinghai Institute. People pointed me in the right direction, but said it was very far and advised me to go only after daybreak.

The streets were wide and the streetlights bright, but there were no vehicles or pedestrians in sight. I decided to set off on foot. The only sound was that of my own footsteps and I felt a surge of fear from the eerie silence. Dawn was just breaking when I trudged up to a sign for the Institute hanging outside its main gate. This welcome sight came almost as a surprise after such a long walk and I heaved a huge sigh of relief.

I made a beeline for Reception and knocked the door, asking for the university offices. Inside the voice of an old man replied in a loud stream of abuse, using Qinghai Mandarin. He was raging, but I couldn't understand a word. Probably, he was just cursing me for disturbing his sleep.

When I looked at my watch, I realised it was only just after 7 am, and I didn't dare knock again. I might as well sit outside the door and wait for the man to get up. As daylight began to take over, many in the Institute buildings came outside to use the toilets. Others emerged and gravitated to the rooms for fetching boiled water. Chimneys started smoking.

Just before 8 am, the man in Reception was still in bed. It was cold, I was impatient and I decided not to wait any longer. I would just ask someone else. In the end, I found the Institute Office and felt fortunate to find the door was already open and someone had started work. A young female cadre admitted me. When she heard I had come from Chengdu, she seemed to know all about me, and was very welcoming. She said she was also from Chengdu and called another cadre to come and lead me to my wife's home so I could rest.

Ying taught the college preparation course, and was head of the teaching group for 'revolutionary history' – namely, the history of the Chinese Communist Party. She lived in a single-person room in a dormitory, less than 20 square metres in area, with a single bed, an office desk, a cupboard, an iron coal-burning stove, brick walls and an earth floor.

On the morning I arrived, Ying asked a couple of students for help. They brought two wooden planks and two single stools, and arranged them to enlarge the single bed into a temporary double bed. With the freezing weather, most people were wearing tall cylindrical felt boots and leather caps. I was not so well equipped, but only had the short cotton overcoat I had worn when leaving Chengdu two days before. I sat all day beside the stove, trying to keep warm and not daring to go outside.

To me, this was a completely new start. Within a few days, I was sent to the Political History Department to report for duty. I was assigned to the history teaching and research office, together with a teacher from Shanxi who had been transferred from the Beijing Teachers' University. We lived together in a dormitory bedroom which doubled up as our office.

Our most important piece of furniture was the coal-burning iron stove. We kept a careful eye on it, continually adding coal and attending to its needs. We would often be found sitting on our beds, covered by quilts trying to keep warm, either reading or writing. At weekends, I went to Ying's for a break. The other teacher remarked that he felt even colder on the two nights I was away, and was simply unable to get to sleep, instead staying up late and smoking more than usual.

Food was rationed at the time and everyone received 10 kg of rice per month. In the mornings, we were provided with a bowl of soup, prepared by boiling some vegetables together with a little paste made from flour and water. At lunch and dinner, we each received two steamed rolls, with some boiled vegetables. Each steamed roll was supposed to weigh 100g, but in fact, they weighed something not much over 50g and together fell far short of sating one's appetite.

Day and night, we were hungry, as if our bellies had been licked clean by a cat. Nearly all the men were afflicted to some degree with swollen legs and faces. Those most seriously affected were not able to stand up again after sunning themselves in the courtyards, paralysed by hunger, and died in their seats.

In all directions, the countryside was bare, with trees consisting of bare branches. There was nothing green in the open fields, which were almost as neat and tidy as the sports fields. You might occasionally see one or two people digging, looking for something, maybe grass roots. Above the surface of the earth, there was nothing.

As usual, there was a university holiday on the first day of the new calendar year. Our food that day was slightly better than usual. At lunch, we received a bowl of noodles and a little fried mutton, while in the evening, everyone enjoyed a bowl of mutton dumplings and received 250g of flour for making their own dumplings. But festival celebrations were just a memory. In practice, all anyone could think of was having one satisfying meal.

To survive the winter, some research students who had graduated from the better universities decided to resign from the Institute to return home. Some students stole and ate a couple of steamed buns, and were punished via re-education through labour. As soon as the winter holidays began, people from other provinces assembled at the railway and bus stations to make the journey home. Locals who owned their own homes also set out in full force, none remaining.

Everyone knew the winter of 1960/61 in Qinghai was going to be freezing, a season when hunger would threaten our very existence. People's faces were blanched with fear as they crammed onto trains and buses, as if fleeing some calamity, taking off towards the east.

Within a month of my arrival in Xining, the winter holidays began. Ying and I also boarded a train, from Xining to Chengdu. I stayed in Chengdu while Ying went on to visit her parents and our daughter in Kunming, and to spend Spring Festival there.

In Chengdu at that time, it was also difficult to find food. I had to queue a whole morning to buy 40g of sticky rice dumplings. I heard you could buy food in the neighbouring countryside and followed others there, going from one market to the next, buying maize pancakes or other light refreshments to stave off the hunger. Occasionally, I was able to buy rice or noodles. In some places, you could buy 'wine' that had been made with fermented vegetables. Hunger improves any dish and for those couple of weeks, I was able to eat enough to satisfy.

When I returned to Chengdu, I learned that they had implemented the policy of Deputy Prime Minister Chen Yun. Sweetshops were suddenly supplying limitless quantities of expensive light refreshments. If you did not have enough food coupons for a meal, you could buy such refreshments to keep going, assuming you had enough money.

Ying returned from Kunming on schedule. Together we set off back to the Institute in Xining. We had survived the winter vacation safe and sound, one which had been characterised by the most difficult of circumstances.

On that winter train journey, the loving care that Ying showed towards me was greater even than that of my own dear mother. She ate less herself so I could eat more, whether rationed mooncakes on the train, barbecued chicken bought with food coupons at the Baoji station waiting room, or food we had brought from Chengdu. Ying's kindness on the journey left an unforgettable impression. How was she able to be so kind to me then?

A new semester began in March and the Political History Department established a new nationality history teaching and research group, of which I was the leader. My group was responsible for writing teaching materials on the history of Tibetan and Mongolian people.

Observing Minority Education

Soon after the spring semester began in 1961, the Institute director invited me for a chat. There were plans to organise a research group to examine minority education, and he asked me to be group leader. The group would consist of six people, including others from different departments. I was to oversee several days' study of the outline of the proposed investigation, and to clarify everyone's responsibilities.

Afterwards, the group would divide up as follows: one person to Yushu, two people to Hainan, one person to Haixi, and two people to Guoluo. Investigations were prescribed to last a month, beginning at the end of April. Living conditions were likely to be very difficult and no one knew for sure if they would be able to return safely after setting off.

I went with Mr Fu to Guoluo, where we stayed at the prefectural guesthouse. Apart from us, only the guesthouse manager and cook were there. We ate steamed buns and braised wild horse meat. We could only have one steamed bun per meal and one portion of wild horse meat. I remember the horse meat seemed tasteless, and insufficient to satisfy my empty stomach.

Although the sun was shining brightly on 1st May and I was wearing a short leather coat, I still felt freezing the whole day. Fu and I visited the Provincial Communist Party Council Chairman Li Xi Cai Dan. He had been born into a Han household in County Hualong and was a Living Buddha: namely, a senior lama, selected in accordance with the rules of incarnation in Lamaism. He spoke Tibetan and welcomed us into his home for the afternoon.

We soon discovered that Cai Dan was married to a short woman who had given birth to a plump baby boy. Mother and son were sitting on a Tibetan rug on the floor, eating *zanba* (a staple food for Tibetans, roasted barley made into a paste). As we left, I asked Cai Dan, "As a Living Buddha, how come you married and had a son?"

He replied that in the past he used to be a less important Living Buddha. Only after Liberation had he first made contact with the People's Government, whereupon he became the prefecture's first Living Buddha ever to marry. This demonstrated progress and paved the way for him to become Chairman of the Provincial Party Council. I asked whether other Living Buddhas had followed suit and married. He replied they hadn't.

The next day, Fu and I split up, going to different Tibetan communes. In the communes, each individual received rations of five kg of barley per month. There were large amounts of butter and dried meat in the storehouses, so no one was hungry. There were lots of carp in the river and you could have used a washbasin to scoop up fish. There was a taboo, however, on eating fish, and in any case, people did not really need the fish to ward off hunger.

The party cadres there looked healthy and were busy with their work. They hardly experienced any of the starvation-panic prevalent in the rest of the country. They listened thoughtfully as I reported that teachers and students at the Institute were going hungry, that many were suffering from oedema and that some had died while sitting out in the sunshine.

A cadre who spoke with a Shanxi accent, who had been demoted into leadership at that commune, tore off the page of a calendar, wrote a note on the page and handed it to me. He instructed his manager in writing to sell me two kg of butter and two kg of mutton. This was like an act of salvation and his kindness still remains fresh in my memory.

The main problem in interviewing the Tibetans was that few of them spoke Mandarin. Primary school teachers were all lamas (spiritual leaders in Tibetan Buddhism) and used Tibetan language and literature. Formerly, they had taught young monks in the temples to recite scriptures and prayers, whereas in modern times, they were teaching ordinary children from society at large. Textbooks were in the Tibetan language.

A commune cadre responsible for culture and education explained that every year the authorities assigned Han teachers to come, but because they did not understand Tibetan, they were unable to teach, and sooner or later gave up and went back. The cadre asked us to train teachers who could teach in Tibetan.

One of the lama teachers, however, said frankly that Tibetans eat *zanba*, speak Tibetan and write Tibetan, whereas Han people eat rice, speak Mandarin and write Chinese characters. For generations it's been like that and you can't change these customs. The antipathy towards studying Mandarin was fairly universal among Tibetans.

The commune cadre said that all the cadres there were Tibetans. If the authorities circulated information in Mandarin, no one would pay any attention. Documents would pile up and no one would know what they said. Locals didn't even want to know, fearing the requisitioning of butter, beef or mutton. When authorities investigated, people would simply reply, "We didn't understand." Many things would be delayed in this way, though Tibetans were very strict with their own people. The ordinary people still bowed down and kow-towed to the cadres, and did whatever they were told. They never dared to say the word 'no'.

Farmers in County Banma lived in houses made of sun-dried brick, which was not fired. There was a prison there and inmates were local Tibetans. Prison guards were also Tibetans, belonging to the civilian army corps. The guards enjoyed drinking and after drinking too much, some would themselves become offenders, casually calling out inmates to beat them. There never used to be any records of such misdemeanours and after amusing themselves, they would just send the prisoners back. Some would simply strike prisoners on sight, just for fun.

The authorities never investigated such behaviour, and strange to say, inmates became used to such treatment. They just hung their heads in shame, but with hardly a trace of fear. When, however, they saw a Han cadre or soldier, they would promptly become fearful, warning, "Han people have come!" They would shrink back, for fear of being led away. Apparently, they did not so much fear being physically beaten as being taken away, because nine out of 10 who were taken away never returned.

Originally, to build the prison, inmates had used cowhide ropes to carry great rocks on their backs. Foremen shouted out repeatedly, "You're building a house for yourselves to live in. No goofing off!"

A few days later, I went to County Maqin to research the circumstances of herdsmen there. The commune cadres gave me directions to the tents where herdsmen were living. They were said to be at the foot of the mountains, about five kilometres away. I went alone, empty-handed, towards the prairie.

Suddenly in the distance, I saw an animal loping towards me. It was hard to distinguish whether it was a wolf or a dog, but as it approached, I realised it was massive and seemed to be accelerating. Looking around, all I could see were endless grasslands, no other company than the sky above my head and the earth beneath my feet. I felt helpless, about to be mauled by a wild animal. Terrified, I crouched down as my legs turned to jelly. All of a sudden, the animal slowed down. It stood there in front of me for about a minute, dumbly staring straight at me. Finally losing patience, it turned and walked slowly away, stopping now and then, as if reluctant to leave, but never looking back until it had disappeared. I heaved a sigh of relief and stood up, resuming tentative progress towards my distant goal.

At the foot of the mountains, there were four or five tents, each with a great Tibetan dog on a leash guarding the entrance. Seeing a stranger, they started prancing around madly, desperate to welcome me in their customary way. The tent where I was to stay was normally occupied only by an old woman, for younger relatives were away grazing cattle and would only return every couple of weeks. A young cadre from the provincial capital was also there doing some research, staying in the old woman's tent.

That evening before going to sleep, the woman unleashed her dog, which came wandering into the tent looking for food. It came up to the young cadre's bed and woke him. He didn't dare to move, except to grab a pistol and load it; then he coughed a little.

The dog turned and nosed my bed, and I was shocked to hear the fearful sound of its breathing up close. It pressed with its paw and simultaneously emitted an appalling howl. Abruptly, it grabbed my right foot in its jaws, quilt and all, and seemed to be biting and pulling with all its strength, trying to tear the foot off. It was growling fiercely and the tent was shaking, when the old woman shouted at it in Tibetan, striking it ferociously with a wooden stick. The bloodthirsty dog turned tail and ran off, but not before it had bitten into my right ankle, and my blood had lent a dark red dye to the quilt and bed sheet.

There was no doctor nearby, so the next morning the woman led over an emaciated horse, and the cadre organised for a local Tibetan to accompany me on horseback to the commune hospital. I had managed to find the tents, but was unable to do any real survey. Instead, I encountered two life-threatening situations. I thank God I didn't lose my life in the grasslands of Guoluo.

Working at the Cadre Training Department

I presided over the minority education research group in its investigation of six prefectures, and presented a written report to Institute leaders at the start of the autumn semester. Provincial leaders subsequently decided that a course on Tibetan language and literature should be offered at the Institute and all cadres in the province should take it.

Thus in autumn of 1961, the Institute established a department for training cadres involved in managing the affairs of minorities. The Institute transferred me, together with two others from the Political History Department, to the Cadre

Training Department, to lecture using the text *Nationality Problems and Nationality Policies*. Six or seven people shared the lecture load.

My job was to teach 20 periods and be involved in panel discussions in the afternoons, listening to ideas and answering questions raised by the students. I followed this routine, but my non-working hours were still relatively many. My hobby-cum-addiction from an early age had been reading and writing. Basically, I had no other interests.

Apart from weekends, when I spent two nights and Sunday at home with my wife, I spent my spare time alone in my bedroom, with my head buried in three Russian books, translating them into Chinese: *Nationalities of Mankind*, *Nationalities in Australia and Oceania* and *Latest Theory on Questions of Soviet Nationalities*.

I was engrossed in research and translation and ignored much else, with the result that I became estranged from some colleagues. At home, I was more emotionally detached than before. I inadvertently gave others the impression that I was able to invest my hope in something they knew nothing about.

It was still difficult keeping body and soul together. Everyone planted their own vegetable plots. Though Ying was several months pregnant with our second child, she dragged herself to tend two plots on gardens dedicated to staff of the college preparation course. On weekends, usually Sundays, Ying and I would go together and work on those plots.

Once Ying fumbled around on her own in the dark, watering sugar beet, right up until 10 pm, and she wouldn't allow me to help. Instead, she urged me to stay at home and concentrate on writing a research article about the book by Engels: *The Origin of the Family, Private Property and State* (1884). When she returned, she was exhausted and famished. I gave her a steamed roll, but she couldn't bring herself to eat it and quietly placed it in a rice bowl. The next morning at breakfast, she drank her mixed vegetable soup and made me eat the steamed roll from the previous night.

For lunch and dinner, we usually each ate a steamed roll and a big bowl of swede, boiled in water. Ying gave me most of two steamed rolls and a bowl of vegetable, and broke off just a little of her roll for herself. She refused to take her full share, saying that I had a bigger appetite. In fact, she was prepared to go hungry so that I could be better fed.

Ying's vegetable plots resulted in an autumn harvest to gladden our hearts. A large quantity of swede, sugar beet and potatoes was piled up in one corner of her room. She often ate swede boiled with potatoes, and every day saved up one or two steamed rolls. She sent me home at weekends clutching potatoes and noodles, and this certainly improved my lot.

Ying was afraid I would starve and she came to see me three afternoons a week. She would be wrapped up in cotton, heavy with the five- to eight-month pregnancy, and come limping along with a heavy bag of potatoes and swede. It was typically a while before her panting subsided.

Ying would hardly have time to talk before putting the pot on to boil the potatoes and pulling out two or three steamed buns from the bag, smiling and saying, "Have something special to eat!" Finally, she would sit down and enquire how I was doing. I don't know how many times this scenario played itself out in the autumn and winter of 1961.

The train network in Yunnan had still not connected with the rest of the country, but of all provinces, Yunnan had the best supply of food that year. You could still eat rice or noodles on the streets of Kunming for only one or two food coupons. Some restaurants didn't even require coupons, and you could pay cash as usual. Cadres, teachers, staff and students from other cities and provinces flocked to Kunming for holidays, using family or friends as a pretext for visiting. The common goal was to eat your fill. You could still buy things that were simply unavailable outside Yunnan – cigarettes, for example, or liquor, sweets and cakes.

The due date of our second baby was sometime in the winter vacation. Ying wanted me to go with her to Kunming for the birth. We travelled by train and road. It took days to travel from Sichuan to Kunming.

Ying straightened up her pregnant belly. Travelling was tough, for the weather was freezing and you couldn't buy enough food to satisfy. I felt sorry for her, but I was at a loss as to how to improve her lot. I could only stay nearby and maintain a watchful eye over her, horrified at the prospect of a premature labour.

Ying, however, seemed immune, always smiling, chatting and laughing, not betraying any trace of suffering from hunger, cold or travel. On the contrary, she spent her time more concerned about me. Once she noticed that the tobacco in my pipe was finished and there was nowhere to buy more. That evening, we walked together to a crossing, where people were selling individual cigarettes. Ying pulled out some change and gave it to me, telling me to buy a couple of packets.

Weining was particularly cold and I was only wearing a thin cotton coat, at risk of catching cold. Ying took her own woollen shawl and draped it over my shoulders. She treated difficulty and danger as if they were the norm and did not falter in the face of hardship. In retrospect, when I think of Ying, my conscience feels seared, and my heart is still full of pain and guilt that is difficult to express.

At last, we arrived safely in Kunming. It was the first time I'd met my parents-in-law, and I did not even know at first how to address them. Ying seemed to understand, and did not complain at all about my sense of inadequacy. We took out gifts from the bag we had carried: a few large potatoes dug up from Ying's own garden, and a kilogramme or two of persimmon cakes that we had bought in Baoji. Smiling, her parents remarked that they had never seen such big potatoes, and my father-in-law said he loved persimmon cakes. Their words reassured me. They were both kindly people, going out of their way to be gracious.

No matter what anyone said, however, such gifts could hardly be regarded as adequate. Even if we had been poorer than we actually were, the gifts would still not have been good enough. I blame my own naivety with regard to etiquette: at the time I felt ashamed, disgraced even, not knowing what to say and standing to one side as if petrified. I was dogged by the Dong tradition of estrangement between a son-in-law and his parents-in-law. I felt subdued and awkward with my in-laws, behaving unnaturally in both what I said and did. I was cautious and meticulous, ever afraid of making a mistake and being disdained. While staying with them, I felt more like a guest than a relative.

My father-in-law had been a respected intellectual. From start to finish, he smiled at me. He never spoke just for the sake of it, and never worried about promoting his own personal opinion. My mother-in-law was diligent in her household duties. At each meal, she quietly placed some special portions in my bowl, then added rice to overflowing. On receiving such kind hospitality, I just didn't know how to respond.

Just after Spring Festival in 1962, Ying gave birth in hospital to our second daughter, Tao, by Caesarean section. While there, she was notified that she had been approved to join the Chinese Communist Party. Delightedly, she jumped out of bed and stood up, then sat down again, tranquil in spirit. Twice she said to me, "Quan, I'm a Communist Party member," and delivered a few sweets into my hand, telling me to eat them quickly to share her happiness. The news actually made it difficult for her to rest. She promptly indicated she would leave hospital the next day. When I advised her to stay a day or two to recuperate, she behaved as if she hadn't heard.

When Ying left hospital, we returned to her parents' home. There was some bleeding at the incision, but Ying had to continue breast-feeding, for we had no money to afford alternative nourishment, and her parents were also poor. In the mornings, they would eat rice porridge, supplemented by rice and fried dishes at lunch and dinner. Meat and fat were rare luxuries. Ying became even more emaciated than before and seemed sick. I wanted to share her suffering yet could not, and felt distressed night and day.

After Spring Festival, the Kunming weather changed from warm to hot, better than the mid-summer mountain weather in Xining. Wherever you looked, the streets were bustling, with young men and women wearing shirts and skirts. The new semester was about to begin, and while Ying still had a towel wrapped around her head – traditional for the first month after giving birth – she was nevertheless in high spirits. She was constantly taking care of the baby and seemed to be over the worst of any health problems, so I could afford to relax a little.

Ying suggested I return first to the Institute, for the new semester was about to begin and it was better not to delay. She would spend the rest of her maternity leave convalescing in Kunming and then return to Xining.

That semester, my work in the Cadre Training Department was the same as before and I still lived in the same bedroom in the middle of nowhere. A young cadre lived next door, where people played mah-jong at practically all times of day and night. Every now and then, there would be loud bursts of menacing clamour, which by day were tolerable but deep in the night felt frightening. After waking with a start, I'd often spend the rest of the night unable to get back to sleep.

Before long, the Deputy Director of the Institute visited the Cadre Training Department to report that the Institute had recently unearthed the existence of a local counter-revolutionary organisation. We felt appalled. There were many Tibetan cadres at our Department and other non-Tibetan trainees were mostly from Tibetan regions. They became the focal point of investigations and we had to take many precautions.

Staff armed with guns started a rota for night patrols. By day, we arranged for guards at the Institute entrance. In addition to lecturing, teachers had to spend time with students, collecting any sensitive information. Lecture content quickly moved towards the left. Everything was explained by the red thread that *nationality problems are essentially problems of class struggle.*

Everyone felt tense and nights were anything but calm. People continued to congregate in the room next to mine, alternately quarrelling and laughing. Sometimes the noise was fierce. The actual words were mostly lost through the wall. My imagination, however, filled my mind with horrific thoughts and kept me from sleep, forcing me to focus instead on my translation work. That was my means of lightening the load, and I quickly completed the translation of *Nationalities of Mankind.*

Within a couple of weeks of breaking the news about the counter-revolutionary organisation, provincial leaders stationed a *four purifications* working group [purifying politics, ideology, organisation and economics, a movement running for four years until 1966] at the Institute. Its first job was to administer a test to Institute leaders. Whoever passed the test could 'go downstairs'.

The Deputy Director of the Institute was repeatedly examined but was never permitted to 'go downstairs'. The working unit mobilised cadres, teachers and staff in every department to convene meetings for sharing opinions and reporting offenders, ostensibly to gather materials to help with the movement of leaders 'downstairs'.

One morning, around 6 am, the Deputy Director hurriedly got out of bed. He grabbed a pistol and shouted to his wife, who had been sleeping in the next room, "I can't stand it any longer!" Then he shot himself twice in the stomach and fell down dead.

Provincial leaders rushed to the scene. Afterwards, we were simply told that the Deputy Director had committed suicide by shooting himself. Nothing else was made public. A few months earlier, when he had first announced the existence of a counter-revolutionary movement, no one could have foreseen that he himself would commit suicide. Such crises when added together were perplexing, and made the underlying problem seem more serious and complicated.

The Qinghai Institute became a key focal point for provincial leaders, who went to great lengths to discover the reasons for the suicide. The *four purifications* working group suspended administration of the 'going downstairs' test, but at the same time became a fixed presence at the Institute. Their new role was surreptitiously to investigate the circumstances and ideology of various people connected with the Institute, and this contributed to an atmosphere which remained extremely tense.

I myself was politically unaffiliated, so hardly anyone paid any attention to me, except in the work sphere. I rarely even spoke to anyone, so I was particularly lonely at that time. Except when engrossed in translation, I felt oppressed by the prevailing atmosphere of terror.

A Brief Divorce

It was probably May 1962, at the end of the cold season in Xining, when Ying returned to the Institute with Tao on her back. She brought many gifts for me from her parents: cans of pork, other snacks and cigarettes. When I saw all this, I appreciated even more their kindness and generosity. I owed the two old folk a great debt of affection, a debt which troubled me for a long time to come.

I continued to visit Ying where she lived in the small single-storey building for staff of the college preparation course, joining her there on Saturdays. On Monday mornings, I returned to the Cadre Training Department, while she lectured, worked in the office, attended meetings and served as head teacher of a class. For Ying, eight hours a day were filled with work, and she also had to take care of the baby, who was not yet six months old. How could she manage all that? She had to pass the baby into day-care during office hours, collect her after work and continue busy until after 10 pm.

When I went to be with her at weekends, I observed Ying doing all kinds of housework in addition to breast-feeding; nose-to-the-grindstone, never resting. She once asked me to go to the River Huangshui to draw water for the baby to drink, for the local spring water was too hard and difficult to digest. I consoled myself with the thought that I was able to help her in this one small thing. Thereafter, every Sunday I would take an empty pot and set off on the journey to the river, happily doing that job. She was still doing too much, however, and it was taking its toll on her; and also on me, for I felt deeply guilty about it.

Why did I not dare to take the initiative and help her by sharing some more of her work? It was still a case of 'not daring'. I was afraid that what I did might not be good enough to satisfy her, that she would somehow be displeased, and I was too easily humiliated. The Dong custom of separating the work of the sexes – a man not doing a woman's work, and vice versa – had left its mark on me, and I couldn't shake free of it. I was already in my thirties, and it felt impossible to break the habit.

By summer 1962, the Institute was tense, with a prevailing perception that class struggle was acute, affecting every sphere of life and work. Everyone viewed everyone else through the prism of class struggle, even within the same family, with clear categories having been spelled out, especially for cadres and teachers. There were Party members, league members, activists, black sheep, landlords' children, workers' or peasants' children, students, staff, people with historical problems, those who had had incriminating relationships before Liberation, those who had overseas connections, those who had been taught by Soviet people, those who had other connections with Soviets, those with family members in prison, or in care, or who had been killed. Even those who knew Russian or English comprised separate categories. Many such categories were grounds for suspicion when the *four purifications* were being implemented.

In this environment, the toleration, understanding, affection and mutual dependence Ying and I had formerly shared, were all undermined. With such categories, even I myself became doubtful about what kind of person I was. She was, however, clearly a Chinese Communist Party member, and she was obliged to make some kind of stand concerning me.

Ying observed me cutting myself off from everyone and burying my head in the sand of reading Russian books, as if I were a prince. She thought I was working my way into a dead end, and that in the prevailing atmosphere of the fierce struggle against 'revisionism', my behaviour was really dangerous. [In the international communist movement, 'revisionism' was defined as anti-Marxist tendencies disguised as Marxism.] There would be problems sooner or later. She was both disappointed in me and worried about me, and became cool, distant and detached.

In those days when I saw Ying talking and laughing with others, warmly and enthusiastically, I felt excluded, left out in the cold, as if Ying was spurning me. We both knew in our hearts exactly how things stood, and we knew we couldn't maintain our marriage like this. We didn't quarrel, however, so when we went to the civil administration department to apply for a divorce, the reason given was simply 'alienation'.

A few days after our divorce, the summer vacation began and Ying again delivered our young daughters to Kunming, so their grandmother could take care of them. 'Alienation' had been the reason for divorce under our bilateral agreement, but it was not really legitimate. We had been married five years and had two daughters, and in normal times, we would still have been committed to each other.

We were, however, different from many others in that our love for each other was relatively introverted. It was as if we kept it secret, as if we each hoped that others would not notice. We were together for days on end, but our love was mostly concealed. I *did* write the words 'I love you' in my letters to her, but when we were out for a walk holding hands, or sharing the same bed, I never plucked up the courage to say directly to her, "I love you." By contrast, Ying was bold in this regard and had frequently said those three words to me.

When we were together, we chatted little, each getting on with our own thing, never bossing each other about, mostly passing the time together quietly. It was as if our relationship had been rooted in the motto: 'Respect without the need for action, trust without the need for words'. Even without words and deeds, we were still closely knit together, and in our heart of hearts, we depended deeply on each other.

After the divorce, the roots of our former love were still strong; we could never be divorced from those feelings. So it transpired that we still normally spent Sundays together.

While we had been going through divorce proceedings, the focal point of the *four-purification* investigations had been the Political History Department, where three teachers had been found guilty of holding revisionist viewpoints. Inspections and criticisms were duly launched. At the time, there were still no problems at my Cadre Training Department or at Ying's College Preparation Department, so this gave us opportunity to see more of each other than usual. In the end, in January 1964, we remarried, having been divorced for over a year. We had found it nearly impossible to live without each other.

After remarrying, our feelings for each other were the same as before. Each weekend, I went home to Ying's place to spend Sunday there. Gao, another female teacher at the college preparation course, from the south of China, often came to spend time with Ying at weekends. She sometimes helped our family by caring for the children, and when Ying and I were not on the best of terms, Gao served as mediator. We knew each other well and she was practically part of the family.

Travel with Children

At Spring Festival 1964, Ying asked me to go and bring our daughters back from Kunming. On the way there, I returned to my old home in the village of Liukai, Guizhou, to visit my mother, who was living unobtrusively with my daughter in a small wooden shed, containing only a bed and a fireplace. It was quite a squeeze for the three of us to sit down together around the fire.

I listened as my mother, weeping as she spoke, described recent events. Seeing my cadre's clothes and hearing I was a university lecturer, she was pleased, though she was still crying. She said that seeing her son return helped her retain the will to live a few more years. We thought we would see each other again, for there might be good days just around the corner. I stayed three days then took my leave.

When I arrived in Kunming, Spring Festival had just begun. Taking advantage of the fact that there were relatively few travellers just then, I started quickly with my two daughters on the journey back to Qinghai. The elder daughter was now six years old, and the younger was two. On the fourth day of New Year in 1964, we said goodbye to their grandparents and set off on the long journey by train and bus. We changed vehicle more than 10 times and travelled thousands of kilometres, the whole journey lasting half a month.

When we boarded the train in Kunming, my younger daughter was on my back, while the older was holding my hand. The children were happy to be with their father. They sat beside me, well behaved and in good spirits, frequently looking up at me and looking out of the window. Both were obedient, never saying 'no' and never causing any trouble.

We stayed overnight in Zhanyi before boarding a bus the next day for Guiyang. That night, we ate our fill in a restaurant and I drank some liquor against the cold.

Perhaps my little daughter was not used to eating so well, or her tummy was more used to rice porridge than oil. That evening, she ate her fill on fried meat and vegetables, with rice. Shortly after returning to our room, it seemed her tummy was sore, but the night was dark and there was no help to be found. Beads of sweat formed on my forehead. My heroic elder daughter hugged her little sister, comforting her, "Don't cry, Tao. It'll soon be better…" After an hour, Tao eventually went to sleep.

Afterwards, a doctor said the problem had probably been induced by eating a lot of rice on an empty stomach. I felt sorry the child had probably been hungry for nearly two years in someone else's home.

The bus stopped overnight and everyone stayed in a motel. On hearing the engine of the bus starting up the next morning, we all hurried out to board. It was freezing. I was carrying luggage on my back and leading Tao by the hand, fumbling along in the dark, while Ou Ou followed behind. Suddenly, Ou Ou slipped and fell, crying out, so I let go of Tao's hand and pulled Ou Ou back to her feet. She stopped crying and followed me again, but soon after, she stretched out her muddy hands and started crying again. I helped wipe her hands clean. She wanted to cooperate and stopped crying, taking Tao by the hand. Then I took Ou Ou's hand and we walked on slowly in the dark until we reached the bus.

On the bus, I told my daughters they had an aunt in Guiyang, whereupon my poor girls behaved like orphans, begging eagerly to see their relative. Ou Ou kept asking if we could see their aunt when we reached Guiyang, where did she live, and were we nearly there. The aunt's home, however, was in the suburbs, far from the railway station, there were no direct buses there, and she had no telephone. In the event, we had to stay at a motel near the station and await the next northbound bus.

For a while, Tao had not been able to pass stool, so I determined to take her to the railway hospital for treatment. It was still Spring Festival holiday, most people had not yet returned to work, and there were only two duty nurses available. They used soap to extract some dry stool, only with difficulty. They advised me to bring Tao back again the next day, and again the soap helped. This all delayed our journey by a day.

After reaching Ganshui by bus, we boarded a train to Chongqing, and then bought train tickets from Chongqing to Chengdu, changing trains several times.

We arrived safely in Chengdu, stayed a night at a motel by the station and bought tickets on to Baoji. The next day, I told my daughters not to leave the room, for I had to go and see an old friend at the Southwest Institute. The children were generally so obedient that when I left them I was unconcerned.

When I returned about three hours later, however, the girls had vanished. Panicking, I rushed to ask a hotel worker if she knew of the girls' whereabouts. It turned out the woman herself had taken the children out. When I questioned her later, Ou Ou said it had been past lunchtime, and the auntie had invited them to go and drink some water. It shocked me to think how easily my children might have been abducted.

We arrived in Baoji that evening and waited at the station for the next train. The northwest felt so much colder than the southwest, and the two girls were still dressed for the warmer Yunnan weather. I draped my coat over Tao and led her by the hand, while Ou Ou, with a small satchel on her back, followed close behind. It was about midnight and everyone was queueing for the connection to Gansu, Qinghai and Xinjiang.

It was so crowded. I was concentrating on Tao, and just assumed that Ou Ou was close behind, but people were jostling and it was all fairly chaotic. When I looked around, there was no trace of Ou Ou. Scared stiff, I rushed around with Tao, and in the end found Ou Ou in the company of some people from Sichuan. Thankfully, we had not yet boarded or she might have been lost. I asked why she had gone with strangers, and she replied that she had lost sight of me, so had opted to go with them instead. It was night-time and the lamplights were dim. I had almost lost our child, and I still shudder today when I think about it.

After Spring Festival, returning students jammed the trains. The three of us squeezed onto two seats but later, when it became even more crowded, we made do with one. Ou Ou climbed onto my lap and fell asleep.

Even though it was so crowded, we still felt frozen in the cold draught. With so many people, it was difficult for anyone to move around, and we stayed in our original seat the whole night long. No one came around to sell food or offer boiled water. We were hungry and thirsty, but when the children woke up, they didn't complain. Instead, they simply accepted the situation, with a maturity beyond their years.

Some Shanxi students returning to Lanzhou University were sitting nearby. On noticing I carried a red card from the Qinghai Institute, they were very polite. When Ou Ou woke, one of the female students squeezed up so that Ou Ou could sit beside her, while Tao stayed with me. That student kindly helped care for the children most of the journey, like a stand-in mother.

The students disembarked in Lanzhou and as they were leaving, our new friend invited the children to visit her there. I never would have imagined we would meet such a kind person in such a crowded and chaotic environment; though at the time, there were still many such people.

We arrived in Xining late at night. The children's mother Chen Ying and our female teacher-friend Gao were waiting at the station, and found us as soon as we disembarked. Ying quickly advanced to pick Tao up, but Tao didn't recognise her and tried to dodge her, clinging to me. We assured her this was her mother and after a while, she assented to leave me and go with her mum. Ou Ou was already six years old and naturally recognised her mother, but she was happy for Gao to lead her by the hand, while Ying took care of Tao. I carried the luggage and followed behind.

At that time of night, there were no buses, so we walked back from the station to the Institute middle school, where Ying was teaching. It felt like going home.

It had been a great adventure, bringing our daughters back from the distant city of Kunming, having had to change vehicles so many times, and arriving at long last back with their mother. We had shared hardship and comfort, horror and rejoicing, so that the two girls and I developed deep bonds.

Ying happily remarked that with the children back home, we were at last a family, and now we could begin family life. In the years just after Liberation, I hadn't had a family, though I'd yearned for one. Hearing my wife speak like this, it dawned on me that we were indeed a happy family. My dearest dreams had been realised.

Chapter 15
Punishing Revisionism
(Xining, 1964-66)

China's First Revisionist

Within a few days, a movement to 'Oppose Revisionism' had been established in Qinghai, and the Qinghai Institute was named as the main focal point for the whole province; indeed for the whole northwest region. The whole issue of revisionism had become extremely serious. [In the 1960s, the Chinese often referred to the Soviets as 'modern revisionists'. This was part of the Chinese campaign to attack Nikita Khrushchev and the Soviet Union over various ideological and political issues, for the original friendship of China and the Soviet Union had soured, over differing interpretations of Marxism-Leninism.]

The *four purifications* working group suspended prosecution of the three 'revisionist' teachers in the Political History Department, and instead concentrated attention on me. This was because my supervisor when I had been a research student in Beijing had been from the Soviet Union. They knew I had translated a Russian book and assumed I still had connections with the Soviet Union. Such background consigned me to the 'revisionist' category.

People even spread the rumour that my translation conveyed some secret communications. Russian names in my translation referred to Nikita Khrushchev, and the paper I had written about three kinds of nationality community had been a revisionist attack on Marxism-Leninism.

Added to my alleged revisionist sentiments, I wore western-style clothing. I was accused of treason. The more they mulled it over, the more serious my offense became, so that in the end I was regarded as a 'dangerous element', an enemy of the highest order. In this way, I became the target of the movement to oppose revisionism. The Qinghai Institute had been nominated to lead the movement, and had taken aim at me. Everyone else only had to practise self-criticism.

At the time, I was still living in my office in the Cadre Training Department. The same noisy stranger was living in the room next door. He fired raucous abuse directly at me, sometimes clearly audible. Occasionally, there would be random bursts of accusation late at night, which seemed menacing to me in my loneliness.

My wife was still working by day and looking after our two daughters. She was overworked and had to deal with the added pressure of allegations that she was married to the first main perpetrator of revisionism. She seemed to be cornered. After visiting her, and observing her melancholy disposition, I would cry dejectedly. How could I set her free?

No medicine could bring a cure. To make matters worse, my accuser next door seemed bent on more evil. I felt unbearable agony and despair, until one evening I went to the clinic to purchase some sleeping pills. Desperate in my depression, I prepared a note to be read after my death.

The next evening, however, I woke from a state of unconsciousness and realised the room door I had locked was no longer locked. The floor showed signs of the footprints of many people. I made my way unsteadily home and found my wife attending routinely to household duties. Though she must have known of my suicide attempt, she did not mention it.

Like everyone else at the Institute, Ying knew I had been under investigation for revisionism, but she had still harboured illusionary hope. When, however, the Institute sent me from the Cadre Training Department to a hospital department, to study 'opposing revisionism', her hope subsided.

Despite my objection, Ying had gone privately to the army hospital for an abortion, removing a boy at the three-month stage of pregnancy. This tested our marriage to the point of snapping. Now without explanation, she refused to converse or answer my anxious questions, and this obviously made things worse. She first ignored me, then told me never to return.

When I subsequently returned, Ying grabbed the girls, marched out and slammed the door behind her. We still shared the same bed but dreamt different dreams. She suspected I was a revisionist, while I suspected she was involved in an affair, that she was torturing me at someone else's instigation. Such suspicions turned to conflict, culminating one evening in an angry argument and slapping each other on the face.

After this, the Institute personnel department notified me I was no longer permitted to go home unless accompanied by two 'guards' Zao and Yang.

Any time I left my room, especially when I went to my wife's home, those two had to accompany me. They sat down together with Ying and me. When I was present, she was supposed to keep open house, so that others could come and understand my situation from her and I could 'be helped'. It was repeatedly asserted that my two guards had been appointed to 'help' me.

Whatever was said or done to me was on the instructions of the leaders. Being guarded and publicly isolated in this way, how could I talk about personal family issues with my wife? I was timid anyway and didn't dare to say much in front of the two observers. It seemed more like she was being visited by the two guards, though at least husband and wife could reassure each other we were okay.

During the *four purifications*, Zao had been criticised for holding revisionist opinions and Yang had been regarded as 'having historical problems'. Often those two would sit in my dormitory trying to coax me into conversation. Zao would say how he had understood the 'three peaces and two alls' [all nations and all parties should coexist in peace, compete in peace and transition in peace]; how Nikita Khrushchev had shaken hands and talked with the Americans; and how allowing certain Russians to return to their country was tantamount to 'capitulation' and 'betrayal of the revolution'.

Zao had watched the broadcast of Lu Mengba being arrested and observed how the audience applauded. Khrushchev had watched him die, and this too had betrayed the revolution. Kenji Miyamoto [leader of the Japanese communist party] was living on a strict diet and had been influenced by Soviet revisionism. Khrushchev had been deploying missiles in Cuba, demonstrating 'capitulationism'.

On one hand was the intense struggle to survive, involving fierce class struggle in socialist countries; on the other was the theory that in such countries the class struggle no longer existed. The Soviet Union had declared that it had eliminated social class, having abolished proletarian dictatorship. Zao parroted such things over and over again.

Every day, such stuff blasted my ears, like bitter torture, making me yearn for sleep. Yang lacked eloquence and sat there to one side, keeping us company and smoking. When his mouth became numb, he would eat a few pills and have another smoke, or smear tiger balm on his forehead, to stave off sleep. You could see that this assignment was hard for him to endure. It lasted through the spring until in summer 1964 I initiated divorce proceedings with Ying a second time.

My guards meticulously fabricated the facts. In reports to leaders presiding over the movement to oppose revisionism, they claimed that as I had attempted suicide, I had been shouting, "Long Live Khrushchev!" Afterwards, the backbone of false allegations in all the meetings was that 'Ou Chaoquan heralded the name of Nikita Khrushchev as he was committing suicide!' This was repeated *ad nauseam*, but it was just a figment of their imagination. I had never uttered any such slogan.

No one had witnessed my suicide attempt, or could verify I had ever shouted such words. In view of the powerful ultra-left emotions opposing revisionism, however, I did not dare to say this, fearing that even a couple of words of confrontation would be misappropriated, tantamount to a death sentence.

In 1964, I wrote two academic articles that enraged the *four purifications* working group and the anti-revisionist stooges.

In August 1964, the first article 'Three kinds of nationality unity' was sent to *Academic Research*. It was never published, for it contradicted the opinions in other journals; but it was never returned to me either.

The second article was about 80,000 characters long, building on the foundation of the first, and expanding upon it: 'On three kinds of nationality unity: tribe, clan and modern nationality'. It expounded the theory of Marx and Engels, using relevant Chinese and foreign references to substantiate my ideas. After I'd finished the first draft, it was confiscated by an Institute leader. I asked repeatedly for it to be returned, until one evening I confronted the leader in the canteen. His shame turned to rage and there in public, he answered me fiercely, "I'm *not* returning it to you. What are you going to do about it?" So the article disappeared forever.

From then on, Institute activists spread rumours that I had been disseminating a systematic theory of revisionism, transforming a simple academic paper that had almost nothing to do with politics into evidence of the crime of propagating revisionism.

My personal drama soon entered a more intense phase. Not only was I forbidden to see or speak to my wife and children, I was also denied access to the library. I was *persona non grata* at the auditorium when the film Early Spring (1963) was screened, so that after buying a ticket and taking my seat, I was brusquely ordered to leave. I was forbidden to participate in the National Day parades. During the National Day holidays, I was not permitted to leave the Institute grounds, but instead my surveillance was intensified.

Such measures emphasised to me, as if I needed to know, the seriousness of my plight. Day and night, I was subjected to psychological pressure. When I realised that my wife had also begun to treat me as an enemy, I realised, too, that she hardly had any choice. Her back was against the wall. My principal concern became to avoid implicating her further, along with my children, and I decided to withdraw conclusively from this family that had in any case already disintegrated. I proposed a divorce and we completed the formalities by the end of 1964.

After this, I stayed alone in my room and read a few English textbooks, occasionally listening to Beijing Radio. Now and then, of an evening, I would attempt to drown my sorrows with alcohol. The leaders did not trust me, and sent Sheng to live with me.

Sheng would sit all day at the office table, or lie on his bed reading, often boiling water for tea. On scorching hot days, he used to burn coal in the fire, creating a cloud of black, noxious smoke to add to the already overpowering heat. I asked him to install a chimney, but he only remarked, "The smoke won't kill you."

Sheng's bed and table were on the bright side of the room beside the window, while my bed was in the corner where you entered. We didn't talk to each other, though if I wanted to leave the university premises, I had to ask his permission. In that case, he would interrogate me until he knew every detail of my plans.

When Sheng went home to celebrate New Year, he was replaced by a man with a Shanxi accent. The new guy liked to chat and often asked about my home village. When he discovered my mother was still alive, he asked solicitously if she had anyone to look after her, divulging incidentally that he thought I would be unable to go back there.

My heart sank, for I realised they were going to imprison me. The next day, I gathered my bits and pieces of clothing together, and posted my graduation diploma to the graduates' office at the Central Institute in Beijing for safekeeping. I burnt all my photos and letters, then sat down and 'relaxed', awaiting my fate.

In spring 1965, the *four purifications* group punished a number of people in succession. Some were demoted, others were expelled and sent home and yet others were sent off for re-education through labour. People were conjecturing about my fate.

Mr Duan, an administrator, instructed me to go to a building site, take over from Mr Sha and do some manual labour; but since I had a cold and high fever, I couldn't go immediately. This of course aroused resentment. Three days later, when the fever had subsided, I was again commanded to go and take over from Sha. I was still, however, incapable of doing physical work.

Duan accused me of simply refusing to work, while Sha hated me. Two more had joined the ranks of my enemies. Duan told the leaders he would soon cure me of my illness. Every time Sha walked past my room, he shouted intimidating threats or wild rumours.

Ying's friend, Gao, was almost as close as family and after I divorced, I frequently went to Gao to enquire about my two daughters. I was hoping she could somehow arrange for me to see them. She always told me the girls were fine, that their mother loved them very much and was looking after them well. She urged me to relax; but the girls' mother still did not permit them to see me.

Otherwise, Gao was full of reassurance. I went to see her several times and our conversation was always cordial. Gao was the only person at the time who showed any sympathy for me, who could understand my heart's yearning.

It never occurred to me that these simple meetings were seriously annoying some of the activists. They spread rumours that I was going to marry Gao during the 1st May holidays. Such rumours shocked the university establishment and spread to the provincial level, where plans were hurriedly made to sentence me before 1st May.

One evening, Duan came to talk to me. At first, he was smiling and amicable, saying many enticing but deceitful words. He said that he, too, had been guilty of wrongdoing, but since his self-criticism had been profound and his confessions sincere, he had not been further investigated. Now his superiors trusted him. If only I made good confessions and transformed my behaviour, all would be well. Many other Institute comrades had experienced such repentance and restoration. Colleagues had not rejected them, but had helped them and taken their side.

With this, his tone changed and an element of urgency was introduced, along with a trace of menace. "This time you must make some concession or you will not be able to move on." He wanted me to outline any relationships or dealings I had had with the Soviets, and to admit that I was in cahoots with other Chinese revisionists. Only if such a confession were clearly made would I have done my duty.

I replied that I had never researched politics and was naïve about the politics of the Soviet Union. The tiny fraction of what I understood about the Soviet situation was from public opinion in China. My research-student supervisor had of course been Soviet, but I knew nothing about him except his academic research. True, I had often discussed research questions with a Soviet student, whose main research focus was the Guizhou Miao people, but he also was just an academic acquaintance.

None of my Chinese friends, relatives or teachers, embraced a revisionist point of view and none had had a negative influence on me. I only knew what 'revisionism' was from the 'nine essays' opposing Soviet revisionism.

Thus, I did not succumb to Duan's deceit, but relied instead on my own conscience, resolutely declining to implicate anyone else. Duan's hopes were dashed and his smiles evaporated, as he simply remarked, "You are too stubborn," and told me to prepare my confession.

Duan said they would convene a rally the next morning to criticise my revisionist words and actions, and they would expect me first to make a detailed self-criticism and public confession. If the confession was good and I accepted the criticism, I would pass the test. On leaving, he sent someone to supervise the writing of my confession and to ensure I didn't get any sleep.

The next morning, Duan presided over a meeting of teachers and staff of the Institute. He first called on me to read aloud the full text of my self-criticism. I did this. Afterwards, a cadre read out a repudiation of me, slandering me by repeating the fabricated Nikita Khrushchev slogan. These proceedings were made public at the Institute, with the result that I was casually insulted on campus.

The night before, Duan had told me I would 'pass' the test, but his words had been empty. I was declared a revisionist and would be sent for three years of re-education through hard physical labour, in hope of a complete change of character.

On 17th April 1965, two guards escorted me by car to number 6 Nanshan Street in Xining, to begin my custody and toil. Several months after I was locked up, my accusers processed the formalities for my three-year sentence at the provincial office for reform-through-labour. There were, however, never any formal documents outlining my crime or punishment. I never saw my so-called case-material.

Why was I treated like this? I had been condemned as a revisionist. Basically, illegal processes had been used, hiding behind the slogan of 'opposing revisionism', to borrow authority to implement personal and subjective judgements.

The whole case violated common sense, arbitrarily attaching the title 'revisionist' to a politically unaffiliated intellectual. It also violated the main policies of the Chinese Communist Party at the time, subjecting me to persecution though I was patently innocent. Thus, it transpired that in the 1960s era of 'opposing revisionism', I became the first person in China to be officially declared a 'revisionist'.

After 'my' rally, I was led to my room to await an escort. At that time, the person who had read my repudiation came to ask, "Do you have anything more to say?" I replied that I was from a distant minority community and my elderly mother was still alive. I would like to go home to see her.

My divorced wife Ying came to see me, along with Mr Duan and Mr Sha. I asked Ying to take some clothes back for the children, but she refused.

Duan told me to prepare to leave. When I went to the restroom, I saw through the window our friend Gao leaving. She was wiping away a flood of tears. She was young and had never before witnessed such cruelty. It seemed to me she was shedding tears of sympathy.

My former wife Ying, on the other hand, did not seem moved at all, perhaps because everything seemed to be unfolding so calmly before her eyes. They deceived her by saying my reform-through-labour would last only three years. I would be able to read and study, listen to the radio and afterwards, return home. She believed all this, so she harboured the hope of seeing me again and buried that hope in her heart.

Although Ying had ultimately reported my 'revisionist' words and deeds, and energetically struggled against and criticised me, I could only think of the heavy burden she had now inherited of raising the two girls. After I had become a black sheep, she had still persevered with our marriage for the children's sake, and held out against all kinds of alienation and rumours. She didn't honestly want to divorce me. So no matter what happened during my various hardships, I never said a word against her.

Neither Ying nor I could have foreseen that she herself would later be accused and condemned, several months after I was incarcerated. She was transferred out of the Institute and had to serve at the counters of the Sisters' Department Store in County Huangzhong, Xining. During the Cultural Revolution, she was expelled from the Communist Party and suffered the humiliation of public criticism. Her accusers even seized her five-year-old daughter and made the little girl stand on a stool beside her mother. Then they extorted a confession from Ying about how she had been influenced by me. She almost died.

Locked up and Tossed Around

At first, I was locked up at number 6 Nanshan Street in a southern suburb of Xining, the first reform-through-labour location in Qinghai Province. Most of those imprisoned were men and women of around 30 years of age, wearing their own clothing, which often supplied clues as to their origin.

There were more than 100 people assigned to male and female working teams. The men's work was heavy, mainly agricultural – planting vegetables, watering and digging fields, spreading manure, weeding and tilling – but also carrying bricks, sand or earth for construction projects. Our rations were 500g of noodles a day; never enough.

Beginning at 8 am every Sunday, the square behind number 6 was covered with visitors who brought foodstuffs, to spend the day there.

The family of the incarcerated 60-year-old Director of Norman Bethune Hospital would sit on the ground eating and chatting, enjoying the fellowship of family life for a day. When they parted, however, the old director would weep and wail inconsolably. Cadres would drag him inside, as he struggled to stay with his family. This weekly drama was heartrending.

On Sunday evenings, as people dispersed, there was always much weeping and wailing. No one visited me, evidence of the fact that my family had been destroyed, and leaving me feeling all the more devastated.

How I missed my Guizhou home! Often on those visiting days, as I observed the visitors, I secretly shed tears. The food delivered by visitors sustained the other inmates, but I was so hungry I couldn't sleep at night. By day, I only had one thought: food. To distract myself from starvation and grief, I started reading English again, and it really did help.

On the day of the Dragon Boat Festival in 1965, our team leader led us down to the river to collect sand, using two-wheeled hand carts, each manned by two people. Pulling nearly 500 kg uphill was extremely heavy work, but we viewed it as a rare opportunity, for we were able to walk the streets and observe some of the old familiar everyday life. It felt as if we were breathing the fresh air of freedom again.

So some of our group were in high spirits, but my mood was different. The Dragon Boat Festival commemorated the day the ancient poet Qu Yuan committed suicide by jumping into a river. I was mulling over his epic, tragic story, imagining how it might be to leave behind the torment of this God-forsaken Qinghai-Tibetan plateau, in the middle of nowhere; and my tears flowed straight down onto my belly.

A burst of heavy rain the previous night had rendered the river fierce, with deep water rushing angrily eastwards, though the overhead scene was blissful sunlight and blue sky. An intense tug-of-war was going on in my mind, first imagining myself drifting off with the rushing water like Qu Yuan, but then realising that activists would denounce such action as suicide prompted by my own guilty conscience.

Going to meet God with such a tarnished reputation would simply be too dishonourable and cowardly, and in any case, the sad, grey-haired image of my old mother kept floating around in my head, along with the features of my wretched, starving daughters. I couldn't bear to inflict on them even more sorrow, so in the end decided to follow everyone back from the river's edge to the land, dragging the heavy sand.

In the spring of 1966, megaphones were hung from the electricity poles in the courtyard of number 6, and all day long programmes were broadcast repudiating Deng Tuo, Liao Mosha and Wu Han. They were said to be a dark, sinister gang, trying to 'subvert the regime of the proletariat'. Afterwards, broadcasts branded Peng Zhen and some of the central leaders as revisionists. This was one year after I had been declared a revisionist and the whole country seemed to have risen up against revisionism.

In May 1966, an urgent notice came to the effect that the inmates of number 6 would have to be evacuated. The building was to be re-constructed as a family courtyard.

People gossiped. One theory was that the Soviets had discovered the location of the prison. Early one morning, we were packed into several open trucks and driven off towards the northwest. We crossed a mountain range and kept on driving, until we finally arrived at our destination, known as Eight Treasures Farm.

Chapter 16
Eating the Mosquitoes
(Farm Life, 1966-79)

Eight Treasures Farm

Eight Treasures was about five kilometres from Qilian county town and had been established in the 1950s at the time of 'opposing rightists', being the largest reform-through-labour farm in Qinghai. When first established, it was just for rightists and admitted many people from other provinces. It was said that at its peak, it was home to 10,000 people.

Afterwards, the farm also received non-rightist inmates, and by the time we arrived, there were only two groups of rightists remaining. One of the inmates said that in the past many residents had come from 'the two Guangs', Guangxi and Guangzhou, and many had starved to death in 1962, when food had generally been scarce. Waving at the mountain behind, he said, "It's just full of graves."

I was the only one who had been convicted of being a 'revisionist', and the authorities sent me to the second 'rightist group'. No one there knew a thing about me. They simply eyed me up curiously, and quickly realised I was disillusioned and lonely.

The physical work was heavy, digging earth and burning grass, scattering ashes and harvesting wheat. We were each prescribed much work and we desperately worked overtime to meet demands. I remember harvesting wheat until 8 or 9 pm, under a full moon. Observing that I was last to finish, a middle-aged man with a northern accent whispered in bewilderment, "Why is this young man incarcerated here?"

By day, there was hard labour, while in the evenings the *four purifications* group convened meetings. Once a cadre made an announcement refuting rumours that the Soviet Union was sending an airborne division to Eight Treasures Farm.

At the beginning of autumn 1966, we worked on the hillsides reclaiming wasteland. One day down in the distance, we could make out crowds of people marching along, celebrating noisily in the streets of Qilian. People told us it was a demonstration of Red Guards opposing the 'Four Olds' [Old Customs, Old Culture, Old Habits and Old Ideas; one of the official goals of the Cultural Revolution was to do away with the Four Olds]. The Cultural Revolution had reached Qilian.

Within a few days, farm cadres were all wearing the Red Guard emblem on their sleeves. One Sunday, some staff and workers burst into our dormitory and turned everything upside down. All my books, Chinese and foreign, were seized. Even the photographs my Soviet supervisor had given to me were confiscated, along with some photos of my own. They poured petrol over the books and burnt them. People whispered to each other, "These former-prisoner Red Guards are even harsher than those in society at large." From that time onwards, the Cultural Revolution had an enormous impact on Eight Treasures Farm.

Restrictions on me became stricter. On Sundays, I was not allowed to go shopping in Qilian like everyone else and any letters to or from me were handed to my team leader for prior inspection.

One evening in late autumn 1967, there was an announcement that everyone was to be transferred elsewhere within three days. An armed garrison was stationed at the farm and Eight Treasures was swiftly transformed into a military farm.

So in the late autumn of 1967, I was sent along with others in an open truck to Kangyang Farm beside the Yellow River, another reform-through-labour farm. I had been detained at Eight Treasures Farm for about one-and-a-half years.

Kangyang Farm

Kangyang Farm was more than 50 kilometres from Xining. The climate was warm and the area abounded in apple and pear trees, and watermelons. The farm cultivated apple orchards, watermelons, and wheat. I was allocated to the third team, with light work, normally eight hours a day, and fairly relaxed supervision.

When not working, we could swim in the Yellow River. Most evenings we ate beef noodles and *mantou* [Chinese steamed buns], and practically every day we ate meat and vegetables. On Sundays, we rested and were allowed to go to the county town, to eat in a restaurant or do some shopping. Local farmers rather envied members of the third team for their light workload and their relatively high standard of living. Some even asked if they could join us.

All the cadres at Kangyang wore an 8.18 'Red Guards' armband, a mark of top-notch cadres. [Chairman Mao had addressed a rally of 800,000 Red Guards in Tiananmen Square on 18th August 1966.]

One morning in the early summer of 1968, an army cadre from the squadron responsible for overseeing discipline appeared with a document in hand, to inform me that authorities had approved my release according to schedule, but I must nevertheless remain a prisoner.

Not for the first time, I asked why I had been condemned to three years of reform-through-labour in the first place. I had never seen any documents justifying my conviction. The cadre replied that relevant documents certainly existed, but when I demanded to see them, he simply repeated that they authorised my detention and re-education. Why on earth would I want to see the documents now anyway? What use would that be? Forget it. Simply work well and reform myself.

Convicts were occasionally forbidden in this way to go home. Thus, another tragedy had befallen me: I was being subjected to an open-ended prison sentence.

Xiangride Farm

A year into my time at Kangyang, after the autumn harvest, farm leaders decided to set up a 7th May Cadre School there. So in winter of 1968, we set off again on open trucks, driving further away from Xining. After driving for more than two days, we arrived at our destination around midnight. This was the Balong section of Xiangride Farm. At that time, just at the end of 1968, the weather was freezing.

Xiangride Farm succeeded Eight Treasures Farm as the largest reform-through-labour farm in Qinghai. All around was vast wilderness, with little trace of human habitation, but home to a diverse range of wild animals, especially bears and wolves. If you lost your way, there was a danger of being savaged to death. If you tried to escape, you would have difficulty surviving in the wilderness, and you might be attacked and killed by bears or wolves. People called it a 'natural prison'. The Balong team was located in the most westerly part of the farm, the most remote corner.

Two young ex-convicts from Shanghai had lost both feet, and shifted along the ground using their arms. Their legs had had to be sawn off after being frozen, when they had tried to escape one winter. People said it was lucky they were found by day, for if they had been out at night, they would have been meat for hyenas.

Another prisoner escaped but could not find his way out of the wilderness. He lived in a mountain cave in a valley for over two weeks, lighting a fire by night and going out to scavenge by day. In the end, he was mistaken by a local hunter for prey and shot dead.

My three-year sentence of reform-through-labour had been a kind of deceit. I had now been moved even further from my family and from society at large. For the four years from 1969 to 1972, I was hidden away in the obscurity of the Balong team.

Not much grew in the half-desert surroundings, apart from sand willow trees. Every fine day in summer, mosquitoes and other insects rose up in swarms, so many it seemed there was a thick curtain in the sky. Cows and horses would make for the mountains. Weaker ones, unable to escape, were often bitten to death by mosquitoes. We had to tie our trouser legs at the bottom, to wear gloves and straw hats with gauze veils, and endlessly to wave a stick like a horse's tail to fend off the insects.

We went to work every day as usual. Activist self-reformers used to scream, "We'll eat the mosquitoes; we won't be eaten by them!" The insect-season lasted a month, whereupon, as if to meet an appointment, the insects disappeared within a day. It was like this every year.

Tuosu Lake is three days' walk from the nearest county town and 4,500 metres above sea level, a world of bears and wolves. Upon entering this territory, no one was apt to leave the company of others. It was an even more secure 'natural prison'. I was sent there in 1973 to dig irrigation channels, chop firewood, carry rocks and dam the turbulent flowing water. It was very heavy work.

We lived in a cave. At night, it was difficult to sleep well, for rocks would sometimes tumble down and cause injury. Only those who were sick could stay in tents. I always had to stay in the cave, where heaps of beef and mutton were stacked. In the winter, the meat needed to be sawn into pieces as it had frozen solid, but there was no way of eating it, for we had no firewood there. The lake was full of fish and we could catch them using our washbasins. After it rained in summer, the ground was full of mushrooms, and the summer lake was frequented by wild ducks, which migrated south during autumn.

With the scarcity of oxygen up there, we did not have much of an appetite, often eating nothing more than fire-roasted *mantou*, washed down with black tea. Any kind of alcohol was regarded as a precious commodity and was only supplied to those of us who went into the water to build dams. According to a doctor there, anyone who came to this area lost any sexual desire. It's true I just felt overworked and physically drained, with no desire even to talk. This place tormented me for more than a year.

In 1996, over 20 years later, there were reports in the national news that space aliens had lived there, and deposited all kinds of metal objects in the caves around the lake.

After I had asked for compassionate leave to bury my mother and been denied such leave, the farm authorities chose to detain me in this place from which it was least possible to escape.

After eventually leaving Tuosu Lake, I was sent to work in the fourth team of the first unit, mostly consisting of personnel who were about to finish their sentences and be released. There was still a tall watchtower at the main entrance, however, and it was strictly manned. Since it was close to the Qinghai Tibet highway, guards were always at the entrance, and they had two big dogs, fiercer than wolves. Strangers would not dare go anywhere near the dogs.

In 1976, the democracy movement opposing the Gang of Four was suppressed by military force. I was subsequently viewed with increased suspicion and subjected to stricter supervision. Around the time Chairman Mao passed away in September 1976, the atmosphere worsened.

In the summer of 1978, cadres from the Qinghai Institute came to the farm to see what was going on and to work out what to do with me. After they left, I remained locked up in the 'number one work unit' where I experienced nearly a year of 'horror before the dawn', physical torment that left me several times at death's door. I survived, and in the end walked away from Xiangride Farm.

Chapter 17
English and Gob-Stoppers
(Torment, 1965-79)

How I Was Viewed Politically

Soon after I had been imprisoned in 6 Nanshan Street, the provincial *four purifications* group at the Qinghai Institute was re-stationed to number 6, and daily demanded that I write something for their inspection.

I had never been interested in politics, regarding the political road as a dangerous one. I harboured absolutely no 'revisionist' point of view, and couldn't have developed such a view if I'd tried. The *four purifications* group, however, like the organisation for opposing revisionism at the Institute, insisted I should read and re-read the 'nine essays' and write a review of the things that were repudiated therein.

I was a Dong nationality bookworm, completely helpless, alone and trapped, terrified of confrontation with people of other nationalities. So I felt compelled to write a pile of nonsense, as instructed, and present it as my report. When they saw that what I had written did not much differ from what I had previously been forced to confess, they upheld the decision to brand me a revisionist. This title was regarded as a cap I had to wear, making me an enemy of the people. This was at the very time when there were constant radio broadcasts in Beijing repudiating sinister gangs and revisionism.

In the summer of 1966, I was escorted along with others to the Eight Treasures Farm. The campaign against Wu Han, Deng Tuo and Liao Mosha, was running in Beijing at the time; opposing 'black lines' (cultured people, including writers, singers and philosophers) and gangsters.

Having dug deeply into the backgrounds of my 'rightist team' members, the *four purifications* group declared seven or eight mutual friends in the team to be a 'sinister gang', and convened rallies outside working hours to expose and denounce them. The rallies were tense, but they did not raise the issue of 'revisionism' and fortunately, I was not personally denounced.

Wherever the *four purifications* groups went, they were at pains to determine or re-determine the status of each person, to ascertain what 'cap' they should wear. Winter of 1966 was the high tide of the Red Guards. Beginning in Beijing, the Guards designated toppled senior leaders as 'counter-revolutionary revisionists', and no longer simply 'revisionists'. The provincial governor in Qinghai, Wang Zhao, was overthrown and publicly denounced. The Guards declared he was a 'counter-revolutionary revisionist', yelling through loudspeakers in high-pitched voices, using captions and headlines in large letters and drumming up a clamour throughout the province.

The *four purifications* group of the 'right-wing team' was naturally agitated by such developments. When they announced new caps in winter 1966, they had added the words 'counter-revolutionary' to my former title 'revisionist'. When I asked why my title had changed, the cadres replied, "There is a new wind blowing. We only did as instructed by provincial leaders. The former provincial governor also has this cap and you two are the same."

I was politically unaffiliated, an ordinary citizen. Wang Zhao was a high-level leader in the Chinese Communist Party, a provincial governor. Where was the similarity? We had the same caps, but this was just symptomatic of an escalation in my persecution. My label as number one enemy of the Cultural Revolution was fabricated.

The next 10 years witnessed the turmoil of Cultural Revolution. Working groups similar to the *four purifications* group often turned up and settled at Xiangride Farm, doing similar work. They were labelled 'military control' groups. They had little contact with us, nor did they convene mass meetings in the evenings, but they were stationed there to inspect records and archives and listen to team leaders report on reform progress. Afterwards, they examined and approved everyone's 'caps', in whichever way they pleased.

I remember in 1971, when Sino-Soviet relations were still tense, there were conflicts at the national borders and the country was preparing for war. One afternoon, the farm leadership convened a general meeting. They announced everyone's cap, including counter-revolutionaries, bad elements [that is, thieves, swindlers, murderers, arsonists, hooligans or other evildoers who caused major damage to social order], rightists and landlords. I listened intently from beginning to end, but never heard my name.

This generated a glimmer of hope and after the meeting was adjourned, I asked my team leader why my name had not cropped up. He told me emphatically, "Your cap is the same as before – revisionist." I simply accepted what he said, not daring to ask again. It never occurred to me that the 'military control' group at the farm, when examining and approving the status of inmates, had come across my original 'revisionist' materials and changed my status to 'counter-revolutionary'. They kept me in the dark about this.

In 1976, when I received compassionate leave to go and visit the grave of my deceased mother, the term 'counter-revolutionary' was written on my leave-permit. I was astonished and asked one of the cadres why my 'revisionist' label had inexplicably been changed. He replied: "Revisionist is the same as counter-revolutionary. A revisionist opposes Chairman Mao, and anyone who opposes Chairman Mao is a counter-revolutionary."

After five years of asking, I had finally obtained permission for home-leave and I was afraid that if I asked more about my cap, my leave-permit would be withheld. I simply stomached the new name. Later, when I discussed the change with a friend, he warned me, "It's a dangerous change! They're not able to kill revisionists! Someone must have wanted to execute you, so had your cap changed to 'counter-revolutionary'!"

So during that period, I felt terrified. I was often threatened, "You can forget your dreams. If the Soviet revisionists fight their way here, we'll kill you first. We certainly won't let you live to see them."

After 1979, although authorities accorded me complete rehabilitation, restoring me to my former position at work, and although I was completely exonerated from the charge of counter-revolutionary, they never admitted the injustice of the case they had fabricated against me. This kind of injustice was frequently seen in China at the time, but otherwise has rarely been so systematically implemented on the face of this earth.

How English Kept Me Alive

After the dawn of 'revisionism', people spread rumours about my infatuation with translating Russian books into Chinese, stoking an atmosphere of paranoia.

At the time, I was in no mood to read Chinese newspapers, magazines or books. Nevertheless, my habit of reading and writing had been deeply ingrained. When I was not engaged in physical labour, I always felt the urge to read.

One evening before my incarceration, I discovered two English texts left over from my pre-Liberation study of English at middle school. Upon browsing the books, I realised that I still knew many of the words and understood most of the texts. Pronunciation of unfamiliar words was clarified by transcription in the International Phonetic Alphabet, which I had studied, and their meaning was explained via Chinese translation. My interest in English was re-ignited, and gradually increased.

During the campaign 'opposing revisionism', when my wife warned that I mustn't read foreign books, I volunteered not to read Russian books, for people said they were revisionist, but maintained that reading English should still be okay. She disagreed, however, and repeatedly snatched the English books out of my hands. In the end, I only read when my wife was not paying attention.

Before long, I had bought more English books and English/Chinese dictionaries. In my spare time, all I did was read those books. During the period of 'opposing revisionism' and also after I had divorced, my English reading helped diminish the sense of melancholy that otherwise threatened to overwhelm me. It also eased my anxiety. From then on, no deprivation was strong enough to force me to abandon the habit.

Before I was sent to 6 Nanshan Street, I tucked all my English books in among my clothes. As long as I complied with regulations at number 6, working hard and writing self-criticisms, the cadres there allowed me to read the books.

It felt humiliating to share a heated brick bed with other people's visitors. All I could do was open a book and start reading, blocking others from my field of vision and line of thought. I became totally absorbed in reading and also used this as a diversion from hunger pangs.

After lights-out in the evenings, I was so hungry I couldn't get to sleep. To no avail, I would try to force myself to sleep. In the end, I would get out of bed, walk beneath the street lamps outside and read another hour or two of English. After returning to bed, I would often fall asleep immediately. As a result, my English proficiency improved and I was able to survive over a year of near-starvation.

Thus, I was not only very interested in English, but discovered that it helped reduce my anguish, and also reduced the power of hunger over me. It became my alternative sustenance during those 15 years of imprisonment and toil.

After I was transferred from number 6, and moved from one farm to another, it felt like anything in my wardrobe was expendable, except the books wrapped up in my clothes. By the time I left Xining, I had finished reading my two original texts and had purchased a set of textbooks simply entitled *English*, along with a series of three books entitled *Selected Readings in English*, plus some miscellaneous pamphlets. In addition, I still had some dictionaries.

The books felt like family and friends, keeping me company. Eventually, however, some were seized and confiscated, while others were taken and burned. It felt as though I had lost precious treasure, but in the course of time, I devised ways of hiding and holding onto one or two books. Throughout the 15 years, there wasn't a day when I didn't have at least one English book. If I was hungry, I could read a little; if I was afraid, I'd feel better after reading a few sentences.

There were others in the 'rightist team' of Eight Treasures Farm who owned English books which I occasionally set eyes on. The team leader at the time did not prohibit them, or criticise anyone for reading them, so after work we could read without fear.

One evening, while everyone was relaxing, chatting and laughing, I pulled out a book from under my pillow and began to read. I became so engrossed I did not notice a man nearby staring at the book in my hands. He did not understand English, but noticed the Chinese translation of the English word 'necklace' and shouted loudly, "He's reading English stuff about necklaces!"

Several activists gathered around. They discovered the Chinese characters for 'necklace' in a dictionary and asked cautiously what I was up to. I told them the title of the text I was reading was 'The Necklace'. It was a story by a 19th century French author named Guy de Maupassant, a university English text. It had been approved at the national level and they could rest assured there was no problem with its content. This, however, only made them more agitated, and blood drained from their faces.

The team leader snatched the book from me and ran off towards headquarters, while two others sat on either side, guarding me in case I tried to run away. Before long, the leader returned with a cadre, who scolded me, "English is full of bourgeois propaganda. You've come here to reform and you are still worshipping imperialism! You are such a reactionary!"

Thereupon he focussed on necklaces, wondering what a necklace was, and if anyone had ever seen one. Other inmates insisted they had never seen a necklace. This led to detailed interrogation. The cadre wanted me to explain to everyone about this necklace. I could only describe to them what was written in the text.

When they heard that a necklace was a kind of jewellery worn by women, some with hatred in their voices wanted to start beating me up, riding a torrential surge of abuse. At this point, the cadre suddenly became democratic, and asked them what should be done. One said the book should be burned. Another suggested I should be forced to submit a self-criticism and confession, to dig up the origin of my ideology. Our team leader concurred and burned that English book, one of my favourites, on the spot, walking backwards and forwards, stamping and spitting on it savagely. He commanded me to write my confession that very evening.

The cadre added that I should dredge up the origins of my failings, listing the names of anyone I had known before Liberation who understood English and of any foreigners I had ever known. I should research my current thinking according to its source. Was I or was I not thinking of treason? I should also mention my social class background. If my confession was not clear, I would not be allowed to 'pass' the test.

I had not dreamt that reading an English book would annoy others so much that it would create such a major crisis for me. They insulted me that whole evening, and I felt terrified.

It seemed as if it would be easier to die than to pass muster in this court of activist ex-inmates. The question of what to do jammed my mind and I didn't sleep a wink that night. Though I didn't know the answer to the question, I knew I didn't want to die or to abandon reading English. It was just agony; I didn't know how I would survive.

The next evening, a general meeting was convened to denounce me, or so I assumed, and I was scared to death. As the cadre read the roll and my name was announced, he criticised me for reading the English 'necklace story' and I was stared down with many indignant glares.

I thought they were about to pull me out, and others thought the same and sniggered. To my surprise, however, the cadre changed the subject. He announced that a sinister gang had wormed its way into the team, intending to organise activities opposing reform. This meeting was being convened to mobilise everyone to speak frankly and report offenders. From today onwards, we would focus on this question and we would not relent until everything had been cleared up. They thus dropped the matter of my reading, and privately I felt elated.

So I did not abandon reading English, though thenceforth I did my best to read in secret. On Sundays, as the day was dawning and others were lying in, I quietly left the dormitory and read aloud outdoors. When people saw me, they thought it strange: why did this man go outside to study English so seriously while others were still sleeping?

The rumour spread that I was preparing to abscond to the enemy and commit treason. A cadre remarked nonchalantly that he was going to confiscate all my English books and burn them. An acquaintance interceded on my behalf to beg for mercy, and succeeded in persuading the cadre to spare me a few books, pamphlets and dictionaries.

The rumours were false, for I was never inclined to run away. Dong people are most attached to their native place, reluctant to leave home. When they do travel, they feel acutely the strangeness of everything new, finding it difficult to adapt. Of course, there are many things to admire about life outside the Dong world, but Dong people don't usually choose to venture into the unknown. Instead, I was energetically reading English out loud simply to satisfy the demands of my morale. My academic interest had once again developed into an addiction.

During that period, I had a deep sense of emptiness. The pain of physical labour and of psychological pressure gave birth to a sense of despair. Only English was able to relieve the pain and void, to help me bear that miserable plight. Reading between the lines, I could discern much by way of human feeling and human reason, and this all appealed to my innermost being.

It just felt as though reading English was like going home. Or again, it was like entering another world and lingering there, forgetting to return. Others may not have had any key for understanding the magical power created by English in a 'revisionist', suffering injustice and loneliness during his period of imprisonment and hard labour. Thus, unfounded rumours spread easily.

In the third team of Kangyang Farm, my physical work was light and administration of inmates was relaxed, so I was at liberty to read English when not working. Mr Hong was a fellow team member from Guizhou, about 60 years old. He was nicknamed 'the shepherd', for he grazed sheep. Before Liberation, he had served as a professor at Guizhou University. In 1958, he was transferred to Qinghai Teachers' Institute, lecturing on Chairman Mao's *On Practice*. In the course of his teaching, he had expressed a few 'erroneous' ideas and was forced to wear a 'counter-revolutionary' cap, and to reform-through-labour.

Hong's elderly mother was still alive at home in Guiyang, but he himself was unmarried. He loved to chat, although at the time he didn't feel like reading. He asked if I had any English books, whereupon I loaned him a small book with some stories. Within a few days, I loaned him another book. He remarked that for him eating rice was like taking medicine, but reading English was like eating meat. He really enjoyed the books. While reading, his melancholy and predicament also receded to the back of his mind.

Although the Kangyang cadres did not prohibit it, they were united in feeling that reading English was equivalent to opposing reform. They tried to curtail such reading. One day, I slipped a small dictionary into my pocket as I went off to work, so I could look over vocabulary during the 10-minute work break. My group leader unexpectedly came over with a cadre who seized the book and refused to return it. Then they searched my bed and confiscated several other English books. At roll call that evening, they scolded me, and ordered me to do a self-criticism in my small group.

In 1968 and 1969 when Chairman Liu Shaoqi was being framed, people wearing the 8.18 Red Guard armbands made a fuss about my being a revisionist, 'the most dangerous enemy of China', 'a descendant of Nikita Khruschev' and 'the offspring of Liu Shaoqi'. Many such 'caps' were pressed down on my head.

There were many rallies denouncing me, but my accusers found no evidence of 'revisionism', and cursed me instead for 'opposing reform' through reading English.

At that time, they 'uncovered' someone else, Mr Xu, and made him stand beside me, then forced us to kneel down. We suffered three nights of denouncement. Xu had been sent to reform-through-labour just after university graduation, assigned to raise chickens along with a female 'rightist'. He bought an English edition of *The Selected Works of Chairman Mao* and took refuge in studying that, thinking that if he studied the *Selected Works*, he would be immune from attack. When I was being denounced, however, someone remarked that he, too, was studying English and 'opposing reform'. Then he was also picked out and forced to kneel down, to share my shame and abuse.

Xu understood a little Russian, but had never studied English, and he was unfamiliar with the International Phonetic Alphabet. So he could not really read the words in Mao's *Selected Works* and he was unfamiliar with English grammar. He just followed the words, without reading aloud, and compared the English with the Chinese, thus using a 'learning by reading' method of studying English.

It was almost inconceivable that he could learn that way: at best, excruciatingly difficult. By day, however, Xu was never without a book in hand and in the evenings, he'd lie on his bed reading by the light of a torch. The woman who cared for the hens with him testified that he was only ever reading; so much so that if hens flew out of the coop, he would often not even notice. She would sometimes observe them flying away and shout the alarm, and only then would he jump into action.

Xu only read the Mao book, so intensely that it felt like his Bible. He was resentful about being denounced for studying Mao's Works, insisting his detractors had been opposing the red flag. He persisted in reading, but did not dare to do so by day, only by night, by the light of a torch underneath the blankets in bed. He maintained he had become addicted to Mao's *Selected Works* in English and could not bear to break the addiction. It surprised me that someone who did not know how to pronounce the English, but only knew the words' meanings, would have such a deep interest in reading them.

English possessed a mysterious power over us, trapped and persecuted as we were. It rescued us by lending strength to endure suffering. The average person may find this impossible to grasp.

Xiangride Farm was a reform-through-labour prison, but also a prison for ex-inmates, who still had to reform-through-labour. Workers were subject to strict supervision and heavy work, but I never saw any rules forbidding the reading of foreign books. I endured the pressure of heavy work and weakness, for I was losing blood and feeling ill because of haemorrhoids. I was close to the limit of what I could physically bear. I often thought of my solitary old mother, who suffered various illnesses, and of my former wife with our two poor daughters. Then there were the dark clouds that hung heavily over our nation. Night and day, I wept, privately and silently, until my heart was broken and the tears dried up.

How could anyone in my circumstances survive? In the numbness and silence of my heartbroken and tear-exhausted state, I relied on English. Reading helped me to banish the merciless reality of my situation, escaping into each word, sentence and paragraph of the texts, so that I temporarily forgot my adversity.

The Xiangride authorities tried to stop me reading. They extended my work periods and destroyed my clothes, discriminating against me when it came to dishing out food. They provoked arguments, so that I became the target of others' rage, and this deprived me of much free time.

I still took risks, doing all within my power, to be able to read. During the mosquito season, I would read through my gauze mosquito veil. Before the water was released, I'd read in the fields. On rare non-working days, others would rest, but I would read, after mending my clothes. If there was any free time at all, I would use it to read.

At last, I finished the English textbooks and an *English Anthology*. Then I studied a book about *English Verbs* which I borrowed from a fellow inmate Mr Qian, to improve my knowledge of passive tense and verb properties. I also read the two English books, *Selected Works of Mao* and *Quotations of Chairman Mao*. Afterwards, I read *Up from Slavery* [the 1901 autobiography of Booker T Washington] borrowed from fellow inmate Mr Liu, and translated that into Chinese. I also translated Brooks's Readers [1907, published by the American Book Company] which Qian had loaned to me.

All were read in a race against time, and my translations were rough and ready, not systematic. During those 14 years, English and I were best friends. The language was my only buddy, supporting my continued survival. Without it, I'd have long since been buried.

Others in the same predicament, such as Mr Wu, found alternative means of self-preservation. Wu had graduated from a medical school in the south of the country. In 1965, relatives abroad sent him a gift of a few thousand American dollars. His work unit had been examining his correspondence and secretly arranged for payment of his salary to be suspended. A month later, he was designated a 'counter-revolutionary' and sent under escort to reform-through-labour. His chosen means of survival was not to say a word.

Wu was not on my team at Kangyang, but we were transferred together to Xiangride, and there we ended up on the same team. When anyone asked him a question, he responded by covering his mouth with his hands and turning his pockets inside out. Then he said something in Cantonese, difficult for anyone to understand. Thus when he did speak, his words were obscure, so unless absolutely necessary, no one spoke to him. He wandered around pouting, as if he were annoyed.

One morning, we two were scattering fertiliser over the fields. The work was heavy and we were pressed for time. In addition, the plateau was high and we could hardly catch our breath. Nevertheless Wu was not so sullen any more, breathing and yawning normally.

We sat down for a rest on a ridge between the fields, when I noticed his hand fetching something from his pocket and his mouth becoming swollen again. Puzzled, I asked if he had put something in his mouth. He smiled, took a wooden thermos-flask stopper from his mouth and handed it to me. When I asked why on earth he wanted to put that thing in his mouth, he replied without hesitation.

Others had warned him his thinking was reactionary; he had been declared a counter-revolutionary and sent to reform-through-labour. He was afraid that if he spoke, people would use his words to condemn him, so instead he stopped up his mouth. That way, he couldn't say anything, whether sad, happy or angry. For the last three or four years, he had indeed avoided public denouncement or flogging. He advised me to contemplate some similar strategy and urged me not to divulge his secret to anyone.

Wu conversed eagerly, in Mandarin with a slight Guangdong accent. He asked if I was not worn out by this kind of work, admitting that he only asked because he himself was too tired to stand up any more. I replied that I, too, was totally exhausted, but indicated some people in the distance and pointed out that we two had scattered more fertiliser than the three of them together. It was unfair, for they were used to farming, but we had never done it seriously before.

I explained to Wu how I was often bullied by those guys. Agitated, he rose and paced about in front of me. He repeatedly said that it was not really those people who were bullying me. They were just activists, citizens without political caps. It was their superiors who wanted them to transform us, so they were being forced to keep a strict eye on us.

Wu now seemed completely different, speaking solemnly like a seasoned campaigner. He thought I didn't understand and wanted to educate me a little. He declared that the camp was just a proletarian dictatorship and we were its victims. We shouldn't blame those workers for taking unfair advantage of us. Wu was a doctor, but after beginning hard labour, he had never received any professional privilege.

Later, Wu was assigned to a different group. On Saturday evenings after dinner, however, he always came to look for me, inviting me to bring some books to his place and read them there. I often brought the *English Anthology*, and would read by the light of the small oil lamp hanging from the wall above Wu's bed. He made me read sentence by sentence, translating into Chinese and explaining the grammar. He had learned some English at university, but had forgotten most, and wanted to re-learn from me.

He didn't really dare to study seriously, but just took advantage of those Saturday evenings when others would be playing poker to learn a little in this way, to avoid forgetting English entirely. Wu said that on the weekend evenings, he really missed his mother and hometown. When he read English with me, he had no time to be so homesick.

Before long, however, the activists threatened us both. Since they couldn't understand English, they accused us of speaking reactionary words and plotting some treasonous act. Subsequently, we didn't dare to read together or even to greet each other in passing. We acted as if we did not even know each other.

One year at winter training, Wu's group denounced him because of the wooden stopper in his mouth. They abused him for several days but he refused to talk. The cadres instructed different groups, including mine, to gang up on him and criticise him.

Wu's group leader and activists turned a stool upside down and forced him to stand on its legs. The stool rocked about shakily, and as he was about to crash, Wu finally opened his mouth and shouted, "I'm going to fall!" The activists then pushed him over roughly, demanding a self-criticism. When his self-criticism was not good (meaning not strong) enough, or his attitude bad (meaning he refused to speak), they forced him to stand on that upturned stool again. Such meetings were convened for over a week.

Since I had been Wu's friend in the past and read English books with him, I was apprehensive, surmising I would have to share his punishment. During his denunciation meetings, I hung my head, not daring to proffer an opinion. They declared, however, that I was the one who best understood Wu and insisted I should tell them anything he had said to me.

I casually mentioned what he had already confessed in his self-criticism; for example, that he had put a wooden stopper in his mouth because he was afraid of saying something that would be construed as wrong. They said I sympathised with Wu and was myself a reactionary thinker, and ordered me to surrender my English books. Finally, they insisted that I should have no further contact with Wu.

After those denunciations, Wu's gob-stopper was confiscated. If he were to use such a device in future, he would be denounced again. Moreover, the next denunciations would not be so 'civilised'.

Wu never used a gob-stopper again, but still declined to say anything. Although he worked with others, he and they never really knew each other. He kept his own counsel right up until 1980, when the policy of sending people back to their original work units was enacted. Only then did he slowly come out of his shell.

Deprivation

Sustained heavy labour depleted my physical strength. I suffered from haemorrhoids, losing blood each day, and from anaemia. It felt like my belly was empty, and I was starving, desperate for nourishment.

While at Xiangride, my staple diet was *mantou* made with wheat bran. My non-staple was boiled Chinese cabbage or potatoes.

When I was with the Balong team, steamed rolls were small and rationed. The one who dished out rice was nicknamed Xie Bapi [after Zhou Bapi, the landlord who was said to get his workers up early by imitating the sound of a cock crowing]. He had been instructed to discriminate against me and consistently selected the smallest portion for me. I couldn't bear the hunger and once challenged him, "The buns in the steamer are nearly all the same size; why do you do your utmost to give me the two smallest ones?"

"I'll take and weigh them then!" he roared. He took the buns and weighed each in turn, then bellowed, "You have too much!" With that, he chopped about a third off each of the buns and threw them back into my bowl, creating in me a flood of involuntary tears.

We rarely tasted meat, but occasionally had some camel meat or horse meat. Exceptions were on National Day and for a month or so around New Year, when we had beef, mutton and pork, along with roast potatoes and radish.

The rare feasts inspired Xie Bapi to be particularly unfair. One day, my bowl was filled with potatoes and radish along with soup and a couple of bones; but when I glanced at the bowls of others, they were full of fatty meat. It felt as if someone had stolen my wallet, as if I was losing blood, and disappointment froze my heart. With a quivering voice, I asked, "Why does everyone else have lots of meat while I only have radish and a couple of bones?"

"Because the ladle has no eyes," he replied. "Whatever is scooped up is what you get."

Some in the queue beside me chipped in, "Who asked you to be a revisionist...or to oppose reform?" On festival days, it always seemed to be like this. It felt like I was victimised like this throughout my decade at Xiangride. I was pricked over and over again by a sense that something rightly belonging to me was being stolen, and developed a sense of horror towards those celebratory feasts.

A fellow Balong inmate with connections to my home area had pity on me, and for several years, he helped me buy beef or mutton. While I was working in the fields, a Mongolian man once asked me if I would like some meat, but despite my predicament, I didn't dare to say yes.

In later years, some others took pity on me, including a Hui staff member from eastern Qinghai, who had earlier studied Tibetan. He had earlier received corporal punishment, but now worked as a shepherd. After observing my deprivation, he helped me buy beef or mutton from Tibetan or Mongolian inmates. He said, "If they won't give you meat, I'll help you buy it."

In another group, there was a man called Min, whose passage into the throes of reform-through-labour I never understood. Whatever it was, he usually remained silent. At that time, you could buy about half a pint of strong liquor once a month. Min didn't like liquor, and would quietly pass me his ration. He only ever asked the usual asking price, not a penny more.

Min seemed to me like an angel. His was a family-style consolation, granted without words. It carried on steadfastly for several years, always without conversation. As I remember him, Min was a good person who carved out a sense of gratitude in my heart. I still don't know why he treated me so kindly.

For years, I suffered from haemorrhoids and blood loss, but despite this, I was invariably assigned the heaviest labour. Often I was coughing with a bad cold, but there was a rule that if a man's temperature was not over 38.5 degrees Centigrade, he was not sick. Although I was often sick, I never received a day of sick leave. Instead, my sickness accompanied me to work in the fields.

One day when I was working at the Lake Tuosu reservoir, with a cold and fever, I was forced to go into the deep water to shift sand and stones. When I asked for leave, I was initially given permission to go and see a doctor, but was called back after only 200 metres.

At roll call that evening, our team leader accused me of abandoning my work. He dramatized the matter, saying, "We Chinese are not like you Soviets and don't practise the Soviet system. We need to force you to reform-through-labour, implementing proletarian dictatorship."

Some days I returned from work to find a hole had been poked through my only food bowl, or through the basin I used for washing.

The buttons on my clothes were frequently pulled off and my chest would be exposed on freezing winter days. The crotch of my trousers was often torn. After being mended, the clothes were again spoiled. While others rested, I would be busy fixing things; a bitter experience. The day after I bought it, my thermos flask no longer retained the heat, for someone broke the small inner glass bottle.

If my things were not destroyed, they were often commandeered or hidden by others. In my already exhausted state, I would look everywhere. Sundays were for rest, but if I wasn't mending things that had been tampered with, I would be looking for things that had been moved or hidden.

In the reform-through-labour farms, the routine often caused inmates to go crazy. Some went mad with anger because of the injustice of their sentences.

In the summer of 1966, at Kangyang, I observed a short man, about 24 years old, rushing out of the dormitory, hair dishevelled. Agitated, he walked to the centre of the courtyard, with only two buttons fastened on his jacket. He took off his shoes and flung them onto the roof of an adjacent building, walking on in his bare feet.

The man was from Sichuan, a geography graduate of Beijing Normal University. After graduation, he had been sent to teach at a university in Qinghai, while his girlfriend was assigned to work elsewhere. He spent his days dreaming of his girlfriend. His girlfriend, however, had gone with another boyfriend and broken off relations with him.

During the *four purifications* period, the young man was said to have had wrong opinions: his thinking was reactionary. He was designated a rebel, and sentenced to three years of reform-through-labour. He spent whole days, however, lying on his bed in silent meditation. He simply didn't eat, unless someone kindly brought him food.

We were moved several times and this young man was always in my team. His behaviour didn't much change. The team leader reported that he didn't work, but needed to be fed. In the end he was assigned to the team that fed the pigs; they could feed him at the same time.

He hardly spoke, and hardly got out of bed – for 15 years. After the demise of the Gang of Four, inmates were able to discard their caps and his 'rebel' cap became a thing of the past.

When he heard this, he started to get up and perform simple tasks of personal hygiene, and do light work such as collecting straw for the fire. He began to reply when spoken to. He was chosen to read from the newspaper for others to listen, but he couldn't, saying he didn't recognise the characters. It had been 15 years and he had forgotten everything! This university graduate had regressed to a state of illiteracy.

In 1980, cadres contacted his hometown, with the intention of repatriating him there, but his mother declined to have him back. She blamed the cadres for transforming her clever son into that feeble state, and pleaded she would be unable to care for him.

Cadres instructed his former college to take him back, but the college dragged its heels. When I left the farm, he was still there. As people were rehabilitated one by one and returned to their former jobs, he showed blithe indifference, as if he had lost all sense of self-awareness. He still didn't talk much, or express what he was thinking. I'm not sure what happened to him in the end.

I had suffered injustice, persecution and agony, but in 1979, I didn't dare to complain or blame anyone. After all, I hadn't gone crazy or committed suicide, but had endured everything, and survived.

As if to excuse their excesses, the farm cadres often said, "We make different policies for different situations."

Among all the inhumane and merciless persecution, there was one good policy: encouraging ex-inmates, who had finished their prison sentences, to marry and bring their wives back to the farm to live. They would be allocated relatively good jobs, such as collecting data and making announcements, releasing water, driving a horse and cart, guarding potatoes, planting vegetables or preparing meals. There was one family to one house, with different households living together in courtyards.

In my team at Xiangride, there were many voluntary workers with wives. The women did not do heavy labour and their families did not have to worry about food or clothing. Even firewood was provided. Life was comfortable, leading many to pursue this option, voluntarily becoming the solid core of the farm.

This fantastic family provision for ex-inmates represented a peculiar and incongruous contrast to all the persecution I received during those years.

Hard Labour

From ancient times, it had been customary for adults in my native village to engage in physical labour. By day, practically no one stayed idly at home, because they were all working in the fields.

From childhood onwards, however, I had been a student. During my teens, I left the village behind to study at Chinese institutions, until at 35 I was sentenced to hard labour. I had become an old-fashioned scholar, who could hardly distinguish one season from another, one crop from another. Beginning heavy labour in middle age felt unimaginably arduous.

During those 14 years of labour, the farming work became heavier as year followed year. The working hours at Xiangride, between 1969 and 1979, were the longest, and the work itself was the heaviest.

In 1969 when I joined the Balong team, I was assigned to the group responsible for irrigation, and remained in that group for the following 10-plus years. Irrigation was the most time-consuming and onerous work. Between December and April, there was no irrigation, for the water froze. After the snow melted in April, however, we had to work day and night, channelling the water.

Both ends of my working day were often dark. I would only just have gone to bed when the call would come that water had arrived and I had to set off again for work. Just before autumn harvest, I would often work day and night without rest. If I stopped digging, I would fall asleep standing up.

Meals were sent to the fields, but the irrigation work could not stop and we were not permitted to sit down and eat. We had to eat our food while working. Nothing could stop, even when we dealt with toilet issues. Foremen pressed us to keep working, as if we were water wheels.

In winter, the hardest labour was levelling the land and digging the field borders, in summer it was irrigation. Gathering fertiliser, planting vegetables and raising pigs were all light by comparison. Guarding the potato cellar was the plum job, while driving the horse and cart required just a little expertise. Collecting data and writing notices on the blackboard almost made one feel like a cadre.

When I was still a relative newcomer to the Balong team, a fellow-inmate quietly advised, "You are a bookworm. Why did they arrest you and send you here? You know why? They're afraid you'll become a voice of protest. You should forget everything that's gone before. If possible, you should even forget how to read and write. Only then will they release you."

Afterwards, the activists often said that only when I had forgotten everything I had studied – Russian, revisionism and writing – would they help me transfer and do lighter work. This may have been the Discipline Department's doing, advising me of my only recourse to freedom.

Besides irrigation, I also worked on levelling the ground and reaping the harvest, both heavy jobs. In summer, the rule was that we planted, ploughed or weeded, while scattering fertiliser or irrigating. We were often doing two or three jobs at the same time.

For the spring sowing, we were ordered to save as much water as possible; to prevent the springtime water from flowing away. When the ice in the mountains was melting, we did manual labour by day and waited with lanterns in the fields for water by night.

Having been overworked by day, we would sit waiting dreamily in the quietness of the night, enjoying the warm gentle breeze and staring up at the moon and stars. It was then that I missed my Dong family and village the most. As soon as the cry went up, "The water is coming!" I stripped off clothes and began to work like mad, as far as possible controlling the water's direction, causing each square inch of land, high, low or in-between, to be irrigated.

Sometimes the person controlling the flow released too much water. Then the field borders would be pierced or the soil would become more alkaline, unable to contain the excess water. The controller would then curse and beat us, later denouncing us in the evenings.

The work depleted my physical strength, so I had no strength left for conversation, laughing or crying. Yes, I was still alive, but I'd be numb and silent. When I realised water was coming, I would persevere, but when I heard people ordering me around, I seemed to lose the ability to react.

My irrigation companion worked hard. Once on the way back home from work, he startled me by saying, "They'll only release you once they have made you illiterate." He meant to give me a straw of hope to cling onto: I only needed to become illiterate.

He told me about a neighbouring-team member, who had been lecturing at Chongqing University. After finishing his original sentence, he was detained to do extra-heavy work at the farm. He became too tired even to stand. One evening, he bought a bottle of Tibetan wine and sloped off to some remote fields to drink. After becoming drunk, he lay down on the grass, resigned to his fate. The next morning, workers found his dead body there. It seemed as if that fellow-worker was suggesting, "Why do you not do the same?"

Everyone wore water boots for the irrigation work. After I had bought a new pair of boots, someone must have poked a hole in each of them by night, after I'd fallen asleep. When I entered the water the next day, the boots leaked. I patched them up, but they were again vandalised.

Daily, I was losing blood through haemorrhoids. I was not allowed to have warm water for washing. The activists would say to me, "Can you not accept reform according to the customs in your own nationality?"

Harvesting wheat in late autumn was also heavy work, and my physical strength and technical ability could not compare with the others. We would leave for work before dawn and finish by around 10 pm. One evening, a fellow inmate had pity and helped by sharpening my sickle, supplying me with a decent implement to use the next day. The sickle was placed under my pillow.

The next day it was blunt, however, as though it had never been sharpened. I suspected my fellow inmate had deceived me. When we talked about it, he grew angry and thereafter ignored me.

Ten-plus years were like a day: always the same. Although most of the educated inmates sympathised with me, they did not dare to say a word. After glancing at me, people hung their heads as if asking themselves, "How is he going to survive if it goes on like this?"

But the activists would say, "Whoever helps him is a Soviet revisionist, opposing reform."

I was persecuted in various ways, not just for political reasons but also because of my minority identity. The combination explained why some people were so unscrupulous, so merciless. At the end of my tether, I contemplated running for my life, but I might just as well have been a castaway on a desert island. This natural prison spread far and wide to every horizon. Any thought of escape was nothing but a pipe dream.

Compassionate Leave

In the spring of 1970, after five years of imprisonment, I was granted compassionate leave to go and visit my ageing mother.

On the day I went through Xining, on my journey home, I was able to look for the place where my daughters were living. That night, I found it. Their mother answered the door, but on seeing me, shut it again. She refused to let me see my daughters and there was nothing I could do about it.

The journey was smooth and I arrived safely back in the village. The year before, it had been ravaged by fire and by 1970, my mother was living in a small wooden shed, less than five square metres in area. Now only my aged mother was left from the former Big House, her strength declining, living alone in that little shed.

Mother's heart was throbbing with pain, as if pierced by a knife. Daily she had been sitting patiently at the entrance to her shed, waiting for her son to return. Now he was here. Mother prepared a meal of boiled noodles and chicken soup, my last meal with her. An aunt kept us company.

Sitting by the fire weeping, mother related softly how someone from Big Village had framed her, reporting to a leader there that she had emptied his fields of water, then stolen his fish and shrimps.

Mother had been dragged out in front of everyone. They urged her to confess honestly. Some even cursed her, trying to force a confession. That whole night she was verbally abused, but she simply maintained her innocence. After all, she was no longer even physically able to make her way down to those fields.

As she told the story, she broke down and sobbed, her tears flowing like a fountain. How could an old person like this climb down into a muddy paddy field and steal fish and shrimps? Those who attended the communal meeting must have known this was impossible. Everyone, however, parroted what the team leader said, "You like fish, don't you?" This was used as evidence to show that she had burst the dam and stolen the fish.

During that short time with me, mother was constantly weeping. She had been victim to merciless injustice, spending days and nights in fear and misery. The weather was cold, windy and rainy. How many more days could she survive? The sadness of her plight seared my soul and I later left the village with tears pouring down my cheeks like rain.

The next day, before I left, I went up the mountain to chop two poles of firewood. Propped up on crutches, mother then hobbled along to see me off at the head of the village. She knew she didn't have much longer in this world. Still sobbing, she said in a whisper, "Son, I don't think I'll see you again."

On the way back to the farm, I again went to try and see my daughters. Their mother saw me as I entered the courtyard and immediately sent the girls inside, leaving me outside the closed door.

Early the next morning, with a broken, ice-cold heart, I boarded a vehicle heading westwards. On that journey, I again felt deeply sorry for my former wife, left to raise the children on her own. Her decision to abandon me had obviously not changed, nor did she show me any pity. My attempts to help her, in any miniscule way possible, had been simply rejected. Why, however, had she not yet remarried? I still wondered if she were not possibly waiting for me. Thus, I was clutching at this fanciful straw, almost certainly doomed to disillusionment.

When saying goodbye, mother and son had both understood we were seeing each other for the last time. One mid-day in early summer, a year later, when I had just returned from scattering manure in the fields, the duty-officer handed me a letter from home, written by my paternal cousin. It informed me that my mother had recently passed away, and they had already given her a rough and ready burial. I should go home to take care of her affairs.

I was devastated, but the people at the farm behaved as if I was invisible. No one asked what was wrong. For three or four days, I could only think of screaming in dismay, but I didn't dare to break regulations even in the most insignificant way. Instead, gritting my teeth, I dragged my bedraggled body off to work.

What followed was the season when mosquitoes rose up in swarms, when everyone used a gauze veil to cover his head. A fellow inmate quietly remarked, "Don't look so sad. See. We are all in mourning for your mother!" His remark was a joke: the veils resembled the headscarves worn by mourners at a funeral. The cadres would not actually have tolerated a genuine show of solidarity for a deceased relative.

In those days, I yearned to go home and visit my mother's grave, to find out how exactly she died and whether she had left anything behind. There was a camp rule permitting inmates to go home and bury their parents. I asked for compassionate leave and my team leader applied for authorisation. He encouraged me to work hard for the right to leave and each day I re-doubled my efforts, often working to the limits of my endurance. A fixed quota of people could go home each year; but that year was not for me.

My leader informed me that my leave had not been authorised, encouraging me to keep working hard and maybe next time. The next time, about a year later, my name was still absent from the list, and again I suffered devastating disappointment.

During the years I applied for home leave, certain other inmates went home twice, but my own hopes were repeatedly dashed.

Then they transferred me from Balong to the reservoir at Tuosu Lake, far from any trace of human habitation. Only small groups of people grazing yaks and camels dared to come and go from the lake area. Having stationed me there, they could rest assured I would not escape, for any 'escapee' would be attacked by wild animals.

After I returned to Balong from Tuosu, I was transferred to the 'end of imprisonment' team, where I was strictly supervised. Whether in the Balong team, at Tuosu Lake, or in the 'end of imprisonment' team, I persisted in applying for leave, but my applications were not approved.

Since I was bereft and resentful, I eventually left my team, intending to escape and go home, but could not break free completely. I was forced to return and suffer as the butt of abuse and criticism. Again, I contemplated escape as my

232

only resort, as I became the subject of even more ruthless persecution and evidently now had even less hope of permission for leave to visit my mother's grave.

After rehabilitation, I discovered why my leave-applications had been repeatedly rejected. My former wife had remarried and expressed concern to her new husband, saying that when I had last gone home to Guizhou, I had twice come to disturb her. What would happen if I came to find her again after she had remarried?

Ying's new husband then visited the farm leader, an old military comrade from the same province, to ask the farm to withhold permission for my leave, for fear that I might go and destroy his marriage. This was the hidden reason why the rules for compassionate leave at Xiangride were violated in my case for so many years.

In March 1976, after five years of pleading, permission was finally granted. In January, Premier Zhou Enlai had died. People throughout the nation were grieving his death and in many quarters the darkness and decadence of the Cultural Revolution were even more deeply regretted. My personal abhorrence of the Cultural Revolution had become progressively more intense.

On my way home to the village, while in Chongqing waiting for a train, I drank some rice wine with a meal, whereupon my anti-revolutionary emotions seemed much harder to control. In the small station garden, I started to think out loud, lashing out at the Cultural Revolution and its crimes, its persecution of revolutionary cadres and intellectuals. I reasoned that Zhou Enlai's premature death had been caused by such persecution, which had exacerbated his illness, and I appealed to all Chinese people with any conscience or courage to rise up and oppose the persecution. I called for a democratic movement, like a volcano, to erupt against the fascist dictatorship of the Cultural Revolution.

Such talk may have seemed heroic. I had a constantly changing audience of travellers, stopping to listen and moving on again. No one interfered. The alcohol loosened my tongue. I waxed eloquent, giving vent to my indignation for several minutes – fury that had been suppressed for years. Afterwards, I went on into the station, boarded the train and left Chongqing.

The first thing I noticed on returning home was that the small wooden shed where my mother had lived had disappeared. I discovered that in the early spring of 1971, when the weather had been at its coldest, my mother in her declining health and general weakness, had become incapable of propping herself up with walking sticks and going out to collect firewood. She had no fire for warmth or cooking, and the wind was howling through the wooden planks of the shed. She could not endure the cold and hunger, and could only lie down on the bed and pull over the quilt. Once she lay down, she was unable to get up again.

My paternal cousin's family, five or six people, sat around the fire chatting and laughing, in a large house with several storeys, next door to where my mother lived. Mother originally helped that cousin find a wife, and then gave him timber for his house and paddy fields for his rice. He had always expressed gratitude for how kind my family had been to him.

After Liberation, however, there had been an earth-shattering change. My cousin's family assumed the high status that our family had formerly enjoyed. They moved into Big House and daily poured their dirty waste water onto the small wooden shed behind. Their home was busy and lively, full of laughter, coming and going, wining and dining.

The little wooden shed at the back was also inhabited by a member of the Ou clan. Before Liberation, the clan had felt like one large family, all of whom treated my mother with great respect. After she had grown old, weak, hungry and weary, however, none of these relatives remembered her former kindnesses – and withheld from her even the little help she needed.

For three days, mother lay on her bed cold and hungry. The person who usually called on her to help her in the mornings stopped calling, and no one pushed her door open to see what was happening. Over the next few days, they waited for the old woman to die, quietly gossiping. When my paternal cousin got wind of this, he was shocked into action. Early on the third morning, he ventured into the shed, calling, "Aunty!" Then he discovered her body already stiff, for she had been dead for several hours.

My cousin stood at the altar to Sa Sui and called the important members of the clan together. Under his direction, relatives trooped out of the village and buried my mother at our clan's burial site. When she had been cold and hungry, about to die, no one went to see her, so she was unable to leave behind any last words and did not bequeath any of her ragged possessions from that pathetic little wooden shed. Those possessions and the shed itself had since completely disappeared, along with my mother.

Having discovered all this and having paid my respects at the small grave, which was just a mound in the earth, I felt sorely grieved. Our large family had scattered for survival. Now that mother had died, only my brother and I remained. He was still in prison, reforming through labour, and I was stuck at the farm in Qinghai. I didn't dwell too long on the future facing the two of us.

On my way back to the farm after visiting the grave of my mother, wiping tears away as I left my 'home without a home', I heard about the dramatic 5th April incident. At Tiananmen Square, people had pasted posters, large and small. There had been a mass rally, a massive demonstration, with speeches grieving for Premier Zhou and exposing the crimes of the Gang of Four. Later the authorities dispatched troops to suppress the rally and the troops arrested VIPs, who were fleeing in all directions. There was an investigation and the Gang of Four accused Comrade Deng Xiaoping of being behind the rally. Thereupon they intensified their campaign of oppression and the whole country was enveloped in an atmosphere of terror.

When I was back in Xining, I returned to the place where my former wife had lived, to try to see my daughters. Someone in the courtyard told me my former wife had remarried and moved away. My daughters were studying at one of the local middle schools.

My heart froze. Now everything had really been lost and I was completely in darkness. I stood there dumbstruck. A stranger asked me whom I had come to seek and I was startled back into the present. Silently, I walked on through the courtyard. That whole night I did not sleep. I did not know any of the circumstances, but simply surmised that Ying had been unable to wait for me any longer and had finally remarried. I felt so sad for my young daughters and sorry for my wife. The fantasy of a happy reunion for my small post-Liberation family, which I had entertained for so many years, had been conclusively dashed. I had been discarded, as if a gale-force wind had blown me off-course to a distant wilderness. The chances were that I would never again have a permanent home.

The next morning, I found the middle school. When I mentioned my daughters' names, however, no one recognised them. Upon hearing a more detailed description, one of the female teachers realised who I was looking for. She told me they had changed their names and had not come to school that day anyway, for they had asked for a holiday. She also advised me not to come again for there was no chance they would see me.

While I was waiting four days to catch a train in Xining, I discovered I was under close scrutiny. At every moment, there was someone nearby, watching me, staring occasionally at the small badge on the left side of my chest, which stated 'The Worldwide Proletariat Unite'.

My train drove right up to the farm headquarters. Someone among the crowd that alighted addressed the people who had come to take custody of us, "He's back. Keep an eye on him and interrogate him well. Make sure you deal with his problem." Actually, though, no one really paid any special attention to me. I was driven back to my former team in a tractor.

When I returned after paying respects at my mother's grave, the events of 5th April were still having repercussions on the farm. Rallies were being convened denouncing Deng Xiaoping. With raised arms, the convenor rabidly yelled slogans condemning Deng. A cadre standing beside me with arms raised was yelling the same crazy slogans, while keeping a close eye on me. Observing me to be silent, he glared at me resentfully.

One day when I was irrigating seedlings, that cadre sat on the ridge nearby to converse. He was asking things like, "Will they be reversing the verdict on Deng?"; "Why are you not outraged by the 5th April anti-Cultural Revolution incident in Tiananmen?"; "Are you even sympathetic to the cause of those people?"; "Are you upset at the repudiation of Deng Xiaoping?" During the rally when everyone else had been shouting, only I had kept a low profile.

The cadre wanted me to confess and to condemn anyone with similar views I had met on my journey. He criticised me for being unrepentant, for persisting stubbornly with revisionism, and for resisting the opposition to Deng Xiaoping. He insisted I should meditate on my problems day and night, leading to self-criticism and confession.

After this, the water-regulators oppressed me even more and said even more frightening things. They released more water, bursting through the field borders, giving them more reason to denounce me.

Fresh and Final Persecution on the Farm

When major challenges to the Cultural Revolution were underway, such as the February Adverse Current of 1967 [efforts by Party veterans to oppose the ultra-leftist radicalism at the beginning of the Revolution], the period of repudiation of Liu Shaoqi between 1966 and 1969 [Liu was the First Vice Chairman of China's Communist Party from 1956 to 1966, and had been publicly acknowledged as Mao's chosen successor in 1961] and the 5th April movement in 1976 [the protest in Tiananmen Square against the central government], farm leaders identified me as a target of criticism, declaring that I wanted to 'overturn the negative verdict' on such movements, that I was opposing change, and that I supported reversal of the verdicts on Liu Shaoqi and Deng Xiaoping. I was the despicable progeny of Nikita Khrushchev, a first-rate enemy of the Cultural Revolution, just like Liu and Deng. Those who had finished their prison terms and were launching a career on the farm treated me as a key adversary.

On 9th August 1976, Chairman Mao passed away and during the following days, everything in my team continued as before. No new rules or prohibitions were announced. We just observed that there were no longer any smiling faces among the cadres and they indulged in less screaming than before. Things seemed unusually calm as if some new force was being nurtured, waiting for an opportunity to pounce.

In October 1976, the Gang of Four fell from grace. It would be forbidden in future to express any opposition to Deng Xiaoping. The past would be generously overlooked, but from now on, a stricter approach would be adopted. Thus, a new set of rules was established ignoring the fact that formerly mass meetings had been convened refuting Deng.

There was a rare Sunday of rest and everyone asked for permission to leave the farm. I asked if I could go to Balong to try to get some butter there, for I had been losing weight. I was the only one whose request was not granted. At dinner, I drank a slug of tiger-bone wine for pain in the joints. I didn't think anyone would mind about this, so I was unsuspecting when I saw someone from the Discipline Department come marching across the courtyard.

The cadre stood at the office door glaring, as if searching for someone. I had no idea he was intending to discipline me and actually approached him to ask why I had not been allowed to leave the farm. With bulging eyes he retorted, "Why did you hail the name of Nikita Khruschev?" Naturally, I again denied ever uttering any slogan involving Khruschev.

In the past, they had fixed a placard on my head with Khruschev's name, before shouting it out, to associate it with me. They would simultaneously shake me, so becoming 'warriors opposing revisionism', as if doing so were an accomplishment in the cause. Metaphorically, they would climb higher by standing on my head.

On this occasion, the cadre's attempt to trap me was wasted. His humiliation turned to anger and he struck me on the face, bellowing. He ordered two 'heavies' to tie me up, trying to force me to confess. When I demurred, he became more flustered. After more screaming, he sent me to headquarters under escort. It was dusk and I was terrified they would concoct some murderous scheme, but I was still determined not to change my plea or beg for mercy.

After casually asking a few questions, one of the leaders at headquarters locked me up for the night in the petrol warehouse. Beside me were two massive canisters of petrol, exuding a suffocating odour. The two guards outside kept flicking on their lighters and smoking, saying, "Let's just cremate him here and now, and have done with it."

At midnight, I was escorted back to the team, to face another false accusation: that I had opposed Deng Xiaoping! They wanted to compel me to admit this, and for over a year afterwards, I worked by day and was denounced by night.

By day, I did the heavy work of pushing tonnes of water through the irrigation channels so that my body ached unbearably. Only with difficulty was I able to walk back from work, or even lie on my bed. When there seemed to be no other choice, I started to use acupuncture with silver needles donated by a fellow-inmate, with the nickname 'Go Fishing'. I pierced my own body according to the standard practises of acupuncture, experimenting to see if I could obtain any relief from pain or reduction in fatigue.

I often had to stand up and 'confess', suffering denunciation in the evenings, after days of heavy labour. Others would already be sleeping on their heated brick beds, exhausted from the day's work. Only the group leader and secretary organised the sessions. On rest-days, I had to stand and endure criticism while everyone else was patching clothes or sewing buttons. Whether by day or night, certain people would jump up to accuse, incite or criticise, striking or kicking me with their fists or feet.

This all became a kind of leisure pursuit, a distraction from the hard labour that otherwise filled the men's lives. There were, however, only two or three men who were fully engaged in persecuting me. They had instructions to force me to admit that I was a Khruschev supporter, and that I had been committed to opposing Deng Xiaoping.

There were two reasons why I was being forced at that time to admit this latter offence. One was to double up my personal trouble, but the other was to gloss over the guilt of others who had stridently opposed Deng. Certain leaders thus remained in key positions.

Those who were framing me were tainted by their own past political activities. Thus, they mobilised others to conduct a campaign criticising *me*, forcing me to admit trumped-up charges.

They continued such coercion for more than a year, and even stronger people could not have coped with it. I fainted many times. I soon resembled a leaf in water, buffeted and driven in all directions by stormy waves, completely bereft of strength, entirely manipulated at their whim. The person presiding used to say to everyone, "Don't be put off by his obstinacy. If you just keep going, he'll come around and no longer be so stubborn."

On the day I was officially rehabilitated and leaving the farm, I encountered that very person who had cruelly abused me. He quietly remarked, "It was Mr

Xu, the team leader, who ordered me to treat you like that. If I hadn't done so, I would have become the victim of such treatment myself."

You could sense that his conscience was seared, but he was not really repentant. He knew very well I had been the victim of injustice. He simply feared that after I was rehabilitated, I might expose his behaviour, and was already busy abdicating responsibility and making it appear as though he was just a pawn in someone else's misdemeanour.

Soon after the death of Chairman Mao, the Gang of Four was broken up, and this should have heralded a grand new phase. Unexpectedly, during this time when good was replacing bad, rogues were still able to frame the innocent.

What I suffered reflected what has always happened throughout history. Innocent people can't help being tangled up in such things, used as scapegoats. At least after the Gang of Four, I was the only one on our farm who had to experience such dark and merciless treatment.

Terror Before Freedom

The Qinghai Institute for Nationalities established a Rehabilitation Office, but staff there did not know where I was. In the end, they encountered Liu, a former inmate, and he informed them I was at Xiangride.

In spring 1978, three Institute cadres arrived in a specially commissioned vehicle to look for me. They explained they had come to help me, and asked if I had any special requests.

My brain could hardly adjust to this unexpected turn of events, to think clearly about what to say. My answer reflected my circumstances at the time. "I'd like to leave here and re-join society. Returning to my home village would be okay, but I'd prefer to return to the Institute. I'd be willing either to resume teaching or to do manual labour there."

I didn't dare to say more, but the three cadres seemed entirely sympathetic. They said they would receive me back to the Institute to resume teaching, and advised me to await notification.

After this, I continued heavy work as usual. Water was released in great quantities and surged with immense force. The guard in control stood silently, staring angrily like a tiger, looking fierce enough to cause palpitations. I only managed to endure by knowing that daybreak was at hand.

In the summer, the water-guard doubled up as group leader and became even fiercer. He supervised my work with a long iron shovel in hand, constantly increasing the water flow, and bossing me backwards and forwards to heighten the borders and block up the holes, until I was hardly able to catch my breath.

Once when a flood was bursting through a large break in the borders, I yelled at the guard to stop until the hole was mended. Instead, he ran at me wielding his shovel in the air. I fled towards headquarters to appeal for help. He was hard on my heels, flailing the shovel and yelling, "Run, but I'm going to slash you to death." Only when I disappeared into the office did he turn around and return to the site.

Such incidents happened frequently. The guards would urge each other, "Beat him as much as you like. It won't matter if you beat him to death." It was strange that every time they beat me, the cadres were nowhere to be seen. Our team cadre never investigated such beatings.

One night in the pitch-dark, as my nemesis was chasing and beating me, I risked my life groping to the bank of the river and then climbing a steep cliff. For two days and nights, I stayed away, without food, until finally I made my way back to the farm headquarters to look for help.

The farm cadres knew that plans were afoot to release me and their attitude towards me had changed for the better. They only insisted that I should not run away again. The next day, they arranged for me to return to my team by tractor.

Back in the team, masses of water were released as before and again I was the victim of vile cursing and contempt, bullied into doing this and that. In the evenings, I was denounced and unlikely scenarios were conjured up to frame me. The object seemed to be to find some pretext for beating me to death. Several times, I was warned, "Be careful! You're in a very dangerous situation!" As if I didn't know.

Someone asked me, "Is there anyone left in your family who would need to know if an accident happened to you?"

When I replied, "No, there's no one," he shook his head and said nothing. So they intimidated me in this exceptionally cruel way. Afterwards, I learned that the Institute office already delivered documents to the farm in spring 1978 to initiate my reinstatement, but the farm authorities were slow to respond.

Several years before, I had witnessed a terrifying incident in the Balong team. The government was implementing an amnesty to former members of the Chinese Nationalist Party, whereby former Nationalist spies could return home. But one night such prisoners were killed by fellow-prisoners and the building where they had been staying was burned to the ground. When I was about to be freed, I remembered that incident and trembled with fear.

When I finally returned to the Institute at the end of July 1979, the comrade at the office there broke into a smile and said, "How come the farm didn't send you back earlier? If you had delayed a few more days, we'd have sent a car to collect you."

By that stage, I was so relieved I just felt pleased. The next day the office arranged for me to sign documents enabling me to return to work. The re-investigation reports that followed explained clearly that my earlier conviction and sentence to hard labour had been wrong. After all, my reputation was unsullied, for there had been no evidence to suggest I was a revisionist. The accusations at the time of my conviction were refuted. Thus, I was rehabilitated and restored to my former position.

Only after I had signed did the comrade from the policy office allow me to see my case materials from 14 years before. The more I read, the paler and cloudier my complexion, for I had been framed from beginning to end. On many matters of principle, I felt shocked. These were the grounds upon which I had suffered ruthless persecution for 14 years, the 'case materials' which I had been asking in vain to see. That day they were completely overturned, though the office comrade insisted I was only permitted to read the materials, not to take them away.

A few days later, the policy office instructed me to return to Xiangride to process formalities for shifting my residency registration away from the farm. This went smoothly and was completed in only two days.

A Zhuang man from Guangxi Province, a former fellow inmate, invited me for a meal. He helped carry my luggage to the bus and as I watched him return silently to his team, I felt so sorry for him. I rode the bus to the discipline section of the farm headquarters to complete formalities there. As I was about to leave, the section leader asked me, "What work will you be doing when you return to the Institute?"

I hastily left the farm where I had been incarcerated doing hard labour for more than 10 years, and returned to work at the Qinghai Institute. I was 49 years old. Persecution, in the name of opposing revisionism, had deprived me of the best years of my life.

Chapter 18
Wedding and Working
(Xining, 1979-95)

Marriage and Family

By the time I returned to society, my mother had died and my own family – my wife and children – had vanished. The place where I had worked was still there, but I had no family and no one to rely on. I'd already lived half a century on this earth. How much I yearned for family, to give warmth to my desolate, sorrowful heart.

My former wife Ying was still at the Institute, teaching history of the Chinese Communist Party. A mutual acquaintance persuaded her to allow me to meet our two children in the home of teacher Hu. Ying advised me to start a new family, but my feelings were so mixed I did not know how to respond, and said nothing. I just asked my daughters, now 21 and 17 years old, if they were well, but neither replied. The younger began to cry and the atmosphere was heavy with grief. I felt so sorry for the girls; it was so excruciatingly sad for us all. We spent just over 10 minutes together.

Ying's new husband had a high position in the Party and in view of my status as a returned convict, I did not dare to seek further meetings with my daughters. When by chance I saw them out and about, I usually felt afraid because of Ying and her husband.

One morning, however, my daughters turned up unexpectedly, carrying brooms and buckets. They were busy for quite a while at my place and left everything clean, neat and tidy. This moved me to tears and generated terrible agony. There seemed to be a wall between us, an intangible wall that had separated father and daughters for many years. It was as if the devil, scheming to sabotage, had declared emphatically, "Destroy his family," and had imposed eternal estrangement, not allowing us to see much of each other. My daughters, however, were young and innocent, and completely unable to discern their father's agony.

Half a year after returning to work, I enjoyed my first winter vacation for 15 years. By now, there was no trace of my old family in a Guizhou village, but my elder brother was working in Guiyang after completion of his prison sentence. Before Liberation, he had been happily married. After Liberation, he and his wife had been separated for many years, each suffering a generous share of political disaster and surviving only against the odds. Now they lived in Wangwu village, a suburb of Guiyang. I really wanted to see my brother, as he was the only member of my parental family still alive.

I stayed with him for a few days at his home in Wangwu. He and his wife were unstinting in their hospitality. In keeping with our old village tradition, they invited guests to keep us company and killed chickens to host us all.

My brother did not in the least resemble the sad person I had been over the past 15 years. It seemed instead as if he had swallowed all his melancholy, and he wore the same smiling face I had earlier known him by, doing his best to feign happiness. I was delighted to see him.

On my third evening back in Guiyang, my sister-in-law insisted on introducing me to her friend, Ms Duan. She was hoping to have me settle down and marry as soon as possible. She accompanied me to Duan's home and we arrived just as Duan was having dinner. Beside her stood two daughters, one just over 10 years of age and the other a few years younger. They invited us to sit down on small wooden stools. The electric light was dim and there was a cold wind blowing through cracks in the doors and windows. Everything indicated the family was poor and living in straitened circumstances.

Ms Duan had been an outstanding primary school teacher, before being transferred to the Education Office to serve as a cadre. She was popular, seven years younger than me, and frequently entertained guests. The first time we met, we just made polite conversation. We both appreciated my sister-in-law's introduction, and our first mutual impressions were good.

Afterwards, I often went to visit Duan, talking a lot, while she listened. She never discouraged me and her daughters always expressed a welcome. Education Office colleagues witnessed our growing friendship, and they, too, seemed supportive. It felt like everything about Duan was familiar and amiable, nothing in the least jarring; and she seemed to feel the same about me. From the similarities in our personalities and backgrounds, we could often discern each other's meaning without so much as a word being said. Although we had only known each other a short time, we found it difficult each time we separated.

At the time, I was staying in a hostel. Every day when Duan finished work, I would go and accompany her back home. She suggested we visit my hostel, but I was reluctant, for I felt embarrassed about staying there. She didn't ask why and didn't raise the issue again, seeming to trust me.

When I proposed, however, she hesitated, saying that marriage would only be possible after I transferred back to work in Guiyang. The Guizhou Institute for Nationalities had agreed to employ me, but had not yet applied to the Qinghai Institute. Neither of us could say when that would be resolved and we would just have to wait until it was. Every day, she went to work, taking care of her two daughters after work, thus keeping extremely busy. She faced and overcame many hardships.

Just before Chinese New Year, Duan was given a bonus by her work unit. So at New Year, she bought lots of food, including meat, and on New Year's Eve spent the whole day preparing a sumptuous feast to which I was invited, along with my brother and his wife.

That night for the first time, I observed Duan really happy, chatting and laughing with my sister-in-law, though she remained more solemn towards me, not engaging me in conversation, and so maintaining the traditions of our respective home villages. I felt pleased with her and she in turn was I think enamoured with me.

The winter vacation passed by quickly, but by the end, Duan had still not accepted my marriage proposal, leaving me ill at ease. One day in the drizzle at dusk, I had to say goodbye to her, since the new term was about to begin. After returning to Qinghai, I wrote several letters to her, but she only replied briefly three months later, saying she was very fond of me and would like to remain friends, but she was unable to make a lifelong commitment.

Duan had decisively declined my proposal and I felt devastated. From our meetings three months before, although she never said that she loved me, never laughed when alone with me, and did not talk much but mostly listened to my non-stop chatter, I felt she was sincere, tolerant, non-argumentative and trustworthy. Maybe partly because she seemed not so very different from me, she left a good impression.

After hearing from Duan, I decided not to request a transfer to Guizhou. My loneliness, however, was accentuated by working at the same Institute as my former wife, who had remarried and was raising a family. I yearned for a family atmosphere, to help me face whatever lay ahead. Two friends expressed their willingness to help, though I felt impatient, while they conscientiously did what they could, eventually introducing me to a potential partner.

At our first meeting, there was no serious problem and the second meeting was arranged soon afterwards. Before long, this new friend was spontaneously coming to visit, though we were not yet formally courting, for we still didn't know each other very well. Her name was Xiao Jiang, from Harbin, a city in northeast China, and she had completed senior middle school. Now she was a carpet designer, unmarried, and about 18 years my junior. That was about it, just a fairly superficial knowledge of her.

The boldness I observed in Xiao Jiang actually made me feel rather timid and I thought I should wait a little before leaping into marriage. The delay, however, turned out to be only a few days, and the wedding was arranged for 1st May 1980. On that day, Jiang moved in with all her clothing and other luggage. She invited cooks from her factory to come and prepare food, and also invited women to come and tidy up my flat.

There was only one table of guests, mostly my colleagues. It was not customary at the time to give presents, and soon after they had eaten, the guests got up and left. The cooks had been busy all day long and did not ask for remuneration. Nor did they themselves feast on their sumptuous food or indulge in wine at the meal. Their assistance was altruistic, supporting our transition to life as husband and wife; they were endued with a selfless kindness.

We lived in a room in the general dormitory for Institute staff, where a double bed occupied most of the floor space. In the mornings, as day dawned, Jiang went to work in the factory, while in the evenings, after returning home, she continued to work hard.

At lunchtime, we went to the dining hall and ate together and usually did the same at dinner in the evenings. Only on Saturday evenings and on Sundays did we use a kerosene stove to cook our own meals. At long last, I had re-established a household, and family life resumed in these Spartan circumstances.

In the second half of the year, we moved to a new dormitory building, where our flat had one bedroom and one living room, with toilet and kitchen, altogether 40 square metres. This represented a huge improvement, making us feel very contented, with more than we needed.

Before long, I travelled to Beijing to participate in an academic symposium and returned to Xining one night. Upon my return, my new wife burst noisily into tears, telling me how someone from the neighbour's family had blocked our window view by piling up coal outside, and had even scolded her. It was a long story and she felt deeply hurt. Then she brought in a delicious hot meal and set it before me. After 15 years, I was gratified to be able to taste again the width and warmth of family life.

Jiang was hard-working and everything at home was well organised, without my lifting a finger. She cooked good, healthy meals. By temperament, she was outspoken, calling a spade a spade. She didn't pay much attention to etiquette, so it transpired that she easily offended others. Often because she spoke one or two sentences out of turn, others would bristle in response, and I too often quarrelled with her as a result. People frequently said, however, that she was kind at heart, without a bad bone in her body. Through experience, I came to realise the truth of this, so I was able to make allowances for her temperament.

After the wedding, work went smoothly and we experienced good times, each enjoying the warmth and happiness of our small family unit. Neither of us was a Party member, however, and I realised we didn't have support at hand from any organisation or close relatives. We seemed isolated and vulnerable. Although we had settled down, there was still an element of anxiety about the future.

Two years after our wedding, Jiang's work began to take her out of the drafting room, and she frequently travelled on business trips. In 1983 while she was in Tianjin, I fell ill with appendicitis, experiencing awful and intense pain. By the time the Institute doctors diagnosed the problem, the appendix had burst and I had to be admitted to hospital for an emergency operation.

There was no one to drive me, so fighting against pain I squeezed my way onto a crowded public bus to the hospital. I found a doctor to examine me and completed admission procedures. There were no close relatives on hand to sign, to agree for me to have the operation.

It just so happened that there was a power cut as I was being pushed into the operation room, but once the power returned, some liquid medicine was rubbed over my belly as anaesthetic. Before the operation was carried out, two nurses bound my hands and feet to the operation table. My screams shook the whole building.

After the operation, there was no intravenous drip and during the night, there was no one to keep an eye on me. When I was discharged a week later, there was no vehicle to take me home. A kind-hearted former classmate cycled to the bus station to help me board a bus and go home. There was no one there waiting for me, for my wife was still away in Tianjin. With great difficulty, I prepared some food and organised myself. The next day I went to the Institute as usual to report for duty and to teach.

That whole experience with appendicitis instilled a general terror in me towards hospital operations. The fact I was able to come out the other side made me think my general health was quite good after all, and I was also the beneficiary of good luck. At the same time, I had experienced again the difficulty of not having close relatives to hand.

In early autumn that year, not long after Jiang returned from Tianjin, the factory leaders sent her off again to study carpet design, in Urumqi city of Xinjiang, this time for half a year. I stayed at home alone, keeping myself busy preparing and teaching classes, and writing research articles.

Soon after Jiang returned from Xinjiang having completed her study there, she was summoned by a female manager in the provincial foreign trade office and asked to transfer there to lend a hand. In spring the following year, the manager decided to take Jiang with her to participate in a trade fair in Guangzhou city. Before leaving for Guangzhou, Jiang had already been showing signs of restlessness. She frequently returned home only at midnight, clearly behaving as though she preferred to avoid my company. It seemed to me as if, after being promoted to the foreign trade office, she had constantly been at loggerheads with me.

When Jiang returned from the trade fair in Guangzhou, the situation deteriorated further. She seemed to treat me with disdain and we frequently quarrelled, until in the end she asked for a divorce – only after I had already felt despair. We went and signed divorce papers at a law court, and two days later Jiang left again, to study in Beijing.

As a result, the official letter confirming our divorce was only delivered to me. Jiang's letter was not delivered but retained at the court. So I knew I was a divorced man, but there was still a trace of uncertainty on Jiang's part, of which I was oblivious. As far as I was concerned, the judgement had been passed, and that was that. Our small family had ruptured and my former status as a solitary bachelor had boomeranged. That half-year had been a circuitous, bumpy journey. My efforts to resolve our relationship problems had fallen short.

A few days before the beginning of the autumn term in 1985, Jiang returned to Xining from Beijing. The female manager from the foreign trade office accompanied her home and mediated between the two of us, raising many different issues. She made Jiang pledge that in future she would not repeat her noisy clamour for divorce. I put to one side my own injured feelings, in the hope that our small family could be resurrected after all. So we accepted advice and agreed to return to the court and process formalities for remarrying. Thereafter, we continued our relationship as husband and wife.

Soon afterwards, the carpet factory decided to send Jiang to the Qinghai Institute to study fine arts, so when she was not attending classes, she was at home, keeping me company. In the end, her two years of professional training passed peacefully in our monotonous little home, with Jiang cultivating the custom of staying at home and not running wildly all over the country on business trips. After her studies, Jiang chose not to return to work in the factory, but applied instead for permission to retire on health grounds, so she could stay at home and be with me. Her application was approved.

I kept very busy teaching by day, or otherwise working in the office, and preparing lessons at home in the evenings. Jiang handled all the household duties, our lives were stable and I was able to concentrate on work. At that time, we were still living in the little 40-plus square-metre flat in a block of flats. The four households above belonged to minority nationality cadres.

It never occurred to me to install a filter in the drain of the kitchen sink. Carelessly, we used to wash the dirty dregs from our meals down the drain, causing the pipes to be blocked. Sewage overflowed from the drain under the sink into our kitchen, so there was nowhere to put your feet. We went upstairs to beg the people there temporarily to suspend releasing their dirty water through the pipes.

No sooner had we returned downstairs, however, than the people upstairs flushed their sewage as usual and the dirty water again spilled into our kitchen. We placed bricks on the floor so that our feet wouldn't step into the sewage. We scooped up and poured out the stinking water every day. Institute plumbers kept being delayed. Our kitchen was flooded throughout the 15 days of Spring Festival. Even with doors and windows open, the stench made us feel dizzy.

After all the trouble maintaining our marriage, this chance adversity brought extra pressure to bear on our relationship. In November 1986, our daughter Lulu was born, and then Jiang's mother came for more than two months to lend a hand. The kitchen crisis of rising sewage often recurred and besides, our flat was just too small. We were unable to convince Lulu's grandmother to stay longer.

The following summer, new teachers' accommodation was built and the Institute allocated housing there according to seniority. They allowed us to abandon the flat where we had been savaged by sewage and to live on the third floor of the new teachers' building. Come what may, we would never again dare to live on the ground floor of a building.

The new flat was 75 square metres in area, with three bedrooms and one living room, along with kitchen and toilet and two balconies. This was bigger than before and the flat was better. Lulu was not yet a year old, and Jiang stayed at home to feed and take care of her. I was busy with work but around that time I also began to take responsibility for meals, and after a personal crash course in the art of cooking, I never again frequented public canteens.

We were no longer afflicted by the feeling that everything was too cramped or cumbersome. Being on the third floor was neither too high nor too low. It was far enough away from rubbish on the ground outside, and there was no longer any fear of sewage overflowing. The balcony faced the sun and in summer, our potted plants were in full bloom.

Outstanding among them was the cactus, the reddest of red, blooming year after year. Surveying the distant scenery from our third-floor balcony, I felt carefree and relaxed. Indoors, each room was bright. On hot days, it felt cool and refreshing and the air was fresh and clean. In winter, we could rely upon central heating, and it felt like spring inside. This housing was better than we had ever experienced, and my heart was full of gratitude to the Institute for such good living conditions.

Within a few days, however, after cheerfully and optimistically moving into the new flat, baby in arms, we discovered that loud noises from the floor above were destroying our tranquillity.

The residents above and below our new flat were Han nationality associate professors. We did not anticipate any problems. When the family above us moved in, there were five people, but later their number had increased to nine. Among them, two young people were working shifts. Their movements upstairs were noisy, day and night. I heard that they didn't have a very good reputation.

Sure enough, within a few days I knew from personal experience that our new upstairs neighbours entertained no scruples. All kinds of noise came through the floor of the flat above. Metal heels clicked around, and there was banging and stamping, a tremendous cacophony.

The noise often roused our infant daughter from sleep. Once, with my wailing baby in arms, I went upstairs to beg the occupants to try to be a little quieter, but they blamed the residents above them in the fifth-floor flat…who were away on a trip at the time.

With the years, the problem only grew worse. My sleep was often disturbed. During a routine physical examination around 1990, I discovered that I had coronary heart disease. I asked staff at the Human Resources Department for advice, and they simply advised we change our housing.

After I retired in 1992, the noise from the floor above seemed to grow even more bothersome. It seemed almost as though people were taking turns to annoy us.

Jiang had been running a small bookstand at the entrance to the Institute, employing our nephew to watch the stand. In the summer of 1994 our nephew left, and Jiang felt compelled to abandon child and chores to take responsibility for buying and selling books. She took our Tibetan dog Bao to the bookstall and spent the nights there guarding the stall.

During that period, we moved Lulu's small wooden bed beside mine. Every evening after she had fallen asleep, I began work until midnight, after which I dropped into bed. Just then, however, noise from the floor above would often wake Lulu, and coaxing her to sleep again would be really difficult. I often went without sleep and during the days, I also had to cook, boil water, send Lulu to school in the mornings and meet her in the evenings. There was not a drop of sleep to be squeezed out of lunchtime, because of the noise from above, and it felt as though I was incessantly busy.

This all created a deep sense of confusion, as if my head was constantly spinning and I was living in a kind of trance. My speech became stressed and hurried, sometimes slurred and incoherent. Lulu was also suffering from sleep deficit, and on the way to school, she would frequently still be half-asleep, crying and making a fuss. Jiang, however, was still resolutely committed to the bookstand, day and night.

It was not until 1995 that I applied to go home to Guizhou province and find a place to settle down. The newly appointed Institute party secretary promptly approved my application, thus rescuing my family. At the time, some staff opposed my departure, but one of the Institute leaders retorted impatiently, "You make people suffer until they are almost mental cases! Why not let him go?" No one could contradict him.

My elder brother had been sentenced to reform-through-labour, and he served nearly 30 years. In 1979, he was discharged and was able to re-marry immediately, but he and his wife had no children.

In summer 1985 when I went to Guiyang for some research, I discovered my brother was suffering from cancer and had been hospitalised for an operation. I went to visit him, but he was so thin and weak I couldn't recognise him, until he called out to me. Seeing his condition, my heart sank. His wife said doggedly he would only be discharged after the illness had been cured, thus expressing the thin thread of hope she was hanging on to.

By the time I went to see him a week later, he had returned to the Wangwu clinic to be nursed on the ward there. He was saying, "I'll be better soon," and did indeed seem better than before. When I went to see him after another week, he was at home, having been discharged. He was there on his own so I prepared a meal for him, after which he kept saying how tasty it had been.

Again, after another few days I went to see him, after he had moved to his wife's home in Qinglingxi Road, Guiyang. The summer weather was at its hottest and he was lying on a straw mat on a wooden bed. There was no doctor or nurse and his wife was out working all day. She only returned in the evening and then prepared food for him: green boiled vegetables.

My brother's cancer consumed him, until there was practically nothing left of him. How could he eat this diet? How could it renew his strength? It seemed to me that his wife's compassion had already been exhausted, but he never whispered a word of complaint, not a word against anyone, nor the least hint of criticism. Instead, he just lay there calmly, from time to time humming a little with pain.

I tried to console him saying he would soon be better, but he just smiled and responded with silence. He surely sensed he did not have long to live, but never passed on anything that could have been construed as last words or wishes. After all, he didn't have a penny to his name.

The day before I left Guiyang, I brought him a watermelon against the heat. He couldn't bring himself to eat any, but said I should leave it until the next day. I left him a little money for something nice to eat, which he put in his pocket as if he had received a rare treasure – so resembling people from our home village in the days before Liberation! Even if he hadn't been ill, he would have died of starvation if forced to depend on his wife's cooking.

As his only visitor, I found myself wondering: what strong and capable man has ever fallen into such a plight and yet remained so stoical? He evoked both my pity and admiration. As I said my final goodbye, I couldn't help shedding some tears, cut to the heart. Within a month, I heard he had passed away, less than four months after his operation.

My brother had tasted a full dose of suffering throughout the 30 years he had spent in a reform-through-labour team, exhausting his strength. After all that, he was worn down by serious illness and staunchly finished his 58-year life in the throes of pain.

My parents' family had been good and honest people. All had passed away sadly, one after another and now only my own little family still survived. My native place remained, but there was no family there.

I, too, had eaten my fill of suffering and now I wanted to bring my little family back home, at least to Guizhou Province, to settle there. On the one hand I was pleased about this prospect, on the other, anxious. I was pleased that I could save my life by leaving that sleepless home. My fate in life thus far, however, had not been good and I was anxious about the unpredictability of what lay ahead.

Work

Before 1964, I had written several academic papers. After I was reinstated at the Institute, my writing ability was recognised and I was assigned to work in the editorial office for scholarly journals.

The Institute published a quarterly journal, with each edition containing around 10 articles. Five people worked in the editorial office and there were not that many manuscripts to read, meaning there was lots of free time. In those days, I felt very energetic, endowed it seemed with endless resources of strength. I was reluctant to rest during the idle times, having become accustomed to working non-stop.

During half a year of working at the office, I wrote evaluations of various manuscripts, along with recommendations for improvements. In addition, I myself wrote two articles. This small quantity of work did not take up even 10% of my working time.

During that half-year, I slept on a single bed in the office. My teaching programme had not yet been set in motion. To be without substantial work made me feel restless. Wherever I observed anything that needed doing, I took the initiative to go and do it.

Departments were supposed to take turns to clean the corridors outside the offices, but after I arrived, I did all that cleaning myself in the mornings, so that those who didn't know me thought I was a janitor.

Three times a day, I went to collect boiled water, turning the taps off one by one, so as not to waste any.

On Sundays, I would often lend a hand to families of colleagues who needed to carry coal, happily doing this for hours on end, with sweat pouring off my forehead.

In those days, I rarely went to bed before 12 midnight. I was accustomed to using the early-morning hours for reading and writing. It became my settled custom not to 'waste time', engaging in various academic projects, writing and translation.

Within a month of being reinstated, I was instructed to teach a course on Nationality Affairs to three research students from the Chinese Language Department. This was like an examination. Fortunately, before I had been imprisoned, I had taught this very course for several years to students in the Cadre Training Department. In one week, I finished teaching the main content of Nationality Affairs, and this developed into the skeleton outline of a lecture course.

An army garrison outside the Institute invited me to go and teach for a morning. They paid me a little for my trouble and invited me to lunch, the first time I had ever enjoyed remuneration for teaching, my normal salary excluded. I felt both pleased and slightly embarrassed. During the half-year I was editing, I also substituted for an absentee teacher for more than a month, teaching English to children in a local primary school.

While on the farm, I had not been at liberty to rest. So when I returned to the Institute, I was constantly itching to work, and I was usually busy from early morning until midnight. Even so, it felt like my strength and energy could not be depleted.

The haemorrhoids that for years had caused loss of blood, healed quickly and naturally, and I recovered completely. Sleeping on my own in the office, as part of my duty to keep an eye on things, felt like such a luxury. It was so spacious and I felt relaxed and cheerful there. Life was good.

In spring 1980, I was transferred from the editorial office to help establish a Nationalities Research Institute. The director of the new Institute was a Tibetan cadre. Several others were to teach Nationality Affairs, but none was well versed in anthropology or nationality research. I was the only specialist in those fields.

My new colleagues and I began work in the Research Institute, busy with teaching and administration. Everything developed quickly.

During the early days, no research was done. The staff threw themselves into teaching minority affairs and minority policies and it was purely a teaching department.

Minority affairs and minority policies became core courses for all students at the Qinghai Institute. Each of these two subjects involved more than 40 periods of teaching, and each member of staff had to teach two classes of students. The greatest challenge was that there were no pre-set teaching materials, and the workload was accordingly heavy.

In the second half of 1980, the State Nationality Affairs Commission convened meetings involving teachers from 10 Nationality Institutes nationwide. As a result, in June 1983 a textbook was published for the Institutes, entitled

Nationality Theory and Policy. Before this, we had compiled teaching materials ourselves.

My speciality was anthropology and I already had several years of experience lecturing in the subject. I taught anthropology and nationality studies right up until retirement. In fact, I taught more periods during that time than anyone else at the Qinghai Institute.

During the first year without official teaching materials, my lectures focussed on introducing the book *Marxism and Nationality Affairs*. The Qinghai Institute approved my course and feedback from students was positive. The result was that the course was incorporated into teaching materials published in Beijing.

My students asked me to distribute lecture notes. I compiled my notes into a draft manuscript and passed this to the Research Institute Director for review. My name was subsequently deleted from the work. By way of explanation, it was said that teaching materials developed during the Cultural Revolution had also omitted the authors' names. I asked to be permitted to write an editor's introduction to my notes, but was informed that such an introduction would be tantamount to a claim to authorship.

Thus, the printed Teaching Outline issued to students did not betray any hint as to authorship and students mistakenly assumed it had been written during the Cultural Revolution. It required some further explanation before they were reassured enough to read it.

In 1982, the Research Institute embarked on its first research project, to write a book entitled *Minority Nationalities in Qinghai Province*. I was designated the task of writing about the Kazakh people of Haixi, with a population of less than 1,000, which involved a research trip to Golmud city. The book was published in 1987.

After national teaching materials had been received, I adapted those for my classes and no longer wrote my own lectures. Instead, when there was time, I wrote about other issues. There was always debate and disagreement about the designation of nationality identity, and this was one of my themes. In 1964, I had written about three kinds of nationality community, and I researched more as I taught the nationality theory course.

My book *A Review of Anthropology* was published in 1988. It received first prize from the State Nationalities Commission in the philosophy and social sciences section. This was the highest award won by any publication from Qinghai Province up to that time.

In 1986, I was promoted to the position of Associate Professor in Qinghai Province, in the field of nationality theory and policy. Slowly but surely, Institute colleagues teaching the same courses raised their standards. Ultimately, my mission to support their progress was accomplished.

In the 1950s, I had chosen anthropology as my main field of study, being the first person in China authorised to pursue anthropological research. At no time did I ever contemplate changing the focus of my work.

During the 10 years after the Qinghai Nationalities Research Institute was established, I published various articles about nationality theory. At one scientific symposium, Mr Wu Zelin, a renowned ethnologist in China, privately commended my work, saying he had read it all, and it would have a great positive impact on the development of anthropology in our country.

From 1988 to 1994, I served as an editor of the journal Qinghai Social Sciences.

After retiring and returning to my native province, I published the book *Basic Anthropology* in 1999, with a revision in 2007.

While working at the Qinghai Institute, I was proactive in promoting anthropology. Colleagues teaching nationality theory were afraid anthropology would clash with their courses and did not want me to teach undergraduates. Instead, I could only teach anthropology to Master's degree students who were studying nationality history. To each year's intake, I taught 50 lecture hours, discussing much of my own research. Feedback from the course was generally positive.

In the end, permission was granted to teach anthropology to undergraduates as part of the core curriculum of the Politics Department. From 1988 to 1991, I did so, 80 periods each semester. I developed my own teaching materials, distributing them to students. At first students were unfamiliar with the course content, and found it difficult. With my lectures, however, they soon understood and interest was aroused. The Law and Minority Language Departments subsequently developed plans to teach this course. When I retired, however, anthropology classes retired along with me.

Academic Activities

The Cultural Revolution resulted in the disbanding of organisations engaged in nationality research. The period just after the Cultural Revolution, however, was nicknamed the 'spring season for science'. Those who had previously done nationality research embraced the slogan: 'Go back to your work unit!' Many returned to their posts.

In August 1980, the Qinghai Institute sent me and another colleague to Beijing, to participate in a conference at the Central Institute for Nationalities.

This was my first return to the Central Institute after my time as a research student there. I came across a former classmate and colleague, Mr Wei, who during the anti-rightist period had victimised me terribly. When I saw him again, however, it was as if we had been transported back to the more innocent time when we had been together at the Southwest Institute for Nationalities. He greeted me smiling from ear to ear and brought me back to his home for a meal. He was most cordial, and we chatted about anything and everything, as though the whole anti-rightist thing had never happened. It was, however, the elephant in the room. In our hearts, there was still private anguish.

That evening, Wei brought me to visit Mr Wu Zelin, who had formerly been my office neighbour in Chengdu, and we chatted in his tiny bedroom-cum-office. He had suffered all kinds of torment in the intervening 15 years, and looked even thinner and more worn out than before. He asked me how I had been keeping all these years and how I was doing now. We were both in a solemn mood.

On the day the conference ended, a former classmate from the Southwest Institute in Chengdu approached me with her husband to invite me to their home for a meal. They had just been transferred from Inner Mongolia to Beijing. Their home was small and cramped, and they placed the dining table outside the main door, where we sat, eating, drinking and chatting freely. This all left a deep and positive impression, but afterwards I never had opportunity to see them again.

In October 1980, I was invited to the first Chinese anthropological symposium in Guiyang. On the day we divided into discussion groups, staff from the Guizhou provincial television station came to produce a live show, and invited some teachers to say a few words. They all diplomatically declined, however, and none of the younger attendees seemed up for the opportunity. There was an awkward silence – until I finally took the bull by the horns, and made a short speech.

In September 1982, the second such anthropological symposium was convened in Xining. I presented a paper entitled 'Socialist nationality relationships in China'.

In May 1985, I responded to an invitation from the Chinese World Nationalities Research Association to attend its second academic symposium in Beijing, submitting a paper entitled 'A brief description of nationality languages in India'.

The vice-president of the Association, Professor Li Yifu, was proficient in both Russian and English. He had been my Russian teacher when I was a research student, and on seeing him 20 years later, I was delighted and deeply moved.

During the symposium, my younger daughter Tao, who was now a second-year student at the Beijing Sports College, came to see me and we ate dumplings together at a restaurant. As we were eating and reminiscing, it dawned on me how frugal my student-daughter was, how unwilling to waste even the smallest scrap of food. This left a sad impression, reminding me of my thrifty, diligent ex-wife Ying.

In November 1985, I travelled to Nanning to attend the third anthropological symposium with the theme 'Commemorating *Origins*'. We discussed the ideas of Frederick Engels in his work *The Origin of the Family, Private Property and the State*, first published in 1884. I submitted a paper entitled 'Discussing tribes', using Engels' book as a theoretical basis.

In October 1987, the Institute sent me, along with four others, to Tianshui in Gansu Province, to attend a week-long symposium on northwestern nationality affairs.

In September 1989, I returned to Beijing to attend the fourth Chinese anthropological symposium, at Beijing University. The Tiananmen incident of 4th June was fresh in people's minds, and students had not yet returned to university. [A pro-democracy demonstration in Tiananmen Square involving around 100,000 people had been suppressed.] At night, fearful cries could be heard from time to time from tall buildings in the distance.

The Russian AM Lieshe Tuofu was there. He had been a research student at Beijing University in the 1950s. Back then, I saw him once a week.

During discussions of my paper 'Tibetans living in the Songpan grasslands', AM spoke up. He had aged a lot, had recently broken a leg and was using crutches. I didn't recognise him, but I was later re-introduced by someone who explained I had been persecuted for 14 years, accused of revisionism. AM expressed sympathy and immediately became friendly and familiar, inviting me back to his room. He said that in recent years he had researched questions relating to Mongolian children. He asked me about the Tu nationality in Qinghai and the Tuomao people in County Haiyan.

AM and I struck up correspondence for a while. Then the Soviet Union broke up and place names and work unit names changed, and this put a stop to our communications.

At this symposium, I also became acquainted with an American anthropologist from Oregon University by the name of John A Young.

On the last day of the symposium, I presented a paper with the theme: 'Changes in culture of the traditional pastoral economy among Tibetans in Qinghai Province', which was well received.

At a special session in the Central Institute for Nationalities, 'Celebrating 50 years of teaching by Professor Lin Yaohua', many of the professor's former students participated. Lin was then still vice-president of the Association. When the celebration was announced, everyone wanted to join in. There was a big crowd bustling with excitement. People were competing with each other to honour the professor, and at the request of some of my old classmates, I also gave a short speech.

Professor Lin himself was really old. He sat motionless and speechless on a sofa, simply listening. I advanced to shake his hand, and he just said, "So you came!" This was to be the last time I would see him, and those were the last words I heard him speak.

An old classmate invited six of us former classmates for lunch, together with AM Lieshe Tuofu. Our host was warm and enthusiastic and had prepared a great feast. I proposed a toast to AM. Afterwards, many private conversations developed. Someone mentioned his difficulties during the anti-rightist era, whereupon our host was embarrassed, and left the table. I too felt embarrassed and took my leave early.

In July 1991, the Chinese Anthropology Association invited me to a meeting in Yanbian Korean Autonomous Prefecture, to discuss the promotion of anthropology as an academic subject. For the first time, I tasted the wonderful hospitality of the Korean minority people in China. On the last day of the meeting, Mr Fei Xiaotong [a well-known Chinese sociologist, 1910–2005] gave a plenary lecture, before a group photo.

Shortly after I returned to the Institute, I received a letter from Professor John Young in Oregon, in his capacity as Chairman of the American Anthropological Association. He invited me to Memphis, Tennessee, to attend the annual meeting of the Association there, and then to do some teaching as a visiting scholar at his university. A Chinese scholar in Chicago had already urged me several times to go to America as a visiting scholar. He wrote that the payment for each hour's teaching was 80 US dollars, a sum undreamed of at the time in Qinghai.

I was intent on accepting the invitation to the USA. The Qinghai Institute agreed, contingent on my completing the normal retirement formalities.

To process a passport, provincial foreign affairs officers needed stamps of approval from relevant Institute departments. Reluctantly, in accordance with Institute requirements, I retired, abandoning aspirations for promotion to the position of full professor and surrendering my salary. All the necessary materials, including a letter of invitation from the American Anthropological Association, the Institute's political investigation and the Institute's approval, were finally supplied.

For over six months, I waited for my passport to be issued. I visited the Foreign Affairs Office regularly to expedite the process, during which time I was in regular correspondence with Professor Young. Then one day, the Office informed me that the Education Department of the Chinese embassy in the USA had faxed saying the American side had not invited me after all. Therefore, the Office could not issue me with a passport.

This was a bolt from the blue and I was totally perplexed. When I asked to see the fax, I was informed it had been addressed to the Office and I could not see it. The staff member waved it in front of my nose. I was unconvinced the fax was genuine. It felt like I was being cheated.

I had retired early and had been busy with this application for more than six months, leaving so much work undone that would otherwise have been done. After this, however, the chicken had flown the coop and all the eggs were broken. Of course I felt aggrieved, but I had no choice but to admit defeat. I posted to the US the paper I had written for the meeting.

Professor Young wrote to express regret that I had been unable to attend the meeting myself. At the same time, he renewed his invitation to visit the USA, saying I would be welcome to visit his university.

At the time, I had been lecturing in anthropology to Politics students. When I was unexpectedly forbidden to leave, some Institute leaders sympathetically announced that my retirement formalities, which had already been processed, would be suspended. They invited me to continue teaching. I was employed for one more year until August 1992. This was just the time when my promotion to full professorship would have been considered and I was afraid that opportunity had already been lost.

In August 1992, my extra employment period expired, and my retirement formalities were again processed. Thereafter, I stayed at home helping my wife take care of our daughter and performing various household duties, including cooking. In spare moments, I worked on *An Outline of Chinese Anthropology* and researched Tibetan history and culture.

In summer 1993, I was invited to host the Japanese Professor Gukou Fangnan from Dongyang University, who was making a trip to Qinghai to research the nationality situation.

Professor Gukou arrived in Xining with a research team of about 20 people. The morning after their arrival, they came to my home, filling up two rooms there, before going to look around the Cultural Artefacts room. Afterwards, we conducted informal discussions.

We had arranged to have lunch in my home. I was apologetic that we ate dumplings rather than rice, but the guests were full of compliments and thanks. An interpreter accompanied them on a visit to Qinghai Lake and altogether they spent three or four days in Xining.

After their departure, I often corresponded with Professor Gukou. He was friendly and generous. He offered to give me a computer and 2,000 *yuan* (about 250 US dollars at the time) towards publication of *An Outline of Chinese Anthropology*. I tactfully declined both offers, instead posting him a camel-hair jacket, to thank him for his good intentions.

Full Professorship

During the Cultural Revolution, there were no academic degrees and there was basically no academic world. Research students graduated without degrees, without professional titles. Instead, they were addressed by the general name 'cadre', or 'teacher' or 'research worker'.

In 1981, the tradition of appointing academics to academic positions was renewed throughout China, and I was approved as a lecturer in Qinghai.

In 1982, the Director of the Research Institute invited me to his home to inform me of his intention to nominate me for the position of Associate Professor. There were only two other such nominees from the Research Institute. Junior staff unanimously supported my nomination.

The Party secretary, however, intervened. "You junior staff now say that Ou Chaoquan should be nominated. When we convened a nomination meeting, however, why did no one nominate him? Why are you only now saying he should be nominated?" The audience fell silent.

Promotions were then suspended for three years, until 1985. By then, you did not need to be nominated but could simply apply. This time my application passed smoothly through various evaluation panels.

In January 1986, the provincial government approved promotions, including my own to the position of associate professor of nationality theory and nationality policy.

The rule was that there needed to be a minimum of five years between promotions. In summer 1990, after I had been working as associate professor for more than four years, new regulations were issued in relation to promotions. This led to establishment of assessment committees.

My assessment scores were above 90%, but this was somehow interpreted as 'average'. Half a year after the appraisals, I retired. Then the Institute finally arranged my promotion, issuing an application form that I completed in one evening. I was told to treat the matter urgently, and staff in Human Resources rushed it through as if their lives depended on it.

In 1991, only two full-professor promotions were available, and these were awarded to the Research Institute director and vice-director, who were both Party members. My qualifications and test results had been better than theirs and I had satisfied all the requirements. By the time my application was revisited, 1992 was already coming to a close. The delay felt like a conspiracy.

But after all, I was promoted to the position of full Professor of Anthropology, the first to hold such a position in the whole country. At the time, 13 members of the Qinghai Institute's staff were promoted to full professorship.

My promotion became effective on 11th December 1992, after I had retired. In the past, people in my position would have been called 'emeritus professor'. Some melodramatically labelled me the 'top-score professor', as if I had gained the highest score in the old Imperial examination system. Institute administrators referred to me as the 'retired professor'. Although I had been doing the work of a full professor for a long time, I had only ever received the salary of an associate professor. I was still bleeding, as it were, from the wounds of discrimination.

A few days before my promotion was announced, my wife Jiang's bookstand was destroyed for no good reason. Jiang had asked her two younger sisters to manage the stand for a few days, but one of those afternoons, we arrived and found five or six thugs tearing it down. Jiang frantically begged for help. I found one of the ringleaders observing at a distance and went to reason with him. After I handed him my business card, he rose and called the others to stop.

The next day, Jiang stuck a cloth banner on the bookstand, with the slogan written large: 'Defend socialist human rights'. This triggered more ire, curses and disturbance, and the banner was pulled down. We felt vindicated but hopeless, and Jiang raged that she would have to leave.

Within a few days of those dark experiences, the red document about my promotion arrived and the names of all new professors were made public. The time-tested routine of our lives seemed to be that before experiencing something really good, we had first to endure a nightmare.

Mr Wei who lived above us and whose family was disturbing our sleep missed out on full professorship; though his salary was still higher than mine. That night, he gave vent to his resentment, swearing at me. Thereafter, the noise from above seemed louder than before. We couldn't sleep, I couldn't work in peace, and it almost drove me mad.

Chapter 19
Returning Home
(Huaxi, 1995–2002)

The Journey to Guiyang

Long-term sleep deprivation made me confused and jittery. One day in 1994, Professor Zhang came to say goodbye. He was about to retire and return to his home region to settle down. He explained there was a policy at provincial level allowing senior teaching and research personnel, who had arrived in Qinghai in the 1950s and early '60s, to settle back in their home regions. Large subsidies were available to help with the purchase of a new home. He said I was perfectly well qualified and should apply.

Since leaving Guizhou, I had been working outside for 44 years, but in my heart, there had been no time during those years when I had not missed my native place. Reminiscing about home, I was often smitten by waves of melancholy. The changes during those years, however, especially cultural changes, had never clearly dawned on me. Frankly, homesickness was born of nostalgia, and such nostalgia can easily deceive the heart of the traveller far from home.

It was thus with high expectations that I set my heart on speeding home, as a falling leaf returns to its roots. In my home village, however, there was no surviving family, no house and nothing belonging to me. Now with the opportunity to go home in my old age, my preferred location could only be the provincial capital, Guiyang.

In Guiyang, there was a teacher whom I knew well, who was now vice-president of one of the schools of higher education. After I was rehabilitated in 1979, he had invited me to transfer to his Institute. Some of my former classmates lived there. Many fellow-Dong people were also there, and seemed eager for me to return to Guiyang. An acquaintance from Beijing in 1958 was now head of the Provincial Nationalities Research Institute in Guiyang.

Such circumstances spoke in favour of moving to Guiyang. At Jiang's urging, I decided not to shy away from the disruption inherent in such a move and made myself busy with preparations to spend my old age in Guizhou. Jiang had her own plans and outlined them in a torrential downpour of chatter. She wanted to open a bookshop and in a few years' time, she would buy a flat. She had studied fine arts, and after arriving in Guiyang, she wanted to study Miao nationality batik [colour printing on cloth using wax]. This would be her self-development project in the new place, representing light at the end of the tunnel. In Qinghai, we had experienced too many years of what felt like discrimination.

I, too, was optimistic. Guiyang would provide the environment in which I would finally be able to concentrate on research. Surely, there could hardly be any persecution in this new environment, for old friends and family would be only too pleased at any success that might come my way.

So I cherished such dreams, intending to continue with anthropological research after going home. I would concentrate on making a contribution in my retirement. Then my life would be complete.

Within a few days, I had submitted an application to the Institute department for retirees. My application was approved and passed on to the provincial office for retirees, which decided to give me an allowance of 50,000 *yuan* (about 6,250 US dollars) for buying a flat in Guiyang. If this were not enough, I would have to supplement from my own savings. Arrangements for buying a flat would be up to me.

I had never been a businessman. Now at the age of 65, I was entering the unfamiliar territory of buying a flat, and it seemed like a challenging proposition. I lacked courage to do it myself, having no idea how Guiyang had changed and even less idea about house prices.

With my lack of know-how, my university vice-president friend in Guiyang came to mind, a student-friend from the 1950s. We had often corresponded, exchanging New Year's cards and academic articles. We were both minority people, from the same autonomous prefecture.

So I wrote to this friend, explaining my desire to buy a flat and settle down, and enquiring about Guiyang house prices. He replied immediately, welcoming my imminent return and informing me that as it happened, his university was just then raising funds for a building project. He invited me to send the 50,000 *yuan* to him and he would use it to buy a flat for me, 100 square metres in area.

I felt sure of his integrity and not long before the start of the new term, I arrived at his university and we discussed arrangements. He was cordial and reassuring, guaranteeing he could help me buy a house. The money only needed to arrive at the requisite account and I would certainly have housing in return. I did not see any housing, however. He only said they were about to begin work and would soon finish.

The Qinghai office for retirees advised on contractual matters. Eventually, my friend suggested a second visit to Guiyang to deal with the development company and complete the transaction myself.

I had no alternative but to return to Guiyang in summer 1995. It transpired that the contract was not for purchase of a flat built by my friend's university, as he had earlier proposed. Instead, it was for a flat being sold on the open market by a development company in Huaxi, a university suburb of Guiyang. The flat was on the fifth floor of an eight-storey building and was 75 square metres in area.

The 50,000 *yuan* given by the Qinghai provincial authorities was insufficient and I had to find another 10,000 *yuan* to buy the flat.

On 10th August 1995, I led our little family party of three, including my wife Jiang and our daughter Lulu, onto a train in Xining, bound for Guiyang, via Lanzhou and Chengdu.

When we left Xining, no one came to say farewell. I felt so sorry that all our acquaintances stayed at home. Most would have liked to leave Qinghai themselves. Some were resentful and sent me off only with ill wishes.

Since sleeper tickets for Chengdu to Guiyang were sold only three days in advance of departures, we stayed for a while in an army guesthouse near the main railway station in Chengdu. The guesthouse felt chaotically busy, with people constantly coming and going.

I tried to persuade Jiang not to go out while we were waiting for the train. It seemed so easy to lose your way. I tramped around the streets a little on my own. Crowds were thick and my main impression was that Chengdu had never been so crowded before.

We arrived at last in Guiyang, exhausted but without hitches. At first, we stayed in the home of Ms Gan Yingtang, my cousin, while waiting for the container with our belongings. Three days later, we were notified of the collection point and two young relatives came with me to collect the luggage. For a day, we were busy transporting goods from the container to our new home. We had arrived.

Teething Problems

Construction of our new flat had finished just a month or so before. Apart from door and windows, it was absolutely bare, with nothing even for cooking a meal. Luggage, furniture and bits and bobs were stranded on the floor, and we improvised by using luggage as temporary stools. Unfortunately, Lulu had a fever, so Jiang took her out for antibiotics, while I busied myself about the flat.

Our flat eventually turned into a home and we gradually settled down. Our daughter was still only eight years old. We were strangers to Huaxi and everything was unfamiliar, so we felt rather vulnerable. How would we deal with any hardships?

First of all, how could we cook? A relative suggested we buy an electric hotplate. It immediately came in useful, but we didn't realise that if you had it on for too long, its lead and socket were prone to burning out.

The hotplate had other defects and we had constant problems. One of my nephews was an electrician, but after he helped to fix the hotplate, I turned it on, only to see smoke emerge and turn into fire! The flat was almost burned down and I had to buy a new hotplate after all. My nephew never fixed anything for us after that.

Any time we hosted guests, keeping an eye on the hotplate was an all-consuming preoccupation. Visitors would peer around into the kitchen to see what was going on, and say, tentatively, "Will we not be able to eat after all?"

We looked forward to cold weather, when we would light the coal fire and be delivered of such trouble. We eventually purchased a metal stove, together with kindling and coal.

There were two other flats on the same floor, but no one had yet moved in, or into the floors above and below. The building seemed to be full of empty flats.

We felt apprehensive about the balcony outside, for there was no railing and the wooden balcony door was not yet secure. I spent the next two weeks fitting a metal railing on the balcony, and then fixing a secure metal door at the flat entrance, to guard against thieves.

Before Liberation, I had spent two autumns in Guiyang but I could not remember ever feeling autumn to be particularly cold. After moving to Guiyang 48 years later, I felt the cold biting early in October. We had just come from a very cold climate, but everyone in Huaxi was saying, "This autumn is really cold."

Jiang's bedroom was next to the balcony and the wind blew straight in, along with the rain. On wet days, it seemed as though she were sleeping outdoors and obviously she could not sleep soundly.

We hung big cotton blankets as protection against the wind. The result was far from perfect and a cold wind still seemed to fill the room. We were shocked. Why should the weather in Guiyang seem even colder than in Xining?

Autumn rains continued into winter, and the autumn cold turned into winter cold. Our metal stove in the living room, cast locally in Guiyang, was 50 kg and unwieldy. We tried to light the fire as we had done in Qinghai, with newspaper and coal, but without success. Then we tried burning wood before adding coal, but the coal remained dark black.

After receiving advice, I tried with charcoal between the coal, paper and wood. The fire ignited and burned well at first. The thick iron stove, however, remained icy cold and the coal itself still did not burn. Instead, the room was full of smoke and it was difficult to breathe.

Sometimes I was lucky – the coal burned and the family would feel a little warmer. At other times, the coal extinguished the fire, instead of enhancing it. The pool of fire danced red to black and the stove reverted to its recalcitrant chill.

Everyone said it was the coldest winter in living memory, continuously overcast and rainy. Every day, we tried to light the stove, but often it baulked. Every day, we donned our winter cotton and leather clothes, together with leather caps, cotton shoes and woollen socks. We even wore woollen earmuffs. As if the chill were immune to clothing, however, we still felt freezing, and chilblains developed all over our hands, feet and ears.

Nights were harder than days, for it felt like the sheets and bed covers were damp and we could not get warm the whole night long. We wondered if we would survive the winter.

To warm ourselves by day, we would brave the drizzle and walk the streets, surveying the city sights. Before Liberation, Huaxi had been inhabited by Bouyei and Miao people, having just one main street running from north to south, with Han people on either side. By 1997, the area around our home still had Miao and Bouyei homes along a bamboo grove. Some lived in single-storey buildings with slate roofs. Few people would walk through the small lonely alley in front of my flat, and there were no vehicles. It seemed like an ancient town.

The destructive noise of demolition, however, incessantly plagued the ear: explosions, which scattered rocks and earth. These served notice of an impending, rapid change of scenery in this ancient town.

When I went out to warm up, I often visited the urban centre of Guiyang with which I had been familiar decades before. You could still see old properties there, built before Liberation, wooden houses and stores, footpaths, an old noodle store on Shifu Road and the old Dusi Road.

The long-established Nanming Hostel, where I had lived before Liberation, and where I frequently stopped over after Liberation, was still there. All this evoked nostalgia for the old city, for in those earlier years, I had often strolled around these same landmarks.

The next year, however, a massive rebuilding programme was launched in the city centre and most old properties were destroyed. My old haunts nearly all disappeared. Afterwards, I stopped strolling around the city-centre streets.

In those early winter days, friends and relatives often turned up to visit. When they observed our stove's propensity for petering out and experienced our flat's icy cold temperatures, conversation would naturally turn to these difficulties. No one, however, successfully supplied practical solutions to our problems.

No one pointed out that the iron stove was unsuitable, or explained how we should light it, or how to keep the fire going through the night.

No one helped us in such ways until the summer of the following year, when Mr Liu, a friend born in Taiwan, advised us to lay damp-proof palm-fibre mats on our beds and to use electric blankets. He became an instant saint by presenting us with gifts of palm-fibre mats and electric blankets! If we had heard such tips before, we might have avoided some of the deep-freeze torture of the previous winter.

In the second year, we commissioned my niece to make a metal frame for the stove. It performed much better after that. The fire rarely went out, but the stove frame was a little too big, which wasted coal and led to more smoke. In the third year, we decided to buy a new stove and we have used that ever since.

After we moved to Huaxi, postal communication dried up. Letters were not delivered on time, but were either lost or delayed as they made their way via various intermediate stops. Often they arrived after the 'action-date' referred to in their contents. I was often on the lookout for some incoming item of mail, and felt keenly the stress of our postal predicament.

The local logistics department explained that my post was being stymied as a result of the new postal district where I was living. Our street still had no name and different flats had not yet identified corresponding addresses. The post office said I should urge the neighbourhood committee and local police to resolve the problem. These two institutions in turn suggested I ask the development company, and the development company said I should lobby the government office at the Huaxi level, which could help by establishing a name for the street.

If I had asked a friend at the nearby university to receive my letters and pass them on to me, I would have had to search for him each time a letter was due, or he would have had to deliver the mail by hand. After a while, no friend would have had enough patience for this.

When I asked if the Social Sciences Department at Guizhou University could receive my mail, I was told, "It could be arranged, but our department is often closed." The secretary was sick and could not guarantee to be at work on a regular basis.

I could ask the neighbourhood committee to receive and forward my letters, but they had moved premises several times. Not only the postman, but we too had difficulty finding them.

While in Qinghai, I had been in contact over many years with individuals and institutions in the USA, Russia, Japan and Taiwan. Now I was unable to receive their correspondence. With time, I stopped writing, so my academic connections petered out.

The Japanese Professor Gukou Fangnan replied to my letter from Huaxi, but I never received his reply. In 1997, while he was on a visit with his wife to the Guizhou Institute for Nationalities, I was able to meet up with him.

For years, I just put up with this postal problem and waited. By the time the postman began to deliver mail, only my former work unit was still communicating with me. Each year, I received a greetings card at Chinese New Year.

A Dead End and a Rescue

After arriving in Guiyang, Jiang Yanrong, my wife of 17 years, was still inclined to be naïve, with the result that she was deceived and abused by an expert in deceit and abuse. This caused quarrels between us, until on 31st December 1997, she stormed out of our home to live elsewhere, demanding a divorce; and in September 1998, we were formally divorced. Our daughter Lulu stayed with me and was thereafter raised by me.

A family friend had deceived Jiang by promising he could find her a job, but when she applied for the job in the School for Eastern Enterprise, she discovered the School did not exist. That is when he raped her. He subsequently continued to use her, but after our divorce was official, he abandoned her.

Jiang suffered all kinds of abuse and maltreatment and no longer had a fixed abode. Destitute, she tasted in full the calamity and torment of poverty. At the end of her tether, when it felt as if there was no longer any way of surviving, she clutched at one last straw. She wrote to the Party and the People's Government to beg for justice, to save her life.

There flowed a succession of letters accusing the person who had deceived her. She wrote everywhere: to the Discipline Committee of the university where he worked, the Provincial Discipline Commission, the Provincial Legal Commission, the Provincial Police and the Prosecutor's Office. She went to seek audience with those to whom she was writing. She was assured they were on her case and it would be handled fairly. She would be given appropriate compensation, but she must wait patiently for due process to run its course.

Jiang cherished this spark of hope as she waited in adversity. She lived in five different places: Stone Village, Dazhai, Luoping and two different places on the streets of Huaxi. She waited and waited, going occasionally to meet with relevant authorities, and also to confront the man who had cheated her.

Several years passed. Not only was there no sign of compensation, but also no single written response to any of her letters. She did not give up, however, but continued to wander the streets, waiting and hoping.

Close to desperation, she would say, "Here people only support him. He can't be convicted, but he's also had trouble. He is also divorced and his former wife curses him. He no longer has any official position and it's his own doing!"

After four years, she returned one last time to ask about progress on her case. The relevant official paid no attention to her. Though no one officially acknowledged her rights, everyone involved knew the truth. In the end, she dropped the matter.

During those four years, I had seen and heard countless details of Jiang's sufferings. By the time she gave up on a fair hearing, she was simply struggling to survive. Her pension of 350 *yuan* a month was mostly used up on rent and telephone bills, with hardly anything left for food. She was from the northeast and had no one in Guiyang she could lean on. At every turn, she was hard-pressed.

No one gave Jiang any material assistance and she was forced to buy cheap food, including leftover food from the restaurants; even to pick up rotten food that people could not otherwise sell. She was practically living the life of a beggar.

With no proper stove to keep warm in winter, Jiang slept with her dog. She had no money for medicine or treatment when she was ill, but asked others if she could use their leftover medicine.

The painful repercussions of having asked her deceiver to find her a job, this bitter fruit seemed as if it would be her portion forever.

That year, I was busy writing the Dong Culture Dictionary. Lulu was in her third year of study at Qinghua Middle School. By day, I was alone at home. Otherwise, there was just me and Lulu; plus the rats and fleas, which were having a field day in our flat. Lulu and I were also suffering harassment from a neighbour.

While Jiang was in dire straits on the streets of the neighbourhood, we were victims of persecution at home. Although my marriage with Jiang had broken up, our destinies seemed parallel. Just as Jiang had once observed, we were fellow-sufferers, both seeking a way out of trouble.

One afternoon just before winter really arrived in 2002, I went out to buy food and saw Jiang sitting quietly in front of a potato-selling stand. She told me people had been urinating on her front door and she had just been evicted. The rent had been just 180 *yuan* per month. She wore a blue jacket and was laden with grief.

Formerly, Jiang's voice had been so loud it startled people, but now it was feeble. She was sapped of strength, bound up by an abnormal, morbid state of mind. As winter approached, she had walked to the gates of hell in torment. Anyone would have sympathised with her predicament.

On her way home from school, Lulu often saw her mother and realised she was sick and despairing. Lulu also knew it was difficult at the best of times to pass the cold winter months. She said anxiously, "Mum's outside. It's so cold. She's going to die…"

Jiang's deceiver was still at large and had not yet been charged, showing how strong his influence had been. My child and I were also his victims, for he had broken up my marriage with Jiang. Now we could only sympathise with Jiang in her calamity, though she had clearly been an accomplice in heaping hardship on herself, with no recourse for justice.

Jiang was simple in thought and idiotically rapid in speech. She only abandoned us after being tricked. I thought back on our marriage of 17 years, how she had left her relatives in the north to come south with me, and how she had been the mother of my daughter Lulu.

Such memories could never be erased, and I couldn't bear to watch Jiang begging for a living. I didn't have the heart to stand by and do nothing while she froze to death in southern streets, surrounded by strangers. 'Saving someone's life is better than building a seven-floor pagoda.' I talked it over with Lulu and we agreed. To soften the injury in Lulu's spirit and mine, in response to conscience and human sympathy, we agreed to rescue Jiang.

Local police quickly gave approval for Jiang to be listed on our household register, to prevent her freezing to death on the streets. Jiang could help me take care of Lulu, clean the flat and do shopping. Perhaps one more person in the household could help decrease the dread we felt from constant intimidation, not to mention from the rampant rats and fleas. We were all victims of misfortune and perhaps by uniting we could save ourselves.

Jiang was delighted, insisting she would take good care of Lulu and take charge of the household duties. From the second day onwards, the Jiang who had recently seemed so morbid, almost unwilling to speak, gradually became the fount of more and more speech. Her illness and depression quickly disappeared. Within a day, she was back in the normal routine of eating three meals a day.

On hearing that Jiang had 'come back from death to life', the one who had deceived her went on the attack. He published false testimony to frighten us about our humanitarian gesture. He spread rumours accusing me of living illegally in relationship with her. Along with friends, he conspired against us, inciting trouble, torment and terror.

Chapter 20
Filling Gaps
(Writing Books, 1998–2011)

The Kam People of China

One day in the spring of 1998, after Jiang had left home and our divorce was being processed, I was in the offices of a law company when I met the head of the Guizhou University Social Sciences Research Institute. He was a professor of ethnology, and knew about my anthropological research.

Soon afterwards, this professor visited me at my home. He had examined my credentials, and announced that his Institute wished to employ me. In May, I received a written invitation to serve as a researcher in the Language and Culture Research Institute of the Social Sciences Institute, for five years (1998–2003), and was invited to a meeting.

The meeting was convened in the Foreign Affairs Office of Guizhou University. In addition to Institute leaders and staff of the Foreign Affairs Office, the meeting involved two other Dong researchers, both associate professors.

I sat beside two foreign scholars, specialists in Dong language and culture. We were being invited by Guizhou University to cooperate with those foreign scholars to write an introduction to the Dong people, for publication in English. We Dong scholars decided that between us we would write a comprehensive introduction to the Dong people based on nine general themes, of which I would take responsibility for four. The other researchers would take five themes between them. The amount of 'teaching time' each week and the days for teaching were agreed upon, along with the goal of completing the first stage of the project by the end of the year.

The foreign scholars were husband and wife. David Norman Geary was British, from Northern Ireland, with a graduate diploma from Cambridge and a doctorate from Oxford in mathematical statistics. In February 1993, he and his wife Ruth had arrived in Beijing to study Mandarin, and in August 1995, they had arrived at Guizhou University to research Dong language and culture. They began to learn Dong using Mandarin and Dr Geary had already translated and published a book in 1998, *The Dong Language in Guizhou Province, China*. A year later, he and his wife began helping with a bilingual education pilot project in County Rongjiang. The results nine years later were outstanding.

Ruth Geary was German-speaking Swiss. She also spoke Mandarin and Dong. This cooperative project would involve our supplying information about the Dong culture and their turning the information into a book in English.

The next week, we began classes. Each week Dr and Mrs Geary had two or three classes, from 9 to 11:30 am. They paid us for the classes, as stipulated at the joint meeting.

Classes were conducted at Dr Geary's home beside Guizhou University. Among the Dong scholars, my responsibility was greatest, and involved a major effort. I would rise at 6 am, help my daughter leave for school on time, have a bun and boiled water for breakfast and leave home at 8:20 am, briefcase wedged under my arm. I'd walk swiftly to the Gearys' home, arrive in about half-an-hour, and immediately start to teach. Upon finishing, I'd walk back home. I followed this routine each morning I was on teaching duty.

Between 1998 and 2003, intermittently as long as the project continued, I walked back and forth. Although there were buses, I preferred not to take them, fearing there might be some delay, which would interfere with working hours.

We finished the nine basic themes on schedule, by the end of 1998. On 7th December, the Institute presented us with our remuneration, inviting us for duck hotpot to celebrate the end of the teaching. This, however, was only the first phase of the project. After dinner, the other three professors left with their pay and had little further responsibility. Most remaining work fell to me.

Frankly, during this first phase we had only supplied basic information, enough to arouse interest, but not enough for a thorough understanding. Much more work was needed to clarify everything. Such follow-up was passed on to me to oversee. Every week, I walked once or twice to Dr Geary's home as before. In July 1999, this second phase of work was completed. The whole project had taken a little over a year.

The third phase of the project was for the Gearys to write the book. At various points during this process, they raised new questions, to supplement and support existing information, to ascertain the published sources of information, and to prepare maps and select photographs of the Dong areas.

They worked hard on these details and needed my help. There was related work for me right up until the publisher posted a nearly ready manuscript early in 2003.

The resulting book, *The Kam People of China* (296 pages), was published by RoutledgeCurzon in London in 2003. Authors in sequence were Norman Geary, Ruth Geary, Ou Chaoquan, Long Yaohong, Jiang Daren and Wang Jiying.

From the time I began working with Norman and Ruth Geary, they treated me with respect and addressed me as their teacher. During the decade from 1998, we became good friends. They were academically rigorous, declining to dabble in speculation. They were logical from start to finish, repeatedly revising the manuscript to improve its quality and readability. I learned from their academic style, and admired their hardworking mentality in not shying away from difficulties, even venturing deep into the Dong areas to investigate cultural issues.

When I heard that Guizhou University would establish an Institute for the study of the language and culture of local nationalities, I felt heartened and expressed sincere support.

Before long, more than 10 foreign scholars were associated with the Institute, and a flow of research articles and books followed. Researchers included some from the USA, the UK, Germany, Switzerland and Canada. Dr Geary was Associate Director and his wife Ruth served as a member of the Institute. They continued collaboration with me on Dong cultural research.

Dong Culture Dictionary

In preparing for *The Kam People of China*, I discovered that research on the Dong people was relatively shallow and confused, with much duplicated material. Much relevant information was missing, there was little screening of subjective opinions, and there were few articles with objective descriptions of specific cultural elements or historical incidents. There was even confusion about historical names for the Dong areas.

Because of all this, I felt convinced of the need for a book with a thorough, systematic treatment of Dong cultural history and research, and I decided to write a *Dong Culture Dictionary*. While working on *The Kam People*, I began privately to formulate an outline of the *Dictionary*, gathering dictionary entries and related materials.

One day around that time a younger man from my old home area, Comrade Jiang, a Dong teacher from a nearby university, dropped by for a visit. When I mentioned that I was looking for collaborators to write a *Dong Culture Dictionary*, his face lit up. He had earlier researched his own culture and really wanted to do more. He said he was eager to participate. He would be my student and assistant, learning and working at the same time.

Like me, Jiang was a graduate of the Central Institute for Nationalities in Beijing. He was not confident about his forthcoming application for promotion to associate professorship and had been contemplating a change of profession. He was young and biddable, quickly receptive to new things and with a keen desire for knowledge.

I gladly declared that Jiang could join the *Dictionary* team. He recommended a Dong Comrade Yang from a local publishing house, who had also studied at the Central Institute for Nationalities, to join us.

In April 1999, Jiang and Yang came to my home for a meeting about the *Dictionary*. We roughly divided up work as follows. I would draft an outline and a list of dictionary entries. Jiang and I would be mainly responsible for the writing. Yang would be responsible for creating some of the dictionary entries and for publishing. We felt confident as we embarked on the project.

Within a week, I had compiled an outline along with a schedule, and I passed these on to the others for their perusal. They agreed to press on.

Later I invited them to come and discuss dictionary entries, but Yang had left Guiyang for his home village to care for sick relatives. He did not know when he would be able to return, so Jiang and I decided to proceed and divide the work among ourselves, without Yang. Jiang would type the manuscript on to computer and be responsible for printing.

During two years of writing, Jiang came to my home two mornings or afternoons a week, during which he followed my lead. We discussed any difficulties and how we could access relevant resources. Each time we met, we added new entries, and I often asked Jiang to add new content to existing entries. There was mutual respect, our collaboration was pleasant and we made smooth progress.

Jiang suggested I should write in the Guizhou dialect, the popular Guizhou language. Only then would people be able to understand. I replied that writing a dictionary was not the same as writing a novel. The writing should be concise and accurate. The dictionary would not only be used by local Dong people; its main readers would be intellectuals. Moreover it would be available nationwide, so standard Mandarin should be used.

Jiang acquiesced without further ado and abandoned the idea. He learned to write in a way that was less verbose, complying with the style for dictionaries I was advocating.

For more than 20 months, we busied ourselves with this project, writing, supplementing and printing, until the entire text was basically finished in draft. At last, we could take a breather.

In 1996, I had been hired to serve as a consultant to the Dong Association of Guizhou Province. (In 2002 and 2008, my consultancy was twice duly extended.) The Association invited me to participate in its symposium at Chinese New Year 2000, at which I introduced the *Dong Culture Dictionary* project. I was delighted to announce that the book was already nearing publication. When I noted, however, that the book would be authored by me and Jiang, rather than by the Association, the warmth of some participants cooled.

Subsequently, when symposium documents were distributed, the only name absent from the list of participants was mine. In the same documents, my collaborator Jiang was promoted to the Association council, contrary to normal process (for his name had not been on the ballot). They had humiliated one and promoted the other, driving a wedge between us.

We carried on regardless. Night and day, I revised the book, asking Jiang to find supplementary materials where necessary, augmenting and improving. After four revisions, the *Dictionary* manuscript was finally ready. Jiang assured me that even if he had to sell his house to do it, this book would be published!

The Guizhou People's Publishing House provisionally agreed to publish, but recommended that we should look up the Dong deputy provincial governor Ms Long for support.

We drafted a preface to the book and invited Long to revise and authorise it. We added evaluations and endorsement letters from Chen Yi, a Dong professor in Guangxi, Deng Minwen a Dong researcher in Beijing, and Wu Yandong a professor in Guizhou. After Long had seen the documents, she was heard to remark, "Not enough [people have recommended the book]!"

At a publication board meeting, as the manuscript was being discussed, Ms Long did not pass any comment, from which others gleaned she was not supportive. So the meeting did not endorse publication and the project was dropped. Disappointed, we could only bring the manuscript back home.

Jiang confessed he was at a dead end. He no longer bragged about selling his house. The Provincial Dong Research Association kept its distance.

While we were fretting over the question of finances for publication, Jiang suggested that if he were to be first author, he'd be able to obtain publication fees from his Institute, and after publication he could apply for a prize. If I were first author, this wouldn't work, because I was not a member of the Institute. (Jiang also had standing as a Party member.) This suggestion, however, disregarded our original agreement, and I declined to make the change.

Instead, I discussed the issue with Dr Norman Geary, the foreign researcher with similar research interests. He had known about the project and had supported it in principle.

I invited Dr Geary to have a look at the manuscript. He found it interesting and well written. He offered 10,000 *yuan* towards the cost of publishing, agreeing at the same time to translate the Table of Contents and Preface into English, saying that he didn't need any recognition for this in the book itself.

His behaviour seemed like a breath of fresh air. In our country, scholars were trampling over each other with iron hooves and you could hardly find this kind of intellectual, who worked with unselfish dedication. Through according me such respect and trust, Dr Geary made another special contribution to the Dong people, and I'll be forever grateful.

Jiang advised that 10,000 *yuan* was still not enough for a domestic publisher. The Dong president of his Institute, Mr Wu Dahua, suggested the book could be included in a series of which he was editor in chief, entitled Dong Culture Collection. Wu proposed a publisher in Hong Kong, which only charged printing costs, for which the 10,000 *yuan* was enough with some to spare. With no better alternative, we accepted this arrangement.

Day and night, I was busy with proofreading and revising, frequently going to the Guizhou Institute for Nationalities to give directions about layout and design, font size and so on. After about six months, the *Dong Culture Dictionary*, with more than 600,000 characters, having travelled a tortuous winding path, reached its destination and was published in 2002, with 500 copies.

Jiang obtained promotion to the position of associate professor. The Provincial Dong Research Association further promoted him to the position of deputy president. My own situation, however, worsened. With publication of the *Dictionary*, I was shut out by certain Dong people, and felt even more isolated.

The book was groundbreaking in Dong research and was the first such single-culture dictionary nationwide. Dong researchers generally found it useful. Still, some in the Research Association said it was an 'illegal publication', because it had been published in Hong Kong and not on the mainland. I heard that some people read it furtively, keeping it hidden.

My collaborator Jiang had always feared others would not believe he was personally responsible for his part of the writing and would doubt his contribution to the book. In September 2007, more than five years after the book was published, he came to look me up, saying he was applying for promotion to full professorship. For this, he asked me to write a certificate, to testify that he had really written his part of the *Dictionary*, and to say a few words in his support.

During our collaboration, Jiang had worked hard and respectfully followed my guidance, and we had established bonds of mutual affection. Afterwards, others had promoted him and demoted me, to drive a wedge between us. I couldn't blame him for this, so I didn't mind and was still prepared to support his career. In response to his request, I happily wrote that certificate, commending him warmly.

Basic Ethnology

While working for Guizhou University, I had time to complete revision of the manuscript of *Basic Ethnology*. This was around 300,000 characters long, synthesized, abridged and augmented from work I had done before retirement.

In May 1999, I took the manuscript to a member of the Dong Study Association, but after browsing the manuscript, he asked how I would deal with copyright. By this, he meant that if the Association were to contribute to publication costs, it should have the copyright. I withdrew the manuscript.

A few days later, I brought the manuscript to an experienced Dong-nationality editor from the Provincial Nationalities Publishing House. Without even looking at it, he said it would cost 30,000 *yuan* (almost 4,000 US dollars at the time); 10,000 *yuan* per 100,000 characters.

Later still, another Dong-nationality friend, originally from my home area, recommended the book to the Guizhou People's Publishing House. A director there made a few revision suggestions before agreeing to publish. Production costs would be 15,000 *yuan*; 1,600 copies would be published, from which the publisher would give 800 to me and keep 800.

I didn't have that much money, but with a subsidy of 7,000 *yuan* from my daughter Ou Ou I got the amount together. My daughter kindly declined to have her name mentioned in the book.

Basic Ethnology was published in October 1999, but at the time, there was no one at home to join me in celebrating this milestone and there were no congratulations.

In recent decades, the publishing houses have presented authors with book-copies in part-payment. This turns a happy thing into a sad one. The 800 copies supplied to me by the publisher were stacked up in my home. When 400 or 500 remained unsold, I didn't know what to do.

Two episodes occurred wherein significant prospective sales collapsed. I felt bewildered by a sense that friends had been less than straightforward with me. I was informed that the 800 copies of *Basic Ethnology* taken by the publishing house were sold out within a few days of reaching the Xinhua news agency. By contrast, the 800 copies sent to me remained mostly unsold.

When President Wang of the Qinghai Institute discovered the book had been published, he congratulated me and asked me to post some copies to him so he could sell them on my behalf. He had returned to China after studying abroad for a doctorate. This singular college leader bailed me out of this mini-crisis and I'm grateful to him. I soaked up his favour, regarding him as my 'benefactor'.

President Wang praised the book. Since there were some imperfections in the publishing process, however, with content omitted and problems with proofreading and printing, President Wang and the Nationalities Institute Director agreed with my request to revise *Basic Ethnology*. They paid for publication of the revised version.

Surely, there are eyes in Heaven. People in authority helped this book emancipate itself, as if moving a rock that had been pressing down on my heart. Upon receiving their call, I immediately began the work of revision. That was 8th June 2005.

I revised the whole book, enriching and improving the earlier edition. After 20-plus months, in November 2007, revision was finished. I posted the manuscript to be printed at the Qinghai Institute.

From there, it was forwarded to the Nationality Publishing House in Beijing and publication formalities were quickly settled. From front to back, its appearance was new. The professionalism of the publication was outstanding.

It is a basic anthropology textbook, the first such in China, with the title *Basic Ethnology (Revised)*. It's a required text in China in the fields of ethnology and anthropology. The book crystallises my teaching and research in those subjects. I'm gratified it can be regarded as a contribution in the anthropological domain.

Life in a Kam Village

The Kam People of China and *Dong Culture Dictionary* were books reflecting the general circumstances of the Dong people, but there was still no book on the anthropology of a single Dong village. To understand the Dong people better, this gap would need to be filled.

Since I myself am a Dong person, and was immersed in village life for nearly 20 years, I began to wonder if I might write about my own mountain-valley village.

I discussed the idea with Dr Norman Geary, the Assistant Director of the Guizhou University Southwest Minority Language and Culture Research Institute. He approved and encouraged it, indicating he would be interested in translating it into English. So, it could be written anticipating an English readership.

In winter of 2003, I started writing. Parts of it were practically my memoirs, involving episodes from my own experience. Progress was fast, for I had a good foundation, and after just over a year, I had produced the first draft. After revision, a clean copy was typed and presented to Dr Geary, who had it printed. He paid 2,000 *yuan* for research and typing expenses, alleviating my financial burden at the time.

Dr Geary printed several copies and passed them on to the Institute Director and a researcher there, as well as two Dong scholars from outside the university. Their feedback was generally positive. One cadre, however, suggested that the manuscript should be submitted to people in Xiangye to solicit their opinion. This idea seemed oddly left-wing, reminiscent of the Cultural Revolution. It wouldn't get us anywhere to take up the suggestion. The content of the original manuscript was preserved.

After this thorough review, Dr Geary went ahead with plans to translate the manuscript into English. He suggested I add a postscript about changes after Liberation. At that, I prepared to return to Xiangye to investigate the current state of affairs. I was threatened, however, that if I returned to Xiangye, I would be murdered. Someone would open fire at me from the undergrowth, or I would be dragged to the bullfighting arena and beaten up.

I had informed my relatives by telephone that I wanted to return and do some research. They protested that if I returned, people in the village might beat me up. At the time I was suffering terror in my home in Huaxi, my nerves were already shattered, and I was worried about my family. With premonitions of disaster, and ambitions still to do many more things in my life, I did not dare to brave the danger. Instead, I wrote out many questions and asked my grandson, who worked in County Jianhe, to research the information.

There was no news for a very long time. I phoned my grandson who said he had lost the outline. He insisted it was difficult for him to ask such questions, anyway. They were all farmers in the village and couldn't explain anything. He wasn't an anthropologist and had never paid careful attention to his own village experiences. He didn't know how to get the right answers. He advised us to drop this indirect investigation.

While Dr Geary was still working on translation, he found out about the difficulties of my going to Xiangye. He decided to go himself, during the summer holidays of 2006, accompanied by a Dong colleague. They made their way to Xiangye with an introductory letter in hand and stayed there just one night, wandering around the village partly in the company of the party secretary and village head.

In March 2007, Dr Geary returned to Xiangye with an American colleague Dean Schauer, for one more visit. They stopped two nights and were at liberty to wander around taking photos. Dr Geary did not ask much detail about the current village circumstances, but felt delighted with the photographs, for they told a story similar to that of the 1930s and 1940s.

On his way there, Dr Geary had been involved in an accident on a three-wheeled taxi just outside Rongjiang county town. The woman sitting next to him on the vehicle was severely injured. Fortunately, Dr Geary himself was unharmed. When I heard this, I was extremely alarmed and began to perspire.

Dr Geary quickly made contact with a publishing house in Leiden, the Netherlands. The book was published in 2007, *Life in a Kam Village in Southwest China, 1930–1949*. The publisher sent 6,000 *yuan* as authors' fees. Dr

Geary passed 3,000 to me and divided 3,000 between Mr Schauer who took photographs and Mr Zhong who drew illustrations for the book.

Before long, the publisher sent 12 complimentary copies, beautifully presented, each book costing around 800 *yuan*. Dr Geary and I took four copies each, with the remaining four going to Guizhou University, Xiangye, Mr Schauer and Mr Zhong. So this project was completed.

After the book was published, Dr Geary decided to leave for home with his family. His flat was sold, with furniture and bits and bobs given to various people. He was taking only two suitcases home. Whether or not he would return to live in China would be decided in seven or eight years' time. If he returned, there was only a slim chance he would be back at Guizhou University.

Dr Geary and I had cooperated on researching Dong history and culture for 10 years. Together with other scholars, we had written *The Kam People* (2003), and I wrote and he translated *Life in a Kam Village* (2007). He had translated a little of the *Dong Culture Dictionary* (2002) into English, and supplied finances for publication. He had made an outstanding contribution in the domain of Dong language, helping to establish a pilot bilingual education project in a village in County Rongjiang, nurturing Dong students to prepare them for middle school and university studies and in the process helping individual Dong people in many ways.

When I heard that he was about to return to his country, I was shocked. Ten years of working together would abruptly come to an end and waves of melancholy flooded my heart. In and through him I had been able to observe and experience kindness and integrity.

On 1st June 2007, before returning home, Dr Geary came along with his American colleague Mr Schauer, to interview me. He asked about the situation in my family and village before Liberation. I answered 20-plus questions and in the end sang a Dong song and spoke a sentence of blessing in both English and Russian. The whole interview lasted around 90 minutes. After creating a DVD from the interview, they gave me a copy, which I found to be of good quality. [At the time of publishing this book, a 10-minute summary of the interview could be found at https://youtu.be/igfjYnTx-Os.]

On the afternoon of 30th July, Dr Geary and his wife braved the rain to say goodbye, before leaving Guiyang for home the next day. They left their forwarding address. Their two sons and daughter had attended school in Guiyang and were fluent in Mandarin. Such things comprised Dr Geary's wealth. Today he was resolutely leaving China. I felt sorry, deeply sorry, that he was leaving. I'll forever be grateful to him and his wife.

At the time of departure, I had nothing else to give him, but simply wrote a poem To Dr Norman Geary, with a writing brush on paper, and presented it as a souvenir. After friendship from 10 years of cooperation, many days still seemed unfulfilled. The words of the poem are copied below.

To Dr Norman Geary*

You come quietly.
The River Nanming laughs a soft belly-laugh.
Guiyang men and women beckon,
Welcome!
Welcome the British expert from Oxford halls,
Bearing with you fame and glory.

You enter Dong mountain villages gently.
Stilt buildings, verandas, schools and fields…
Male and female, old and young alike are smiling,
Arms outstretched to embrace.
You give them bilingual education, scientific culture,
Dreams and desires.

You leave quietly.
Leaving behind the well-equipped children of Zaidang,
Masterpieces to be passed down through the generations,
And people you have helped.
Saying goodbye,
Taking with you friendship and gratitude.

*[Partly inspired by *Taking Leave of Cambridge Again*, by Xu Zhimo, 1928.]

Outline of Tibetan History

Beginning in 1953 with a field survey of the Songpan Tibetans, I produced various publications about this great minority, with history and culture so broad and deep. During my career, two nationalities became the major objects of my research: my native Dong, and Tibetan.

In the summer of 1991, when I was invited to the US to attend a conference on applied anthropology, I wrote a paper linking ancient and modern, entitled 'An outline of Tibetan history and culture'.

During the summer vacation of 2004, President Wang of the Qinghai Institute came to visit. He discovered I was interested in writing about Tibetan history and expressed full support.

I encountered a shortage of materials. It was difficult to find literature on Tibetan history, or on the general situation in the Tibetan autonomous region. As for pre-Liberation documents or newspaper articles, I could forget about those, for practically nothing was available.

I had to purchase the requisite reference books by mail order from the Tibetan Studies Publishing House in Beijing. Fortunately, I had earlier collected many materials, so already had a good foundation. By December 2008, a draft manuscript had been prepared.

Thereafter, I began with revisions. When I put down my pen after the final chapter, the sight in my left eye suddenly turned black; the retina had detached, though I did not know this at the time. The last book of my last period of academic research had been completed.

In early February 2010, shortly before Chinese New Year, Guizhou Province Cultural Association convened its 20th anniversary celebration in a lecture hall of Guizhou University. The convenor insisted on my participation, and I went along leaning on a walking stick, in my capacity as consultant to the Association. I presented a 25-minute paper about Schools of Thought. I had not expected that this would be my last ever academic lecture and my last get-together with colleagues of the same profession. Before the lecture, the Association presented me with a certificate labelled 'Award for Outstanding Academic Achievement'.

The manuscript of *Outline of Tibetan History* had not yet been cleaned up when I was incapacitated by a broken femur and deteriorating eyesight, but because of financial support from the Qinghai Institute, it was still accepted by the Nationalities Publishing House in Beijing. A copy editor identified remaining problems, and inserted corresponding changes.

After proofreading, experts were asked to examine the manuscript several times and printed a copy for me to revise one last time. I worked using a magnifying glass, reading two or three pages a day, in what was challenging and slow-moving toil. In November 2011, the book was published. This was to be my last academic work in this life.

Chapter 21
Listening to Big Brother
(Harassment, 2000-07)

After retiring to Guizhou, I was even more reticent than before, afraid of involvement in any untoward activity and of becoming the subject of suspicion or misunderstanding. I just wanted to mind my own business and keep out of trouble, so I concentrated on academic research and immersed myself in writing. In turn, I wanted my daughter to concentrate on her schoolwork.

As a result, I was often perceived as an outsider, not 'one of us'. With the poison bequeathed by extreme left-wing politics, my solitary study and my home became targets of persecution. As a result, my family suffered distress along with me.

There were 20-plus households on our staircase. Many were cadres, some still working and some retired. At first, everyone was polite, and our relationships with neighbours were normal.

A Han person named Huang, about 40 years of age, lived on the floor below. I heard he had only been schooled up to junior high (aged around 15), during the time of the Cultural Revolution. He worked for a local college, dealing with salaries, but did not have much to do and often stayed at home. People were afraid of him, for he was known for fighting and swearing. He opened a shop selling bags, with 'Big Brother speaks' on the signboard. Later the sign was changed to the English word 'Skys' (sic). Both signs alluded to his superiority, bragging he was the biggest of all.

At the time trouble began, I was divorced. Only my 14-year-old daughter and I were at home. Once I met Huang outside and addressed him as *shifu* [meaning 'artisan' or 'master' of a certain trade]. This annoyed him and thereafter he seemed antagonistic towards me.

Discouraging My Daughter from Going to School

Before Liberation, very few Dong children went to school and it seemed as if no Dong girl had *ever* been to school. Only well after Liberation did people begin to send their daughters, and even by the 1990s, not all Dong girls went to school.

My daughter Lulu went to school in Huaxi. Huang ganged up on her along with one or two Dong people. They bullied her by shouting in Dong at her, "Our Dong tradition is that girls don't go to school. Why are you going to school?"

When Lulu went to school, she had to pass Huang's door on the stairway. One morning in November 2000 around 7 am, wearing only pyjamas, Huang abruptly opened his metal door into the stairway and tried to grab Lulu, but she escaped quickly down the stairs. He swore at her, saying her going to school was disturbing his sleep.

Huang was *often* waiting at his door when Lulu went to school in the mornings. He would make loud but vacuous accusations, and threaten to smash her head in. My daughter was scared out of her wits. After classes at the end of the day, she'd still be upset.

When Lulu was still at primary school, I would teach her English at home. She really liked it and acquired the habit of reading English out loud for 10 minutes or so each morning. After she entered junior middle school, I made it a rule she should persevere with reading each morning.

When Huang's family heard Lulu reading, however, they complained it was 'disturbing' them and Huang insisted she was not allowed to read aloud or he would kill her. Lulu was terrified, and refused to speak.

In the evenings, I continued to teach English to Lulu but she was in no mood to pay attention. A voice from below would sometimes scream, "You're not allowed to teach her. You're disturbing me!" I spoke more softly when teaching than when speaking normally.

Because I insisted, Lulu reluctantly persevered. At junior middle school, she had to walk about 30 minutes to get to school. Every day she travelled that distance four times. After lunch, she would go straight back again. It was very tiring. Leaning over her homework in the evenings, she was often drowsy. At 10 pm, she'd go to bed.

It was not only from below that trouble came. At midnight, there'd often be a burst of noise from the floor above Lulu's, rousing her from sleep. Lulu became absent-minded. In class, she'd stare blankly ahead, desperate for a nap. During exam periods, her sleep was disturbed even more often than usual. She would often leave in a daze to take her exams.

Huang and his accomplices tried to deceive Lulu, saying she was not really my daughter; I had just picked her up off the streets. Lulu began to have doubts and frequently asked me about this. I told her she was honestly and truly my daughter, without question.

As Lulu was leaving home for school, or at night when everything was quiet, Huang would shout, "Lulu's a worker's daughter. She's a b__! She shouldn't go to school. It's just wasting your money!"

Not Allowed to Speak, Not Allowed Not to Speak

Being old, I often reminisced over past events and was unable to understand the queer and grotesque things that were happening in the present, right in front of my very eyes. I was distressed and wanted to talk things through, but there was no one to talk to, so it felt claustrophobic. The upshot was that I often talked to myself, and certain others heard me talking. They responded with floods of verbal abuse.

I didn't divulge anything that might be useful to eavesdroppers. My lectures to myself were more about tackling corruption and coping with illegal activities, infringements of human rights or the words and actions of despotic rulers.

Since my soliloquys seemed so awful in their consequences, however, it felt I should simply shut up. If no words left my mouth, there should be no problem. Not so, however. If I meditated in silence, the eavesdroppers considered it a sign of rebellion. They'd scream my name outside the flat, demanding, "What are you doing?"

One evening after dinner, I heard someone in the home above saying, "This evening Laozi [the Old Master] will prevent you from sleeping." At midnight, I had just put down my pen and lain down in bed when there was a burst of pounding from the floor above.

I sat up, hearing from time to time the sound of conversation, "How come there's no reaction?" Then they hurled down abuse in Dong and threatened to beat us up. "If he doesn't speak we'll beat him up. He should say something."

During the day as I was preparing food in the kitchen, I'd hear some nonsense about a 'lover', a 'flash in the pan', 'people a thousand miles apart can fall in love'.

More than anything else, they manufactured frightening political rumours, such as: 'XX was involved in a coup d'état', 'There's going to be another World War', 'XX has been arrested' or 'XX has died'. Sometimes they also boasted of sexual exploits.

Demands

As well as intimidating us physically or verbally, Huang made all kinds of irrational demands. He boasted he was the leader of a gang of bullies, the most powerful person in the area. My family was disturbing him, 'Moving the earth above *Taisui*'s head' [*Taisui* was the great gang leader], and he would certainly drive us out.

In old age, you need the toilet more frequently. When Huang heard us in the bathroom, he would scream from below, "B__s, listen to me! Don't use the toilet!"

He demanded we should install our own drainpipe to go out through the window, avoiding their flat.

If I spat into the spittoon, he swore, saying I should go to the toilet to spit. He didn't allow me to move about on the balcony. Every time I took a shower, Huang would scoff, "Go to the river to wash; you're not allowed to shower at home."

My family was practically being forbidden to live in our own flat. Performing daily tasks provoked retaliation.

They didn't tolerate *any* noise. They demanded we change a squeaky stool. Huang screamed we should stop listening to audio tapes while lying in bed. He insisted I go to the corridor outside my flat to grind hot pepper. Scraping rice from the bottom of the rice pot led to more rage.

If I sang, Huang swore and called me a 'lunatic', with 'a mental disorder'. He demanded I go to bed at the same time as his family and rise at the same time.

Huang sometimes suggested we exchange flats. He would live above and I would live below. If not, he'd continue to hammer my door and destroy my flat, or drive me to insanity.

Huang's friends shouted that we should make steps from our balcony to the ground, so we didn't have to pass Huang's flat and could avoid 'conflict'. I replied tongue-in-cheek that building stairs from the balcony to the ground would be illegal. Huang retorted, "We are the special operations unit of the police. You don't need to worry about that."

Not Permitted to Keep a Dog

When my former wife Jiang returned, we kept a dog and named him OK. Jiang and Lulu called him Speck. He was little bigger than a cat but quite clever. He was our burglar alarm, able to distinguish us from enemies, good people from bad people. He was normally so quiet I suspected he had cats for ancestors!

OK was obedient. Each morning, Jiang led him to the waste area outside to do his business and he knew to go to the balcony to urinate. We often bathed him. He understood human nature. Whenever he heard angry words at our door, he ran to the door prickling with protest. If a friend knocked, he usually knew intuitively it was a friend. He would look up towards the door and yap a friendly greeting.

When Huang came to bang on the door, cursing and swearing, we were frightened and so was OK. Each time Huang came, OK leaned against the door, snarling and gnashing his teeth, but simultaneously shivering with fear.

After a while, OK recognised Huang's smell and each time he caught a whiff, he left his den and came trembling up to me to sound the alarm, gazing up at me, as if to ask for an explanation. At night, when people came to bang on the door, OK would bark madly. Huang turned this on its head, accusing the dog of disturbing him by its bark.

Huang said the dog's walking around 'disturbed him'. We had no alternative but to sew special 'shoes' for OK, but this didn't work. Huang still complained, demanding that we tie 'the brute' up.

One night, Huang lodged a complaint with the police, claiming that OK's walking around was disturbing him, though OK had actually been sleeping with Jiang. That night, two policemen arrived. One sat in the flat below listening, while the other, wearing leather shoes, led OK on a lead around my living room. The downstairs policeman came up and announced, "There's noise, a rustling noise."

OK had been registered at the local police station and we had followed all the dog-ownership regulations. The two policemen announced, however, that because OK was making a noise when walking, my family should part with the dog.

We three felt a deep sense of injustice. We said we could not do without OK and would hold on to him. The two policemen retorted angrily, "If you want to keep the dog, we'll pay no attention to what goes on here in future."

Afterwards, Huang banged even more crazily on our door. When I went to report him to the police, they insisted my family should not be keeping a dog.

Attacks on the Door

At first, I made a note of the fierce door-pounding incidents. It happened too often, however, and I soon stopped. In the course of seven years, there were probably several hundred such instances. I reported many to the police, but it seemed that after my police-reports, the problem became worse. The police simply warned us not to open the door.

The flats on our staircase were mostly living quarters for staff of an electronics school where Huang worked. Diagonally opposite Huang's flat was the home of the school's security administrator. Most people on the stairwell were Party members.

Huang attacked my flat for seven years. At the very beginning, only the security administrator remonstrated with him and dragged him away. Thereafter, that man did not intervene further.

Those who heard Huang's violent banging also heard our cries for help, but no one ever came out. When people encountered Huang outside, they typically tried to avoid him.

Despite the many incidents, no one ever tried to get to the bottom of what was happening, or to find a solution. Only one woman said to Jiang, "Huang is bullying you."

Local newspapers carried articles describing how the Guiyang government apprehended people who contributed to the dirty, disorderly state of the city. Citizens should cultivate more civilised habits. In defiance of such propaganda, however, Huang dumped bags of garbage outside my door. He brought a dog to urinate there. At night, Huang dashed upstairs himself and urinated at my door. The passageway piled up with rubbish, quite the opposite of the new sanitary model being urged by city authorities.

I reported all this to the neighbourhood committee and to the Guiyang Evening Standard. Reporters came and wrote about it, but to no avail.

During the years before Huang moved into his flat and the years after he left, we never had a single problem.

Chapter 22
Staring at the Mountain Path
(Old Age, 2009-11)

Loss of Sight

In that atmosphere of intimidation and harassment, I immersed myself in writing the *Outline of Tibetan History*. On the night of 30th August 2009, I finished writing the last sentence of the last chapter, on social customs. It had just gone midnight. When I turned to review the night's work, something was suddenly obstructing the sight in my left eye. I couldn't clean it off and it gradually became worse, until I couldn't see what I had just written.

The next day, my wife led me by the arm to see a doctor at the hospital, and the doctor declared I had cataracts in both eyes. In addition, the retina in the left eye had become detached. Having a detached retina was like taking a photo with film that had been exposed to the light; there could no longer be any picture. He declared that the left eye had become blind and no operation could restore its sight.

Distraught, I returned home and had to make do. All of a sudden, I was unable to read or write. In misery and despair, I began a completely different kind of life.

After 10 days or so, Dr Norman Geary made a long-distance telephone call from Europe to ask how I was doing and express concern. He had heard that I had lost the sight in my eye. The next day he phoned again, saying he'd like to try to help me arrange medical treatment.

He suggested I go to Kunming to see a foreign doctor, an expert in ophthalmology who was working at a hospital there. He might be able to heal my eye. Half the medical expenses would be absorbed by his organisation.

Dr Geary had returned to Ireland with his family more than two years before. I was deeply moved by his willingness to help.

Since the Guiyang hospitals were not prepared to issue me with a certificate to go elsewhere for medical treatment, I would have been unable to claim medical insurance. In Guiyang, I was qualified to receive medical treatment at public expense because of my background as a university lecturer. Moreover, I didn't have the heart to ask foreign friends to spend lots of money to subsidise my treatment. I was already old and it was inadvisable to leave the care of my family. For all these reasons, I decided not to go to Kunming.

On hearing this, Dr Geary contacted an American physiotherapist Ms Meng (Karen Malone). She knew an eye specialist at the Guiyang Medical School Hospital, and Dr Geary asked her to accompany me there. He assured me I could trust her. Ms Meng's kind interventions gave me more courage and confidence and led subsequently to operations on my cataracts and retina.

After Ms Meng's introduction to the Ophthalmology Department, my daughter Ou Ou telephoned and asked Director Wang of the Department personally to treat me. Ou Ou was the Deputy Mayor of Zhengzhou, the capital city of Henan Province. So on the morning of 15th September 2009, Jiang guided me to the hospital.

My grandson Tian Yingchang, the son of my Dong daughter in Xiangye, made a special trip from County Jianhe to visit and stayed a night.

Four directors from the Zhengzhou city government, where Ou Ou worked, who happened to be on an official trip to Guiyang, came to see me, clutching fresh flowers and other gifts, and expressing sympathy and encouragement. That was the evening of the day of the second operation.

Probably because of the medication, I spoke frankly to those visitors about many things on my mind. Distractedly, I said, "I shouldn't have written those six books, for they just caused trouble for me. My friends and relatives here don't want to know me any longer."

One of the bureau chiefs objected, "You can't say that. Those are your accomplishments, your contributions to knowledge – riches flowing from your pen." These words felt like some reward for all my study and resulted in a great deal of comfort.

Some days later, my daughter Ou Ou arrived and helped arrange my discharge from hospital.

After the operations, my left eye had only 1% vision: it was practically blind. My right eye was afflicted by cataracts and I could no longer read newspapers or books. With difficulty, I was able to read large-font print, but after 10 minutes, my left eye would be hurting and I would need to rest for half-an-hour. Without rest, the pain and fuzziness would increase.

This was all tantamount to losing the ability to read and write. Those pastimes I had loved my whole life long had suddenly been lost, within the space of a few days. I have no way of describing the grief I felt. During the day, I'd mostly shut my eyes and sit quietly, but I'd be fidgety and unable to sit at peace, for in my mind, I was distraught.

On the bright side, I could still see the rough outline of the road and shuffle along the footpaths. Every morning, I shifted myself cautiously down the stairs, making my way step by step to the sports field. I would jog slowly twice around the empty athletics track and do a little gymnastics, before making my way home. Although it was difficult, I gritted my teeth and persevered, deeming it profitable for good health; this was its own reward, but also led to a little more optimism.

In the 15 years since I had returned to my home province Guizhou, I had been bent over my desk day and night in the lonely work of writing, and had completed research for and the writing of six books. Five had already been published in China, London and Leiden.

Most of my writing was in fountain pen, both small and nearly illegible. Now I could not see clearly and could not read the draft of the last book, much less revise it. The publishing house agreed to go to the trouble of typing and editing, until it was ready for publication.

Broken Bones

At the beginning of February 2010, at 8 am, on the 8th day of the 20-year celebration of the Guizhou Nationalities Culture Association, I was struggling down the stairs, intending to go to the sports field as usual for my daily exercise.

On the fourth step of the penultimate flight, there was some filthy slippery stuff. My eyesight was such that I completely overlooked this slippery surface, with the result that I slipped and fell. Quickly and uncontrollably, I rolled down all 16 steps, arriving immobilised on the ground at the bottom, screaming, "Ai yo!"

I couldn't articulate any words, but my scream had pierced the whole neighbourhood. Everyone in the building must have heard it, though no one emerged to help.

After a minute or so, a middle-aged man arrived, on his way back home upstairs. I asked him to inform my wife on the fifth floor to come down and help me. When she realised I couldn't move and she couldn't really help me, she phoned our daughter Lulu, telling her to come home quickly. They called an ambulance. All the while, I was screaming with pain.

The X-ray showed my femur had smashed into pieces. Afterwards I felt a chill and began to tremble, then to vomit repeatedly. My blood pressure was perilously high, and a middle-aged male doctor gave me medication to lower the pressure. Next thing, I heard him saying my blood pressure was too low and I had to take medicine to raise it again, but this time it declined to rise.

I never lost consciousness, but observed everything clearly, coherent enough to have misgivings about all that was going on.

After a while, the doctor handed a note to Lulu saying I was in a critical state, and then left.

Before long, he reappeared, and looking askance at me, whispered to Lulu and then left again. With gaping eyes, I watched him leave without doing anything, and with a sense that there was nothing more he *could* do. He had been unable to save me and I was simply going to die of this injury, despite being in hospital. I realised I was going to die!

Reluctantly, I asked Lulu to phone my daughter Ou Ou. I told Lulu my bank pin number and gave her a few simple instructions outlining my last will and testament. My wife Jiang Yanrong was standing beside Lulu, crying.

I had to abandon everything, without having time to give clear explanations. Lulu and Jiang would be unable to manage everything. I thought mainly of the problem of dying. I was afraid of dying. I was leaving behind too many things. Far too many things were unfinished. I wanted to struggle to survive.

When the doctor told Lulu I was critically ill, he also told her he had no way of saving me and I would have to be transferred to another hospital. Lulu was still only 24 and bewildered with anxiety. She just asked, "What should we do? Transfer to which hospital?"

They telephoned the Guiyang Medical School Hospital and were told no beds were available. Just when it seemed I would die no matter what, Ou Ou phoned from Zhengzhou. She had made a dozen calls, trying here, there and everywhere, to find help. She had finally liaised with the Guiyang Medical School Hospital and arranged after all for me to go there immediately.

Since there were traffic jams on the roads, with much stopping and starting, the journey was a critical juncture for me. It took two or three hours for me to transfer to a bed in the Orthopaedics Department of the School Hospital. One Director Liu, with whom Ou Ou had spoken, came to see us and to find a bed for me. After examining me, this old doctor spoke to me frankly, "Your life is hanging by a thread!"

Thank goodness I survived, against the odds. When I recall those cruel moments in a critical state in Huaxi Hospital, more than half expecting to die, I cringe at how awful and painful it was!

My life flashed before my mind's eye. I was just a quiet academic. My books and articles, however, had caused others to be jealous and resentful, especially Dong cadres and intellectuals. I had suffered a double dose of prejudice for I had been born into a 'land-owning household'. I defied my detractors, so they regarded me as a thorn in the flesh, only hesitating over how best to pull it out as quickly as possible.

My daughter Ou Ou, however, saved my life and that is engraved upon my heart and mind. Without her, I'd have been destined to die in Huaxi Hospital. The aged orthopaedics Director Liu of the Medical School Hospital assumed personal responsibility for treating me. He decided to do a major operation after the Chinese New Year holiday. Before that, he would stretch the leg, hanging a three-kilogramme lead weight on it. On the afternoon I was admitted, I lay down and he set up that weight.

I was only able to lie flat on my back, not to sit up, turn over or even move much in any direction. It was just as though I was lying in a coffin. I had to use that position for everything; including eating, drinking and toilet activities.

On the morning of my second day in hospital, my daughter Ling Ling (Tao) and her son Kun Kun flew from Kunming to see me. My grandson Tian Yingchang also came, with his wife, by train from County Jianhe. With such family gatherings, we could only think of the shadow of imminent sadness, and hardly said a thing. That afternoon, they all went their separate ways, leaving me lying in hospital.

Six days later was the first day of Chinese New Year. Along with everyone else, doctors were busy celebrating. One nurse appeared occasionally and otherwise just a carer we had hired. My daughter Lulu and her mother Jiang came to see me daily, taking turns to brave the bitter weather and bring a food box from Huaxi. They stayed with me only a few hours, before leaving in a hurry.

The lead weight dangled from the end of the bed, pulling on my broken leg, day and night. My whole body alternated between numbness and pain, and I was unable to sleep.

On 30ᵗʰ January, Dr Geary's wife Ruth phoned from Ireland to say hello and, when she heard of my predicament, to express sympathy. I spoke bluntly about the unbearable suffering from the lead weight as I lay in bed. As time went on, I was worried pathological changes would occur, and from time to time, I suffered hallucinations. Sometimes it seemed like I was staying in a treasure store, with bright and shiny walls and lights. At either end of the room, there was a frog and the frogs were taking turns to croak at high volume. At other times, it seemed like people were lying all over the floor and the ward was so stuffy I felt I would suffocate.

Apart from such hallucinations, there was the noise of the life-monitoring apparatus at the head of the bed, not to mention the fireworks outside, in celebration of New Year.

At the time, I mainly felt sorry for Lulu and my wife, who were braving the bleak winter weather to come and see me every day. I had no confidence I would survive long enough for the doctors to finish celebrating New Year and perform the necessary operation.

This torment of 'sleeping in the coffin' lasted for more than two weeks. On the morning of the 10ᵗʰ day of New Year (23ʳᵈ February), doctors back from holiday operated on me. As I was being pushed into the operating theatre, I noticed Ou Ou standing in front of the hospital bed. She had flown that morning from Zhengzhou to take care of me. Two days later, after ascertaining there was no imminent danger, she organised everything, then left for home.

Because of the anaesthetic, I have almost no recollection of Ou Ou's arrival and of her care during those days. Lulu and my wife later explained to me what had happened.

The operation, performed by Director Liu, was successful. Within a few days, the lead weight was no longer needed. I was able to begin stretching and moving the injured leg, and gradually I was able to move on to one side to sleep. Thereafter, I was able to sit up and my recovery was quite quick, though I had lost a lot of weight and become extremely weak.

During the four weeks in hospital, Lulu and my wife faithfully took turns to bring me food, but after the two-hour bus-trip the food was icy cold. Lulu tried using a gas heater to re-heat it, but I still had no appetite and couldn't stomach it. When I saw them, however, appearing before me every day, clad in thick clothing and cotton caps, it warmed my heart.

Two weeks after the operation, I was discharged from hospital. An ambulance delivered me to the bottom of our stairs and I was carried up on a stretcher to our flat.

Returning home felt like returning to life after death. Although conditions were Spartan, I was unwilling to leave this home. After two weeks, the American physiotherapist Ms Meng arrived with three Chinese colleagues and taught me how to do certain exercises to help the leg recover. They invited me to their convalescent centre to undergo physiotherapy, explaining that Dr Geary would take responsibility for any expenses, and I wouldn't need to pay a penny. People came several times to try to persuade me, but I just thanked them and tactfully declined, determined that I would not leave this house again.

Two months after my return, my injured leg was still too tender to be set on the ground. I could only either sit or lie on the bed. Eating, drinking and toileting were all attended to by my wife. On the sixth day after my discharge from hospital, Lulu had flown to Beijing to look for work. Jiang attended to all my care, including shopping, and any work inside or outside the home. Whenever I called, she came to help without delay, day or night. On normal days, she talked more than anyone else, but now she talked much less than before.

During this time, I was totally dependent on Jiang. She was my faithful friend in adversity, and without her constant care, I'd undoubtedly have died. When she was out, I often shed tears on her account. I was also afraid that some unexpected mishap might befall her. Every time she went out, I reminded her to be careful, wishing her to be safe and sound and to return early.

In May, as the weather changed from cold to warm, Jiang caught a cold. I suggested she go for an injection, but she was reluctant to spend the money for that. She persevered for a few days but to no avail, and in the end, she lay down on her bed and could no longer get up again. Obviously, she could no longer care for me and between us we could not even get a cup of boiled water to drink. It looked as if we might die there together in the flat. I telephoned the neighbourhood committee to ask them to engage a housekeeper on our behalf. They replied, "We'll tell you later if we can find a suitable one."

A housekeeping company in Guiyang took my call and answered in the same way. In desperation, I phoned a female cousin and asked her to arrange for someone to respond to this emergency. She herself was already over 70 years old, but when she realised our circumstances, she came quickly to help us for two days in a row – boiling water, washing dishes, preparing food and persuading Jiang to go and have injections to treat her fever. With medication, Jiang's fever receded and she slowly recovered.

Previously, Jiang had hardly known my cousin, but now regarded her as a saint, repeatedly thanking her sincerely. When calamity strikes, you most need the support of close relatives. After Jiang had recovered, she cared for me as before.

Slowing Down

On the evening I was discharged from hospital, four or five people carried me back up to my fifth-floor flat, as you would carry a dead body. Nobody knew then how things would develop. They placed me on the bed and quickly left, leaving all future nursing in the hands of my wife.

Day and night, I was confined to my bedroom, like a hermit. My former hobby of reading and writing had been abruptly terminated. Lying on the bed, my body ached with agonising pain and though I wanted to get up, I could only *sit* up with extraordinary difficulty and after a long time of trying. If I sat for long, my body ached again. It took ages to try to stand up, and sitting down again was also difficult. Each movement was extremely slow, difficult and painful. When moving, I couldn't speak, but had to concentrate on my movements, or I would surely have lost balance and fallen over.

Every day, my wife had to go shopping or run errands. While at home, she was either busy with housework or watching television in the living room. If I didn't call her, she didn't come, but when summoned, she listened carefully to any requests and then left. Otherwise, I sat alone on my bedside with little to do, other than think about death.

When she noticed my worried countenance, Jiang often consoled me saying, "Your health is much better than before." Gradually, I began to move around the bedroom.

Because of the operation, my injured leg was slightly shorter than before, so when I stood up, I felt that one side was high while the other was low. My body's centre of gravity had changed, making me inclined to topple over. Leaning on crutches, I learned how to walk slowly between the bedroom and kitchen, where I was able to distinguish the fuzzy outline of the rice cooker. To alleviate my wife's workload, I made up my mind gradually to do some things about the house. In the evening I was able to cook a bowl of noodles or rice, while at lunchtime, I cooked some rice in the rice cooker and placed a small bowl of leftover food on top, to heat up at the same time.

For the three or four months after I left hospital, I ate this kind of food, good for convalescing. Small accidents often happened as I tried to cook, for I couldn't see clearly. Sometimes I'd pour water outside the pot, scoop things out and miss the bowl, miss the cup when pouring water, or put seasoning in the wrong place. At first when I fumbled around doing things, I mostly ended up calling Jiang to come and help out.

Since I was propped up on crutches, I wasn't able to take things with both hands, but had to place cups and bowls in a bag and suspend it around my neck, which rested on my chest as I walked slowly into the kitchen. I used to mock myself saying, "You're like an old horse!" By this time, I was in a much better frame of mind, beginning to think about venturing out of the flat.

Seeing my health gradually improve, Jiang said to me one day, "Let's register to remarry. Otherwise, if you have to have an operation in future, I'll not be able to sign on your behalf."

My recent illness had been very serious and Jiang had really stood by me. She'd attended to all my physical needs and waited upon me around the clock. She'd sympathised with me in my suffering and had shared in my fear that I would die. Many times since my accident, she had quietly shed tears, and I felt sorry that otherwise she had no one to rely on.

Lonely and weak, with no one to lean on, she had experienced the full force of endless bullying, humiliation and hardship. When she had been at her wits' end, I had made an effort to save her, demonstrating loyalty at her time of greatest need. Now she had done the same for me.

Neither of us had forgotten our mutual debt. We had both been deeply moved by such loyalty. So we agreed to remarry, changing our status of 'calamity-friends' back to that of husband and wife.

When we applied to remarry, registry office personnel were unwilling or unable to show any flexibility in handling the application. They insisted that I personally go to the office along with Jiang and only then would they handle the remarriage formalities. My vision was indistinct, my broken leg had not yet fully healed and I didn't yet dare to go down the stairs.

Faced with such exigency, however, we both waited painfully for my condition to improve and then we could go. On 1st September 2010, Jiang supported me step by step down the stairs and we took a car to the necessary office to complete the remarriage formalities. Members of staff wished us a happy life together until we were 100 years old, a sentiment in keeping with my cherished dreams. Frankly, my life is inextricably linked to Jiang's. If she were not around to help, I certainly could not keep going. She cares for me, is able to bear hardship and weariness and is constantly loyal.

Guiyang has a long winter, like a long, dark night that's difficult to endure. At night, the bones in my body ached and I could hardly sleep, always needing to get up for two or three hours. By day, I closed my eyes and meditated silently, waiting impatiently for spring to come. On sunny mornings, I ventured out on crutches, depending still on the support of my wife. We walked twice around the nearby university sports field and slowly made our way home again.

Persevering thus with physical exercise, my health improved markedly. Some passers-by saw the old couple, my wife and me, going every morning hand-in-hand for exercise, and complimented us saying, "Those two really are growing old together until they are 100 years old!"

Jiang often said to me, "You can live longer by persevering daily in going out for a walk. By living longer, you can frustrate those people who used to curse you."

The manuscript of the *Outline of Tibetan History* that I had posted to the publisher was printed and proofread. In a process that took almost a year, experts twice examined it carefully. Then in March 2011, the editor Li Zhirong posted the revised manuscript back to me for revision.

When I saw it, I was overjoyed, so appreciative of their investment in the project. On receipt of the manuscript, I proofread and revised meticulously, with the help of a magnifying glass, working for 20 minutes at a time, before my eye was painfully swollen and even fuzzier than usual. Then I would simply have to stop, close my eyes and rest a while. Progress was painfully slow, at two or three pages per day.

After more than four months, I finally finished reviewing the whole manuscript and posted it back to the publisher on schedule. I thought to myself, "If I hadn't become blind, I'd still like to have written another one or two books."

The Dong people have a proverb, 'When bulls die, they leave their horns; when people die, they leave their songs,' as a legacy for later generations. My life's legacy lies in having taught a few students and having written a few million characters' worth of academic prose. Feeling vulnerable to the vagaries of politics and society, I don't dare to say I have made any significant contribution, but I look forward to brighter days, when history and conscience will re-evaluate everything. I look forward to spring, when mornings will break earlier and I can walk hand-in-hand with my wife to the sports field.

Sitting idly, trying hard to remember the past, I recall one early morning 60 years ago. I am wearing light clothing, following a villager who is seeing me off. We march through the drizzle without umbrellas, leaving my home village, my mother and family, and the 'Big House' where we had lived.

Not long afterwards, my mother and her extended family are driven out of their home. My relatives are scattered, and one after another they leave this world, unable to bear its suffering and torment. I alone am left, drifting around in the world outside the village. Now I've reached old age and ailments are wrapping themselves around my body.

Living far from my native place has proved lonely and bitter. How much I miss and long for the village of my childhood! But my native place no longer possesses anything of mine, and there is no way of returning there. Some unconscionable Dong people rub salt in my wounds, saying, "Your home was destroyed long ago, and you would not be allowed to go back home."

In fact, one large house in Zhanmo, seven kilometres from Xiangye, still remains in my family. It is a large three-storey, five-roomed, tile-roofed house, once bought by my father and used for storing grain and as a home for tenant farmers.

In the course of 60 years, that house passes through many hands. Its residents often hear cries of warning, "They're coming back [to retake possession of the house]!"

Their complexion pales in alarm as they sigh repeatedly, "Then what's to be done? What's to be done?"

The main entrance and veranda of the house face the mountain path frequently traversed by its former owner. Day and night, they keep watch, as if waiting for the owner to return. Years pass – wind and rain invade and attack – and the beams and pillars rot.

Before long, the big house staring at the mountain path and beyond, waiting for its owner, will be unable to endure any longer and will topple over. Then everything belonging to the clan of that big house will have disappeared. Only the mountains and rivers will remain as they have always been. The world of human relationships will have changed forever.